Kemalist Turkey and the Middle East

To better understand the lasting legacy of international relations in the post-Ottoman Middle East, we must first reexamine Turkey's engagement with the region during the interwar period. Long assumed to be a period of deliberate disengagement and ruptured ties between Turkey and its neighbors, the volatile 1930s, Amit Bein argues, was instead a period during which Turkey was in fact perceived as taking steps toward increasing its regional prominence. Bein examines the unstable situation along Turkey's Middle Eastern borders, the bilateral diplomatic relations Ankara established with fledgling governments in the region, grand plans for transforming Turkey into a major transit hub for Middle Eastern and Eurasian transportation and trade, and Ankara's effort to enhance its image as a model for modernization of non-Western societies. Through this, he offers a fresh, enlightening perspective on the Kemalist legacy, which still resonates in the modern politics of the region today.

AMIT BEIN is Associate Professor of Middle East History at Clemson University. His previous publications include *Ottoman Ulema, Turkish Republic: Agents of Change and Guardians of Tradition* (2011).

Kemalist Turkey and the Middle East

International Relations in the Interwar Period

AMIT BEIN

Clemson University, South Carolina

CAMBRIDGE
UNIVERSITY PRESS

CAMBRIDGE
UNIVERSITY PRESS

University Printing House, Cambridge CB2 8BS, United Kingdom

One Liberty Plaza, 20th Floor, New York, NY 10006, USA

477 Williamstown Road, Port Melbourne, VIC 3207, Australia

4843/24, 2nd Floor, Ansari Road, Daryaganj, Delhi - 110002, India

79 Anson Road, #06-04/06, Singapore 079906

Cambridge University Press is part of the University of Cambridge.

It furthers the University's mission by disseminating knowledge in the pursuit of education, learning, and research at the highest international levels of excellence.

www.cambridge.org
Information on this title: www.cambridge.org/9781107198005
DOI: 10.1017/9781108182072

© Amit Bein 2017

First published 2017

Printed in the United Kingdom by Clays, St Ives plc

A catalogue record for this publication is available from the British Library

Library of Congress Cataloging-in-Publication data
Names: Bein, Amit, 1970– author.
Title: Kemalist Turkey and the Middle East : international relations in the inter-war period / Amit Bein.
Description: Cambridge, United Kingdom : Cambridge University Press, 2017. | Includes bibliographical references.
Identifiers: LCCN 2017026235 | ISBN 9781107198005
Subjects: LCSH: Turkey – Foreign relations – Middle East. | Middle East – Foreign relations – Turkey.
Classification: LCC DR479.M54 B45 2018 | DDC 327.56105609/042 – dc23
LC record available at https://lccn.loc.gov/2017026235

ISBN 978-1-107-19800-5 Hardback

To Roi, Omri, and Ira

Contents

List of Figures		*page* viii
List of Maps		ix
Acknowledgments		x
1	Not-So-Distant Neighbor	1
2	Degrees of Separation	25
3	Ties That Bind	62
4	Great Expectations	107
5	The Turkish Model	139
6	Strolling Through Istanbul	179
7	A Distant Neighbor	215
Notes		241
Bibliography		280
Index		291

Figures

3.1 King Faisal and Mustafa Kemal   *page* 77
3.2 Reza Shah and Mustafa Kemal Atatürk   84
3.3 Mustafa Kemal Atatürk and the Emir Abdallah   92
4.1 Turkish cigarette factory   108
4.2 Turkish cigarette advertisement in a Palestinian newspaper   109
4.3 "Toward Iraq and Iran" celebratory sign, Diyarbakır   131
5.1 Miss Universe Keriman Halis on the cover of the Egyptian
    journal *al-Musawwar*   146
5.2 Keriman Halis hosted by the Egyptian daily *al-Siyasa*   149
5.3 Keriman Halis hosted by the Turkish community in
    al-Mansura   154
5.4 Huda Shaʿrawi traveling abroad   159
5.5 The İsmet Pasha Girls' Institute in Ankara   163
5.6 Cooking lesson in the İsmet Pasha Girls' Institute   164
5.7 An Arab caricature of the Kemalists booting the Greeks
    out of Anatolia   176
6.1 The Egyptian friendship delegation   188
6.2 Syrian scouts in Istanbul   194
6.3 *Cumhuriyet*'s headline celebrating the continuation of the
    Istanbul-Alexandria maritime line   197
6.4 The Young Men's Muslim Association delegation in
    Istanbul   199

Maps

1.1 Kemalist map of the Treaty of Sèvres   *page* 9
1.2 Turkey's borders in 1926   14
2.1 The borders of Syria as envisioned by Arab nationalists
    after World War I   44
3.1 Turkey and the Eastern Mediterranean, 1926–1938   63
4.1 The Tabriz-Trabzon Road   113
4.2 Turkey's railroad system, 1937   132
6.1 The Taurus Express   207
7.1 Turkey and its neighbors on the eve of World War II 219

Acknowledgments

The research for this book was facilitated by the staff of the National Library of Turkey (Milli Kütüphane) and the Turkish Republican Archives (Cumhuriyet Arşivi) in Ankara; the British Library and National Archives in London; the Library of Congress in Washington, DC, and the National Archives at College Park; and the Central Zionist Archives and the National Library of Israel in Jerusalem. I owe a particular debt of gratitude to Clemson University's library and its interlibrary loan service.

I am thankful to a number of colleagues and friends who commented on parts of the book, reviewed some chapters of it, or invited me to speak about sections of it, among them Şükrü Hanioğlu, Ebru Boyar, Kate Fleet, Erik Zürcher, Mike Reynolds, Ryan Gingeras, Eugene Rogan, and Mustafa Aksakal.

I would like to thank the Institute of Turkish Studies for a sabbatical grant and Clemson University, its College of AAH, and the Department of History for a number of research grants that supported my research. I owe a special debt of gratitude to my colleague Billy Terry for his invaluable assistance in drawing the maps for this book. Last but not least, I would like to thank my editor Maria Marsh and all the fabulous support staff in Cambridge University Press.

1 | Not-So-Distant Neighbor

Ahmed Umar, the Turkish Consul-General in Jerusalem, was traveling on the Jerusalem-Nablus highway in April 1936 on official business of the single-party government of the Kemalist republic. These were the very first days of the Arab Revolt in Palestine (1936–1939), and he was therefore taken by complete surprise when his car was stopped at a roadblock set by a group of armed Arab rebels. Bullets were flying, and the Turkish diplomat had every reason to fear for his life. But he was pleasantly surprised that once the rebels noticed the Turkish flag on his automobile, they immediately ceased fire and apologized for the inconvenience they caused him. They then allowed him to evacuate a passerby who was injured in their attack and sent him off on his way to Jerusalem with loud chants of "Long Live Mustafa Kemal! Long live Turkey!" After he duly reported the startling, yet ultimately reassuring, incident to his superiors in Ankara, the story was distributed for publication in the Turkish press. Commentators presented the incident as indicative of the prestige accorded to the Kemalist republic and its leader and contrasted it with the derision that led to an Arab revolt against the Ottoman government only two decades earlier.[1] A few weeks after that incident, the Turkish press reported at some length on the participation of Feridun Cemal Erkin, the Turkish Consul-General in Beirut, in the inauguration ceremony of the Turkish pavilion in the Damascus Industrial Fair. The declared goal of the Kemalist republic's participation in this and similar fairs in Egypt and Palestine was "to display to the Eastern peoples the great advances of our republic, particularly in industrial production, and to develop new export markets through the advertisement of our products." Commentators in the Turkish press were therefore incensed when reports arriving from Damascus a few days later suggested that the display in the pavilion was underwhelming and not up to the task of presenting Turkey in a positive light. Ankara took the complaints seriously. The officials in charge of the pavilion were summarily sacked and recalled to Turkey,

1

even as the Turkish Consul-General in Beirut and several officials and
specialists from Turkey were dispatched to Damascus to reorganize
and upgrade the display. The pavilion was then reinaugurated with
much pomp and fanfare in July 1936, in a ceremony attended by the
French High Commissioner, the President of Syria, Syrian government
ministers, and many other local notables and religious dignitaries.[2]

Turkish, Arabic, and Hebrew periodicals in the 1930s featured these
and many other instances of diplomatic and other types of engagement between Turkey and the Middle East. News items and commentaries in the Turkish press regarding the Middle East, and vice versa,
were at times positive, at others negative, and at yet other instances
simply descriptive. Regardless of tone, such reports remained ubiquitous throughout the tumultuous decade that preceded the outbreak of
the Second World War. The topics of the reports varied widely, as the
types of engagement were diverse. They could range from reports in the
Palestinian press in 1931 on Turkey's donation of a revered hair of
the Prophet Muhammad to a mosque in Acre, to stories in the Turkish press in 1933 on Egyptian royals vacationing in Istanbul, to warnings in the Syrian press in 1937 that Turkey was harboring designs on
Aleppo and northern Syria.[3] More generally, political, cultural, diplomatic, and economic developments in Turkey and the Middle East were
approached from various perspectives in the Turkish, Middle Eastern,
and international press. For example, the Kemalist ideological reorientation of Turkey toward Europe in general, and the assertive secularist policies of the Turkish government in particular, were especially
polarizing topics. But whereas contemporary Turkish, Middle Eastern,
and European commentators could differ widely in their attitudes on
this and other aspects of the Turkish state and society in the interwar period, virtually none assumed that the demise of the Ottoman
Empire and the emergence of the Kemalist republic spelled the abrupt
end of Turkey's involvement in the Middle East, nor the beginning
of a deliberate long-term process of unmitigated mutual dissociation
and disinterest. Indeed, many statesmen, officials, and commentators
throughout the region and beyond suggested in the late 1930s that
Turkey's involvement in the region would likely increase in the near
future, following the anticipated loosening of the British and French
grip on much of the former Ottoman territories in the region. The veteran Austrian diplomat August Ritter von Kral expressed a common
perception when he argued in 1938 that "the absolute necessity for

Turkey to interest herself actively in the events occurring in the States of the Near East results from their immediate neighbourhood and their common history."[4] He and many others at the time believed that the geopolitics of Turkey and the Middle East necessitated mutual engagement, regardless of ideological tenets that could have been understood to dictate otherwise during the heydays of Kemalism in the 1930s. A German expert on Turkey indeed explained in 1939 that Atatürk "did not conduct foreign policy from theory, but according to the dictates of geography and the needs of the time," and thus "emphasized and strengthened [Turkey's] dual position as a European and Asiatic state."[5] Accordingly, Suad Davaz, the Turkish ambassador to France, did not hesitate in 1939 to author a very laudatory preface to a French book entitled *La Turquie: Centre de Gravité des Balkans et du Proche-Orient* (Turkey: The Center of Gravity of the Balkans and the Near East), shortly before leaving Paris for a new assignment as Turkey's ambassador to Reza Shah's Iran.[6]

And yet, if an interested reader in the early twenty-first century were to consult books and articles written in the last few decades, it is most likely that they would encounter a very different view on Turkey's position vis-à-vis the Middle East in the interwar period. The dominant narrative in the historiography of Turkey and the modern Middle East, the foundations of which were laid during the Cold War period, all but consensually deemphasized Turkey's engagement with the Middle East in the 1930s. Instead, a narrative of deliberate cutting of links and dissociation is ubiquitous in histories of the period. David Fromkin, in his well-read *A Peace to End All Peace: The Fall of the Ottoman Empire and the Creation of the Modern Middle East*, presents this prevailing view succinctly and emphatically. He asserts that with the setting of the new post-Ottoman borders in the early 1920s, "Turkey, which for 500 years had dominated the Middle East, departed from Middle Eastern history to seek to make herself European."[7] Published in 1989, just as the Cold War was coming to an end, the book reflected the general tenor in the historiography of Turkey and the Middle East in the preceding decades. For the most part, studies on the Middle East in the interwar period largely disregarded Turkey, and vice versa. Regarding a few specific topics, scholars could not completely discount a few well-known instances of Turkish involvement with the region in the 1930s. This was the case with the Treaty of Saadabad of 1937, which was a nonaggression pact between Turkey, Iraq, Iran, and Afghanistan, and with the separation of Alexandretta/Hatay from Syria in 1938 and its annexation to Turkey in the year that followed. Still, these instances were either downplayed, as in the case of the former, or placed within a narrative of conflict and dissociation, as with the latter. In a recent commentary on Turkey, a well-respected journalist could thus state very emphatically that "Mustafa Kemal Atatürk, the secularist army officer who founded modern Turkey in 1923, sought to sever his land's ancient bonds to the Middle East."[8] Indeed, the general tenor of studies of the period either asserted or implicitly assumed a process of deliberate and mutual disinterest, alienation, and severance of links during the interwar period, which was driven by ideological considerations, lingering ethnic animosities traced to the closing years of the Ottoman Empire, and the new post-Ottoman colonial-dominated political realities in the region.

There is an evident and striking difference, then, between the way contemporaries described the engagement of Turkey and the Middle East in the interwar period and the ways in which it was related by later historians. This sharp discrepancy has to do mainly with the radical change in the local, regional, and international circumstances of Turkey and the Middle East in the wake of World War II. The global conflict and the decades-long Cold War that followed the Second World War affected radical changes in the geopolitics of Turkey and the Middle East. With the multipolar world of the 1930s giving way to the bipolar world of the Cold War, Turkey transformed from a proud symbol of nationalist self-assertion into a state heavily dependent on the United States and its European allies, even as major countries in the Middle East became independent from European colonial control and were led by pan-Arab regimes that adopted a nonaligned stance but developed close relations with the Soviet Union. It was during this period that official alienation, disengagement, and formal hostility became a feature of Turkey's relations with many of its Middle Eastern neighbors. And it was during this time, particularly from the late 1950s, that many of the later developments were projected back to the early republic. The presentation of developments in the interwar period as leading linearly toward the policies of Cold War Turkey was used to justify and legitimize Turkey's dissociation from the challenging and troubling developments in the Middle East. Atatürk was widely and officially venerated in Turkey, and it therefore appeared sensible and convenient that the course set under his leadership was followed by his successors in reorienting the republic toward becoming what Erik Zürcher termed succinctly "Atlantic Turkey."[9] This narrative was touted by the Atatürkist establishment, particularly in the wake of the first military coup in 1960, and was also picked by Western scholars of modern Turkish politics, foreign relations, and history. At the same time, governments in the Middle East and scholars of the region mirrored that narrative, largely writing Turkey out of the history of the post-Ottoman Middle East. At most, modern Turkey was presented as a pro-Western threat, or at times as an unjust occupier of Arab lands in Alexandretta/Hatay. The narratives of the modern history of Turkey and of the Middle East converged in this respect in the shared assumption that the crucial stage in the dissociation of Turkey from Middle Eastern affairs took place during the time of Atatürk in the interwar period. Indeed, by the end of the Cold War, it had become all but an orthodoxy in the historiographies of Turkey and the Middle East to view their respective histories as advancing separately with very limited and mostly inconsequential interaction between them since the early 1920s. In this telling, "Atatürk decided to cut his country's traditional ties with the Arab world, and [thereafter] Republican Turkey distanced itself from Middle Eastern politics."[10]

The post–Cold War period witnessed a Turkish pivot to the Middle East since the 1990s, and more vigorously under the premiership and presidency of Recep Tayyip Erdoğan since 2002. The increasing engagement between Turkey and the Middle East in the early twenty-first century has been the topic of numerous academic studies as well as reports and commentaries in the popular press. In a great many of these publications, this renewed interest in the region has been juxtaposed not merely with the situation in the previous decades but most particularly with Mustafa Kemal's purported severance of ties during the early days of the republic. Thus, in reference to the reengagement with the region in the 1990s, one scholar suggested in 2000 that since the 1920s, with only "the exception of a brief period in the mid-1950s, Turkey has assiduously pursued a cautious and low-profile policy toward its southern neighbors."[11] Writing a decade later, shortly before the 10-year anniversary of the rise to power of the Justice and Development Party (Adalet ve Kalkınma Partisi, AKP), scholars yet again contrasted the new activism in the Middle East under Erdoğan's government with "the original guiding values underpinning Turkish foreign policy, [which] were firmly established by the founder of the

Republic, Kemal Atatürk," based on "a Western-oriented, isolation-ist and passive foreign policy stand."[12] This ubiquitous juxtaposition, hinging on the assertion that "Kemal Atatürk had no interest in pur-suing an active Middle East foreign policy," indeed has become all but a dogma in studies of Turkey's recent relations with the region. This purportedly deliberate Turkish disengagement from the Middle East in the interwar period is often explained in ideological and sentimental terms. In this telling,

distancing the [Turkish] Republic from Middle Eastern affairs was... congruent with the Turkish-Arab mistrust that had originated in the first two decades of the twentieth century. From the Turkish perspective, the Arab Revolt, which helped the West destroy the Ottoman Empire during the First World War, had represented an unforgivable stab in the back. From the Arab perspective, the Ottoman imperial domination of most of the Middle East and the repressive regulations of the Young Turks had unforgivably ham-pered Arab national development.[13]

Along these lines, major recent works on Turkish foreign policy have very little to say about Ankara's relations with the Arab countries of the Middle East during the interwar period.[14]

This book suggests that Turkey's engagement with the Middle East in the interwar period was in fact much more multifaceted, intricate, purposeful, and intriguing than the dominant narrative of disengage-ment and disinterest allows. This was very evident to contemporary observers in the 1930s but is not reflected in the historical literature on the period. This book is an effort to write Turkey back into the history of the Middle East in the early post-Ottoman period. Such a reexami-nation of the relations between the Kemalist republic and neighboring countries and societies in the region is beneficial and timely in several respects. First and foremost, it offers an opportunity for a reevaluation of interregional relations in the early post-Ottoman period, in a field of study mostly focused on the impact of European colonialism on the Middle East in the interwar period. That impact was obviously piv-otal and decisive, but regional dynamics, involving Kemalist Turkey, also played a not inconsequential role in the history of the period. Questions about the durability of the new post-Ottoman borders and political arrangements, diplomatic relations between newly established regional powers, economic interests and plans coupled with geostrate-gic considerations, and persisting and newly nurtured social and cultural ties across new national borders were all parts of those regional dynamics during the interwar period. An added benefit of the reexamination of Turkey's relations with the Middle East during that period is that it allows for a reassessment of the legacies of this era of the early republic for Turkey's engagement with the region in the decades that followed, from World War II to the present. A reconsideration of the formative period of the post-Ottoman Middle East thus has the potential to amend and enrich the historical record on the period and to provide a revised perspective on the precedents set in that period and its impact on developments in the decades that followed.

The drawing of Turkey's borders with its Middle Eastern neighbors was formally concluded in the mid-1920s, following the signing of the Treaty of Lausanne in 1923. It was the end of a protracted and complicated process that began on the eve of World War I and proceeded more dramatically in the aftermath of the Great War. The drawing of Turkey's borders with Iran was the least painful and complicated because the borders were based on the centuries-old Ottoman-Persian frontier lines. A border treaty signed in 1913 served as the basis for the Lausanne borders of Iran with Turkey. In the intervening decade, there were several efforts by both sides to change the demarcation line, but the postwar settlement set it back to its prewar line. It nevertheless was not free of challenges and amendments in the interwar period. Still, the setting and demarcation of Turkey's borders with Syria and Iraq was much more complicated, as it could not rely on any prewar international agreement or long-standing frontier lines. Instead, these borders were set after years of fighting, attempts at imposed agreements, and, finally, reluctant territorial compromises. The Treaty of Lausanne determined the borders with Syria in 1923, but the border with Iraq was finalized only in 1926, after further maneuvering, negotiations, and arbitration. Yet, the protracted, convoluted, and conflicting developments that led to the demarcation of these borders produced much suspicion, contesting territorial ambitions, unsettled frontier regions, and political uncertainties that in turn generated doubts about the long-term sustainability and viability of the new borders. In retrospect, we know that the new borders set in the mid-1920s mostly remained intact in the decades that followed. But throughout the interwar period, and particularly in the volatile 1930s, it was far from certain that the new borders might not prove ephemeral and changeable.

The first steps toward the partition of the Ottoman Empire and the demarcation of new borders in the region were taken by the Allied powers during World War I. In 1915 and 1916, after months-long multilateral negotiations, the British, French, Italian, and Russian governments inked a number of agreements regarding the territorial division of the Ottoman lands at the end of the war, which became popularly known as the Sykes-Picot Agreement. They stipulated the maintenance of a small Ottoman-Turkish principality mainly in parts of northern and central Anatolia, while Italy was to be awarded control over parts of southern Anatolia, Russia domination over Eastern Anatolia, and France authority over parts of Southeastern Anatolia, Syria, and northern Mesopotamia. Britain was to receive control over Ottoman territories farther to the south. But when the hostilities between the Allies and the Ottomans formally came to an end with the Armistice of Mudros in October 1918, these agreements were not implemented as conceived. In the intervening years, the Bolshevik Revolution pulled Russia out of the partition plans, while the American entry into the war required reformulation of old imperialist goals within the new parameters of the League of Nations and the powerful idea of the right of self-determination, as conceived by President Woodrow Wilson. Furthermore, since it was mainly imperial British forces that actually occupied almost all Ottoman territories south of Anatolia, London was inclined to secure control over larger territories than were awarded to it in the Sykes-Picot Agreement, largely at France's expense. Finally, Britain sought to find a way to integrate into the postwar settlements various commitments it gave and promises it made to its Arab allies in the region and to the Zionist movement. It took many months of, at times contentious, negotiations and a significant amount of arm-twisting and machinations between the wartime allies until they reached in April 1920 an agreement for the partition of the Ottoman Empire. Heavy pressure was then put on the Ottoman authorities in Istanbul to accept the Allies' dictated terms, which the government of the Sultan finally felt compelled to accept in the Treaty of Sèvres in August 1920. The new partition plan differed in certain respects from the wartime Sykes-Picot Agreement. Britain, rather than France, was now awarded control over northern Mesopotamia, Greece over parts of Western Anatolia, and Armenia over territories in Eastern Anatolia that were previously designed as areas of Russian domination (Map 1.1). Furthermore, the treaty stipulated terms that were

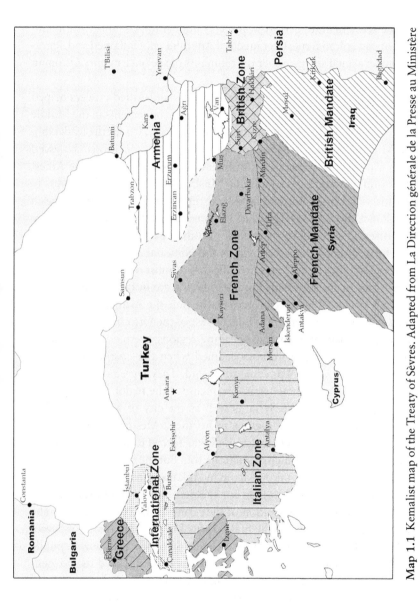

Map 1.1 Kemalist map of the Treaty of Sèvres. Adapted from La Direction générale de la Presse au Ministère de l'Intérieur, *La Turquie Contemporaine* (Ankara, 1935), 45.

likely to lead to the establishment of a Kurdish state in parts of Eastern and Southeastern Anatolia in the near future. But rather than settling the territorial conflicts over Anatolia and ushering in a new postwar peace settlement, the effort at forceful imposition of non-Muslim and European colonial rule over much of Anatolia only inflamed and aggravated an armed struggle over the remnants of the once mighty Ottoman Empire.

The advance of European colonial forces and Allied powers helped elicit the emergence of a number of resistance movements in the Middle East in 1919 and 1920, most notably in Anatolia. Under the leadership of Mustafa Kemal, various local resistance organizations coalesced into a powerful nationalist movement aimed at thwarting the Allies' partition plans and at maintaining Muslim sovereignty over the mostly Turkish-speaking Ottoman heartlands in Anatolia. The Ankara-based resistance movement laid out its own territorial demands, which were endorsed in early 1920 by the last Ottoman parliament in Istanbul in the form of a document known as the National Pact (Misak-ı Milli). The document virtually accepted the loss of most of the Arab-majority territories of the Ottoman Empire, which were in fact already almost entirely occupied by Allied forces by the time the Armistice of Mudros was signed in October 1918. But the rest of the Ottoman territories, in mainly Turkish- and Kurdish-speaking regions in Anatolia and immediately to its south, were not occupied when the hostilities formally ended and the Great War came to an end. They were now claimed by the National Pact. These territories included the region of Aleppo and other parts of northern Syria as well as the city of Mosul and adjacent Kurdish-dominated regions in northern Mesopotamia. The feeble Ottoman government in Istanbul was forced to forgo any claim to these regions, and to much of Anatolia too. But the fledgling nationalist government that was taking shape in Ankara under the leadership of Mustafa Kemal vowed to fight for the derailing of the European partition plans and the realization of the terms of the National Pact. The nationalist forces landed the first serious blow to the Treaty of Sèvres when, in late 1920, they defeated the army of the fledgling Republic of Armenia, shortly before a Bolshevik invasion quashed its independence by the end of the year. Facing common enemies in Britain and France, Moscow and Ankara established a strategic cooperation, buttressed by mutual diplomatic recognition and an agreement in March 1921 on their common borders in Eastern Anatolia. The Ankara government focused thereafter on the more formidable task of thwarting the territorial claims of Britain, France, and their allies and securing control over the territories stipulated by the National Pact.

A series of military victories against French forces in Cilicia and Southeastern Anatolia in 1921 prompted France and then Italy to negotiate a territorial settlement with the Ankara government. France resolved to focus its attention on securing its hold over Syria, and Italy determined that its position in Anatolia was untenable in view of problems closer to home and of tensions with Britain. Turkish-French negotiations resulted in October 1921 in the Treaty of Ankara, which ended the hostilities between the two sides and drew a line of demarcation between French-controlled Syria and the emerging Turkish state. The unofficial border ran from the northern part of the Gulf of Alexandretta to the Tigris River just south of Cizre (Jazirat Ibn 'Umar), much of it along completed parts of the Baghdad Railway. France thus conceded regions north of this line, which were first pledged to it in the wartime Sykes-Picot Agreement and later in the postwar Treaty of Sèvres. Conversely, the Ankara government conceded to French-ruled Syria territories that were demanded in the National Pact, such as the District of Alexandretta, areas around Aleppo, and the Jazira region. Ankara and Paris negotiated and signed the agreement without any regard to Arab and Kurdish nationalist claims for any of the frontier regions, let alone to Armenian hopes to secure control over some Anatolian regions in which the Ottoman authorities initiated the deportations and large-scale annihilation of Armenian communities during the Great War. The last stage of what came to be known after World War II as the Armenian Genocide thus ended with almost no Armenian presence left in Eastern and Southeastern Anatolia and with large numbers of survivors concentrated in northern Syria. Not all of them gave up on the nationalist vision of Armenian sovereignty in their lost homelands. Arab nationalists in Syria, who only a year earlier saw their fledgling government in Damascus crushed by French forces, were meanwhile outraged that France conceded to Turkey control over Cilicia and other lands north of the demarcation line, which they claimed as unalienable parts of Syria and the larger Arab homeland. Their protestations were completely disregarded. In 1923, the Lausanne borders between Turkey and Syria were based on the demarcation line set by the Turkish-French agreement two years earlier. It was a border liked neither by many nationalist Kurds and Arabs nor by nationalist

Turks abiding by the National Pact, and thus its legitimacy and perma-
nence were questioned on both sides of the border.

The demarcation of the Turkish-Iraqi border proved much more protracted and not less controversial and frustrating for the states and
communities affected by it. After the Italian forces withdrew peacefully
from Antalya in June 1921, and the Greek forces were routed in August
1922, the Eastern Anatolian frontier between Turkey and the British-
controlled Kingdom of Iraq remained the most contested and volatile
of Turkey's border regions. Even after all other borders and most other
territorial issues were resolved by the signing of the Treaty of Lausanne in July 1923, the future of the Turkish-Iraqi border remained
hung in the balance. Turkey laid claim to the city of Mosul and adjacent Kurdish-dominated regions in northern Mesopotamia, in accordance with the stipulation of the National Pact. It complained that the
British forces occupied these regions unlawfully after the signing of the
Armistice of Mudros in October 1918 and insisted that ethnic, historical, geographic, and economic considerations dictated that the region
and its peoples should be part of Turkey. Britain responded, on behalf
of Iraq, that northern Mesopotamia should rightfully remain tied to
Baghdad and the newly established Iraqi monarchy. Moreover, British
officials demanded that the region of Hakkari, farther to the north and
controlled by Turkish forces, should be also annexed to Iraq, so as to
allow for the return to it of Christian Nestorian (Assyrian) tribal populations that were driven out of their homeland by Ottoman forces
and their local auxiliaries during the Great War. London and Ankara
failed to resolve their differences, and the determination of the border
was therefore handed to the League of Nations. While the arbitration
and deliberations went on, a demarcation line known as the Brussels
Line was set as a provisional line separating Turkey and Iraq. Throughout 1924 and 1925, Britain and Turkey not only invested efforts at
building a strong legal and diplomatic case to support their claims but
also aided and abetted rebellions aimed at weakening their adversary's
hold over the territory on the other side of the line. This only intensified the instability in the region and the distrust and mutual suspicions between all involved. Finally, the League of Nations determined
in 1926 that the Brussels Line should become the permanent border.
Turkey accepted this outcome very reluctantly, after further ironing
out of conditions and details in negotiations with Britain. This was a
painful concession for Ankara, after years of public vows not to give

up on territories demanded by the National Pact, compounded by the loss of northern Mesopotamia's considerable oil resources, strategic transportation routes, and sizable Turkmen and Kurdish populations to which Turkey claimed ethnic affinity. It was on a much grander scale than the territorial concession made to France in Syria and came after years of persisting public pledges by Ankara not to concede these territories in northern Mesopotamia. Many nationalist Turks indeed felt that British machinations robed their country of important regions that belonged to it by right, even as nationalist Kurds demurred that they were left without any national state of their own, and Assyrian leaders in northern Iraq were bitter that their ancestral lands in Hakkari remained under Turkish rule (Map 1.2).[15]

The formal drawing of Turkey's Middle Eastern borders left very few of the involved governments and communities satisfied and many more of them frustrated and desirous of changes. Turkey was particularly dissatisfied with the handing of the Mosul region to Iraq and with the inclusion of the District of Alexandretta in Syria. This dissatisfaction was no secret. And it resulted in persistent wariness in Baghdad, Damascus, London, and Paris regarding Ankara's intentions in these regions. Of most immediate concern were suspicions regarding Turkey's motivation for aiding and abetting subversive activities and rebellions by Kurdish and Turkmen populations in northern Syria and Iraq. On its part, Turkey had very similar concerns. Even after the new border agreements were signed and ratified, Ankara continued to be worried that neither London nor Paris was completely reconciled to the failure of the Treaty of Sèvres. Turkey remained suspicious during the interwar period that the two European colonial powers were supporting Kurdish, Arab, Armenian, and Assyrian subversive activities and rebellions aimed at destabilizing the Turkish hold over Eastern and Southeastern Anatolia. Similar mutual distrust and suspicions extended to the Turkish-Iranian border as well. The government in Tehran still remembered well that Ottoman armies occupied Iranian Azerbaijan during the Great War and sought to spread the ideology of pan-Turkism among the local Turkic population. And Ankara was well aware that during the negotiations on the postwar settlement Iran laid claims to significant territories in Eastern Anatolia. The fact that the interwar period indeed witnessed repeated rebellions of frontier populations in Turkey, Syria, Iraq, and Iran fed into these at times exaggerated multilateral suspicions. The regional distrust they

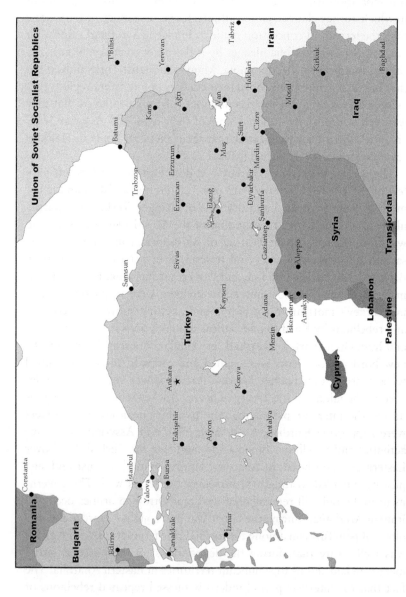

Map 1.2 Turkey's borders in 1926 (map drawn by William Terry).

nourished persisted with ups and downs throughout the period between the two world wars, and beyond, with particular spikes during the international crises and uncertainties of the 1930s.

The military balance in the region played an important role in managing threats in the frontier regions and influencing the levels of threat perceptions between regional powers. Britain and France were obviously global powers with military forces, weapon systems, and resources far superior to any country in the region. Yet, political, economic, and imperial considerations prompted both colonial powers to seek to decrease their military presence in the Middle East during the interwar period as much as possible, without compromising their core interests in the region. Uprisings and rebellions at times forced them to send significant reinforcements, but the interest in limiting their permanent military presence in the region without risking their strategic, political, and economic interests remained intact throughout the interwar period. Indeed, by the late 1930s, many observers speculated that the growing Italian and German challenges to their interests elsewhere might convince Britain and France to defer the defense of much of the Middle East to Turkey. The *New York Times* reported along these lines in June 1938 that Ankara, London, and Paris were moving toward a strategic alliance so that Turkish troops "would be in a position to invade Syria if she becomes troublesome to France or to enter Iraq if she makes trouble to Britain."[16] This unfounded report reflected widely held perceptions at the time regarding Turkey's regional power. Indeed, within the region, Turkey had by far the largest armed forces during the interwar period. In the 1930s it had 120,000 enlisted men under arms, and the number ballooned to 1.5 million after the outbreak of World War II. Iran's military was the second largest. Reza Shah expanded it from 40,000 at the beginning of his reign in the mid-1920s to 90,000 men at the end of the 1930s, and then to 127,000 after the outbreak of the Second World War. The armed forces of Turkey's other Middle Eastern neighbors were either very limited or all but nonexistent until they secured a level of autonomy from their colonial overlords. In Syria, for example, the French mandatory authorities prevented the local government in Damascus from organizing under its control any significant armed force. The British acted differently in Iraq, even before the end of their formal colonial rule as a mandatory power over the land in 1932. The Iraqi army was already 12,000 strong when the country was awarded its formal independence. Thereafter, however, the Iraqi military was rapidly expanded, reaching 43,000 men under arms by the early 1940s, which was admittedly still much smaller than the armies of Turkey and Iran. The relative size of these countries' armed forces also correlated with the number of airplanes, tanks, and other modern weapon systems at their disposal.[17] All three states deployed their armed forces regularly to quell insurrections in their frontier regions, primarily led by ethnic minorities in their common border regions. At times they cooperated against these rebels. But in many instances they suspected each other of encouraging or assisting rebels on the other side of the border. The level of distrust was in fact significant enough that these mutual suspicions did not dissipate even after the three countries signed in 1937, along with Afghanistan, a nonaggression pact known as the Treaty of Saadabad. Across the Mediterranean, in Egypt, the British finally allowed the government to gradually begin the formation of a meaningful if small armed force only after the signing of the Anglo-Egyptian Treaty in 1936. The clear military imbalance between the fully independent, partially independent, and colonized lands, and the constant mutual suspicions between them all, was the context within which the regional and colonial powers made recourse to diplomacy during the interwar period, to manage their differences and protect their interests through nonviolent contacts and negotiations.

Diplomatic ties and engagements involving the major European powers were of prime importance, but not to the complete exclusion of diplomatic relations within the region. The government of Iran, and from the early 1930s those of Iraq, Egypt, and, to a much lesser degree, even Syria, conducted their own foreign policy and managed their relations with Turkey. Iran established formal diplomatic relations with Kemalist Turkey already shortly after the establishment of the republic. Turkey's relations with Egypt, Iraq, and Syria were initially managed by their colonial overlords. But Ankara and Cairo established diplomatic relations shortly after the ratification of the Treaty of Lausanne, and Baghdad followed suit after the signing of the Anglo-Iraqi Treaty of 1930, which paved the way for Iraq's formal independence in 1932. Turkey established embassies and legations in the capital cities of these states, and consulates in other major cities in Egypt, Iran, and Iraq, as well as in the French mandates in Syria and Lebanon, the British mandate in Palestine, and in the Saudi-ruled Hijaz. The bilateral relations between Turkey and its neighboring countries involved diplomatic ties, defense and security issues, and economic interests, as well as consular matters of visas, various certificates, property and residency rights, and so on. The division of the former Ottoman territories into separate states indeed left many unresolved issues that were managed by the Turkish diplomatic missions in the Middle East, and by Middle Eastern official representatives in Turkey. From attending to issues of citizenship, marriage, inheritance, and so forth, to collecting information on opposition activists abroad, keeping tabs on political developments, and representing their countries in social, cultural, and diplomatic functions, Turkish diplomatic representatives in the Middle East and Middle Eastern envoys in Turkey played meaningful roles in the nascent regional state system.

The parameters of Ankara's relations with the Middle East were set, however, by broader geopolitical considerations related to Turkey's changing relations with the major European powers. The most stable and productive relations nurtured by the Kemalist republic from the early 1920s and throughout most of the interwar period was with the Soviet Union. In the 1920s, the Turkish-Soviet alignment was largely based on their common threat perception from Britain and France, whereas in the 1930s it, was their common concern with the increasing belligerence of Fascist Italy that contributed to their cooperation in the international arena. Ankara and Moscow were never formal allies and had their share of disagreements. For example, the Kemalist suppression of Communist activities in Turkey was not viewed kindly by the Comintern, and disagreements regarding Turkey's rights in the Straits cooled their relations in the late 1930s. Nevertheless, the two sides maintained good working relations until the eve of World War II, with Ankara being careful to coordinate with the Soviet leadership all its major diplomatic initiatives, including regarding the Middle East, or at the least to secure Moscow's acquiescence. In contrast, Italy emerged in the 1930s as Turkey's main concern in the international arena. The Italians already controlled the Dodecanese Islands, off the Mediterranean coast of Anatolia, since capturing them from the Ottomans in 1912. But it was in the early 1930s that Ankara became particularly concerned with Benito Mussolini's increasingly belligerent and expansionist posture in the Mediterranean arena and the Balkans. The shared concern with Italy's goals and intentions helped pave the way for a gradual rapprochement between Turkey and Britain in the mid-1930s, and later with France too. The improving relations were always fraught with difficulties, because of lingering mutual suspicions from the early 1920s and disagreements regarding border issues between

Turkey, Syria, and Iraq. Nevertheless, by the eve of World War II, Ankara's hope and expectation was to successfully align its rapprochement with Britain and France with the preservation of its cooperative relations with the Soviet Union. One complicating factor in Turkey's relations with all three major powers, but which also incentivized better ties with them, was Ankara's growing dependence on trade relations with Germany in the late 1930s, which in turn provided the Nazi regime with economic clout over Turkey.[18]

In the decade following the onset of the Great Depression in 1929, economic considerations indeed gained added importance in Turkey's international relations, including with the Middle East. The major European countries were Turkey's most important trade partners. This was crucially dictated by their large populations, sizable and advanced economies, geographical proximity, efficient transportation networks, and political clout. Turkish trade levels with neighboring countries in the Middle East were much less important despite their historical economic ties, because many of the conditions that favored trade with European markets were not as favorable. Take for example the sheer difference in population size between Middle Eastern and European countries, even discounting overseas colonial populations. In the early 1930s, the population of each of metropolitan Italy and France was about 40 million people, of metropolitan Britain 45 million, and of Germany 64 million. The population of Turkey at the time was meanwhile only about 14 million people, of Egypt 15 million, of Iran 13 million, of Iraq 3.5 million, and of Syria and Lebanon 3 million.[19] In all these cases, there was a high correlation between population figures and the size of the economy. This meant that even before factoring in levels of industrialization, economic diversity, complementarity of markets, and so on, the potential markets for Turkish trade with neighboring countries in the Middle East were much smaller to begin with. And commercial relations with Middle Eastern countries indeed remained much less substantial than with European countries throughout the interwar period. At the same time, economic relations with Middle Eastern markets were neither perceived as negligible, nor as lacking potential for growth, nor as devoid of strategic importance. For one thing, whereas Turkey ran trade deficits with Europe, its commerce with Middle Eastern economies was for the most part in surplus and earned it desperately needed hard currency. For another, Ankara hoped and expected that the development of new transportation networks with the Middle East would attract to its territory Eurasian transit trade in general, and European–Middle Eastern trade in particular. These were considered to be strategic and economic goals of the first order. But in order to become a major conduit for major transcontinental trade and transportation networks, Turkey was required not only to overcome financial and engineering challenges, but also to secure the cooperation of Middle Eastern governments on the other side of its borders. Deep-seated suspicions about Turkey's regional intentions, as well as competition from other markets and prospective transit routes, necessitated the investment of significant efforts in propagating Turkey's vision of regional economic and transportation cooperation and in lobbying distrustful neighboring governments for its implementation.

Attitudes toward Turkey in the Middle East were not always dominated by suspicions or disapproval, however, with some viewing the Kemalist republic as a model for emulation. The secularizing reforms, legal emancipation of women, and the adoption of economic nationalism, for example, won many admirers in the Middle East, alongside their fair share of detractors. The former were not shy of making their admiration to Turkey be known in books and articles in the press. Whereas critics oftentimes warned against the precedents set in Turkey and denounced the Kemalist regime on ideological or religious basis, admirers countered with positive commentaries on aspects of the Kemalist reforms, and with recommendations to emulate them partially or fully in their own societies. By the mid-1930s, the ruling Republican People's Party defined the basic tenets of Kemalist Turkey as consisting of the principles of republicanism, secularism, nationalism, populism, statism, and revolutionism. In reality, however, Kemalism never became a systematic and all-embracing ideology in the interwar period. Instead, it remained a set of generally defined opinions and attitudes that allowed people of different worldviews – some attracted to socialism, others to fascism, some to liberalism, others to autoritarianism – to all describe themselves as Kemalists and remain part and parcel of the establishment during the single-party rule in the interwar period.[20] In the Middle East, admirers of Mustafa Kemal and his regime were similarly a diverse lot who were attracted to various aspects of the Kemalist agenda and policies rather than to Kemalism per se. Indeed, while many described Mustafa Kemal and his reforms and achievements as an impressive model for success that was worthy of emulation in the Middle East and in other non-Western societies, they more often than not picked and chose specific elements rather than the entirety of Kemalist Turkey's political structure, economic policies, social reforms, cultural reorientation, or posture in the international arena. When advocating and hailing the "Turkish model," admirers in the interwar Middle East tended to focus on only some of these aspects. Just as critics were likely to focus on specific elements of the Kemalist policies and reforms when warning against its emulation in the Middle East.

The Turkish government never aspired to export Kemalism as such, but it did actively present its policies and reforms as an impressive success story that should inspire other "Eastern peoples." As part of its propaganda operations, or public diplomacy in later parlance, Ankara actively sought to project to the Middle East a positive image of the Kemalist republic as a successful model for emulation, and to develop and nurture fruitful relations with admirers and sympathizers in the region. In that vein, the director of the Turkish government's press office, Burhan Asaf Belge, declared in 1936, on the occasion of a visit of a group of Egyptian dignitaries to Turkey, that "the movement that has transformed the economic, social, cultural, and political foundations of society from top to bottom began as a Turkish movement, but it cannot be limited to Turkey alone. There is no doubt that all other countries that live under similar circumstances will learn from the Turkish marvel and be inspired and invigorated by Atatürk, the founder and great leader of the Turkish revolution." A few months later he embarked on a lecture tour in Middle Eastern capitals, aimed at advocating this vision to audiences in the region.[21] This was only one of a number of more sustained public relations and propaganda initiatives of the Turkish government in the Middle East in the interwar period.

At the same time, some of the legacies of the late Ottoman period left uneasy memories that impacted mutual attitudes in Turkey and the Middle East during the interwar period. In Arab nationalist circles this was a period that was remembered and described as a time of political oppression and efforts at cultural assimilation. More generally, the hundreds of years of Ottoman political domination were oftentimes presented by Arab nationalists as a long period of mismanagement that was crucial in preventing progress and modernization in the Middle East. In Turkey, meanwhile, Arab demands for autonomy or independence during the late Ottoman period, and the Arab Revolt during World War I, were depicted as indicative of Arab ungrateful and treacherous attitudes toward their coreligionist Turks, who purportedly protected them and their interests for many centuries. One of the most powerful and well-known purveyors of this viewpoint was Falih Rıfkı Atay, a member of the Turkish Grand National Assembly throughout the interwar period, who also served as the editor-in-chief of the semiofficial daily *Hakimiyet-i Milliye* and its successor *Ulus*. In a book he originally published in 1932 under the title *Zeytindağı* (Mount of Olives), Atay relates his experiences as a young officer on the Palestine front during the Great War. The book was much more than simply a memoir. It was interlaced with observations on the root causes of the destruction of the Ottoman Empire, ultimately arguing that the territories beyond Anatolia were burdensome foreign lands, populated by treacherous people who were undeserving of the great sacrifices made by the Turkish people in defending these regions. The book thus conveys and supports the prevailing Kemalist perception that the end of the multiethnic and multireligious Ottoman Empire and the establishment of the Anatolia-based Turkish nation state was both desirable and all but inevitable. The memoir remained very popular in the decades that followed, particularly in Kemalist circles, but curiously even Recep Tayyip Erdoğan declared in early 2014 that the book is an "essential reading for any aspiring politician" as well as for all young citizens of the republic. Scholars of modern Turkey, meanwhile, have pointed to the book as a prime example of the antipathy in the early Kemalist elites toward the Middle East and its peoples.[22] Not a few students of Turkish foreign policy indeed suggested that ethnic animosities and lingering acrimony from the late Ottoman period were crucial in informing the early Kemalist republic's purported disinterest in the Middle East.[23]

A closer look at the evidence suggests that the Kemalist elites were neither consensual in these positions nor willing to allow sentiment and ideology to trump Turkey's interests in the region. None other than Falih Rıfkı Atay himself made that point in a confidential conversation with a Zionist envoy from Mandate Palestine in early 1938. He confirmed to the visitor his contempt to the Arab peoples, as depicted in his famous memoir, but also clarified that although these sentiments are shared by many others in the Kemalist elites, they do not let their emotions dictate Turkey's policies toward the Middle East. Instead, Turkey's foreign relations with the region are based strictly on their

assessments of Turkey's national interests and its geopolitical circumstances.[24] Furthermore, not all those who were part of the Kemalist
establishment in the interwar period even shared these sweeping negative sentiments toward the Middle East. Indeed, within the relatively
political big tent that the ruling Republican People's Party was during the single-party regime of the early republic, there were important voices that advocated the strengthening of ties with the Middle
East, because it would serve vital Turkish interests, and in anticipation
that societies in the region would follow suit and undergo processes of
progress and modernization like in Turkey.

The Istanbul-based daily *Cumhuriyet*, which was one of the most
popular and influential newspapers in interwar Turkey, was a notable
champion of productive relations with the Middle East. Yunus Nadi,
the journal's proprietor and editor-in-chief, and a loyal and influential purveyor of the government's perspective in the interwar period,
commissioned numerous articles and opinion pieces in support of
expanded ties with countries in the region, and wrote himself many
front page editorials in that vein. While fiercely taking Ankara's side
in cases of diplomatic or political disagreements with Middle Eastern
governments, *Cumhuriyet* defended very consistently throughout the
1930s the benefits of improving and expanding Turkey's economic,
social, cultural, and political ties with states and societies in the Middle
East. It thus gave voice to a perspective shared by various stakeholders, particularly in Istanbul and the Aegean region, which traditionally
have maintained business and social ties to Egypt and the Levant. For
instance, *Cumhuriyet* lobbied on their behalf for the establishment of
maritime line between Istanbul and Alexandria by way of Izmir, and
then campaigned vigorously for its maintenance when it faced financial difficulties. Likewise, it backed efforts to attract Middle Eastern
participants and visitors to the Izmir International Fair, and tourists to
traditional vacation destinations such as Bursa, Yalova, and Istanbul.
Cumhuriyet also advocated closer diplomatic relations with Middle
Eastern governments, as well as public relations initiatives aimed at
improving Turkey's public image in the region.[25]

The foreign policy of Turkey during the early years of the republic
was indeed not dictated primarily by ideological precepts or by contentious sentiments and historical grudges. Ankara established fruitful
cooperation with the Soviet Union despite the Turkish government's
suppression of Communism, and initiated a rapprochement with

Greece in 1930 and with Britain and France later in that decade despite the bitter memories and legacies of the war over Anatolia and the post–World War I partition plans that prompted it. The same may be concluded regarding the factors and considerations that influenced the Kemalist republic's relations with Fascist Italy and Nazi Germany. A recent study on Turkish foreign policy during the period indeed concluded that "during the Atatürk era, ideological considerations were considered less important than power politics in the formulation of foreign policy." It has often been overlooked, however, that Ankara's relations with the Middle East were no exception in this regard. But the same author goes on to argue that the "Kemalist foreign policy was, in effect, defensive realism – state survival through the maximization of power achieved by focusing on strengthening the Turkish economy and military, and establishing friendly relations with all the neighbours through a policy of non-expansionism and the protection of the status-quo."[26] This is certainly the way Ankara sought to project its foreign policy during the interwar period, toward its neighbors in the Middle East as much as toward other near-abroads. Yet, this was certainly not the way it was perceived by many contemporaries in the region, even before the Turkish annexation of Hatay on the eve of World War II. Ultimately, Turkey never resorted to unilateral action to expand its territory, as did Fascist Italy and Nazi Germany during that time period. Ankara opted to remain within the confines of international commitments and agreements. But it did at times issue veiled threats or implied that it might resort to arms, and both neighboring governments and the major European powers in fact operated under the assumption that, should the opportunity present itself, Turkey may well be interested in the annexation of regions in northern Syria and Iraq which were within the bounds of the National Pact. And yet, mirroring Ankara's modus operandi, political realism guided the now cooperative, now strained relations of regional and international actors with the Kemalist republic.

This book suggests that the history of Turkey's relations with the Middle East in the interwar period is not a simple story of abrupt rupture of ties, deliberate mutual dissociation, and moving in separate directions. It could hardly have been, in the volatile international arena of the 1930s. As argued above, none of the principal actors in the region or in Europe could be convinced that the global economic crisis that precipitated serious challenges to the post–World War I international order elsewhere, will not lead to significant modifications in the recently installed post-Ottoman order in the Middle East. In contrast to the retrospective conclusions of historians and other scholars in later decades, contemporaries in the interwar period hardly assumed that Turkey was engaged in a voluntary effort to perpetually detach itself from the region, or was not actively pursuing specific interests in the Middle East. Chapter 2 shows that the post-Ottoman borders in general, and those separating Turkey from the Middle East in particular, were indeed much less stable in reality and perception than has been often assumed in studies of the period. If anything, there were persisting concerns and suspicions in neighboring countries at the time that the Kemalist republic might be harboring revisionist intentions regarding the Lausanne borders. Chapter 3 explores how Ankara was expanding its diplomatic footprint in the Middle East in the 1930s in direct response to changes in the regional and international arenas, and in an effort to protect what the Kemalist leadership perceived as vital Turkish interests in the region. Chapter 4 argues that economic calculations and strategic concerns, having to do with Turkey's geostrategic position between Europe and the Middle East, played a meaningful role in informing Turkey's engagement with the region, particularly in the decade following the onset of the Great Depression. Chapter 5 explores interactions between Turkey and sympathetic observers of the Kemalist reforms in the Middle East and ways in which Mustafa Kemal and his policies were presented as models for emulation in the region. Chapter 6 examines Turkey's efforts to attract visits by Arab journalists, intellectuals, professionals, businesspeople, and tourists, for both propagandistic and economic reasons. Chapter 7 concludes the book with a survey of major developments in the relations between Turkey and the Middle East since World War II and how they measure in relation to the circumstances and policies of Kemalist Turkey during the interwar period. This reexamination of the relations between Turkey and the Middle East during the period between the two world wars, with a scope that goes beyond a narrow definition of diplomatic history, throws a new light on foreign relations and regional dynamics during this formative period in the history of the post-Ottoman Middle East and offers a modified perspective on Ankara's engagement with the region in the decades that followed.

2 | *Degrees of Separation*

It has been often argued that after the establishment of the republic and the signing of the peace settlements in the mid-1920s, Ankara's "energies had been directed to progress at home, while the goal of Turkey's foreign policy was to maintain the status quo."[1] This was indeed Ankara's official stance during the interwar period. It was encapsulated in Mustafa Kemal Atatürk's motto of "Peace within the country and peace with the world," as was stated, for example, by Foreign Minister Tevfik Rüştü Aras in a propagandistic article he penned in 1937 for a special issue of the *Financial Times*. The piece was entitled "Turkey's Domestic and Foreign Policies of Tranquility and Security," and its gist was that Turkey was a status quo power that Britain would do wisely to befriend.[2] The motto was subsequently rephrased to read "Peace at home, Peace in the world," which to this day is presented by official Turkey as the fundamental goals of Ankara's domestic and foreign policies. During the interwar period, however, not many foreign statesmen and observers viewed the Kemalist republic as either beholden to the Lausanne borders or as a country committed to peaceful solution of domestic and foreign disputes. Arab nationalists, Zionist leaders, Kurdish nationalists, Iranian statesmen, and British and French officials usually did not see eye to eye on most issues related to the region in the late 1930s. But in the years leading to World War II, they did seem to share the view that Turkey might in fact be very much interested in finding opportunities to press for revisions in its borders with Syria, Iraq, and Iran. Territories in northern Syria and northern Iraq, which were within the boundaries of the National Pact and were only reluctantly conceded by Turkey, were perceived in European and Middle Eastern capitals as particularly coveted by Kemalist Turkey. This assessment was ubiquitous in commentaries in the Arabic, Hebrew, English, and French press of the period as well as in secret correspondence of local political leaders, colonial administrators, and European diplomats and statesmen. Furthermore, it was no secret that in its efforts to ensure

"Peace within the country," Ankara was willing to deploy harsh measures to suppress any expression of political dissent and unleash very
violent means against rebellious Kurdish populations in the vicinity
of its Middle Eastern borders in Eastern and Southeastern Anatolia.
Turkey was certainly not perceived as particularly reluctant to use military force to achieve its goals. Foreign observers often suspected that
despite the slogan of "peace with the world," should the opportunity
present itself, Ankara might be tempted to occupy territories south
of its borders, either by force or by diplomatic pressure backed by
the threat of force. Indeed, at a time in which the peace settlements
in Europe were facing increasing revisionist challenges in the 1930s,
and various initiatives were launched in the Middle East to redraw
some of the post-Ottoman borders, the durability of Turkey's Middle
Eastern borders was widely perceived as anything but guaranteed and
certain.

The Kemalist leadership, too, had its doubts regarding the commitment of the European and regional powers to Turkey's territorial
integrity. Ankara remained suspicious throughout the interwar period
that Britain and France might be assisting secessionist movements in
its frontier regions in Eastern and Southeastern Anatolia, that they
might be aiding and abetting conspiracies and plots by anti-Kemalist
activists in the Middle East, and that Italy might be coveting Turkey's
Mediterranean shore. Kurdish revolts near the borders with Iran, Iraq,
and Syria were indeed time and again perceived and described as
assisted by the European colonial powers. Armenian, Assyrian (Nestorian), and Syriac exiles from Anatolia, who found refuge in northern
Syria and Iraq after the Great War, were likewise suspected of maintaining territorial claims on Turkey's Lausanne borders and of assisting Kurdish rebellions. The Treaty of Sèvres assigned the territories
claimed by these ethnic groups to other powers. The Turkish leadership remained convinced that even after signing the Treaty of Lausanne, Britain and France did not forgo their ultimate goal of parti-
tioning Turkey along the lines stipulated in the Treaty of Sèvres. This
persistent concern with malicious Western designs for Turkey would
be later denoted the Sèvres syndrome.[3] Kurdish, Armenian, Assyrian,
and Arab nationalists indeed did lay claims to territories under Turkish rule, and in some cases rebels did receive support from across the
border, so Ankara's fears were certainly not completely detached from
reality. The Kemalist leadership was thus persistently suspicious that its

own restive Kurdish population might be conspiring with enemies of Turkey abroad to detach the frontier regions from Anatolia and shrink Turkey's territory.

The durability and long-term permanency of the post-Ottoman borders was never taken as self-evident during the interwar period and appeared as increasingly questionable in the turbulent 1930s. Revanchist pressures, irredentist claims, and revisionist demands in the Middle East were certainly not as extreme, destabilizing, and consequential as they were in Europe of the time. Nevertheless, they did exist and produced unsettling rumors, wild conspiracies, and various forms of deliberations regarding possible changes in the political map of the region. Ankara was therefore very concerned with developments in the frontier regions and also in political developments south of its borders. For example, Ankara was suspicious that either Britain or France might support the establishment of Kurdish, Assyrian, or Armenian political entities in northern Iraq or Syria, lest such entities might lay claim to its territories or serve as staging grounds for rebellions in Anatolia. Similarly, Ankara also followed closely on pan-Arab and pan-Islamic initiatives in the Fertile Crescent and beyond. The former risked the establishment of a potentially powerful political force that could lay claim to territories assigned to Turkey in Lausanne as well as more effectively thwart possible Turkish claims to lands assigned to the mandates of Syria and Iraq. The latter could potentially attract the support of significant parts of the Turkish population that had yet to fully resign to the abolition of the Caliphate and the adoption of secularism as a fundamental tenet of the republic. Either way, Turkey had no interest in seeing any or all parts of the Arab-majority regions of the Middle East being united within a pan-Arab or a pan-Islamic political structure. Ankara was therefore determined to try and hinder any such initiative. At the same time, the fact that Turkey only reluctantly accepted the borders with Syria and Iraq made its neighbors to the south less than confident that Ankara was satisfied with the status quo. To a lesser extent, Iran too was anxious of possible Turkish designs on its frontier regions with Anatolia. In sum, neither any of the neighboring countries nor the European colonial powers perceived the post-Ottoman borders to be inviolable. Indeed, the process of finalizing Turkey's Middle Eastern borders was in fact a work in progress throughout the interwar period, with all involved parties being far from certain by the late 1930s that more dramatic changes were not still to come.

I A Painful Parting

The partition of the Ottoman Empire involved the division between Turkey, British-administered Iraq, and French-ruled Syria of a vast frontier region known during Ottoman times as Kurdistan. Before World War I, this Kurdish-majority region of mostly mountainous terrain was also the homeland of other ethnic communities. Substantial Armenian and Assyrian communities inhabited the northern parts of Ottoman Kurdistan until the Great War, and Turkmens and some Arab populations lived in its southern regions, along with some other smaller ethnic and religious communities. Both the Sykes-Picot Agreement and the Treaty of Sèvres stipulated the detachment of the whole region from Ottoman rule, and its division between the Allied powers. The effective resistance led from Ankara prevented the implementation of these settlements as planned by the European powers. On its part, the fledgling nationalist government in Ankara presented in the National Pact its own demands to all parts of Ottoman Kurdistan, as well as the adjacent city of Mosul and its surroundings. Subsequently, the fate of the vast region became a bone of contention between Turkey and Britain. After they failed to resolve their disagreements in Lausanne and in direct negotiations thereafter, the fate of the regions of Mosul and southern Ottoman Kurdistan was submitted for the determination of the League of Nations. On the ground, meanwhile, British forces secured de facto control over the oil-rich area of Mosul and its environs and the Kurdish-majority mountainous regions to its west. The Turkish forces meanwhile established their presence in Hakkari, the traditional home of Assyrian communities before World War I, which after the Great War became dominated almost exclusively by Kurdish populations. While the arbitration process was ongoing, Turkey and Britain pledged in October 1924 to respect the existing situation on the ground, with the two sides separated along what came to be known as the Brussels Line. The Turkish claim to the territories south of the line was in accordance with the National Pact but in the arbitration process was justified in terms of ethnic affinity with the Turkmen and Kurdish populations in the area and based on economic, geographical, and historical considerations. The British side rejected these claims on behalf of Iraq. In addition, London submitted its own claims to the region of Hakkari, north of the line, in order to repatriate to that area the Assyrian populations that were forced to flee their homelands during World War I, on account of their cooperation with the Allies. Most of the Assyrian refugees were concentrated in northern Iraq and aspired to return to their lost properties after the detachment of the region from Turkish rule. The League of Nations appointed a fact-finding commission and tasked it with weighing the competing claims, and with proposing a permanent border between Turkey and British-administered Iraq.[4]

As the arbitration process was gradually proceeding through 1925, the contested region was very volatile because of tribal revolts aimed at influencing the border settlement. The most dramatic development in this respect was a major Kurdish revolt against Turkish rule in 1925, which for a time threatened Ankara's hold over much of Eastern Anatolia. The Turkish government denounced the uprising, known as the Sheikh Said rebellion, as a treacherous insurrection which was motivated by reactionary traitors. But it suspected Britain of masterminding the revolt in an effort to demonstrate Turkey's unpopularity among the Kurds and to weaken its hold over Eastern Anatolia. Ankara was similarly nervous about the movements of Assyrian populations in the direction of Hakkari. From Turkey's perspective this was part of a British-encouraged effort to establish facts on the ground, in accordance with the Assyrian leaders' demands to establish in Hakkari a national home for the Assyrian people, at least initially within the framework of Iraq. Turkey responded decisively and harshly. The Sheikh Said rebellion was quelled very violently, and the remnants of Assyrians in its territory were deported south of the Brussels Line. When the fact-finding commission finally submitted its recommendations by late 1925, it proposed that the temporary line would become the basis for a permanent border between Turkey and Iraq, leaving Hakkari under Turkish governance, but assigning to Iraq the much larger and more valuable regions in and around Mosul. This was a very bitter outcome for Turkey, but Ankara was finally resigned to accept it as an important step toward the stabilization of its control over the rest of Anatolia. Additional rounds of negotiations finally led in June 1926 to a frontier agreement. The Brussels Line became the permanent border between Turkey and Iraq, but as a sweetener, Turkey was promised 10 percent of the royalties on oil exports from Mosul for 25 years. Overall, however, the new border was very unsatisfying for Turkey, and in contradiction to the National Pact, and was much more favorable to the interests of Britain and the fledgling Kingdom of Iraq.[5]

The Turkish government reluctantly accepted what was widely perceived within the Kemalist elite as an unjust solution to the so-called

Mosul Question. After years of insistence on the purported Turkishness of the region, and vows to secure its unification with the rest of the homeland, Kemalist leaders and intellectuals explained to their people that the overall interests of the republic dictated the swallowing of that bitter pill. And yet, there was no effort to disguise the Kemalist disgust with the new border with Iraq, neither in the immediate aftermath of the official resolution of the controversy in 1926 nor in the years that followed.[6] This is evident, for example, in a lecture to university students given in 1934 by Minister of Education Yusuf Hikmet Bayur, the author of the monumental *History of the Turkish Revolution*, a semiofficial Kemalist version of late Ottoman and early republican history. In his talk, which was entitled "Our Perspective on the Mosul Question" and was reproduced in the daily press, he explained that malicious cooperation between Britain, France, and Fascist Italy produced a resolution that deprived Turkey of its rightful claims to Mosul and its environs. With Hakkari being the exception, the British had their way thanks to their nefarious scheming. Turkey was eventually resigned to accept this injustice out of its desire for peaceful relations with its neighbors in the Middle East, and because of its pressing need to concentrate its limited resources on rebuilding and internal reforms.[7] However, neither Britain nor Iraq was convinced that Turkey might not look for opportunities to revise the new border and gain control over parts of northern Iraq.

The British colonial authorities and the Iraqi government indeed remained concerned that Turkey did not fully come to terms with the loss of the Mosul region. British military plans for the defense of Iraq therefore included a scenario of Turkish invasion from the north. And during the negotiations with Iraq in 1930 toward the end of the mandate, London justified its demand for maintaining an air force base near Mosul in the need to deter Turkey from occupying the region by force. This particular British request was rejected by Baghdad. But the Anglo-Iraqi Treaty of 1930 did stipulate that Britain could keep defensive military forces in the environs of Mosul for five years. The British ambassador to newly independent Iraq explained in 1932 that "Turkey, for the moment, was a safe neighbour [to Iraq], but no-one could be sure that her old claims to the Mosul vilayat might not be revived again later on."[8] The fear of potential Turkish designs on the oil-rich region, and of Ankara's long-term ties to Turkmen populations and its ad hoc cooperation with Kurdish tribal groups in northern Iraq, indeed remained a constant concern for the Iraqi government throughout the 1930s.[9]

By the same token, the treaty of 1926 did not put to rest Turkey's anxiety with Kurdish rebellions and Assyrian claims on its territory, allegedly with Britain's encouragement and assistance. In northern Iraq, significant numbers of Assyrians served in a British-armed militia just south of the border. Even after the frontier treaty of 1926, the Assyrian leadership did not drop its claim to Hakkari, which was publicly stated to be irrevocable. Their public stance was changed only when Iraq gained formal independence in 1932, and tension between Baghdad and the Assyrians increased. At that point, the new Assyrian National Pact included statements which in effect abandoned their claim on their ancestral homeland in Hakkari. At the same time, during the British-Iraqi negotiations over the end of the mandate, the Assyrian leadership demanded to be awarded an autonomous region in postmandate northern Iraq, just south of the Turkish border. Ankara did not believe the Assyrian assurances regarding Hakkari and communicated to the British government and the League of Nations its opposition to the establishment of Assyrian autonomy even inside Iraq. Turkey therefore supported the Iraqi government in its refusal to accept these Assyrian demands. Baghdad was concerned that an autonomy would lead to future secessionist demands, whereas Ankara was suspicious that it might become a basis for seditious activities in Turkey and irredentist claims on Hakkari. Based on similar arguments and concerns, Baghdad and Ankara were likewise opposed to Kurdish demands for autonomy in independent Iraq. At the same time, both countries sought to manipulate the Assyrian and Kurdish competing claims to the same territories, and the tensions they created between the two ethnic groups. Ankara maintained ties with Kurdish tribes in northern Iraq since the early 1920s, partly as a countermeasure to what it perceived as British fomenting of unrest among Kurdish tribes in Anatolia. Turkey was now striving to exploit these ties both as a handle on Baghdad, to the chagrin of the Iraqi government, and as a pressure device on the Assyrians. From Turkey's perspective, its interference in developments in northern Iraq was defensive in character, because it was aimed at preventing the region from becoming a staging ground for insurrections and rebellious activities on Turkish territory. Iraq and Britain, on the other hand, tended to view Turkey's interventions in northern Iraq as unwarranted, meddlesome, and worrying.[10]

The border agreement of 1926 stipulated the establishment of a permanent frontier commission to address misunderstandings and problems between Turkey and Iraq. Both governments pledged to prevent unfriendly activities toward their neighbor in a 75-kilometer-wide security zone on both sides of the largely unmarked border. The commission met annually, which was an occasion for each side to air grievances and demand remedy to problems regarding the implementation of the treaty. In a meeting in October 1929, for instance, the Turkish side complained that armed Assyrian bands were roaming the frontier region and encroaching deep into the Turkish side of the border. In several cases they were detained by Turkish forces and found to be carrying standard British weapons, and to be acting on orders from British officials in Baghdad. The Iraqi side, still operating at the time under the British mandatory authorities, countered that this activity was in response to encroachments of Turkey-based Kurdish tribal groups into Iraq, implying that Ankara might have had a hand in that activity. Both sides agreed to cooperate to prevent future misunderstandings. Yet, in the following year's meeting in June 1930, Turkey not only made similar complaints about encroachments of armed Assyrians into its side of the border but also protested against seditious anti-Turkish propaganda by Armenian and Kurdish nationalist activists in northern Iraq.[11] Bilateral pledges to prevent these and similar unfriendly acts against both countries notwithstanding, mutual complaints about the other side's management of the frontier regions persisted throughout the British mandate period and into the period of formal Iraqi independence after October 1932.

Turkey's complicated calculus regarding the management of the frontier region is evident in Ankara's intricate and fluid relations with the Kurdish tribal leader Ahmed of Barzan. On the one hand, the important Iraq-based chieftain was known to have cooperated with Kurdish rebels in Anatolia. On the other hand, he was seen as an important counterweight to the influence of the British-backed Assyrian militia just south of Turkey's borders with Iraq. Therefore, when the Kurdish leader launched in 1931 a major rebellion against the Iraqi government, Turkey wavered on whether to assist Baghdad in crushing his revolt. Initially, Ankara opposed an Iraqi initiative in May to conduct a large-scale military operation against his supporters near the Turkish border. Hoping to maintain his role as a counterweight to the Assyrian militia, Turkey offered to Barzani its good offices for negotiating a compromise with the Iraqi government, in return for his pledge to desist from any cooperation with Kurdish rebels in Anatolia. The negotiations with the Kurdish leader soon failed. Ankara therefore opted to offer Baghdad its blessing for an Iraqi operation, and promised its cooperation in sealing its side of the border. The dire situation forced Barzani to reconsider his stance. In December 1931 he approached the Turkish government again, pledging his full loyalty to Turkey in return for permission to cross with his supporters into its territory and settle in the vicinity of Hakkari. At that point Ankara already pledged cooperation with Baghdad. Moreover, it had little incentive to offer refuge to the restive Kurdish leader. He was therefore warned that if he will cross into Turkey, the Turkish army will pursue him.[12] The British-Iraqi onslaught forced Barzani in mid-1932 to cross the border nevertheless and surrender to the Turkish forces. He was promptly arrested and removed to western Anatolia, hundreds of miles away from the Iraqi border. The exile did not last very long. A few months later, following increasingly assertive Assyrian demands for autonomy in northern Iraq, Barzani was allowed to return in early 1933 to the frontier region and launch raids into northern Iraq. The newly independent Iraqi government complained to Ankara about his activities, but Turkey claimed no knowledge of his actions. At that point in time, Ankara's concern with the prospect of an autonomous British-backed Assyrian entity in northern Iraq trumped its distrust of Barzani and his Kurdish tribal forces.[13]

The place of the Assyrians in independent Iraq indeed became the center of a rapidly escalating situation that ended in tragedy in 1933, and which indirectly involved Turkey too. As a confrontation between the Iraqi army and the Assyrians militia appeared to become increasingly unavoidable, Britain sought to defuse the situation by again seeking to acquire for them their old homeland in Hakkari. London approached Ankara with an offer to exchange that region, which would be then opened for Assyrian resettlement and would become a semiautonomous part of Iraq, in return for the Barzanis' traditional tribal territories in northern Iraq. Ankara rejected the deal. It made little geographical or strategic sense to exchange Hakkari for Barzan; the Barzanis were only ephemeral allies that Turkey distrusted; and most importantly, the Kemalist leadership had no desire to see the Assyrians establish an autonomous political base in Eastern Anatolia, which might set a precedent for similar demands by other ethnic and religious groups in the frontier regions. Turkey indicated nevertheless that it might be willing to reconsider its stance in return for a steeper territorial price. If the British could convince the French government to cede to Turkey the Kurdish-majority northeasternmost part of Syria, known for its shape as the Duck's Bill, then Hakkari could perhaps be awarded to Iraq. There was zero prospect that France would be willing to consider surrendering this strategic region, and therefore the British-Turkish negotiations reached a dead end.[14]

The tensions between the Iraqi government and the Assyrian leadership finally reached a boiling point in August 1933. On orders from Baghdad, the Iraqi armed forces initiated a large-scale attack which resulted in the massacre of thousands of Assyrians by the army and its tribal allies. Turkish observers viewed with satisfaction the destruction of the Assyrian powerbase in northern Iraq. The Turkish ambassador to Baghdad told British diplomats in no uncertain terms that the Assyrians were guilty of intrigue against the Iraqi government and therefore "have only themselves to thank for the punishment they have received."[15] The Turkish press echoed this sentiment. Articles in Turkish daily newspapers suggested that the Assyrians were paying both for their past treacherous collusion with the Russians and British during the Great War and for their more recent rebellion, which was part of a grand conspiracy against Turkey and Iraq, purportedly hatched by none other than Lawrence of Arabia.[16] Not surprisingly, then, when some Assyrian survivors sought refuge in Turkish territory, they were turned back. According to British reports, Ankara went on to request from Baghdad to remove "the mischievous Assyrian race" altogether from the frontier regions, in accordance with the neighborly relations between the two governments.[17] The Iraqi army thus quashed by force the Assyrian claim for autonomy in northern Iraq, with many of the survivors seeking refuge across the border in French-administered Syria.

The elimination of the Assyrian power base in northern Iraq changed Turkey's calculus regarding its cooperation with the Barzanis. Ahmed Barzani was now pressured to negotiate with Baghdad for his peaceful return to Iraq. He subsequently returned from Turkey to Iraq after reaching an agreement which stipulated that his life would be spared in return for taking an oath of loyalty to King Faisal and accepting internal exile away from his tribal territories near the Turkish border.[18] The frontier region continued to be restive nevertheless, with frequent Kurdish revolts near the Turkish border in the latter 1930s.[19]

The mutual suspicions between Ankara and Baghdad continued throughout the 1930s, but in the second half of the decade, Turkey and Iraq mostly cooperated against Kurdish rebels. In instances of rebellion on either side of the border, the other country would pledge to seal its side of the frontier against the cross-border movements of rebels, arms, ammunition, and propaganda materials. The difficult nature of the mountainous terrain and both countries' limited resources in the region meant that such efforts were always limited in their effectiveness. But in cases in which Turkey believed that Iraq was not doing as much as it could to act in accordance with its pledges, the government in Ankara did not hesitate to use forceful methods of persuasion to do more. For example, during the Dersim Rebellion in Eastern Anatolia in 1938, Turkey concentrated military forces in threatening postures north of the border in order to pressure Baghdad to take decisive steps against the Kurdish rebels' supply lines and purported rear bases in northern Iraq. There were even reports that Ankara might be using the issue as a pretext to pressure its weaker southern neighbor to accept modifications in their common border.[20] No such modifications ever took place. The borderline as determined in the Anglo-Turkish Treaty of 1926 remained unchanged in the 1930s. Indeed, although it was demarcated only following a very bitter controversy and despite being one of Turkey's most volatile frontier regions, the border with Iraq was Turkey's only Middle Eastern border that did not undergo any meaningful change after the 1920s. This did not mean that Turkish suspicions regarding subversive activities directed from Iraq evaporated, or that the Iraqi and British concerns regarding Turkey's territorial designs on northern Iraq dissipated, even after the two neighboring countries signed the Treaty of Saadabad nonaggression pact in 1937. Indeed, even to mid-1939, British and Iraqi military planners continued to view Turkey as a potential military threat to northern Iraq and thus worked on refreshing contingency plans for the defense of Mosul and its environs against a future Turkish invasion.[21]

II A Mountain of Discord

The Turkish-Iranian border was the only Middle Eastern frontier of Turkey that was demarcated before World War I, but it too was very unstable in the interwar period. The environs of Mount Ararat served for centuries as the frontier region between the Ottoman Empire and Safavid and Qajar Iran. But it was only on the eve of the Great War that

Ottoman encroachments into Iranian territory in the region prompted Britain and Russia to initiate prolonged negotiations that finally led in 1913 to a more precise demarcation of a borderline between the two Islamic empires. It left Mount Ararat on the Turkish side of the border, whereas Little Mount Ararat was recognized as Iranian territory. A decade later, the Treaty of Lausanne adopted the prewar line as the international border between Turkey and Iran.[22] In the intervening years, the region witnessed much political and military upheavals that left in their wake a heavy baggage of mutual suspicions. During World War I, Ottoman forces twice crossed the international boundary and occupied parts of Iranian Azerbaijan for prolonged periods. At the same time, Ottoman propagandists sought to spread the ideology of pan-Turkism among the Turkic Azeri population, in an attempt to mobilize their support for the region's permanent political unification with their ethnic Turkish brethren in Anatolia.[23] Following the Ottoman defeat in the Great War, it was Iran's turn to make opposing claims to territories on the other side of the prewar international border. Thus, in the Paris Peace Conference in 1919, the Iranian Foreign Minister argued that the "portion of Kurdistan which formed part of the Turkish Empire" fell within the "natural borders" of Iran, and that its Kurdish inhabitants shared with the Persian people racial affinity and faith in Shia Islam.[24] This remained only a statement of intention. The weak postwar Iranian government was not in a position to contest either the territorial claims of Britain, France, and Armenia to these regions or the Turkish recapture of most of these lands in 1920. Finally, the Treaty of Lausanne upheld the old border as set on the eve of the Great War. By that time, the Iranian strongman Reza Khan, who led a military coup in 1921, and finally became Reza Shah following his coronation in 1926, was seeking to stabilize and improve Tehran's relations with Ankara. The two sides indeed signed a Treaty of Friendship in April 1926. But Kurdish rebellions on both sides of the border and mutual suspicions regarding territorial ambitions in the region contributed to recurring crises between the two governments in the late 1920s.

Iran was highly concerned that Turkey might be still harboring territorial designs on Iranian Azerbaijan and was ready to foment rebellions and collude with the Soviets to advance that goal. The fact that Kemalist Turkey understated the ideology of pan-Turkism during the interwar period did little to allay Iran's concerns in this respect. The government of Reza Shah operated under the assumption that Ankara was only feigning disinterest in fomenting separatism in Iranian Azerbaijan. It was no secret that notable Azeri nationalists found refuge in Turkey and never made full renouncement of their separatist goals. Furthermore, although the official Turkish position rejected any pan-Turkist agenda, well-known ideologues of pan-Turkism from late Ottoman times still occupied important positions in the Kemalist government and in the intellectual life of the republic.[25] Reza Shah did not take the threat of Azeri separatism lightly. As part of a national policy of cultural and nationalist assimilation, his government implemented policies aimed at imposing the adoption of the Persian language as the vernacular of the Azeris, the Kurds, and various other ethnic minorities and, in the 1930s, supplanting their ethnic affiliations with a common Iranian identity.[26] In many respects, these policies mirrored the harsh Kemalist assimilationist measures aimed at the Kurds and various other ethnic minorities in Turkey. The Turkish government indeed neither criticized the Iranian assimilationist policies nor led any meaningful effort to subvert them. And yet, even after the two sides signed a treaty of friendship and security in April 1926, and an addendum to it two years later, their mutual suspicions regarding the other side's involvement in fomenting and abetting Kurdish rebellions in their frontier regions persisted.[27]

The Iranian government was particularly bothered by reports about Turkish cooperation with the rebellious Kurdish chieftain Ismail Simko. After leading a revolt against the Iranian government in the immediate aftermath of the Great War, he was defeated in 1922 and was forced to escape to Iraq by way of Turkey. In 1925, a peace initiative led to his return to Iranian Kurdistan, even as much of Eastern Anatolia was in rebellion against Turkish rule. Ankara was concerned that Simko, perhaps with Iran's green light, might be preparing to assist the Kurdish rebels in Anatolia. The Turkish ambassador to Tehran therefore warned the Iranian government that Turkey would view such an eventually very gravely and would respond to it very resolutely. The Iranian government was requested to warn him not to engage in any action in support of the rebellion. Turkey was in fact concerned that Tehran had an interest in steering the Kurdish chieftain to activity in Anatolia and away from Iranian Kurdistan.[28] The rapprochement between the Iranian government and Simko indeed proved short-lived. After only a few months, the two sides took again to arms, and the Kurdish chieftain was again forced to look for refuge in Iraqi Kurdistan. Three years later, in 1928, reports surfaced according to which Ankara was seeking to mobilize Simko's support against Kurdish rebels in Eastern Anatolia, in return for subsidies and lands in its territory, just across from the Iranian border. Tehran suspected that the alleged deal would also entail a free hand for Simko to raid into its own territory. Such an agreement, if it was ever offered, never materialized. But the level of distrust between Turkey and Iran in the late 1920s was sufficiently high to make these claims believable from Tehran's perspective. Simko was finally tricked into returning to Iranian soil in 1930 only to be ambushed and killed by the Shah's men.[29] His death removed a major headache for Iran but did not eliminate concerns about possible Turkish ties with other Kurdish rebels in Iran. Tehran's suspicions were only enhanced when, on several occasions in the late 1920s and early 1930s, Turkey opened its borders to give refuge to Kurdish rebels and their families, who were fleeing from the heavy retaliatory measures of the Iranian armed forces.[30]

On its part, the Turkish government was as much annoyed with the inability or unwillingness of the Iranian government to help it quell Kurdish rebellions in Eastern Anatolia. The first time the issue threatened to turn into a major crisis between the two states was in 1926, when a major Kurdish revolt known as the first Ararat rebellion shook Ankara's hold over its side of the frontier region. The insurrection broke out only weeks after the signing of a treaty of friendship and security between Turkey and Iran, so the Kemalist leadership demanded from its Iranian counterpart through diplomatic channels to deny the rebels supply lines and escape routes. At the same time, the Turkish press received a clear signal from Ankara to publish biting critiques of Iran's failure to abide by its pledge for good neighborly relations. Some Turkish periodicals went as far as accusing Iran very explicitly of aiding and abetting Kurdish attacks on the Turkish armed forces. The Iranian press responded, undoubtedly with the approval of Tehran, with furious rebuttals of these accusations. The Iranian press suggested instead that the whole crisis was manufactured by Turkey as a pretext for the occupation of Iranian lands, in order to satisfy its imperialist designs on its peaceful neighbor's territories. The public war of words in the press lasted several weeks. Finally, the two governments agreed that toning down the mutual public attacks and engaging in bilateral negotiations would serve their interests better. In the diplomatic deliberations that followed, Ankara argued that the current borderline was untenable because it prevented both countries from sealing the frontier region against rebels' cross-border movements. Turkey therefore suggested a land swap by which it will get hold of Little Mount Ararat, in return for ceding to Iran Turkish territory farther to the south. Iran refused to this deal, and the two sides only agreed, in a new Turkish-Iranian formal protocol signed in 1928, to recommit to mutual cooperation along their common frontier.[31]

The new security protocol neither ended Turkey's dissatisfaction with the continued Kurdish rebel activities in the frontier regions nor eliminated the mutual distrust between the two sides. Turkey's suspicions regarding Iran's reluctance to help it pacify the frontier regions were not unfounded. But Tehran, too, viewed Ankara's request for cooperation as less than sincere. Hasan Arfa, a senior Iranian army officer who had close ties to the Shah, intimated the Iranian leadership's calculus to an American diplomat in September 1930. Colonel Arfa explained that Ankara harbors expansionist ambitions against all its Middle Eastern neighbors but temporarily refrains from aggressive actions only because major European powers are in control of Syria and Iraq. The Iranian officer suggested that therefore "he believes that Persia would be the first to suffer, since the rich Turkish speaking Persian Azerbaijan would make a logical addition to Turkey." He declared that because he knows the Turks very well, "he wholly distrusts their assertions of friendship for Persia" and is fully aware that they "cast covetous eyes on Persian Azerbaijan." He believed that what stopped Ankara from realizing its designs on the region was the fact that "Azerbaijan is separated [from Turkey] by a corridor inhabited by Kurds who are always ready to fight the Turks" and who "for centuries been the frontier guards of Persia." The colonel explained that what Turkey was in fact requesting is that Iran cooperate in destroying these pillars of its defense, so that after their subduing, Ankara could implement its expansionist schemes in the region. That is why, he explained to the American diplomat, "Persia did not desire to diminish the Kurdish strength on the frontier," despite Turkey's protests and complaints. From Tehran's perspective, all Turkey really wanted was "to prepare the road for taking Azerbaijan from Persia."[32]

The resulting tensions between Ankara and Tehran came to a head in summer 1930, in the wake of another major Kurdish revolt in Turkey. The second Ararat rebellion saw the Turkish forces suffering initial setbacks before mounting a major counterattack against the Kurdish rebels. As in the past, the insurgents sought refuge across the border, in Iranian territory near Little Mount Ararat. Ankara was furious. The Turkish government sent Tehran a stern diplomatic note in which it complained about the lack of Iranian security cooperation in the frontier region. It now demanded in no uncertain terms the amendment of the border between the two states to make it more defensible against rebels. The Turkish press, meanwhile, launched a public campaign along the same lines. With Ankara's approval and encouragement, columnists and analysts criticized Iran in the harshest terms for its inability or unwillingness to abide by its treaty obligations and declarations of friendship to Turkey. Some writers went as far as to attack the person of the Shah with insulting caricatures, which was taken as a reflection of the extreme level of anger in Turkey. Indeed, the Turkish government decided to pull out all the stops in its counterinsurgency and ordered its land and air forces to pursue the rebels into Iranian territory near Little Mount Ararat. The Turkish army was then authorized to set camp and establish strongholds in strategic positions, in disregard of the existing international border. Iran immediately protested against the Turkish encroachments into its land and airspace, but to no avail. Ankara responded sternly that it might find it necessary to expand its military actions and presence on Iranian soil even further, if Tehran will not be able to cooperate effectively against the Kurdish rebels. Turkey suggested again that modification of the border through territorial exchange was necessary in order to stabilize and pacify the frontier region.[33] The Turkish measures and threats now prompted the Shah to take decisive actions against Kurdish rebels in Iran, lest Turkey would act on its threats. Indeed, the Iranian assault was so violent that at least one large tribal group opted to negotiate with the Turkish authorities their surrender, preferring the exile to western Anatolia that awaited them in Turkey, to facing the onslaught of the Shah's forces.[34] Turkey persisted nevertheless in its demands for border modifications as a necessary long-term solution, and in an effort to keep the heat on Tehran, maintained the presence of its armed forces on the Iranian side of the border through 1931.

The frontier crisis was finally solved in 1932, with Tehran ultimately acceding to Ankara's demand for modifications in the Lausanne borders. The issue was considered so acute that Turkish Foreign Minister Tevfik Rüştü Aras led an official delegation to Tehran in January, during the dead of winter, to negotiate an end to the two-year crisis.

The high-ranking Turkish delegation traveled to Iran by way of the Soviet Caucasus, and several mountain passes and roads had to be cleared of snow and ice in order to allow it to reach the Iranian capital. The framework for agreement was set in advance. But it took a few more days of negotiations to iron out the finer points of a territorial exchange that ceded Little Mount Ararat and adjacent lands to Turkey, in exchange for a similarly sized territory further to the south. Iran accepted the border modification only reluctantly, largely because Turkish units were anyhow camped in the ceded region since 1930. The Shah decided that resolving the issue was in his best interest, in order to eliminate a point of friction in the relations, which threatened to escalate into a serious crisis in the event of any future Kurdish rebellion in Anatolia.[35] Turkey, on its part, was careful to present the border modification as amicable rather than as a forced imposition on Iran. The new border agreement helped clear the air between the two sides, even if it did not fully eliminate occasional disagreements and persisting mutual suspicions. For example, shortly after the agreement was signed, the Iranian government protested to Ankara that young Iranian Kurds who were due for military conscription were dodging the draft by crossing the border to Turkey. Conversely, Ankara complained that the Iranian border guards were at times reluctant to cooperate with their Turkish counterparts in the administration of the frontier region. Nevertheless, and despite a few more minor amendments to the borderline in 1937, the border agreement of 1932 put an end to the most serious crisis between the two states during the interwar period. With the air of mutual acrimony mostly cleared after the formal transfer of Little Mount Ararat to Turkey, a period of much better Turkish-Iranian bilateral relations ensued in the latter 1930s, albeit without the complete elimination of their mutual distrust.[36]

III The Long and Winding Border

The combined length of Turkey's borders with Iran and Iraq was only a little greater than the Kemalist republic's 500-mile-long border with Syria. The terrain of Turkey's longest Middle Eastern border was also very different. Whereas its borders with Iran and Iraq ran through rugged and sparsely populated mountainous terrain and nomadic migration routes, Turkey's border with Syria cut through more densely populated agricultural lands and historically busy trade routes in lower elevations. The new frontier separated regions and urban centers in northern Syria and Southeastern Anatolia which were socially and economically integrated for many centuries. The demarcation line, first set in a Turkish-French agreement in 1921 and endorsed two years later in Lausanne, ran from the Mediterranean coast to a point on the banks of the Tigris River, just south of Cizre (Jazirat Ibn 'Umar). At its western edge, on the Mediterranean coast, the border ran just north of the District of Alexandretta (İskenderun), a region renamed by Turkey in the mid-1930s as Hatay. This strategic territory at the meeting point of Anatolia and the Levant was located on the shores of a sheltered bay that had the potential to be developed as a major modern port and was positioned very well to serve as a Mediterranean outlet for northern Syria, Iraq, and potentially Iran too. The population of the District of Alexandretta was ethnically diverse, including a significant minority of Turkish speakers alongside Alawites, Kurds, Arabs, Armenians, and a few other ethnic and religious communities. The Ankara Agreement of 1921 and the Lausanne Treaty assigned its administration to French-ruled Syria, but as a separate administrative unit and with specific guarantees to the region's Turkish-speaking population. Turkey fashioned itself as guarantor of their rights and made little secret of its long-term ambition to prevent the region from becoming part of an Arab-dominated independent Syria. Farther to the east, the middle part of the new border ran alongside completed sections of the Baghdad Railway, from Çobanbey/al-Ray, just northeast of Aleppo, to Nusaybin/Qamishli, at the end of the Duck's Bill. The two sides were required to manage the railway service jointly. The easternmost part of the border in the Duck's Bill region had an important strategic value in that it allowed Syria access to the Tigris River before it crossed from Turkey to Iraq and control over the main road connecting Mosul to Syria and Anatolia. Finally, an unusual feature of the new border was that it left a Turkish sovereign enclave 60 miles south of the border, near the banks of the Euphrates. This was the site of the tomb of Suleyman Shah, the grandfather of the eponymous founder of the Ottoman dynasty. For all the above mentioned reasons, and a few others discussed below, the Turkish-Syrian border proved more contentious and even more complicated to manage than Turkey's other Middle Eastern frontiers.

Arab nationalists in Syria were convinced that the new border left on Turkey's side regions that should have been by right part of an independent Syria. These included the regions of Gaziantep ('Ayntab), Şanlıurfa (al-Ruha), and Mardin, which were demanded by the leaders of the Arab Revolt during World War I (Map 2.1) and envisioned in the Treaty of Sèvres as part of the French mandate of Syria. The Turkish occupation of these territories, which was accepted by France in the Ankara government of 1921, was resented by Arab nationalists as one more sin among the many committed by the French colonial administration with the blessing of the League of Nations. Turkey was very unsatisfied with these persisting albeit informal claims of Arab nationalists in Syria to territories north of the border, in Cilicia and Southeastern Anatolia.[37] That is why, while pledging its friendship to the Arab peoples and its support for the future independence of Syria, Ankara in fact was generally content with the divide and rule policies implemented by the French authorities in Syria. These included the division of the mandate territories into smaller "states," such as Grand Lebanon, Damascus, and Aleppo, which were based on geographical basis, or the Alawite State and Jabal al-Druze, which were based on ethnoreligious criteria. This colonial policy hindered the emergence of a unified Arab power south of Turkey's borders, which could conceivably pursue the ambition of unification with Transjordan, Palestine, Lebanon, and Iraq, as part of a Greater Syria or pan-Arab ideological project. Turkey had no desire to see such a potentially powerful force emerge in the Middle East, with possible irredentist claims on its territories. Turkey kept a particularly watchful eye on the administration of the District of Alexandretta as a special administrative region, with every intention to prevent its full integration into Syria.

The routine management of the hardly marked border was very challenging, as the new frontier cut through a formerly integrated social, cultural, and economic zone. In the central parts of the border, crossing the railway tracks was all that was needed to cross the border. The joint management of the service, some parts of which were on the Turkish side of the line and others on the Syrian, required various levels of coordination in security, customs, and administration. Commerce and trade between neighboring communities newly divided by the border were also issues of concern for both the Turkish government and the French mandatory authorities in Syria. In some border regions, agricultural fields and orchards and various other properties of residents of one country were left on the other side of the

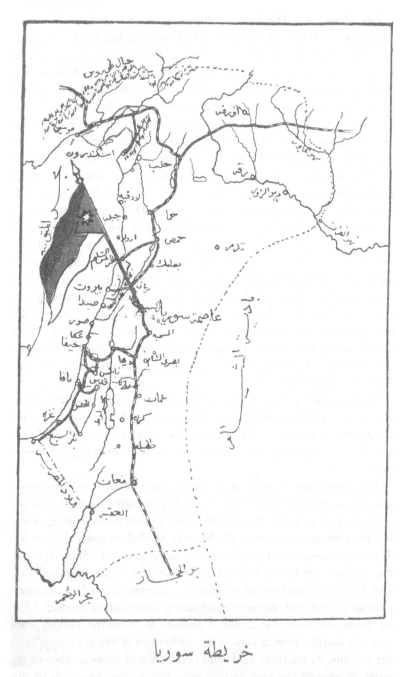

Map 2.1 The borders of Syria as envisioned by Arab nationalists after World War I. From *Dhikra Istiqlal Suriya* (Cairo: Matba'at Taha Ibrahim wa-Yusuf Barladi, 1920), cover.

border, which required their regular crossing of border gates to the neighboring country, and involved complicated issues of taxation as well as residency and property rights for "foreigners" from either country. The most pressing problem, however, was that the new frontier region was rife with smuggling operations, brigandage, and rebel activities on both sides of the border. Neither government found it easy to distinguish between the criminal and political actions, particularly because oftentimes the same people were involved in more than one type of these cross-border activities. The porous frontier thus became the site of frequent violent clashes that were a constant source of irritation. Both the Turkish and the French mandatory authorities suspected that their counterpart might be aiding and abetting the activities of smugglers, brigands, and rebels in effort to destabilize their power in the frontier region.

Some political opponents of the Kemalist government indeed found refuge in Syria, even as some rebels against the French rule in Syria were given political asylum in Turkey. Both governments pledged to prevent these political exiles from engaging in cross-border plots and subversive activities. This included the prevention of the dissemination of anti-Kemalist propaganda from Syria and the organization in French-controlled territories of plots against Mustafa Kemal and other senior Turkish leaders. Conversely, Turkey assured France that political refugees from the Great Syrian Revolt of 1925–1927 would be prohibited from efforts to rekindle the fires of anti-French rebellion. But as antigovernment propaganda continued to be smuggled from both side of the border, and information on cross-border subversive activities flowed repeatedly to the intelligence and security services of the two governments, neither side was satisfied that their counterparts remained true to their pledges.

A permanent border commission was established in the mid-1920s with the intention to facilitate the management of the border regions and solve disagreements between the two sides. The problems kept piling nevertheless. In 1928, for example, the French authorities complained that the Turkish army established permanent border posts on Syrian lands. Turkey reciprocated with complaints that the French mandatory authorities allowed for armed bands to set bases of anti-Turkish operation just south of the border.[38] Negotiations between the two sides led to signing of a new border protocol in 1929, aimed at pacifying the frontier regions. It included minor territorial

modifications in the border as well as an agreement for the declaration of a 30-mile-wide security zone on each side of the border, within
which the activity of groups deemed as hostile by the other government
will be prohibited. Turkey wished the city of Aleppo to be included
within this range, because it was an important center of Armenian and
Kurdish nationalist activities in northern Syria. But the French authorities resisted the demand and insisted that the southern boundary of
the security zone would pass about two miles north of the city. Their
concern was that Ankara was in fact looking for pretexts to interfere
in the French administration of this major Syrian city, out of a long-
term goal to establish Turkish dominance over northern Syria. On its
part, Turkey was suspicious that France was duplicitous in its promises,
and in reality wished to preserve its freedom to assist the organization of anti-Turkish schemes and plots in Aleppo and its environs.
Cross-border raids continued after 1929, alongside with the spread of
antigovernment propaganda on both sides of the border, with Turkey
accusing France of not doing enough to keep its end of the security
agreement, and vice versa.[39]

Even as Turkey and France were unable to eliminate their disagreements and mutual distrust, Arab nationalists suspected both of collusion against Syria's legitimate rights and interests. During the negotiations that led to minor border modifications in 1929, for example,
the nationalist press in Syria warned that France was yet again willing to surrender Syrian territory to the expansionist government in
Ankara, just as it did in 1921. The Damascene daily *al-Qabas* thus
suggested that the French negotiators would likely be willing to betray
Syria's interests by acceding to Turkey's ambition to annex Alexandretta, with Ankara's ultimate goal being to secure control over Aleppo
and the whole of northern Syria. The repeated cross-border raids from
Turkey into northern Syria were interpreted in this context as a war of
attrition to weaken the French willingness to resist Turkey's territorial
ambitions at Syria's expense. Turkey's denial of these accusations could
not convince Ankara's doubters in Syria. Reports in the Arab press
in Syria and neighboring countries were persistent in their warnings
already in the early 1930s that Ankara was looking for ways to pressure Paris to cede Alexandretta to Turkey, perhaps followed by other
parts of Syria. France was time and again rumored to be mulling these
proposals. Insistent Turkish and French denials and rebuttals notwithstanding, warnings against probable Turkish-French collusion that

would undermine Syria's territorial integrity in order to satisfy Turkey's expansionist tendencies, continued to appear quite regularly in the Arab press of Syria throughout the 1930s.[40]

In this context, even what could have been taken as innocent Turkish initiatives to upkeep Ottoman burial sites in Syria, or provide for the commemoration of Ottoman troops, were suspected as conniving schemes. In one such instance, reports on the dilapidated state of the tombs of three Ottoman military pilots in Syria, prompted Turkish interest in the renovation of their place of death and burial sites. The three crushed in 1914 in Ottoman Palestine. They were the first casualties in the short history of the Ottoman air service and were later embraced by the Kemalist republic as its air force's first martyrs. Turkey thus approached the French mandatory authorities in 1928 with a request for extensive renovation of their tombs in Damascus and of the memorial erected in their crash site near the Sea of Galilee. The request included the hoisting of the Turkish flag in both sites. This initiative coincided with a number of other Turkish requests for the renovation and upkeep of Ottoman military cemeteries in Syria and in British-administered Palestine. Both the French and British mandatory authorities were willing to accommodate such requests. They were wary, however, of any symbols of Turkish sovereignty because of the suspicion that Ankara was harboring a secret ambition to later demand their recognition as extraterritorial holdings that are falling under Turkish legal jurisdiction. In the nationalist press in Syria, all these endeavors were presented as a veiled Turkish effort to secure footholds in Arab lands, in order to demand sovereignty in and around them, as was the case with Turkey's extraterritorial control over the tomb of Suleyman Shah. Columnists in the Syrian press warned that Ankara's ultimate goals had nothing to do with care for the tombs and the cemeteries per se, and everything to do with acquiring additional tools for interfering in the internal affairs of Syria and for laying the foundation for Turkish territorial expansion in the Arab lands.[41] This atmosphere of multilateral distrust and suspicion extended to other communities in northern Syria and was fed and intensified by persistent violence in the frontier regions.

IV Cross-Border Plots and Counterplots

The political reconfiguration of the Middle East after World War I left many unsatisfied parties who felt that the new post-Ottoman order did them great injustices. That was particularly true for nationalist movements who were offered no path to nationhood under the League of Nations mandates and in the Treaty of Lausanne. Kurdish nationalists, and even more so Armenian and Assyrian nationalists, believed that their rights and interests were betrayed in Lausanne. Kurdish nationalists were dissatisfied that their national rights were neither recognized nor guaranteed in Turkey, Iran, Syria, or Iraq. Armenian nationalists were perturbed that despite the displacement and horrendous suffering of their people during the Great War, the Armenian presence in Anatolia was virtually erased. Tens of thousands of Armenian survivors were forced to seek permanent refuge in Syria and elsewhere in the Middle East or overseas. The Assyrian community had similar misgivings with their forced displacement from Anatolia during the war, and grave concerns regarding their precarious situation in Iraq and Syria in the interwar period. Some nationalists within these communities pinned their hopes for a better future on the expectation that successful insurrections in Eastern Anatolia might lead to the collapse of Turkish rule in their historical homelands, which would open the door for their repatriation and for the realization of their nationalist political aspirations. Others pursued the seemingly more realistic goal of the establishment of autonomous enclaves for their ethnic communities in northern Syria.

Turkey viewed with grave concern any initiative to establish a political entity for either of these ethnic groups south of its borders, whether in Iraq before 1933, or in Syria throughout the 1930s. Kurdish rebellions in Eastern Anatolia were a recurring problem throughout the interwar period, and in virtually every case Ankara found evidence that appeared to suggest that they were instigated or supported from northern Syria. Turkey was therefore concerned that the establishment of any separate political entity in northern Syria which would be dominated by Kurds, Armenians, and Assyrians would elevate the risk of it becoming the launching pad and inspiration for more revolts in Eastern and Southeastern Anatolia. Such an eventuality appeared feasible because it could fit well with France's policies of divide and rule in Syria. The French mandatory authorities indeed tended to rely on non-Arab or non-Sunni Muslim ethnic and religious minorities in its policing of Syria since the early 1920. And recurring reports in the late 1920s and through much of the 1930s suggested that Paris was willing to consider the establishment of an additional "state" or autonomous region in the Jazira, a strategic region near the Turkey-Syria-Iraq border triangle, which was dominated by non-Arab ethnic groups, including Kurds, Armenians, Assyrians, and a few other smaller ethnic and religious communities. Turkey viewed such an eventuality as a serious threat to its security. Ankara was therefore not resigned to accept a role of passive observer on the political future of northern Syria, but rather was determined to actively resist political developments that it deemed detrimental to Turkey's vital national interests.[42]

Cross-border raids of Kurdish, Arab, and Turkmen armed bands were a common occurrence along the Turkish-Syrian frontier region, originating from Turkey as much as from Syria. Official Turkish and French reports from the late 1920s and early 1930s, as well as news items in the press of the period, are replete with stories of armed assaults of marauders into both sides of the border. In either case, the victim side tended to pin the blame on the government authorities on the other side of the frontier. Ankara stood accused of seeking to foment ethnic tensions and political instability in Syria, as much as it accused the French mandatory authorities of the same purported vices in Anatolia. In May 1930, for instance, the Damascene daily *al-Qabas* accused Turkey of arming Kurdish tribal groups and encouraging them to raid Syrian localities. The Turkish government was censured and warned that it will later find it difficult to disarm these Kurdish bands because they will be unwilling to be left defenseless and risk "suffering the same disasters that befell the Armenians." The Turkish press responded to such accusations with its own allegations, suggesting that Armenian gendarmes employed by the French authorities in northern Syria were aiding and abetting Kurdish raids into Turkey, as part of a nefarious effort to weaken Ankara's hold on Southeastern Anatolia.[43] And so it went throughout the 1930s, with practically any raid on either side of the frontier attributed to malicious scheming of government authorities on the other side of the border. The French and Turkish authorities discussed the need to disarm the frontier populations and elevate the level of their security cooperation in many meetings during the period. But cross-border attacks nevertheless continued apace, and the level of mutual distrust remained persistently high.[44]

Ankara was particularly concerned with what it was convinced was a coordinated undertaking of Kurdish and Armenian nationalists to engage in subversive activities, with French complicity. The Turkish apprehensions were focused on a group of Kurdish political exiles who in 1927 met in French-administered Lebanon and established Khoybun

(or Xoybun), as a political platform aimed at uniting Kurdish nationalists in Syria, Iran, Iraq, and Turkey, in a common struggle for independence. The activists sought to establish in Aleppo a center of planning
and propaganda that would help instigate revolts in Eastern and Southeastern Anatolia. From the outset, they were positively inclined toward
cooperation with the Armenian Revolutionary Federation (Dashnak-
tsutyun), whose members were commonly known as Dashnaks. This
leftist nationalist organization, which was established in the late nineteenth century and was very influential among the Armenian community during the closing years of the Ottoman Empire, secured a position
of dominance among the Armenian refugees in Syria and Lebanon. The
revolutionary organization's ultimate goal during the interwar period
remained, as in Ottoman times, the establishment of an independent
state in what they considered as historical Armenia, but which was
now under Turkish rule and largely free of self-identified Armenians.
Because of the common foe, and because of practical considerations
having to do with the fact that Kurds maintained substantial presence
inside Turkey, whereas the Armenians built much better international
presence and ties, Khoybun and Dashnak leaders sought to cooperate against the Kemalist government from their main powerbases in
French-administered Syria and Lebanon.[45]

Turkey protested to France vigorously against any sign of anti-
Turkish activity of Kurdish or Armenian nationalists south of its borders. Turkish complaints in 1928, for example, prompted a French formal ban on Khoybun's operations in Aleppo. In March 1929, however,
the Kurdish nationalist leader Akram Jamilpashazade was able to flee
Turkey with his brothers and take refuge in Syria. They helped revive
Khoybun's activities in Aleppo and, from the safety of that major Syrian city, sought to initiate uprisings in Anatolia. Turkish agents and
spies were able to collect information on their meetings and deliberations. They reported to Ankara on the Kurdish revolutionaries' efforts
to secure the support of Kurdish tribal leaders through propaganda
and by material support, ostensibly with French and British backing. Their alleged strategic plan was to coordinate a Kurdish rebellion
inside Turkey, with attacks by Syrian Kurds on trains carrying Turkish
military reinforcements along the Turkey-Syria border. Strong Turkish protests to the French authorities led the mandatory government
to order the Jamilpashazade brothers and a few other Kurdish nationalist leaders to leave Aleppo for Damascus, away from the Turkish

frontier. But only a few months later, Khoybun activists still played an important role in instigating the second Ararat rebellion in 1930, despite French reassurances to Ankara that their authorities would suppress the organization's activities in northern Syria. In the years that followed, internal divisions weakened the organization, but Khoybun activists continued to publish anti-Turkish propaganda materials in Syria, Egypt, and several other Middle Eastern countries. Their published pamphlets in Kurdish, Turkish, Arabic, and European languages were aimed at addressing various audiences within and without Turkey. In 1933, for instance, as the Republic of Turkey was celebrating its tenth anniversary, Khoybun published in Egypt a bilingual propaganda booklet in Arabic and Turkish in which the organization pledged to maintain the fight in spite of Turkey's brutal efforts to destroy the Kurdish people's struggle for "their liberty and natural rights." Decrying Ankara's alleged policies of wanton destruction of villages, forced migration and exile of whole populations, and prohibitions on the use of the Kurdish language in education and public life, the organization vowed never to abandon its determined battle until the Kurdish people realize their dream of an independent Kurdistan.[46] Turkey rejected these accusations and dismissed these ideas as the reflection of treacherous separatism but also charged that their purveyors were serving as agents and terrorists on behalf of imperialist powers that harbored anti-Muslim and anti-Turkish agendas.[47]

The Turkish government indeed issued recurring alerts on alleged terrorist plots of Middle East–based groups aimed at assassinating Kemalist leaders and officials. In the early 1930s, the Kurdish Khoybun and Armenian Dashnak organizations were frequently accused by Turkey of the dispatch of teams of assassins from Syria and Lebanon, who were tasked with killing Mustafa Kemal and other senior Turkish leaders.[48] Similar plots against the leadership of the republic were attached to other political opponents of the Turkish government who took refuge in the Levant in the early 1920s. They were accused of instigating assassination plots and of smuggling of seditious propaganda into Turkey.[49] Circassian political exiles associated with Edhem the Circassian (Çerkes Edhem), an erstwhile ally turned a bitter rival of Mustafa Kemal during the war over Anatolia, featured very prominently in such alleged schemes against the Kemalist republic. Edhem was living in exile in British-administered Transjordan, and many of his Circassian associates took residence in the French mandates of Syria and Lebanon, in the British mandate of Palestine, and in Egypt. Among many sensational reports in the Turkish press of the 1930s on plots against the Kemalist leadership which were allegedly hatched in the Middle East, a particularly notable one took place in 1935. The case involved the alleged dispatch of assassins sent by Edhem the Circassian from Syria and Palestine with orders to kill Mustafa Kemal and plunge Turkey into political chaos. The accused terrorists and their collaborators inside Turkey were arrested and their plot was foiled long before they reached anywhere near the president of the republic. The Turkish press followed the case with lengthy and sensational reports on the investigation and the trial. The Turkish government, meanwhile, lodged urgent appeals to the French and British mandatory authorities in request for the arrest and extradition to Turkey of the ringleaders and accomplices of the plot in Syria, Transjordan, and Palestine. Subsequently, both colonial administrations interrogated the persons of interest identified by Turkey, including Edhem the Circassian, but to Ankara's bitter disappointment they were all released shortly, after denying any involvement in the plot.[50] This episode, and a number of similar ones in the interwar period, were seized upon by Ankara as justifying extreme security measures at home. They were at the same time presented as proof of the dangers lurking in the Middle East, with the complicity or malign disregard of the French mandatory authorities in Syria and, to a lesser degree, the British in Transjordan and Palestine.

Turkish diplomats in the Middle East were tasked with assisting in the intelligence collection efforts in the region. Feridun Cemal Erkin, Turkey's consul-general in Beirut in the mid-1930s, relates in his memoirs that reporting on the activities of anti-Kemalist Armenian, Circassian, Kurdish, and Turkish activists and political exiles was an important part of his job. The future Minister of Foreign Affairs in the 1960s further revealed that he collected information on their plots and conspiracies, both through open channels and through sympathetic and paid informants. Some of these agents were Levant-based pro-Kemalist Turkish citizens or from Turkophone populations in the region. Others served as informants primarily for the monetary prize or for some other personal gain. Information gathered was sent to Ankara and at times was communicated to the French authorities in requests to preempt anti-Turkish schemes.[51] France was not at all thrilled about Turkish spying and information gathering activities in its colonial holdings. In 1937, for instance, the French security services in Syria arrested members of the "Turkish-Syrian Friendship Association" on charges of spying and subversive activities. Documents found in their possession appeared to indicate that they were paid agents of the Turkish government who acted under orders from the Turkish consul in Damascus, allegedly for the purpose of spreading pro-Turkish and subversive propaganda in Syria.[52]

The French footing in Syria became less secure in the latter 1930s, at a time of political instability in France and increasing German and Italian challenges in the international arena. In order to maintain its interests in the region while decreasing its commitments and vulnerabilities, various French administrations sought to negotiate with Syrian leaders a treaty along the lines secured by the British in Iraq in 1932 and in Egypt in 1936. In the early 1930s, these negotiations failed time and again. But in mid-1936, after the Popular Front won the legislative elections and formed a new government in France, the Syrian National Bloc and the authorities were finally able to negotiate in September 1936 an agreement that envisioned the formal independence of Syria, albeit with various strings attached to ensure France's continued military and political predominance in the Levant. The new treaty was aimed at stabilizing Syria. Instead, it opened a period of controversy in France on whether the agreement was beneficial and should be ratified or instead was detrimental to French interests and should be rejected. Turkey was particularly incensed with the agreement's inclusion of the District of Alexandretta in the envisioned independent Syrian state. In the two years following its signing, tensions along the Syrian-Turkish border increased dramatically. Cross-border raids from Syria and rebellions in Eastern Anatolia were now suspected by Ankara as encouraged by France in order to diminish Turkey's bargaining position against the Franco-Syrian Treaty. During the Kurdish rebellion in Dersim in 1937, for example, Turkish intelligence sources claimed they have traced logistical supply routes to Syria, and the French authorities were suspected of being complicit in that alleged effort to weaken Turkey's demands on Alexandretta.[53] Conversely, the French authorities and Arab nationalists in Syria were convinced that Ankara was seeking to take advantage of France's weakened international position in the late 1930s to secure territorial gains at Syria's expense. The immediate target of Turkey's revisionist demand was the District of Alexandretta, renamed in Turkey as Hatay since the mid-1930s. But it was widely suspected by contemporaries in the late 1930s that, should the opportunity present itself, Turkey would be more than willing to press the case for the annexation of other regions in northern Syria, and possibly in northern Iraq too.[54]

V Shaken and Stirred

Throughout the 1930s, none of the principal actors assumed that Turkey's Middle Eastern borders were assured for the long term. Turkey was constantly concerned with real and alleged conspiracies against its rule over Eastern and Southeastern Anatolia. And Britain, France, the governments in Damascus and Baghdad, and various other stakeholders were convinced that Turkey did not forgo its territorial ambitions in northern Syria and Iraq. As France's international position weakened from the late 1920s, some in the region came to believe that it may find it tempting to accede to Turkey's assumed ambitions. In as early as May 1929, for example, the American consul-general in Beirut reported that Arab nationalists in Syria were speculating that "Turkey has successfully imposed the condition that she be given control of Alexandretta and Antioch. It is commonly held by Syrians that France will surrender the region about those cities to Turkey to secure the latter's accord on the several questions pending between the two countries."[55] This turned out not to be the case at the time. The Wall Street Crash was still a few months away and the full consequences of the ripple effects caused by the global crisis it triggered was still several years in the offing. Once the rapid destabilization of the international arena became clear in the mid-1930s, however, it affected calculations and relations in the Middle East as well. Uncertainties in the international arena and tensions within the region translated into various nationalist protests and rebellions, followed by initiatives to stabilize the region. Among these, the late 1930s witnessed Iraqi initiatives for unification with Syria, Trans-Jordanian push for the unification of Greater Syria, and British short-lived proposal for the partition of Palestine. In this time of regional and international anxiety, uncertainty, and possibility, Turkey was able to gain greater leverage vis-à-vis France, and to a lesser degree Britain too. The new circumstances placed Turkey in a better position more than any time since the establishment of the republic for potentially securing favorable changes in its Middle Eastern frontiers.

The Italian and German challenges to the post–World War I international order were at one and the same time threatening and inviting from Ankara's perspective. Turkey viewed Italy's aggressive moves in the Mediterranean region, and Germany's challenges to the postwar borders in Central Europe, as matters of grave concern. But Ankara also realized that it could exploit the international crisis to demand certain revisions in its own postwar agreements. The first major instance in this respect was the Kemalist republic's success in securing changes in its rights and sovereignty in the strategic straits of the Bosporus and the Dardanelles. The Montreux Convention of July 1936 expanded Turkey's rights and prerogatives in the Straits, including their fortification. The Kemalist leadership presented this diplomatic achievement as a great national victory that rectified unjust conditions imposed on the fledgling republic in the Treaty of Lausanne. The new agreement was indeed presented in the Turkish press as akin to the heroic defense of Gallipoli during the Great War, which was similarly attributed to Aratürk's capable leadership.[56] With that precedent set, it appeared very plausible that Ankara might look for opportunities to revise other terms of the Treaty of Lausanne, including regarding its Middle Eastern borders. Commentaries in the Arab press indeed warned that the success in securing its demands in the Straits might lead the Kemalist republic to follow the German irredentist agenda in demanding the annexation of Syrian and Iraqi lands to Turkey.[57] The fallout from the signing of the Franco-Syrian Treaty of Independence in early September 1936 became an occasion for testing Ankara's international stature and leverage, and more pointedly, its ability to transform a crisis into opportunity, within the context of escalating tensions among the major European powers.

Turkey's main bone of contention with the Franco-Syrian Treaty was its inclusion of the District of Alexandretta as an integral part of independent Syria. Ankara opened a very public campaign to block the ratification and implementation of the treaty. The multifaceted effort included appeal to the League of Nations, diplomatic pressures on France and its British allies, as well as threatening military maneuvers on Turkey's side of the border, and direct actions in the District through Turkey's supporters in the region. The Kemalist republic insisted that the majority of the people of Hatay shared ethnic, racial, cultural, and historical ties with Anatolia and its Turkish population. The strategic importance of the region as a potential springboard for the invasion of Anatolia or for expansion into northern Syria, and its potential commercial importance as a Mediterranean outlet for northern Syria and Iraq were not less of a consideration.[58] The Turkish territorial designs on the region were neither new nor unknown. For instance, in early 1932, the then Iraqi Prime Minister Nuri al-Said reported shortly after returning from talks in Ankara that the Turks "are hoping that the evolution of Syrian affairs may give them an opportunity of obtaining the cession to them of Alexandretta. It is their belief that France, which formerly abandoned to them Cilicia, may be induced to make this further concession."[59] During earlier rounds of Syrian-French talks in 1933–1934, the Arab press in Syria and in neighboring countries indeed warned that Ankara perceives the District as their Alsace-Lorraine and that securing their hold over that territory is part of a broader Turkish plan to annex Aleppo and adjacent regions in northern Syria.[60] The Turkish government denied the latter accusations but hardly concealed its claim for the Alexandretta region, which from 1935 was denoted Hatay. In 1934 the Turkish press in fact suggested that the "return" of the region to Turkey was on the negotiating table between Paris and Ankara.[61] Turkey's move to defend "its rights" in Hatay in the wake of the Franco-Syrian agreement of 1936 was thus not at all unpredictable.[62]

The main contours of the story of Turkey's success in affecting the detachment of the District of Alexandretta from Syria and its eventual annexation to its own territory are well known. Turkish pressures, on the one hand, and conservative opposition in France, on the other, combined to block the ratification of the Franco-Syrian Treaty in the French Parliament. It thus never came into effect, and the French mandate did not come to an end in the late 1930s. Instead, the long-standing concern of Arab nationalists in Syria that France will eventually cede the region to Turkey was proven right. Ankara and Paris negotiated in 1937–1939 a number of agreements which first led to separation of Hatay from Syria and its constitution as a semi-independent republic in late 1938, and finally to its formal annexation to Turkey in July 1939. Turkey's success in achieving its goals in Hatay benefited greatly from France's desire to secure its friendship in the wake of the European crises of the late 1930s. The German annexation of Austria and the Czechoslovakian Crisis in 1938, and the German occupation of Czechoslovakia and the Italian invasion of Albania in 1939, even as the nationalists in Spain were gaining the upper hand in the Spanish Civil War, all strengthened the Turkish leverage over France. In these circumstances, Hatay was considered in Paris and London as a reasonable price to pay in order to help cement security, defense, and diplomatic cooperation with Turkey. Ankara's victory in Alexandretta was a heavy loss to Arab nationalists in Syria, and to substantial number of the region's residents – including many Sunni Arabs, Armenians, Kurds, Circassians, and Alawites – a considerable number of whom felt compelled to emigrate to Aleppo and other regions of Syria and Lebanon rather than remain to live under Turkish rule.

The annexation of Hatay has been often described by scholars as an aberration in Turkey's general status quo policies, but that's certainly not how contemporaries assessed the situation. In June 1938, a full year before the annexation was formally completed, the Iraqi daily *al-Istiqlal* in fact compared the Turkish ultimate goals to the irredentist policies of Nazi Germany. It suggested that in this case Britain and France actually backed "the Turkish *Anschluss*," with Ankara's purported eventual goal being the annexation of additional Arab lands.[63] Ironically, French officials were similarly concerned that Turkey's territorial ambitions in Syria may not be limited to Hatay. During the Munich Crisis in September 1938, Paris indeed intimated to London its suspicions that Turkey was looking for ways to cooperate with Germany in pressing demands for other territorial concessions in Syria, in addition to Hatay. British officials did not find it inconceivable at all. In fact, in as early as 1937, British Foreign Office officials voiced concerns that from Ankara's perspective, "the Alexandretta dispute was only the first move in the policy of pushing the Turkish south-eastern frontier well towards the south."[64]

The Syrian regions perceived as most susceptible to a possible Turkish territorial claims after Hatay were the Jazira and so-called Duck's Bill territories in the northeast of Syria. It has been correctly pointed out by scholars of the period that Turkey's revisionism in Hatay had been accomplished "in conformity with international law and without resorting to arms. This is the opposite of what revisionist states of the period were doing."[65] From the perspective of contemporaries, however, Turkey's methods to buttress its diplomatic leverage were not necessarily benign or in accordance with international agreements. And those who feared that Turkey might demand the annexation of their territories of residence against their will frankly did not see much legitimacy in deals cut between Ankara and colonial powers, even if in accordance with international law. In the late 1930s, French colonial officials, members of ethnic communities in the region, and Arab nationalists in Syria's main urban centers accused Turkey of undue and damaging interventionism in the Jazira region. The area was home to Kurdish tribes; Christian communities of Syriacs, Assyrians, and Armenians, many of whom were refugees from Anatolia; and a minority of Arab nomadic and sedentary populations. Already from the 1920s, but more intensely as the future of independent Syria was on the negotiating table in the late 1930s, the region became a hotbed of separatist propaganda and activities among the non-Arab communities. Many communal leaders in the Jazira demanded that France accord them an autonomy, perhaps as a first step toward future independence. Both Arab nationalists in Syria and the government in Ankara were vehemently opposed to these aspirations, the former because they perceived the Jazira as an inseparable part of Syria and the greater Arab homeland, the latter because it was concerned that the region might become a launching pad for rebellions in Anatolia and might develop irredentist claims to Turkish territories.[66]

Turkey was in fact suspected of harboring its own territorial ambitions to the strategic Jazira region. The main roads to Mosul passed through the region, oil resources were discovered in it in the interwar period, and it was within the boundaries of the Turkish National Pact.[67] When communal clashes and violence beset the Jazira in 1937–1938, French intelligence sources as well as the Arab press in Syria were convinced that Turkey was helping to ignite the fires of discord by supplying arms and ammunitions to its agents and supporters in the area. This was seen partly as a way to increase the heat on France while the negotiations over Hatay were ongoing and partly as an effort to prepare conditions to justify future Turkish intervention in the name of peacemaking in the region. Turkey rejected such accusations regularly and claimed innocence of any violence across the border, but suspicions regarding its conduct and territorial goals in Syria persisted nevertheless.[68]

The burgeoning strategic cooperation between Turkey, Britain, and France in the late 1930s indeed increased Arab worries about possible Turkish territorial gains at Syria's expense. From late 1938 and through 1939, the Arab press published numerous news items and commentaries on negotiations between Turkey and the two European colonial powers toward an agreement that would give Ankara a formal role in the defense and administration of northern Syria, and perhaps more. Some reports suggested that French and Turkish diplomats were negotiating terms for the transfer of the League of Nations Mandate for northern Syria, or perhaps the whole country, from France to Turkey. Other sources suggested that negotiated terms stipulated that only in the case of a new European war would Turkey be given the duty of sending its army across its southern border to take responsibility over the administration and defense of Syria. None of these reports was accurate, but they gave voice to grave concerns regarding Ankara's intentions and, in turn, amplified and helped disseminate distrust in Turkey and in its alleged collusion with Britain and France. The efforts of Turkish officials and diplomats to quash these false reports proved ineffective.[69] Indeed, concerns in the Middle East regarding secret deals to hand control over parts of the region to Turkey only intensified after Ankara signed protocols for strategic cooperation with Britain and France in May and June 1939, respectively. Immediately thereafter, a new wave of rumors swept over Syria and neighboring countries regarding alleged secret territorial concessions to Turkey in Aleppo and its environs and in Syria's Jazira region.[70]

The reports in 1939 about the handing of Syrian lands beyond Hatay to Turkey were taken very seriously by Arab nationalists in Syria. Some of their most senior leaders even contemplated clandestine cooperation with the Zionist leadership in Mandate Palestine in a joint effort to hinder what appeared to them as a credible and immediate threat. In July 1939, for example, just as Turkey was finalizing the formal annexation of Hatay, a secret meeting was held between Jamil Mardam, Lutfi al-Haffar, and Zionist envoys from the Jewish Agency. The two prominent members of the Syrian National Bloc served consecutive terms as Prime Ministers of Syria from December 1936 to April 1939. In the meeting they warned their Zionist interlocutors that Turkey was intent on breaking up Syria and devouring parts of it, before proceeding to reoccupy other former Ottoman lands in the region, including Palestine. Similar assessment about Turkey's purported ambitions to expand southward into Syria, and perhaps beyond, were also expressed to the Zionist representatives by Abd al-Rahman Shahbandar, the major nationalist political opponent of the National Bloc in Syrian politics. A year earlier, in mid-1938, the Turkish consul in Jerusalem inquired with Zionist leaders what might be the Jewish reaction in the event of Turkish annexation of Aleppo and its environs.[71] The Arab concerns about Turkey's purported revisionist intentions therefore did not appear a figment of their imagination to their Jewish interlocutors. Nevertheless, the Zionist leadership pursued its own agenda and was not interested in cooperation against Turkey's purported expansionist intentions. Elsewhere in the region, Kurdish activists, Armenian political operatives, and some officials in the British and French governments shared the assessments of Arab nationalists in the late 1930s that Turkey harbored territorial ambitions in Greater Syria and, if the opportunity presented itself, in the Mosul region and northern Iraq too.[72]

The annexation of Hatay eventually proved to be the last and most important revision in the Lausanne borders, but this was far from evident when it took place in July 1939. The intensifying crisis in Europe, on the one hand, and the subsequent warming relations between Turkey, Britain, and France, on the other, appeared to many observers at the time as precipitating additional Turkish territorial claims in the Middle East. Indeed, even in as late as October 1939, already after the outbreak of war in Europe, the Iraqi government sought urgent reassurances from London and Ankara that the recently signed treaty of friendship and mutual assistance between Turkey, Britain, and France did not include a secret protocol that authorized a Turkish occupation of northern Iraq.[73] As the interwar period was coming to an end, Turkey's post-Ottoman borders with the Middle East were yet to be viewed either in Europe, Turkey, or the Middle East as a guaranteed long-term fixture. Ankara's persistent fears of Western efforts to foment rebellions aimed at detaching Eastern and Southeastern Anatolia from Turkey somewhat subsided in 1939, although even more serious concerns took their place after the outbreak of war in Europe. In the Middle East, meanwhile, at no point during the interwar period was Turkey considered, as claimed by Turkish spokespersons, as a status quo power that was "satisfied with existing frontiers" and was intent on refraining "from pursuing irredentism . . . in lands containing Turkish minorities."[74] Throughout the interwar period, and into World War II, Turkey was in fact widely perceived as a country with clear revisionist tendencies when it came to northern Syria and Iraq and, from Tehran's perspective, perhaps Iranian Azerbaijan too. However, in contrast to contemporaneous revisionist states in Europe of the late 1930s, Turkey was more averse to dangerous adventurism, which the Kemalist leadership believed doomed the Ottoman Empire under the Young Turks. The government in Ankara was not loath to taking some calculated risks in its foreign policy in general, and regarding the Middle East in particular, but it did not seek to challenge or undermine the post–World War I international order and was careful not to take actions that would isolate it in the international arena of the 1930s. This relatively moderate approach certainly did not mean passivity, however. Instead, it meant that aside from managing its frontier regions, Ankara put a premium on diplomacy in its interactions with the Middle East during the interwar period, in order to advance its regional goals, protect its interests, and reassure anxious political elites in the region that it did not harbor hostile intents toward them and their fledgling states.

3 | Ties That Bind

The Great War resulted in the retreat of the Ottoman flag from the Middle East. The Ottoman suzerainty over Egypt was abolished by the British in 1914, its armies were driven out from Greater Syria and Mesopotamia by late 1918, and its diplomatic presence in Iran was suspended until after the end of the hostilities. The Ankara government's triumph in the war over Anatolia and the international recognition it received in its wake precipitated the gradual return of the crescent and star flag to major cities in the Middle East, albeit now flying over diplomatic missions of the Republic of Turkey. By the early 1930s, Turkish consuls and ambassadors of various ranks served in Tehran, Tabriz, Cairo, Alexandria, Baghdad, Beirut, Damascus, Aleppo, Antakya, Jerusalem, Jeddah, and a few other localities. At the same time, ambassadors and consuls of Egypt, Iran, and Iraq represented their governments in Ankara, Istanbul, and a few other cities in Turkey. As in the case of Ankara's relations with European governments, the Kemalist republic had no qualms about developing diplomatic relations with former foes in the region. This was the case with King Faisal of Iraq and his brother Emir Abdallah of Transjordan, both of whom played key roles in the Arab Revolt during World War I, or with King Fuad of Egypt, who first assumed the throne of Egypt under British auspices during the Great War, and was well known for his antipathy toward Mustafa Kemal. Political realism informed by awareness of Turkey's vulnerabilities and constraints on the one hand, and its need to protect important interests in the Middle East on the other, dictated pragmatic pursuit of productive diplomatic relations not only with the British and French colonial powers, but also with fledgling and existing local governments in the region (Map 3.1).

The establishment and maintenance of functioning diplomatic relations required Turkey and governments in the Middle East to oftentimes put a nice face on significant animosities and mutual distrust. Bad blood from the Great War, ideological differences, and mutual

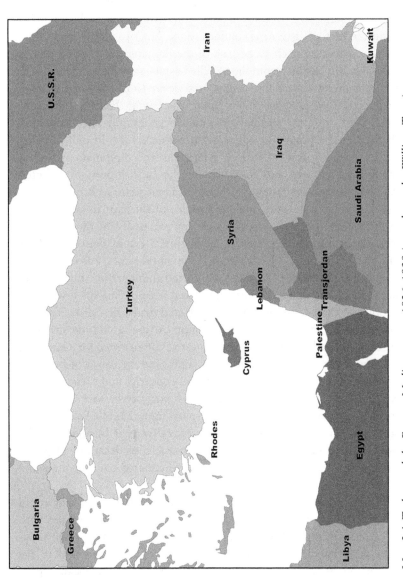

Map 3.1 Turkey and the Eastern Mediterranean, 1926–1938 (map drawn by William Terry).

suspicions certainly existed and complicated the relations between Turkey and the region. In Turkish school books of the early republic, for example, texts were rife with negative stereotyping of the Middle East in general, and of Arabs in particular.[1] And when Turkish Foreign Minister Tevfik Rüştü Aras confided to the American ambassador that Turkey perceived itself to be part of the Balkans and Europe, and as geopolitically distinct from the Middle East, he may have expressed the well-documented Kemalist deep-seated desire to reshape and rebrand Turkey as a progressive country that was facing West.[2] At the same time, there were the stubborn realities of geography and geopolitics that dictated a pragmatic engagement with the East. In public, therefore, speeches given by Turkish politicians and diplomats as well as many commentaries and news items in the Turkish press of the interwar period are abundant with frequent references to the brotherly relations between the Turks and the peoples of the East in general, and with the Arabs in particular, and are rife with calls for the rebuilding and cementing of the cultural and historical bonds between Turkey and the Middle East. The same was true on the other side of Turkey's Middle Eastern borders. Turkish purported colonization and injustices in the past and accusations of enmity and negative intents toward the peoples of the Middle East were inculcated to the first post-Ottoman generation in societies around the region. At the same time, in public speeches official government representatives often opted for a language that emphasized presumed commonalities and measures of cooperation and friendship between Turkey and countries and societies in the Middle East. The questionable levels of sincerity in such statements from Turkish officials or their counterparts in the Middle East notwithstanding, they were indicative and illustrative that in regional relations during the interwar period, pragmatic considerations of political expediency and national interest predominated over ideology and sentiment.

From Ankara's perspective, defusing potential threats that could emanate from the region was a major reason for nurturing ties with governments and political elites in the Middle East. One major concern was that territories in the Eastern Mediterranean and in the Levant might serve as springboards for a renewed European expansionist drive into Anatolia. In the 1920s, Ankara's main threat perception in this respect was focused on Britain and France. But from the early 1930s, Turkey's main concern shifted to Italy. The Fascist regime's military presence in the Dodecanese Islands, just off the coast of south-west Anatolia; its suspected claims to nearby Antalya and its environs; and Rome's increasing belligerence in the Mediterranean arena and beyond became a major cause for concern in Ankara. Turkey was therefore seeking cooperation with other international and regional actors who were as concerned with Italy, primarily Britain, France, the Soviet Union, and, after 1936, Egypt too. They were all opposed to the expansion of Italian influence in the Eastern Mediterranean and in the Levant. Another threat perception associated with the Middle East, namely, pan-Islamism, never reached similar levels of alarm in Ankara. But it was a matter of concern nevertheless, particularly because of various initiatives to revive the institution of the Caliphate. Turkey kept close tabs on such initiatives and made its displeasure with them and opposition to their realization well known. Another matter of concern to Ankara, which required a more subtle approach, was the increasing dominance of various forms of the ideology of pan-Arabism in much of the Middle East and the proliferation of proposals and political programs aimed at the unification of parts or all of the Fertile Crescent into a larger Arab state. Whereas Turkey could reject pan-Islamism publicly as a reactionary and counterproductive agenda that did not befit the modern age, this was not an argument that could be easily made against Arab nationalism by a regime that hailed and celebrated its own ethnic nationalism. Ankara was thus never inclined to criticize pan-Arabism as such, in whatever form it appeared during the interwar period, even as it was fully intent on putting spokes in the wheels of efforts for the unification of Arab-majority countries in the Middle East. Conversely, Turkey was much more straightforward in rejecting any claim for Kurdish, Armenian, or Assyrian nationhood or even autonomy south of its borders.

The fractured political arena and fiercely competing interests and groups that defined the early post-Ottoman Middle East provided Turkey with opportunities to establish cooperative relations in the region. Oftentimes these were ad hoc alignments focused on a specific shared interests or common causes. None involved a strategic long-term and stable alliance. Thus, for example, a common concern with Italian designs in the Eastern Mediterranean helped precipitate a marked improvement in Turkish-Egyptian relations in the 1930s. Conversely, when the Egyptian monarchs of the interwar period appeared to indicate ambitions to assume the vacant throne of the Caliphate,

Turkey found other willing partners in the region in putting pressure to bear against this aspiration. And when various plans were floated for the unification of Greater Syria or of Syria and Iraq, Ankara cooperated with other regional opponents of these schemes to derail them. Obviously, as much as Turkey sought to tend to its interests through the establishment of productive relations and coalitions of interest in the region, so did its interlocutors in the Middle East. Other governments and political actors, too, sought to enlist Turkey's support as a means to advance their own interests. The Kemalist republic certainly did not stay aloof from regional politics in the Middle East during the interwar period, but at the same time Turkey was careful not to become entangled in disputes and conflicts within and between countries in the region. Conversely, Turkey's interlocutors in the region sought to calibrate their ties with Ankara so as not to assist any potential Turkish aspiration for regional hegemony. All these maneuverings and counteractions resulted in an eventful period of intense and very pragmatic Turkish diplomatic engagements with the Middle East, which appeared to contemporaries to be increasing in volume and importance in the late 1930s and on the eve of World War II.

I Headgear, Head Case, and Diplomatic Headaches

The relations between Kemalist Turkey and Middle Eastern governments were not free of occasional tensions and public disagreements, although they were not fully defined by them either. One brief diplomatic crisis in particular, purportedly centered on a headgear, has at times been exaggeratingly depicted as epitomizing an ever-growing ideological, cultural, and political divide between Turkey and countries in the Middle East, and the pettiness that inflicted their purportedly deteriorating relations. The so-called Fez Incident or Tarbush Affair indeed did have shades of all the above. But in its core the crisis was inflamed by the clash of interests between two governments, and its resolution attested to the primacy of pragmatism in the relations between Turkey and Middle Eastern governments in general, and with Egypt in particular. The diplomatic crisis began in the wake of a festive reception held by Mustafa Kemal to the diplomatic corps in Ankara on October 29, 1932, on the occasion of the ninth anniversary of the Republic of Turkey. Among the dignitaries and guests in attendance was Abd al-Malik Hamza, the Egyptian ambassador to Turkey since 1930. He arrived dressed in his ceremonial attire, including a red *tarbush*, a head-gear similar in shape and color to the Turkish fez, which had been out-lawed in Turkey since 1925. The festive celebration went as planned, until toward the end of the evening, Mustafa Kemal rose up and made his way to the door. On his way out, according to an eyewitness report by the American ambassador, he "stopped before the Egyptian Minis-ter, exchanged a few words with him, leaned forward and kissed him on the cheek (a Near Eastern form of salutation when one desires to compliment a friend) and the next thing we knew, the red fez was off the Egyptian's head and was being carried out of the room on a sil-ver salver."[3] The Egyptian diplomatic envoy later reported that he was forced to surrender his national headgear and that the Turkish Pres-ident appended the order with words to the effect that the King of Egypt should learn a lesson from what he did. In the hours that fol-lowed, officials from the Turkish Foreign Ministry hastened to ensure Abd al-Malik Hamza that no offense was intended and that the inci-dent should not be made public. The Turkish government hoped that the diplomatic faux pas will be limited to a matter of gossip within the diplomatic corps and then simply dissipate without any lasting dam-age. This was not to be. Two weeks after the fact, the incident was made public in mid-November, through reports in the British press. In a mat-ter of days, the story made its way to the Egyptian press too, with some newspapers presenting the incident as an affront to Egypt's national dignity.[4] The Egyptian government, hammered by opposition publica-tions for its purported failure to protect Egypt's national honor, now felt compelled to take action. The Egyptian Foreign Ministry leaked to the press its intention to investigate the issue thoroughly, and possibly retaliate by withdrawing Egypt's ambassador from Ankara and down-grading the level of diplomatic relations with Turkey. The Egyptian government's purported deep indignation against Mustafa Kemal's ide-ological antipathy toward the late Ottoman red headgear thus threat-ened to spiral into a serious diplomatic crisis between the two coun-tries.[5]

Neither the Egyptian nor the Turkish government were in fact inter-ested in a diplomatic spat over the issue, but both found it hard to contain the inflammation once the incident became public. Ankara first sought to diffuse the tensions by denying that the Tarbush Affair ever took place. The Turkish press suggested that the whole story was invented by a third party, hinting at Britain, which wished to poison the relations between the two friendly governments and brotherly nations. In Egypt, meanwhile, the incessant criticism from the nationalist opposition led by the Wafd party, prompted the government to submit an official diplomatic note to Turkey in demand of an apology and a pledge that Egyptian diplomats will never again meet a similar inconvenience in the future. This public stance led to an escalation in the controversy. The Turkish government responded with its own note, rejecting the Egyptian demands, which in turn prompted another Egyptian note. The controversy continued to escalate, with the Egyptian press criticizing Turkey's haughty and disrespectful attitude toward a friendly government, and the Turkish press taking their counterparts to task for their audaciousness to criticize Mustafa Kemal and reprimanding the Egyptian government for its willingness to be duped by foreign conspiracies. Ironically, even as it hinted that London instigated the crisis, Turkey approached the British authorities in Egypt confidentially, requesting their good offices to help resolve the crisis. Finally, after weeks of bickering, cooler heads began to prevail. In Egypt, the daily *al-Ahram* began publishing in mid-December columns calling on both sides to put the incident in proper perspective as a minor misunderstanding between two friendly governments. And in Turkey, Mustafa Kemal made a very public gesture of friendship during the official New Year's Ball in Ankara, when he invited the offended Egyptian envoy to his table and explained to him that the whole affair was a misunderstanding, and that he was full of affection for him and for his king.[6] Meanwhile, after weeks of public squabbles, the two sides were finally able to contain the controversy and negotiate its resolution by the early days of 1933. Two months after the beginning of the diplomatic row, the sides came in mid-January to an agreement to put the crisis behind them and restore their friendly relations. No formal Turkish apology was forthcoming; but Ankara gave public assurances that it has no intention to ever intervene with Egyptian diplomats' attire and headgear or to disrespect their nation and its monarch.[7]

The embarrassing incident and its diplomatic aftermath were oftentimes depicted as reflective of excessive pride, boorishness, and pettiness in the relations between Turkey and Egypt. *Time* magazine exemplified the former when it wrote in December 1932 that the crisis was the outcome of an affront by the "progressive dictator" of Turkey who, "flush with champagne & cognac," insulted the "favorite headgear of Egypt's fat King Fuad."[8] Similar sensationalized and demeaning descriptions appeared in other contemporary reports in Europe and North America. Meanwhile, Turkish observers at the time, and in the decades that followed, described the incident as the result of Egyptian provocation aimed at challenging the antifez law in Turkey.[9] However, any suggestion that the headgear was the cause of the diplomatic crisis between the two countries, rather than a trigger, is not very convincing. For one thing, Turkey established diplomatic relations with Egypt in 1925, the year the ban was introduced, but for seven years Egyptian diplomats in Turkey continued to don the red headgear without incident. For another, following the diplomatic crisis, Egyptian envoys continued wearing their *tarbush* while on assignment in Turkey in the 1930s, without any Turkish protest or opposition. In fact, in the months that followed the incident, Mustafa Kemal went out of his way to display his friendliness toward the Egyptian envoy. For the same reason, Turkey hastened to raise the level of its diplomatic representative in Cairo from chargé d'affaires to ambassador in early 1933. And later that year, Ankara let the instance of an Egyptian government's virtual boycott of the annual celebration of Turkey's Republic Day in its embassy in Cairo pass with no response, in an effort to put the bilateral relations between the two states back on track.[10]

The tensions between Cairo and Ankara were in fact more serious than being the result of a perceived slight to an ambassador's headgear, or of his alleged disrespect for the laws of the host country. It is definitely true that no love was lost between the Turkish government and the Egyptian court, at least partially because of King Fuad's barely concealed aspiration for the seat of the Caliphate. But the main irritants on the relations between the two countries were a number of legal and financial issues on which they were bitterly divided. One disagreement stemmed from the inability of Ankara and Cairo to conclude an agreement that would settle questions of citizenship, residency, and property rights. A particularly thorny question in this regard revolved around the rights of members of the Egyptian royal family to acquire Turkish citizenship, while maintaining full ownership of properties in Egypt. Another bone of contention surrounded the rights of members of the substantial Turkish-speaking community in Egypt to acquire Turkish citizenship and enjoy capitulatory privileges on par with the extraterritorial legal benefits that were awarded to citizens of European countries, including to the substantial numbers of Greek and Italian nationals in Egypt. The abolition of such extraterritorial and discriminatory rights for foreign citizens had for long been an important goal of the Egyptian government. Cairo was particularly incensed with this Turkish demand because the Kemalist republic counted the abolition of the capitulations in its own territory as one of its greatest successes in the Treaty of Lausanne. Turkey's demand for capitulatory rights in Egypt was thus rejected by Cairo as hypocritical and immoral. Ankara responded that the capitulations in Egypt should indeed be abolished, but as long as citizens of other countries enjoy these privileges there was no good reason why its own citizens should not benefit from the same extraterritorial legal rights as well. In practical terms, this included the right of Turkish citizens to stand trial in the mixed-court system and to be tried in accordance with the new Turkish secular legal codes, rather than in accordance with Islamic laws and derivative Egyptian legal codes.[11]

Another bone of contention between the two governments focused on Egypt's efforts to block some Islamic Endowment (*waqf*) revenues from supporting institutions in Turkey. In Ottoman times, some wealthy Egyptians, often of Balkan or Anatolian descent, endowed certain income-generating assets and properties to support charitable and not-for-profit institutions and organizations in Istanbul and in various Anatolian cities and towns. Among the beneficiaries were orphanages, infirmaries, schools, and similar social and educational institutions. In the interwar period, the Egyptian government took steps to block the transfer abroad of these funds and to divert them instead to support worthy causes in Egypt. In one notable case in 1933, for instance, the funds of a substantial Egyptian *waqf* that was designed to support Darülfünun, reorganized that year as Istanbul University, were reassigned by the Egyptian government to support Cairo University, known then as the Egyptian University. Turkey protested to the Egyptian government and to the British authorities in Egypt, but to no avail. In this case too, as with the capitulations, Ankara's case was weakened by the fact that in its own territory the Turkish government was itself busy nationalizing and reassigning *waqf* assets and properties.[12] These and other legal and commercial issues were the topic of Turkish-Egyptian negotiations on several occasions in the late 1920s and early 1930s. But neither these efforts, nor initiatives to conclude a commercial treaty that would regulate custom regimes and tariffs between the two countries, reached a positive conclusion by the time of the Fez Incident and the diplomatic crisis that it sparked.[13]

The clash of legal and financial interests that fueled tensions between the two governments was epitomized by the controversy regarding Prince Ahmad Sayf al-Din, King Fuad's former brother-in-law. In 1897, when Prince Fuad was a newlywed in his mid-twenties and not likely to succeed to the throne of Egypt, Ahmad Sayf al-Din shot him for allegedly abusing his wife, the would-be assassin's sister. Fuad was injured but survived, and soon thereafter divorced his wife. His brother-in-law was arrested, assessed as psychiatrically infirm, and was shortly sent to England for indefinite confinement in a mental asylum. During his more than two decades of institutionalization, his very significant estate was taken over by the Egyptian royal court, with various prominent politicians and courtiers assigned to manage it for hefty salaries. During that time, Fuad became the Sultan of Egypt in 1917 and was finally crowned king in 1922. Meanwhile, his former mother-in-law and one of her daughters took residence in Istanbul and sought unsuccessfully to lobby the British authorities and Egyptian government to allow the prince to regain his liberty. Finally, in August 1925, they arranged for Prince Sayf al-Din to be smuggled out from the mental institution and be transported across Europe to Turkey, with the approval of the Turkish government. He was soon declared sane and in a matter of few weeks made known his desire to get married.[14] After a short period the middle-aged prince indeed wed a much younger Turkish girl and was given Turkish citizenship. His mother then opened a legal case in Egypt on his behalf, in request for the restoration to her possession of full control over her son's vast estate. The lawyers she hired in late 1927 were none other than senior figures in the Wafd, the nationalist and most popular party in Egypt of the interwar period, including the party's leader Mustafa al-Nahhas. The party was in the opposition at the time, and its tense relations with King Fuad were well known. But a few months later, the king was forced to ask al-Nahhas and his party to form a new cabinet in March 1928. The legal case became embroiled with the political struggles in Egypt when opposition newspapers published in June documents that appeared to show that newly appointed Prime Minister al-Nahhas and two of his colleagues agreed to receive from the prince's mother a very hefty payment in return for a legislation in parliament that would lead to the wresting of the control over her son's vast properties from the royal court and the transfer of the estate to the prince's mother. The king, in agreement with the British authorities in Egypt, used this pretext to remove from office the nationalist al-Nahhas and his Wafd cabinet. Sayf al-Din's representatives then chose a new legal tactic, which injected Turkey more prominently into the affair. They argued that because the prince acquired Turkish citizenship, as a foreign national the control over the estate should be transferred from the Egyptian government to him. The Turkish government supplied the necessary documents to back this request. But the Egyptian government rejected the claim, arguing that the prince was still mentally infirm and therefore not in a position to receive control over his estate. The Egyptian position suggested that his marriage was fictitious and the whole affair reeked of Turkey-based manipulation by interested parties who sought to exploit the prince's mental situation for their own ends. Furthermore, Cairo insisted that even if the prince were mentally firm, Egyptian royals were in any event prohibited from acquiring foreign citizenships. Subsequently, the case reached a political and legal deadlock that further complicated the already strained Turkish-Egyptian relations in the early 1930s.[15]

The Turkish government was not oblivious to the fact that the Fez Incident was fueled by more weighty issues than the Egyptian ambassador's headgear, or merely matters of national honor. Therefore, in an effort to affect a broader rapprochement with Egypt, Ankara dispatched to Cairo in January 1933 a senior official to explore ways to patch over the disagreements between the two governments. İbrahim Talî (Öngören), a veteran diplomat, former Inspector-General in Eastern Anatolia, and a member of parliament, was tasked with reopening negotiations over all legal, economic, and political sticking points between Egypt and Turkey. But the differences between the two sides soon proved too hard to reconcile. In early 1934, the Turkish ambassador to Cairo therefore approached Miles Lampson, the new British High Commissioner to Egypt, in request for his good offices in the stalled negotiations. He shared with Lampson the Turkish government's willingness to withdraw its demand for formal capitulatory rights as well as to pull back its support from the case of Prince Sayf al-Din, along with his Turkish citizenship papers. Ankara expected in return for these concessions that Egypt would accept certain Turkish legal and commercial demands. New negotiations were duly opened in mid-1934 with the goal of finalizing a treaty of friendship, along with a commercial treaty and agreements on nationality and residency rights. By early September, the negotiations appeared advanced enough for Foreign Minister Aras to suggest optimistically that he may soon embark on a historic visit to Egypt for the signing of the anticipated bilateral treaty and accompanying agreements.[16]

The Turkish optimism proved premature, as the two sides were unable to overcome their differences and therefore concluded no agreement in 1934. The main sticking point remained the unwillingness of the Egyptian government to concede any extraterritorial legal rights to Turkish citizens, while Ankara insisted that even without formal capitulatory privileges, Egypt-based Turkish citizens should fall under the jurisdiction of the Turkish secular legal codes rather than Islamic law and its derivate legal codes as practiced in Egypt.[17] Once the negotiations reached an impasse, the Turkish government rescinded its offer to give up its demand for formal capitulatory rights and to withdraw its support from the case of Prince Sayf al-Din. A stalemate ensued until 1936, when the signing of the Anglo-Egyptian Treaty, the emergence of Italy as a shared threat, and the death of King Fuad would converge to create more conducive circumstances for a Turkish-Egyptian rapprochement. But the bilateral relations between the two Eastern Mediterranean powers was not disconnected from their interests in the Levant, which would become very clear in the late 1930s, but was already evident at the beginning of the decade.

II A King, an Ex-Monarch, and the Syrian Throne

The land often deemed by Syrians as "the beating heart of the Arab world" was one of the least politically stable of all former Ottoman territories in the Middle East during the interwar period. A short-lived Arab state established in Damascus under Faisal in the immediate aftermath of World War I was destroyed by France in 1920. In its stead, the French authorities established a colonial regime under the guise of a League of Nations Mandate. The heavy-handed foreign administration helped provoke the Great Syrian Revolt in 1925, to which France responded with very decisive and violent measures that finally crushed the rebellion by 1927. The French authorities instituted a policy of divide and rule, but the bitter opposition of mostly Sunni Arab nationalists to French rule still made it difficult and costly to pacify the land. By the early 1930s, as neighboring Iraq was moving toward formal independence from Britain, the French government appeared to be willing to consider significant changes in the administration of Syria, which would decrease its commitments and costs but still

ensure France's core interests in the land. Whether this would entail the
maintenance of Syria's existing borders and its republican form of government remained unclear. France was therefore lobbied by various
interested parties in an effort to secure Paris's endorsement for their
preferred solution to the Syrian question. Neighboring Iraq was particularly hopeful in that regard. King Faisal and many of his closest allies
and supporters sought to convince Paris to support the unification of
Syria and Iraq under his crown, in return for strong guarantees for
France's continued preeminence in the Syrian part of the united, feder-
ated, or confederated Arab kingdom. Overcoming France's likely skep-
ticism with handing control over Syria to a man associated since 1916
with British regional designs was the main problem facing that scheme.
But Faisal and his supports were also well aware that Turkey might
also be a major obstacle even should he be able to sway Paris's support. Ankara's response to Faisal's Syrian initiative was indeed far from
supportive and cooperative. Instead, Turkey became actively involved
in opportunist, cunning, and resolute efforts to hinder any prospect of
unification of the lands to its south, with little regard to the displeasure
with which its intervention in Syria's affairs was received in Baghdad
and Cairo.

The Iraqi government's attempt to persuade Turkey to acquiesce to
King Faisal's claim for the crown of Syria, in return for assurances of
friendly relations, was a tall order to begin with. First, there was a
heavy historical baggage between the two sides, extending all the way
to the Great War. Faisal led the army of the Arab Revolt as it marched
from the Hijaz through Transjordan to Syria, with T.E. Lawrence riding by his side. The revolt itself was widely portrayed even in 1930s
Turkey as the greatest expression of Arab treachery against the Turks.
Second, Faisal led the short-lived Arab state in Syria in the immediate wake of World War I, which laid claims to territories in Anatolia
that were still considered by many Arab nationalists in the 1930s as
integral parts of Syria. Third, Faisal played a major role in the successful British maneuvers to annex to Iraq the regions of Mosul and
northern Mesopotamia, which was still remembered in Turkey as the
most painful defeat of the Kemalist leadership since the establishment
of the republic. Finally, Turkey had no interest whatsoever in seeing the
emergence of a large Arab kingdom south of its borders. Intelligence
reports on Iraq's desire to serve as the Prussia of the Arabs, that is,
become a powerful military force that would unite all the Arab lands

under its leadership, were not very reassuring to Ankara.[18] Turkey's distrust and misgivings were well known in Baghdad. Therefore, as Iraq's formal independence in 1932 was nearing, and the efforts to convince France to reinstall Faisal's crown in Damascus proceeding, the Iraqi government was seeking to convince the Turkish leadership of their friendly intentions and of the benefits that Ankara would reap from the realization of Faisal's plans. King Faisal and his Prime Minister Nuri al-Said sought to sway Turkey's support by convincing Ankara that their unification scheme would lead to the stabilization of Syria, the decrease of European military forces in the Levant, and the quashing of any prospect of Kurdish, Armenian, or Assyrian autonomy in northern Syria.

The Iraqi side began sending feelers regarding an invitation for a historic visit of King Faisal to Ankara in 1931, in order to ensure friendly relations as Iraq was preparing for independence in 1932. Turkey's initial responses were polite but disinterested. King Faisal therefore arranged a meeting with the Turkish ambassador to Baghdad in which he intimated to the Turkish envoy his great personal admiration to Mustafa Kemal and his reforms, and his distrust of Britain because of its intrigues against both Turkey and Iraq. He proposed yet again that it should prove fruitful if he would travel to Ankara to discuss issues of mutual interest with the Turkish government. With Iraq's independence around the corner, and many questions regarding the administration of its northern regions still on the table, Turkey reconsidered its previous position and decided to invite the King and Prime Minister Nuri al-Said for talks. The summit was set for July 1931. As soon as the date was set, the pro-government press in Iraq began inflating the historic significance of the planned meeting, trumpeting a narrative of enduring friendship between the Turkish and Arab nationalist movements, led by Mustafa Kemal and King Faisal, respectively. The Baghdadi press indeed suggested that the two brotherly movements followed a similar trajectory. According to that narrative, both nationalist movements liberated their people from Ottoman oppression, and each was able to secure their independence under the heroic military command and political authority of capable and just leaders. The Turkish press was not as generous in pointing to purported similarities between the two national movements and their leaders. But the popular daily *Cumhuriyet* did go as far as describing the impending summit between Mustafa Kemal and King Faisal as "the most important and meaningful event in the Middle East since the end of the World War."[19]

King Faisal arrived in Ankara on July 6, 1931, for the first leg of a European trip to several of the continent's major capital cities. In Paris he was scheduled to discuss various regional and bilateral affairs, and was expected to broach his aspiration for the crown of Syria. Getting Turkey on board with his plans was one of his most important tasks in Ankara. The Turkish government sent a special train to a point just north of Aleppo in Syria, where the king boarded it en route to the Turkish capital. He was received in Ankara's train station with pomp and ceremony, before proceeding to hold working meetings with Mustafa Kemal and the republican leadership (Figure 3.1). His Prime Minister, Nuri al-Said, arrived from Europe to join the discussions.[20] The talks centered on various issues relating to the bilateral relations between the two states, including the situation in their frontier region. But the Iraqi leaders also brought up the topic of the future of Syria. This was a sensitive matter that had to be broached carefully, because Turkey reiterated its special interest in the District of Alexandretta, which the Iraqis took as a statement of Ankara's intention to pursue the long-term goal of annexing the region to the Kemalist republic. But when the option of declaring Syria a monarchy with Faisal at the helm was raised, the Turkish side remained uncommitted and vague. Nothing more than general statements of amity and future cooperation could be attained by the Iraqis. With no concrete political gains, King Faisal's most pleasant part of the visit became its unofficial part, in Istanbul, the city in which he spent most of his childhood. He passed several enjoyable days in the former imperial capital, visiting with family members who resided in the city, and touring "the haunts of his youth" before proceeding to Europe.[21]

Faisal's visit to France, where he sought to secure serious French consideration for his claim to the vacant Syrian throne, appeared to be proceeding successfully. A little more than a decade after he was unceremoniously deported by French forces from Damascus, and still a year removed from Iraq's formal independence, Faisal was fêted and honored by the government in Paris as a respectable head of state. So much so, that the welcoming language used by some of his hosts and the polite responses he received when the question of Syria was raised, convinced the king that Paris was seriously weighing his bid for the

Figure 3.1 King Faisal and Mustafa Kemal. From *Fotoğrafla Atatürk* (Istanbul: Cumhuriyet Matbaası, 1939).

throne of Syria. On his way back to Iraq he made a stop in Amman, where he shared this conviction with his older brother Emir Abdallah. And after returning to Baghdad, he informed the Turkish ambassador of his purported success in convincing France to consider his aspirations in Syria seriously. Subsequently, the press of Iraq, Syria, and Turkey began publishing in late 1931 news items and commentaries that presupposed French willingness to indeed accommodate Faisal's plans. The fact that a monarchist faction supportive of Faisal's restoration to the throne was active in Damascus appeared to lend credibility to the assumption that Paris was weighing seriously the merits of doing away with the republican regime it established in Syria and its replacement with a monarchy.[22]

The information and rumors about Faisal's conversations with the French government were received with grave concern in Ankara. Turkey sounded Britain on the issue, sharing with London its strong objection for the unification of Syria and Iraq or the restoration of Faisal's throne in Damascus. Ankara was concerned that should a measure of Arab unity under French auspices be implemented south of its borders, Paris would later steer the unified Arab power toward laying territorial claims on Turkish territories in Southeastern Anatolia. Britain was therefore requested to seek clarifications from France regarding Paris's attitudes toward Faisal's aspirations. But Turkey was not content to adopt a wait-and-see policy. Instead, Ankara took steps toward complicating Faisal's plans by proposing an alternative candidate for the throne of Syria who could serve as a spoiler. In Emir Abdallah of Transjordan, Faisal's older brother and himself a British protégé with aspirations for the Syrian throne, Turkey found a willing collaborator in its efforts to derail the Iraqi government's aspirations in Syria. When the Prime Minister of Transjordan Hasan Khalid Abu al-Huda traveled to Europe by way of Turkey in late 1931, he held informal talks with Turkish officials regarding the Syrian question. Even though the French government informed Ankara that it never seriously considered Faisal's candidacy for the throne of Syria, Turkey did not trust the sincerity of the response and therefore sought to promote its own candidate to the Syrian throne, with indirect assistance from Emir Abdallah.[23]

The man chosen by Ankara to serve as a spoiler to Faisal's candidacy was Abbas Hilmi, the ex-Khedive of Egypt and the nephew of King Fuad. He was deposed by the British authorities shortly after the outbreak of World War I on account of his pro-Ottoman sympathies, and spent most of the war years in Istanbul. After World War I he sought unsuccessfully to present himself as a viable candidate for the throne of Syria, before dividing the rest of the 1920s between residences in Turkey and in Europe. During the early years of the republic, he nurtured good relations with the Kemalist government in Ankara, became a major investor in the Turkish banking system, and acquired Turkish legal documents after being denied any legal rights in Egypt. From Turkey's perspective, his pro-Turkish proclivities, the fact that he was not related to King Faisal, and his tense relations with his uncle the King of Egypt all made him a very appealing sham candidate for the Syrian throne. Furthermore, in May 1931, the ex-Khedive signed a settlement agreement with the Egyptian government according to which he abandoned any claims for the Egyptian throne in return for a generous annuity and Egyptian citizenship, thus clearing a way to invest his resources and attention elsewhere.[24] His virtually nonexistent relations with Britain were another advantage from Ankara's perspective, because in the early 1930s, Turkey still viewed Britain as a power intent on scheming against Turkey. The Turkish government sought to manipulate the ex-Khedive and sponsor him as a candidate for the throne of Syria out of expediency rather than conviction, but the Iraqi and Egyptian governments and the British and French colonial powers could not be certain regarding the seriousness of Turkey's support.[25]

In December 1931, the ex-Khedive arrived in Turkey for a well-publicized meeting with the Kemalist leadership, before embarking on a tour of Middle Eastern capitals. The Turkish press reported expansively and very approvingly about the visitor and his friendly and productive meetings with Mustafa Kemal and Prime Minister İnönü. From Ankara, Abbas Hilmi traveled to Transjordan by way of Lebanon and Palestine. While in Beirut, he was received for a conversation by Henry Ponsot, the long-serving French High Commissioner for Syria and Lebanon, which added intrigue and appeared to add validity to his candidacy. In Amman, he was received very favorably by Emir Abdallah. In a true Machiavellian way, Abdallah too decided to appear as if going along with Turkey's initiative to promote the ex-Khedive's candidacy to the Syrian throne, simply in order to complicate his younger brother's bid to return to Damascus. An added value was that cooperation with Turkey might help him established a strong foundation for securing Ankara's acquiescence to his own bid for the unification of Greater Syria under his rule. After his meetings in Beirut and Amman, Abbas Hilmi returned to Turkey for a new round of meetings with the Turkish leadership. And when the Prime Minister of Transjordan arrived in Turkey again in early 1932, Abbas Hilmi met with him too, with all these talks gaining publicity through reports in the Turkish press. As a result of Turkey's efforts, this retired monarch and politician who enjoyed virtually no basis of support in Syria, suddenly appeared in the international press and in diplomatic circles as a serious candidate for a throne that neither existed nor was in the offing.[26]

The Egyptian court perceived Abbas Hilmi's candidacy very unfavorably, viewing it as a product of damaging and subversive Turkish interference in regional affairs. King Fuad was enraged that this development took place only a few months after reaching an agreement with his nephew the ex-Khedive, according to which Abbas Hilmi pledged to retire from politics. Once news reached Cairo about his candidacy, the Egyptian government therefore demanded that he withdraw it immediately, in accordance with the agreement. The ex-Khedive responded that he only pledged to retire from Egyptian politics, to which the Egyptian government retorted that the affairs of Syria were also part of Egyptian politics. Cairo concurrently protested to Turkey about its intervention in the internal affairs of Egypt and its royal family. But Ankara responded slyly that the Turkish leadership in fact backed the ex-Khedive's candidacy to the Syrian throne out of conviction that the Egyptian king would be very content if one of his relatives would rule an important neighboring country such as Syria. With neither the ex-Khedive nor Turkey willing to back away from his candidacy, the Egyptian government sounded its strong misgivings to the French government. Paris reassured Cairo that the whole topic of establishing a monarchic regime in Syria was nothing but hot air, but the Egyptian government remained suspicious that France might be bluffing, while conducting secret negotiations with the Turkish government on the ex-Khedive's candidacy.[27]

Iraq was similarly concerned that a Turkish-French agreement on Syria might be secretly negotiated and therefore sought to dissuade Ankara from finalizing it. Baghdad believed that Turkey's aim was to install a friendly monarch in Damascus that would help France preserve its influence in the Levant and endorse a Turkish-French agreement on the secession to Turkey of the District of Alexandretta and Aleppo and its environs. The Iraqi Prime Minister Nuri al-Said sought to use his persuasion skills to convince Turkey not to proceed down that road. As reports on the ex-Khedive's candidacy increased in late 1931, the Iraqi Prime Minister traveled to Ankara to negotiate with Turkey a bilateral trade agreement and treaties of nationality and residence rights and of extradition. The talks ended in the signing of all these agreements in January 1932. The Iraqi Prime Minister took the occasion of his stay in Ankara to also raise with his hosts the question of Syria's political future and the ex-Khedive's candidacy. He suggested to his Turkish interlocutors that the Egyptian royal was beholden to France and therefore would promote policies that were unwelcome to Ankara. Conversely, Nuri argued, a political unification of Syria and Iraq under Faisal's crown, would establish in Damascus a stable and friendly government that would cooperate with Turkey in removing all the foreign elements from their common frontier regions. The "foreign elements" he referred to were Armenian and Assyrian refugees that France was reported to be contemplating their resettlement in northern Syria. Turkey remained unconvinced, which the Iraqi Prime Minister interpreted as another confirmation of Ankara's expansionist intentions in northern Syria, with its ultimate goal being the annexation of the Mosul region too. A similar assessment was shared by Prince Zayd, Faisal's younger brother and his first ambassador to Ankara in 1932, and by Rashid Ali al-Kaylani, Nuri's political rival who replaced him at the helm of the government in March 1933. These senior Iraqi political leaders did not see eye to eye on a great variety of issues. But they all shared the conviction that Turkey's activist policies regarding Syria were a reflection of its desire to block the emergence of a unified and potentially powerful Arab state that might challenge Ankara's territorial ambitions.[28] In public, however, both the Iraqi and Turkish sides maintained a façade of cordiality and unbounded friendship between the two governments even through their disagreements on Syria.

The sudden death of King Faisal in September 1933 and France's evident disinterest in changing the form of government in Syria finally put the kibosh on Abbas Hilmi's candidacy. With the former monarch of the post–World War I short-lived Arab Kingdom of Syria gone, and with France showing no inclination to support the unification of Syria and Iraq, the usefulness of the ex-Khedive's candidacy ran its course. By early 1934, the Turkish Foreign Minister was already willing to admit to the British ambassador to Turkey that his government had supported Abbas Hilmi's candidacy merely as a countermeasure against Faisal's initiative to unify Syria and Iraq under his rule but that "once the maneuver had been successful in blocking the candidature of Feisal, they would have thrown His Highness [the ex-Khedive] overboard."[29] With the question of the Syrian monarchy off the table, Ankara was more than ready to remove this additional irritant on its relations with Cairo, and to end the awkward situation in which a staunchly republican regime was seen as endorsing the establishment of a monarchy in a neighboring country. Emir Abdallah too was satisfied to drop his sham endorsement of the ex-Khedive. He did maintain a common cause with Turkey, however, in their shared opposition to later Iraqi initiatives for unification with Syria in the late 1930s. The question of the throne of Syria in general, and the candidacy of Abbas Hilmi in particular, proved to be a tempest in a teapot. But it did illustrate to governments in the Middle East and in Europe that Ankara would not be resigned to serve as a passive observer on regional affairs. The Kemalist republic's already established status as a regional power was further enhanced shortly after the end of this episode, following Turkey's rapprochement with Iran in the wake of the revision of their borderline in 1932. Iraq's caution not to aggravate its relations with Turkey was at least partially informed by its concern with the possible regional ramifications of the improvement in Turkish-Iranian relations. The January 1932 agreement that modified the Turkish-Iranian border helped alleviate the greatest irritant on the relations between the two states, at the moment in which the ex-Khedive's candidacy to the throne of Syria was most actively promoted by Ankara. Iraq's concern was that after resolving their differences its two powerful neighbors might cooperate to challenge its territorial integrity. Turkey was suspected to be still coveting Mosul and its environs, whereas Iran was making demands for various modifications in the Iran-Iraq border just north of the head of the Persian Gulf. From Turkey's perspective, the indirect effect of its rapprochement with Iran on its leverage over Iraq was just one of a number of benefits it saw in the improved relations with Tehran.

III Neighborly Relations

Political, diplomatic, and economic calculations convinced Turkey and Iran to seek closer relations of cooperation despite the persistence of mutual distrust between the two governments. In the early 1930s, Iran was locked in a dispute with Britain over its demands for a greater share in the revenues of the Anglo-Persian Oil Company, while a border dispute with Iraq complicated its relations with Baghdad. Amiable relations with Turkey carried the promise of better leverage in these disputes, a diminishing prospect for the always alarming specter of a Soviet-Turkish collusion against Iran, and a friendly voice in the League of Nations, which Turkey and Iraq joined in 1932 while Iran was still contemplating whether to follow suit. It finally did in 1934, alongside its eastern neighbor Afghanistan. Turkey viewed Iran as an essential member in a Middle Eastern security system that it was seeking to establish from the early 1930s and as an important trade partner that could become immensely valuable for the Turkish economy. After the Turkish Foreign Minister visited Tehran in early 1932 to sign the new border agreement, the Iranian Foreign Minister reciprocated with a visit to Ankara in October. He engaged in negotiating more bilateral agreements and a new commercial treaty, and the two sides pledged their commitment to friendly relations. The Iranian ruler, Reza Shah, was not content with this level of meetings. He wanted to organize a summit meeting between his person and Mustafa Kemal as the ultimate expression of the close relations of cooperation between the two neighbors. His initial suggestion was for a meeting at a point near the two nations' shared border. But he eventually proposed that the summit would be held in Ankara, to afford him the opportunity to see up close the impact of the Kemalist reforms on Turkey. The Turkish side was happy to oblige, albeit without any indication of a future reciprocal visit of Mustafa Kemal to Iran, as was expected by the Shah. The historic visit between the two heads of state was set to take place in summer 1934.[30]

Reza Shah's visit to Turkey began on a tentative note in mid-June, but concluded in early July as a resounding success. The Iranian side suggested that the Shah may travel to Turkey by way of Iraq, but Turkey insisted on the less convenient direct route across the Iranian border and into Eastern Anatolia. He was to travel by motorcade to Trabzon, where he was to board a Turkish ship to Samsun and from there by car to Ankara. There were some potential problems with the direct route, however. The first concern was the security situation in Eastern Anatolia, in a region that was the site of recent revolts. The Turkish government therefore boosted its military forces along the route. A second concern was the road conditions between the Iranian border and Trabzon. The anticipation that the road will be fully passable by June proved too optimistic. The most recent winter storm left parts of the road in such a bad shape that it was decided in the last moment to lead the Shah's motorcade through a longer but safer detour. A third concern had to do with Shah's health, with intelligence reports suggesting that he might be suffering from a stomach ailment and from mood swings, which the bumpy road might aggravate. Shortly after he crossed the border and was received with pomp and ceremony on

Figure 3.2 Reza Shah and Mustafa Kemal Atatürk. From *Fotoğrafla Atatürk* (Istanbul: Cumhuriyet Matbaası, 1939).

the Turkish side, the hosts found that he indeed suffered from stomachache, and from toothache as well. Worrying reports reached Ankara that the Shah was not in the best of moods and was keeping aloof from his hosts, as they slowly traversed the roads of Eastern Anatolia. But to the relief of the Turkish government, his health and mood improved significantly once he reached Trabzon, and by the time he arrived in Ankara he was fully recovered and in high spirits. The following two weeks were dedicated to pomp and ceremony during the official part of the visit in Ankara and to travels with Mustafa Kemal in western Anatolia and Istanbul in the informal part of the visit (Figure 3.2). The Shah visited Turkish institutions and observed the effects of Kemalist policies, with the intention to emulate in Iran some of the things he has seen. The Turkish and Iranian presses were meanwhile busy celebrating the purported mutual admiration between the two national saviors, and hailing the deep-seated sentiments of brotherhood and affection between their two brotherly peoples.[31] The Arabic press in the Middle East took note too. Whereas in Europe, the visit was overshadowed by the concurrent first meeting between Hitler and Mussolini in Venice, in Arab capitals in general, and in Baghdad in particular, much attention was given to the summit of the Turkish and Iranian leaders. Initial reports on possible Turkish support for Iran's territorial demands on Iraq eventually proved inaccurate, to Baghdad's relief. Indeed, no major agreement or negotiations of any strategic importance were concluded during the visit. But as the Shah headed back to Iran in early July, the positive atmosphere between the two governments appeared to many contemporary observers as laying the foundation for greater political and economic cooperation between the two sides.[32]

The Shah's visit to Turkey helped improve Turkish-Iranian relations further in a way that Faisal's visit three years earlier could never achieve. Both Ankara and Tehran went out of their way to display their commitment to maintaining friendly relations between their nations. During the Shah's visit, he was met with large greeting banners in Persian, which was probably the first time the Kemalist government encouraged such public displays since the alphabet reform of 1928. Similarly, the Turkish press addressed the Iranian monarch as "King of Kings" (Shahanshah), even as traditional honorifics were legally abolished and widely ridiculed in Turkey. In 1936, the Istanbul city council even honored Reza Shah Pahlavi by renaming a street in the vicinity of the city's main railway station the Şehinşah Pehlevi Street, and a street in the vicinity of the presidential palace in Ankara was renamed Rıza Şah Pehlevi Street (decades later renamed again as Iran Street). On its part, Iran named a boulevard in Tehran after Atatürk (after 1979 renamed Ayatollah Kashani Boulevard) and extraordinarily gave the green light for the performance of a Turkish theater company in Tabriz in 1934, at a time in which the Shah's Persianization policy was implemented in full force in Iranian Azerbaijan. The visiting theater company performed 10 plays in Turkish, including *Hamlet* and *Othello*, which did not attract large audiences but was still perceived as symbolically important because it was the first time since the late 1920s that performances in any other language than Persian were allowed in Tabriz. Put together, the combined expressions of mutual friendship and admiration between the two nations and their leaders left a strong public impression that colored popular and scholarly depictions of Turkish-Iranian relations in the interwar period for decades to come.[33]

The reality of the relations between the two states in the 1930s was a little more complicated in terms of their leaderships' mutual trust level than was put on public display by the two sides. The improvement in the relationship was evident when in late 1934 Iran accepted Turkey as a mediator in a land dispute it had with Afghanistan. Ankara had good relations with both governments and no direct stake in the territory, so Turkey was perceived as a fair mediator. With the help of its good offices, the dispute was resolved through negotiations in an agreement signed in June 1935. But Iran was unhappy with the results of the arbitration, despite feeling compelled to accept its results.[34] During the same time frame, however, Tehran dragged its feet for many months on Turkish offers for new bilateral agreements between the two governments. Through 1935 and 1936, Ankara was pressing the Iranian government to sign treaties on a slew of topics from border security to telephone and telegraph connections between the two countries. In November 1936 Turkey finally dispatched to Tehran a high-level delegation to press the issue and finalize the agreements in a matter of weeks. And yet, it took five more months until treaties on the above mentioned topics, as well as on extradition, nationality and residency rights, and customs and tariffs, were finally signed in April 1937. It may well have been the case that Iran dragged its feet, to Turkey's utter frustration, as part of an effort to press Ankara to first endorse Iran's position in the border dispute with Afghanistan and later in a separate border controversy with Iraq. Turkey was not willing to be pressed into fully backing Iran's claims in either case, however.[35] At the same time, in 1937, Turkey was finally able to leverage its relations with Iran, Iraq, and Afghanistan to convince their governments to form a regional defensive pact that Ankara was aspiring to establish since the early 1930s.

IV An Eastern Pact

Ankara's foreign policy in the Balkans and the Middle East since the early 1930s aimed at establishing regional pacts to which Turkey would serve as the linchpin. The Kemalist leadership hoped that nonaggression agreements would help stabilize these volatile regions, decrease the level of influence of the Great Powers on the member

states, and serve as a bulwark against aggressive and belligerent powers from within or without these regions. On its European frontiers,
Ankara found in Greece, Yugoslavia, and Romania willing partners to
its vision, which culminated in the Balkan Pact of 1934. The member states in the pact found a common ground in their opposition to
Italian expansionist ambitions and Bulgarian revisionist aspirations in
southeast Europe. The establishment of a similar nonaggression mechanism among independent countries in the Middle East proved harder
because of mutual suspicions, border disputes, and initial opposition
by Britain. The prospect of a regional nonaggression pact – including Turkey, Iran, Iraq, and Afghanistan – was first broached by Turkey
already during Faisal's visit to Ankara in July 1931, while Iraq was still
formally under the British mandate. The Turkish government again
raised the issue in conversations with British diplomats a year later,
shortly after Iraq became formally independent and joined the League
of Nations. Since Britain continued to maintain much leverage over
Iraq it was clear that such a pact could be concluded only with its
approval. But London's apprehensions regarding Turkey's close strategic cooperation with the Soviet Union, and with Ankara's suspected
hegemonic and territorial designs in the Middle East, combined to
discourage it from supporting any such regional agreement. Turkey
did not give up easily, however. In late 1933, Foreign Minister Aras
reiterated the proposal for a regional pact, now suggesting that both
Britain and the Soviet Union would be given a stake in the new regional
arrangement. With Fascist Italy emerging as an increasingly belligerent
international actor in the Mediterranean arena, and Nazi Germany
rapidly moving to shake the post-war international order in Europe,
Ankara hoped that Britain would now be willing to back its plans.
This proved not to be the case at the time, partly because of London's
distrust of Turkey's peaceful aims, and partly because of its unwillingness to appear as taking an anti-Italian stance. Britain's opposition, as
well as ongoing border disputes between the three other prospective
members in the pact, doomed the Turkish efforts for the time being.[36]
   The deterioration in international relations following Italy's invasion of Ethiopia in October 1935 gradually produced circumstances
more conducive to a regional pact in the Middle East. Britain was still
seeking to prevent conflict with the Fascist regime, but London became
much less dismissive of Turkey's concern with Rome's belligerence than
it has been even in early 1935.[37] With British opposition weakening,

and with Soviet approval secured beforehand, Turkey renewed its initiative directly with the prospective members. A decisive step in form-
ing a defensive pact appeared to have been taken in Geneva in October 1935, when the foreign ministers of Turkey, Iran, and Iraq met on
the sidelines of a League of Nations meeting to initial an agreement
for a nonaggression pact between them, with the stated intention to
invite Afghanistan to join in as well.[38] The conclusion of the proposed
treaty – interchangeably termed the "Eastern Pact," the "Near Eastern Pact," or the "Asiatic Pact" – was described in the regional and
international press as imminent throughout much of 1936. The Palestinian daily *Filastin* described the impending alliance between "the four
Islamic countries" as the brainchild of Atatürk, in his quest for regional
peace and cooperation. And the Iraqi newspaper *al-Istiqlal* hailed the
looming treaty as a historic step toward the substitution of collaboration and cordiality for the previous misunderstandings and strained
relations between the four member states.[39] The Turkish press was
particularly jubilant in celebrating the expected pact as another great
diplomatic victory for Turkey, shortly after the signing of the Montreux Convention in July 1936. It was described as a manifestation
of Turkey's growing international prestige and of its influence in the
Middle East.[40] But an unresolved Iranian-Iraqi territorial dispute, and
Iraq's efforts to convince other Arab countries to join the nonaggression agreement, delayed its realization until 1937.

The long-expected treaty of nonaggression was finally signed in July
1937 by the foreign ministers of Turkey, Iran, Iraq, and Afghanistan
in the Saadabad Palace outside of Tehran. Years of Turkish diplomatic
efforts were crowned with success, but under very different and much
more volatile regional and international circumstances than when it
was first envisioned in 1931. In the Mediterranean arena, Italy has been
increasing its belligerent activities following its occupation of Ethiopia
in 1935 and its intervention in the Spanish Civil War from 1936. Meanwhile, increasingly self-confident Germany was expanding its influence
in the Balkans. In the Middle East, an Arab general strike in Palestine in
April 1936 escalated into a major revolt, Egypt and Britain signed in
August a treaty leading to formal Egyptian independence, Syria and
France concluded in September an agreement aimed at leading to Syrian independence, and a military coup in Iraq brought to power a new
government in October. The cumulative result was regional instability and uncertainty, which appeared to create openings for potential

Italian subversion and aggression in the Levant, even as the future of the District of Alexandretta became a hotly contested issue between Turkey, Syria, and France. In these circumstances, Ankara expected the Treaty of Saadabad to help stabilize the region, discourage Iraq from siding with Syria on Alexandretta, and help reassure other member states of its lack of territorial ambitions at their expense, while adding a complicating factor to any Iraqi aspiration for any measure of unification with Syria. The post-coup government of Iraq established good relations with Turkey, even though Ankara offered asylum to some of its political rivals. The Iraqi Foreign Minister visited Turkey in April 1937, and the Turkish Foreign Minister reciprocated with a visit to Baghdad in late June. It was during this visit that the final sticking points in the treaty of nonaggression were ironed out, and after Iran and Iraq reached a compromise on their territorial dispute, the last obstacles on the road to the pact were removed. It took almost another full year, however, for the treaty to be ratified by all four member states, before it finally came into effect in June 1938, just as the European crisis was beginning to intensify.[41] The Treaty of Saadabad turned out to carry much less importance than was expected by many contemporary observers in the late 1930s. It was a weak regional alliance which was fraught with mutual suspicions and no strong mechanism of cooperation – so much so that between the ratification of the treaty in June 1938 and the outbreak of the European war in September 1939, the member states held only one formal meeting, in April 1939. Moreover, their foreign ministers apparently had more pressing issues to attend to, so the meeting was led by lower ranking diplomats. It was much less meaningful than the Balkan Pact of 1934, which in itself proved ineffective by the eve of World War II.[42]

The Treaty of Saadabad did not lead to dramatic changes in Turkey's position in the Middle East, but it did offer Ankara various advantages in its regional policies in the late 1930s. Turkey's leadership role in the pact elevated its international image as a regional power, which improved its bargaining position vis-à-vis Britain and France on the eve of World War II, as well as versus governments in the region. In Iraq, the government that came to power in the wake of the military coup of 1936 came to an abrupt end only a month after the signing of the Treaty of Saadabad. The succeeding Iraqi governments had much stronger pan-Arab proclivities, but they nevertheless sought neither to discredit the pact nor to challenge Turkey on the issue of Hatay. Egypt did not join the nonaggression pact, despite repeated reports in the Turkish and Arab press that it might, but the government in Cairo too was reluctant to question Ankara publicly on its assertive pursuit of the gradual detachment of Hatay from Syria in 1937–1938, and the region's eventual annexation to Turkey in 1939.[43] The growing Turkish regional clout in the late 1930s indeed left Syria mostly isolated and convinced at least one important claimant to the rule of Syria that the road to Damascus might be going through Ankara.

V Eyes on Syria

From the time he accepted the position of the Emir of Transjordan in 1921, Abdallah never stopped dreaming of finding a path to establish his rule over Greater Syria. In the 1930s he sought ways to coordinate his regional policies with Turkey, in the hope that Ankara may be able to help him fulfill his dream of establishing his rule in Damascus. At the beginning of the decade, Abdallah was operating in a prevent mode, supporting Ankara's efforts to block King Faisal's ambition to reassume the Syrian throne which he lost in 1920. After his brother's death in 1933, and with the international instability in the late 1930s appearing to open new opportunities for changes in the region, Abdallah began promoting himself more openly than before as a candidate to the rule of Greater Syria. Subsequently, he was as opposed as Turkey to the Franco-Syrian treaty of 1936, because it envisioned an independent Syria within the mandatory borders and under a republican regime. With Turkey's status as a regional power appearing to be on the rise, and with British and French influence in the Middle East facing increasing challenges from within and without the region, Emir Abdallah calculated that coordination with Ankara might help buttress his push for greater independence from British tutelage in Transjordan, and for a larger role in Syrian and regional affairs. He could offer Turkey in return to help block Syrian efforts to mobilize regional support against Ankara's policies on Alexandretta or potentially even acquiesce to the annexation of the region if given the opportunity to establish his rule in Damascus.

Turkey was guarded in its reactions to Abdallah's overtures because of concerns that uncalibrated response might arouse concerns and inflame tensions with Britain. Abdallah first approached the Turkish government in mid-1934 and again in early 1935, in request for an invitation for an official visit to Turkey. This was a time in which a new wave of publications in the international press suggested that the signing of the Eastern Pact was imminent, and when another round of French negotiations with Syrian leaders on the future of the country was ongoing. Separately, this was a period in which Turkish concerns with Italy's intentions prompted it to seek a rapprochement with Britain. Ankara's response to Abdallah therefore needed to be weighed carefully. On the one hand, cooperation with Abdallah carried the promise of derailing Syrian efforts to mobilize a pan-Arab front in opposition to Turkey's designs on Alexandretta, by demonstrating that Ankara was not hostile to the Arabs and by gaining for Ankara an ambitious ally who might be gaining in regional importance. On the other hand, Abdallah was ruling under British tutelage, and Ankara was well aware that Britain would likely perceive a formal invitation as requested by Abdallah as a form of Turkish unwanted intervention in a British sphere of influence. Subsequently, Ankara opted not to accommodate the emir's request for an invitation for an official visit, but as a sweetener, Turkey accredited its consul-general in Jerusalem as a non-resident consul-general to Amman too.[44]

The signing of the Franco-Syrian Treaty of Independence in late 1936 modified Turkey's calculus, as it was seeking to isolate Syria in the Alexandretta dispute. This was in opposition to the stated goal of the Syrian Committee for the Defense of Alexandretta, which aspired to turn the dispute over the future of the District into a pan-Arab cause like the conflict in Palestine.[45] In February 1937, a report was leaked to the press according to which the Turkish consul in Jerusalem traveled to Amman to meet Abdallah, and the two "have had a long conversation concerning Transjordan's attitude over the Alexandretta dispute." For good measure, it was added that "Turkey may establish a consulate in Amman."[46] Abdallah enjoyed the attention and sought to capitalize on the Turkish interest in preventing the controversy with Syria from becoming a pan-Arab cause. The emir was himself unsatisfied with the Franco-Syrian agreement, because it distanced him from fulfilling his vision of the unification of Greater Syria under his rule, and he also hoped to secure Ankara's backing for his claim to the rule of Palestine. The timing therefore appeared as fruitions to again request an invitation to Ankara for discussions on the future of Syria and regarding his goal to secure greater measure of independence from Britain. This time Turkey obliged, and the British government agreed too, so long as

Figure 3.3 Mustafa Kemal Atatürk and the Emir Abdallah. From *Fotoğrafla Atatürk* (Istanbul: Cumhuriyet Matbaası, 1939).

the visit was considered informal and apolitical. It was to be presented simply as an occasion for the emir to meet Atatürk and observe in person the results of his laudable reforms. At the same time, the Turkish hosts nevertheless planned on receiving Abdallah with full honors, such as were usually accorded to a head of state. Turkey hoped to send a strong public signal to the National Bloc, the dominant nationalist party in Syria which negotiated the Franco-Syrian agreement and was at odds with Abdallah's regional ambitions. The visit was set to May 1937, when Abdallah was scheduled to return from Europe, after visiting London for the coronation of King George VI.[47]

Abdallah was received with pomp and ceremony when he arrived in Turkey in late May 1937, and his visit was covered heavily with reports and photos in the Turkish and Arab press (Figure 3.3). The emir was first met by Prime Minister İnönü and then treated to one of President Atatürk's signature late-night socializing events, which that time lasted until six in the morning. In this alcohol-infused all-nighter, Abdallah left a good enough impression on the Turkish leader to prompt Atatürk to dictate a note addressed to the British government, in which he recommended the broadening of the emir's political authority and the elevation of his position to that of a king. Abdallah was delighted with this unexpected endorsement, regardless of the nondiplomatic circumstances in which it was produced. Until that point in the visit, he was accompanied by his British aide-de-camp, formally in order to assist the emir, but in reality as his handler on behalf of the British government. Once receiving the note, Abdallah was sufficiently excited to instruct his ADC to leave immediately for Jerusalem to hand-deliver Atatürk's message to the British High Commissioner for Palestine and Transjordan as soon as possible. The British government simply disregarded the note, but the British colonial authorities were utterly furious that it gave the emir a pretext to temporarily get read of his ADC, hold private meetings with Turkish officials to which London was not privy, and issue statements to the Turkish press without British preapproval.[48]

Abdallah's visit to Turkey while the dispute over Alexandretta was heating up, and his laudatory public statements about the Kemalist republic, infuriated supporters of the National Bloc in Syria. In 1937, there were rumors swirling in the Middle East according to which Abdallah was seeking the establishment of an Arab kingdom under his rule, which would include Transjordan, Palestine, and the southern parts of Syria, with the northern parts of Syria ceded to Turkey.[49] Statements made by Abdallah while in Turkey, which appeared to suggest that he secured Turkish support for the Arab position on Palestine, but refrained from explicit opposition to the detachment of Alexandretta from Syria, increased suspicions regarding his dealing with Turkey. He was therefore pilloried by the nationalist press in Syria as a collaborator with Turkey's anti-Arab policies. Abdallah refuted these accusations, arguing in interviews he gave to the press that "Turkey contemplated no territorial expansion in the Sanjak of Alexandretta" and that Atatürk assured him in person of Turkey's unconditional support for the Arab cause in Palestine. These clarifications did not impress his critics in Syria, and ferocious attacks on his purported collusion with Turkey continued apace. The level of anger against Abdallah was in fact so high that the British colonial authorities forced him to change his travel plans. Originally, he planned on riding the train from

Turkey to Syria and then proceed by car back to Transjordan. Instead, he first spent a few days of vacation in Istanbul, before boarding a steamship that took him to Haifa, from where he traveled by car back to Amman.[50]

The Syrian government of the National Bloc was particularly annoyed with Abdallah's talks in Ankara, because in 1937, it still held some hope for fruitful direct negotiations with Turkey. Syrian Prime Minister Jamil Mardam visited Turkey twice that year, once before and once after the emir's visit to Ankara. In February 1937, Mardam met with Turkish leaders on his way to Europe for negotiations in France, and in December on his way back from talks aimed at saving the increasingly moribund Franco-Syrian Treaty. Meanwhile, the veteran Syrian nationalist Adil Arslan, a scion of a princely Druze family, was appointed to serve as an informal diplomatic envoy of the Syrian government in Ankara. But notwithstanding various public declarations of the two sides regarding their mutual friendship, and regardless of Turkish statements of support for full independence to Syria, they could not come to any agreement on Alexandretta. The increasing communal violence in the District, and Ankara's success in pressing Paris to gradually accept its demands, finally brought the Syrian diplomatic efforts in Turkey to an end. The signing of a Turkish-French agreement in July 1938, which led to the formal independence of Hatay on terms favorable to Ankara's demands, was the coup de grace to the Syrian-Turkish ties. The Syrian government was invited by Turkey to sign the agreement, but expectedly declined, and the relations between the Kemalist regime and the already tenuous National Bloc government in Damascus were all but severed.[51]

Emir Abdallah and the Turkish government, meanwhile, sought to build on the positive atmosphere that was created between the two sides during his visit to Turkey. The Turkish Consul-General in Jerusalem met with Abdallah quite regularly in 1938, and the government in Ankara invited him to visit again in late October, for the planned festivities on the occasion of the republic's fifteenth anniversary. The British government was very unhappy with this turn of events, despite the marked improvement in British-Turkish relations in the late 1930s. Both London and its colonial officials in the Middle East were concerned that Ankara was looking for ways to increase its influence in the Middle East, which they found unwelcome. They suspected that Turkey was trying to manipulate Abdallah to back Ankara's policies on Hatay, in ways that will make him the focus of even more intense Arab nationalist criticism and animosity, which was undesirable from a British standpoint. The emir sought to reassure his British overlords that he was not blind to Ankara's purported goals in the region. He explained that he was well aware of Turkey's aggressive territorial demands in Syria but suggested that strengthening his relations with Ankara will help him keep in step with the British-Turkish rapprochement and that the friendship of Turkey would prove much more valuable to him and the British than anything his pan-Arab nationalist critics in the region could ever offer them. London remained unconvinced and therefore vetoed his request visit to Turkey again, only a year after his first visit to Ankara.[52]

The British roadblocks did not hinder Abdallah from seeking alternative ways to strengthen his ties with Turkey. Shortly after Atatürk passed away in November 1938, the emir approached his successor İsmet İnönü regarding the Turkish government's willingness to invite his son Nayef to undergo military training in Turkey. The request came at a time when Abdallah was trying to convince the British government to accept his desire to appoint Nayef as his heir apparent in place of his eldest son Talal.[53] İnönü obliged and extended the requested invitation to the Transjordanian prince. He proposed that the grandson of the leader of the Arab Revolt during the Great War would train and serve in the Ankara-based Presidential Guard Regiment (Riyaseticumhur Muhafız Alayı). When informed of the offer, the British authorities were yet again hesitant to authorize this initiative. British officials were concerned lest Turkey might establish long-term influence over the 24-year-old prince, secure a new opportunity to expand Ankara's influence in the Middle East, and give more ammunition to pan-Arab critics of Abdallah. Harold MacMichael, the High Commissioner for Palestine and Transjordan, cautioned that "the Arabs, who realized the possibility of eventual Turkish designs upon Syria and the countries lying south of it, and who bear no love for the Turks, might see in this move an attempt to gain an ally for designs contrary to their interests, and the French might regard it askance for similar reasons." Abdallah yet again sought to assuage these British concerns by explaining to his colonial overlords that he was well aware of Ankara's nefarious intents to expand its clout in the Middle East. But he suggested that his experiences in Turkey will actually illustrate to his son Nayef why the Arab Revolt against the Turks was so necessary and justified and will help him gain "more knowledge concerning the Turkish danger which still threatens Arab countries, and I pray that he might become a worthy successor of his father and of his House as well as a loyal preserver of our traditional friendship with Great Britain." To up the pressure on London to approve his plan, Abdallah leaked to the press that his son was definitely going to Turkey, all the while holding "numerous interviews with the Turkish Consul-General at Amman." The British government finally relented. The prince traveled to Ankara by way of Syria in late April 1939, where he was appointed honorary ADC to President İnönü. He remained in this post through the period of the annexation of Hatay in July and until shortly after the outbreak of war in Europe in September.[54]

The budding relations with Abdallah served Turkey's efforts to prevent the formation of an Arab front against its policies on Alexandretta, and to expand its regional clout. The late 1930s was a time in which the end of direct colonial rule in the region appeared imminent, albeit still with strings attached, as was the case with Iraq in 1932 and with Egypt in 1936. Greater Syria was still administered by Britain and France under the mandate system, but the future independence of Syria, Lebanon, Transjordan, and Palestine was on the negotiating table too in the closing years of the interwar period. In these circumstances, it made perfect sense for Turkey to nurture relations with both formally independent countries in the region and with likely future independent governments, like that of Transjordan. But if the prospect of a restructured and more limited British and French colonial presence in the Middle East carried the promise of more opportunities for self-rule in the region, it also appeared to potentially entail a greater opportunity for Italian penetration and expansion in the Eastern Mediterranean in the late 1930s. It was this perceived threat which helped precipitate a Turkish rapprochement not only with Britain and France but also with Egypt, an Arab state far more important than Emir Abdallah's Transjordan.

VI An Odd Couple

Italy's increasingly aggressive ambitions in the Eastern Mediterranean and the Balkans in the late 1930s impacted Turkey relations with Egypt more than with any other Middle Eastern country. Following the Italian invasion of Ethiopia in 1935, Egypt and the Anglo-Egyptian Sudan

became sandwiched between Italian Libya and Italy's colonial posses-
sions in the Horn of Africa. As the Fascist regime's expansionist ambitions in the Eastern Mediterranean and Red Sea were well known, and
the importance of the Suez Canal for its leader's imperialist plans was
self-evident, Egypt was concerned that it might soon be the next target in Mussolini's crosshairs. This perceived Italian threat, which was
shared by Britain too, played a crucial role in creating conducive circumstances for the negotiation of the Anglo-Egyptian Treaty of 1936.
The agreement secured Egypt's formal independence from Britain and
the end of the capitulation regime in its territories, and paved the way
for its acceptance into the League of Nations in 1937. The treaty did
not end Britain's hegemony and military presence in Egypt, but it did
allow the Egyptian government more leeway in conducting its foreign
policy and establishing an independent albeit small military force. It
was in these circumstances and in view of their shared desire to keep
Rome's ambitions in the Eastern Mediterranean at bay, that Turkey
and Egypt began moving cautiously on the path of rapprochement in
the late 1930s. The death of King Fuad and his succession by his son
Farouk in April 1936, and the signing of the Anglo-Egyptian Treaty
four months later, cleared some of the major hurdles for a marked
improvement in Turkish-Egyptian relations. Some other issues continued to hamper the bilateral relations between the two Eastern Mediterranean neighbors. These included the Egyptian royal court's flirtation
with the idea of claiming the empty seat of the Caliphate for young
King Farouk, indignation in pan-Arab circles with Turkey's policies on
Alexandretta, aversion toward the Kemalist reforms in pan-Islamic circles, and broader Egyptian suspicions toward Turkey's regional ambitions in the Middle East. Nevertheless, a gradual thaw in the once
tension-filled Turkish-Egyptian relations was evident in the closing
years of the interwar period in response to developments in the international arena.

The gradual rapprochement between Turkey and Egypt began in
1936, at a time when the two countries were both relishing new
political achievements and being alarmed by regional developments.
In Turkey, the Montreux Convention of July 1936 allowed the government a firmer control over the Straits. In Egypt, a Wafd cabinet
was established in May, and by August it finalized negotiations on
an agreement that set parameters for the country's formal independence from British rule. At the same time, the growing instability in the

international arena in general, and in the Mediterranean region in particular, became a matter of major concern for both countries. Both
sought a certain level of British protection from what appeared like
a growing Italian threat to their territorial integrity, but without sub-
jecting themselves to full dependence on London's power and dictates.
Egyptian suspicions regarding possible Turkish hegemonic ambitions
south of its borders, and Turkish concerns with Egypt's potential to
become a powerful influence in the Levant persisted. But the two sides
gradually concluded that the new regional circumstances and their
shared interests called for better relations and higher degrees of cooperation.

Turkey's interest in rapprochement was reflected in numerous
reports in the Turkish press of 1936 on efforts to solve past problems and negotiate new agreements between the two states. Ankara and
Cairo resumed long-stalled talks on a nationality and residence agreement, a commercial treaty, and other bilateral agreements. The two
sides declared their determination and resolve to remove any obstacle on the path of restoring the historical relations of brotherhood
and friendship between the two peoples.[55] The improvement of the
atmosphere between the two governments was evident in late October, when the Turkish embassy in Cairo held its annual festive reception on the occasion of Turkey's Republic Day. In 1933, on the one-
year anniversary of the Fez Incident, the Egyptian government all but
boycotted the event, and in the two years that followed, it dispatched
only low-profile representatives to the event. In October 1936, however, the list of guests included many prominent Egyptian politicians
and dignitaries, including Prime Minister Mustafa al-Nahhas, and al-
Azhar University's rector Mustafa al-Maraghi, who was considered a
very close confidant of King Farouk. Following the event, the pages of
Egypt's newspapers were graced with photos of the smiling guests, and
with laudatory commentaries on the strong fraternal bonds between
the Turkish and Egyptian nations, striking a very different tone than
in the wake of the Fez Incident exactly four years earlier.[56]

The improved atmosphere led to concrete results after Egypt became
formally independent in early 1937, although in a slower pace than
expected by Turkey. In April, the two sides concluded a treaty of friendship which was accompanied by agreements on various issues that they
failed to resolve in previous rounds of negotiations since the late 1920s.
These included treaties of nationality and residency, issues related to

the allocation of *waqf* funds, matters of legal jurisdiction and several other legal matters. Turkey, meanwhile, supported the acceptance of Egypt into the League of Nations in May 1937, and some consideration was given on both sides to the possibility of Egypt's admission to the Eastern Pact, albeit without any concrete result. Egypt was generally cautious regarding regional commitments at the time, thus also rejecting a separate Iraqi initiative for a bilateral Egyptian-Iraqi agreement.[57] Turkey was content with leaving Egypt outside the pact. But it did hope to accentuate its warming relations with Egypt with an official visit of Foreign Minister Aras to Cairo in late 1937. Ankara intended for the visit to serve as an occasion for a ceremonial signing of the new bilateral agreements between the two states, shortly after the signing of the Treaty of Saadabad was presented as a great Turkish diplomatic success, and at a time in which Turkey was aiming to demonstrate that the conflict over Alexandretta did not damage its relations with most Arab governments in the region. The Egyptian government did not like these optics and the visit was therefore postponed.[58]

The visit of the Turkish Foreign Minister and the ratification of the bilateral agreements finally took place in April 1938, after a new government came to power in Egypt. Yet, the new Muhammad Mahmud ministry did not initiate a fundamental or rapid change in the cautious regional policies of the previous al-Nahhas government. Aras's visit thus did not entail any immediate breakthrough in the relations, although it was a propaganda success for Turkey at a time in which the future of Alexandretta was still hanging in the balance. The visit of the Turkish Foreign Minister to Egypt lasted five days, during which Aras met with King Farouk, Egyptian cabinet ministers, parliamentarians, bureaucrats, and dignitaries, and attended receptions and parties organized by the Egyptian government, the Turkish embassy, and the Turkish colony in Egypt. The agreements reached a year earlier were signed and ratified, and public declarations of friendship and brotherhood abounded. But reports in the international and Egyptian press in the preceding weeks about possible Egyptian entry into the Treaty of Saadabad proved incorrect. Neither was Egypt interested at the time in joining, nor was Turkey thrilled about adding another major Arab state into the pact and risking diminishing its relative dominance among its members. Ankara was content with improved relations that militated against an Egyptian or Iraqi opposition to its policies on Hatay, either in the League of Nations or in public statements, and laid the foundation for a meaningful anti-Italian alignment in the Eastern Mediterranean at a time when the British-Italian Easter Accords created much regional uncertainty regarding London's position vis-à-vis Rome.[59] In the same vein, the well-publicized visit of the Turkish naval training ship *Hamidiye* to Alexandria in June 1938, even as the regional press was full of almost daily reports on violence between pro-Turkey and pro-Syria activists in Alexandretta, was a propaganda coup for Ankara. The old Ottoman cruiser was received with a 21-gun salute and much fanfare, with large crowds reportedly receiving the visiting sailors with chants of "Long Live Atatürk!"[60] Ankara wished to make an even stronger statement with a visit of King Farouk to Turkey. However, the death of Atatürk in November 1938 and preparations for the politically arranged marriage of the king's sister to the Iranian crown prince Mohammad Reza Pahlavi in March 1939 gave the Egyptian side convenient pretexts for postponing the visit indefinitely. The Egyptian court was instead toying again with the idea of reviving the Caliphate, to Turkey's dismay, and did not wish to appear as too closely aligned with Ankara, and thus risking the ire of radical pan-Arabists and pan-Islamists.[61]

The intensifying crisis in Europe in 1939, and particularly the Italian invasion of Albania in early April, gave new impetus for efforts to establish a defensive alignment in the Eastern Mediterranean. The German-Italian Pact of Steel in late May, shortly after the nationalists completed their victory in the Spanish Civil War, increased the urgency to check Italy's expansionist ambitions in the Balkans and in the Eastern Mediterranean. It was within this context that Britain and Turkey declared in mid-May their intention to sign a defensive pact against aggression in the Mediterranean, followed by a similar Turkish-French declaration in late June, after Paris acceded to Ankara's demand for the formal annexation of Hatay. At this point in time, Turkey expected that the signing of defensive agreements between the two democratic allies and the Soviet Union, with which Turkey maintained generally good relations of cooperation since the early 1920s, would create a defensive front from the Baltic Sea to Red Sea by way of the Eastern Mediterranean, which would serve as an effective deterrent against Italian belligerency. Egypt was expected to anchor the southern edge of that defensive front. The dangerous international situation appeared to be calling for better coordination between Cairo and Ankara. Thus, even as Turkey and France were finalizing the agreement for the annex-ation of Hatay to Turkey, the Egyptian Foreign Minister Abdel Fattah Yahya traveled to Ankara in mid-June 1939 for high-level talks with the Turkish government. As fate would have it, Yahya was the same man who in an earlier term in office was the Foreign Minister who managed the Turkish-Egyptian diplomatic crisis in the wake of the Fez Incident. The veteran politician was now tasked with strengthening the friendly relations between the two governments.[62]

The official visit was formally a reciprocation of the Turkish Foreign Minister's visit to Egypt a year earlier, but the Turkish press hailed it as a historic event pregnant with symbolic and political meaning. The first visit of such a senior Egyptian official to the republic was applauded as a manifestation of Turkey's friendship with all the Muslim peoples, and particularly with the Arab world. On his part, the Egyptian min-ister visited Atatürk's temporary tomb in the Ethnography Museum in Ankara, in a public display of respect to the "Eternal Leader" (*Ebedi Şef*) and his legacy. Speculations were raised that in addition to bilat-eral agreement on civil and economic issues, the visiting minister was also engaged in talks about the possibility of closer defense and secu-rity cooperation between the two sides. In previous years Egypt was disinterested in joining the Treaty of Saadabad, but in 1939 there was indeed some reconsideration in the Egyptian government of the pos-sible merits of such moves. Eventually Cairo did not initiate such a step, however, because the probable downsides in the Egyptian, Arab, and international arenas were deemed as outweighing the potential benefits. Instead, the visiting Egyptian Foreign Minister made do with asking for Turkish assistance in the training of officers in the fledgling Egyptian army. Turkey responded favorably. The Turkish government also extended again an invitation for an official visit of King Farouk, as the ultimate display of the warming relations between the two coun-tries.[63]

The prospect of defense and military cooperation between the two Eastern Mediterranean nations was welcomed by the pro-government press in Egypt, but received with hesitancy by Britain. The weekly *al-Thaqafa*, for instance, hailed in July 1939 the strong indications of security cooperation between Cairo and Ankara, coming on the heels of the public declarations of Turkey's intention to formally ally itself with Britain and France. The journal suggested that these developments were positive and essential steps toward a regional defense of the Eastern Mediterranean and the Red Sea against the aggressive and expansionist ambitions of Italy.[64] The British and French governments were similarly supportive of such an alignment,[65] but Britain was not enthusiastic regarding direct Turkish-Egyptian defense and military cooperation. London's reluctance was informed by lingering suspicions about Turkey's intentions in the region, as well as by concerns that Egypt might become too independent of Britain's military stranglehold. The British therefore opposed any direct ties between the Turkish and Egyptian militaries. When rumors spread only a few days before the Egyptian Foreign Minister's visit to Turkey that Cairo was intending to request the dispatch of a Turkish military mission to Egypt for training and instruction purposes, the British government immediately made its displeasure known to Prime Minister Muhammad Mahmud. He hastened to reassure the British Embassy that these were baseless rumors. London was therefore utterly dismayed when it transpired that during his visit to Ankara the Egyptian Foreign Minister requested Turkey to host a group of 20 to 30 Egyptian officer cadets for training in Turkey, as well as discussed the possibility of dispatch of Turkish military officers to Egypt. Turkey responded positively, but neither Ankara nor Cairo shared any information on this topic with their British allies. London had to gather it from its own intelligence sources, including reports that Egypt was considering a request for Turkish officers to serve as commanding officers in the fledgling Egyptian army. When Prime Minister Mahmud was confronted with this information by a British official in mid-July, he yet again flatly denied it.[66]

The British authorities were therefore flabbergasted and dismayed when not a week passed before reports were leaked to the Egyptian press about the government's intention to dispatch a military mission of 15 army officers to Turkey for training purposes, with the expectation that the Turkish military would reciprocate with a similar mission to Egypt in the closing months of 1939. A British official again hastened to meet the Egyptian Prime Minister in request for clarifications, but this time received a very different response from the senior statesman. Only weeks before the outbreak of World War II, Prime Minister Mahmud insisted that his government had the right to conduct its foreign policy as it saw fit, and that thinly veiled British threats disguised as advices will not be acceptable to him. He was adamant that the exchange of military missions between Turkey and Egypt will take place as planned. London was obviously very dissatisfied with what British officials saw as potential opening for the establishment of Turkish influence over the Egyptian officer corps. But since the exchange of military missions was already made public, and because Britain did not want to risk straining its relations with neither Ankara nor Cairo just as war in Europe appeared increasingly imminent, the British government decided to swallow its pride and not to stand in the way of the initiative that Egypt and Turkey hatched behind its back.[67]

The visit of the Egyptian military delegation in late August 1939 came at a very inopportune moment, as the clouds of a new major European war were gathering over the continent. Led by an army general, the Egyptian officers arrived in Turkey on August 19 in time to observe the annual maneuvers of the Turkish army in Eastern Thrace. They were then scheduled to visit Turkish military installations in Anatolia, to study from their Turkish counterparts methods of military training and logistical organization and lay the foundation for friendly and cooperative relations between the top military brasses of the two countries. The Turkish press reported at length on the visit. The visiting officers were received enthusiastically upon arriving in Istanbul, were reportedly impressed by the capabilities of the Turkish army as displayed in the maneuvers in Eastern Thrace and enjoyed tours of the Turkish General Staff headquarters in Ankara, an air force base in Eskişehir, and a number of other military installations in Central and Western Anatolia. In statements to the press, the delegation's commanding officer attested that "the undeniable combat capabilities of the Turkish army have left on us a strong impression and filled us with pride." He was further thankful for the cordiality and fraternity of the Turkish hosts. However, according to information gathered by the British upon the delegation's return to Egypt, the true picture was somewhat less idyllic. It transpired that the Turkish hosts were very guarded in their interactions with the visiting Egyptian officers, being quite reluctant to share with them detailed information about drills, weaponry, organizational methods, and finances of the Turkish armed forces. They were apparently concerned of spying, or at the least the leakage of valuable information about their military preparedness. This Turkish attitude could be at least partly explained by the dramatic political developments which took place in Europe, and to a lesser degree in Egypt too, while the Egyptian military delegation was still in Turkey. The Egyptian officers arrived in Istanbul when clouds of war were already hanging over Europe. By the time they boarded a ship back to Alexandria in early September, the *Wehrmacht* was already on the march in Poland, Britain and France were in a state of war with Germany, and Prime Minister Mahmud was just replaced in office by Ali Mahir Pasha.[68]

VII Defensive Stand

The Molotov-Ribbentrop Pact of August 23, 1939, and the war in Europe changed Turkey's calculus, as its sovereignty and territorial integrity came under threat in the early 1940s. Turkish strategic planning in the late 1930s hinged on Soviet backing of an anti-Italian front in the Eastern Mediterranean, in which Egypt would be a junior but willing partner. Despite some strains in the relations with Moscow since 1936, and difficulties in Soviet-British and Soviet-French relations in late 1939, nothing prepared Turkey to the shock of the Soviet-Nazi agreement. When the Soviet armies invaded Poland in mid-September, evidently under an understanding with Berlin, it set off alarm bells in Ankara because of fears that the German-Soviet agreement might have included secret clauses about Soviet territorial demands at Turkey's expense. Ankara's declared intention to sign strategic defensive agreements with Britain and France now threatened to place it in Berlin and Moscow's crosshairs, and suddenly it was the Soviet Union rather than Italy that rapidly emerged as the most serious potential threat to Turkey's territorial integrity. In Egypt, meanwhile, new Prime Minister Ali Maher, was much less interested than his predecessor in regional affairs and more inclined to adopting a position of neutrality in case of a major European war.[69] The British concern in July 1939 that Turkey and Egypt might be developing a too cozy defense and security relations became rapidly irrelevant and faded away. A Turkish military mission was never sent to Egypt. The dramatic developments in Europe altered Turkey's priorities rapidly and cut down any intention Ankara may have entertained only a few weeks earlier about an expanded political footprint in the Middle East.

Turkey's cordial relations with the Soviet Union throughout most of the interwar period factored prominently into Turkey's relations with the Middle East during the period. Although Soviet-Turkish relations were not devoid of suspicions and disagreements, the relations with Moscow in the interwar period were nevertheless more stable than with any other European major power with any stake in Turkey's geographic vicinity. Maintaining good relations with the Soviet Union indeed remained a cornerstone of Turkish foreign policy since the early 1920s, even as Ankara was seeking a rapprochement and better relations with Britain and France in the 1930s. Any major Turkish diplomatic initiative in the Middle East was coordinated with the Soviets, or at minimum, initiated after consultation with Moscow and securing its acquiescence. Moscow's support, at times real and at others assumed, was oftentimes a source of suspicion against Turkey among stakeholders in the Middle East, particularly in London, Paris, and Tehran. But it also allowed Turkey to project a more powerful position than it would have had on its own, and to operate in the Middle East and Mediterranean arenas under the assumption that its Soviet frontiers were relatively secured and unthreatened, even after relations somewhat cooled in the wake of the Montreux Convention. The widely held assumption in the Middle East of the late 1930s that Turkey might be trying to take advantage of the international crisis for territorial gains south of its borders in fact assumed Soviet acquiescence to such moves. Thus, as the new administration of President İsmet İnönü was taking full control over the state by early 1939, Paris and London were concerned that Ankara might seek to exploit their preoccupation with the European crisis to expand Turkey's clout in the Middle East, and advance its territorial ambitions through subversive activities in Syria and Iraq. Indeed, when during the Czechoslovakian Crisis in late 1938 France approached Turkey regarding the possibility of negotiating a mutual defense treaty, its diplomats came out of the meetings with the impression that Ankara demanded in return a stake in the oil resources of Syria.[70]

The declaration of Turkey's strategic alignment with Britain and France in May and June, respectively, elevated concerns in the Middle East regarding Ankara's potential territorial ambitions. The three governments were prompted to action by the German imposition of its control over the Romanian economy in late March and by the Italian invasion of Albania in early April. But many observers in the Middle East suspected that secret clauses in the projected agreement between the three countries might hand Ankara control over additional territories south of its borders with Syria and Iraq. In northern Syria, a reported increase in Turkish propaganda and subversive activities in Aleppo and its vicinity in late 1939 was understood by some observers as a preliminary stage before imminent occupation with French consent. The existence of a significant faction in Aleppo that supported intimate ties with Turkey despite the loss of Alexandretta only exacerbated such concerns.[71] The Iraqi government too, and even Iran, two members of the Treaty of Saadabad, were similarly concerned with Turkey's purported territorial designs on their territories and with Ankara's projected European allies' willingness to accommodate them. Both Baghdad and Tehran therefore asked for assurances from Ankara and London that the anticipated Turkish-British defense agreement would not include secret clauses with adverse ramifications for the territorial integrity and national interests of the two countries. Even Emir Abdallah, with his dreams of the Syrian throne still very much intact, made known to the British government his opposition to Turkish occupation of any Syrian land beyond Hatay.[72]

Although Ankara did conclude the planned strategic agreement with Britain and France in October 1939, Turkey was increasingly committed to a defensive mode at that time. The world war reversed, at least temporarily, what appeared in the 1930s as a shift toward greater regional autonomy and independence for local governments. It was within that prewar context that Turkey sought to expand its diplomatic footprint in the Middle East in the decade before World War II. By late 1941, however, all the countries south of its borders, from Iran in the east to Egypt in the west, were under the effective control of Britain and its post–Operation Barbarossa Soviet ally. As the greatest global powers were engaged in a mighty struggle over the fate of Eurasia and the world, all of Turkey's investment in regional diplomacy in the Middle East in the 1930s came to naught, at least in the short term. The rude awakening to Turkey's aspirations for an influential role in the Middle East, and also in the Balkans, had similarly negative ramifications for Ankara's hopes to leverage its international standing and Anatolia's geostrategic position to gain important economic benefits from its ties with the Middle East.

4 | Great Expectations

One of the greatest challenges facing Turkey during the interwar period was to overcome the devastating economic effects of the long years of war from 1913 to 1923. The economy was therefore a subject of great importance in Turkish politics, particularly in the wake of the global economic crisis after 1929. In the 1930s, statism (etatism), a form of command economy, was adopted by the ruling party as a major ideological tenet, envisioning the nationalization of vital sectors of the economy, government-led industrialization and expansion of transportation networks, and centrally created multiyear plans for an increase in agricultural production and trade volumes. These measures played a role in helping Turkey to overcome some of the worst effects of the global economic crisis and actually grow its economy in the decade before World War II. But the all-important agricultural sector of the economy still faced problems as a result of a precipitous decline in the prices of all major crops in the early 1930s, and the consequent decline in the value of Turkish agricultural exports. Meanwhile, Turkey was finding it difficult to attract foreign investments, and faced a constant shortage of hard currency.[1] The Middle East appeared to offer some intriguing possibilities in this respect, partially as a market for Turkish agricultural exports and manufactured products, and more importantly, as a promising partner for European transit trade by way of Turkey.

Ankara did not overlook the significance of its trade relations with the Middle East, even though European countries were by far Turkey's most important trade partners in the interwar period. Egypt, the largest and most prosperous Middle Eastern economy during this period, was the most important regional destination for Turkish exports. Ankara was actively trying to expand these commercial ties in the 1930s. As part of this effort, the government-controlled İş Bank (formally denoted at the time as the Bank of Affairs), opened a branch in Alexandria in 1932.[2] Celal Bayar, the bank's general manager,

Figure 4.1 Turkish cigarette factory. From La Direction générale de la Presse au Ministère de l'Intérieur, *La Turquie Contemporaine* (Ankara, 1935), 97.

who shortly thereafter was appointed the Minister of National Economy, traveled to Egypt in person to inaugurate the new branch. The future Turkish Prime Minister (1937–1939) and President (1950–1960) tasked the office with increasing the volume of Turkish exports to Egypt. Two years later, in 1934, the newly established national import and export agency, or Türkofis, also opened a branch in Alexandria, followed a year later by the opening of another branch in Haifa, which in the early 1930s was envisioned by British planners as a future hub for European trade with Iraq, Iran, and possibly India too. Turkish exports to the Middle East were mainly agricultural products such as dried fruits, grains, timber, livestock, tobacco and opium.[3] The latter two were particularly lucrative. Tobacco was exported both in the form of loose tobacco leaves, for cigarette factories in Egypt and neighboring countries, and as Turkey-made brand name cigarettes (Figures 4.1 and 4.2). Ubiquitous advertisements in periodicals in Egypt, Iraq, and Palestine of the interwar period bear witness to the concerted effort to promote Turkish cigarettes, either Turkey-made or locally manufactured with imported Turkish tobacco, under slogans such as "Smoke cigarettes with original Turkish tobacco!" or "The original Turkish cigarettes!"[4] In 1935, Turkey opened in Egypt a cigarette factory aimed

السجاير التركيه الاصليه

المصنوعة بادارة الريجي في استامبول

الجـودة

الوجاهة

الاتقـان

جميع هذه الصفات تجدها في السيجارة التركية

جوسكيه كلوب * غازي * يالوه
تورك * ينيجه * خانم * ا كسترا   الاصناف
ا كسترا * برجي ا كنجي

الوكيل العمومي : يوسف البينا

Figure 4.2 Turkish cigarette advertisement in a Palestinian newspaper. From *Filastin*, February 11, 1936, 8.

at expanding its stake in the country's thriving cigarette industry. Although the factory could not find success, allegedly because its operation was sabotaged by Greek and Armenian competitors in collusion with corrupt Egyptian officials, its establishment was another demonstration of the Turkish government's awareness of the potential significance of Middle Eastern markets for its exports.[5] Opium and its derivatives were another important export item from Turkey to the Middle East and to farther destinations in Asia and Europe. In the early 1930s, the Turkish government established an opium monopoly and sought to build a powerful international cartel of the most important opium producers, along with Yugoslavia and Iran. The Balkan state did sign with Turkey a cooperation agreement in 1933, but Iran refused to join the envisioned cartel, in spite of Turkish efforts to leverage the improved diplomatic relations between Ankara and Tehran for that purpose. A more serious problem was the international pressure on Turkey to suppress the illicit production and smuggling of opium-derived drugs such as heroin and codeine, oftentimes through Egypt and the Levant. Following intense international pressures, which created tensions with Cairo because of Egyptians accusations that Turkey was ignoring the criminal smuggling of drugs to Alexandria, the Turkish authorities began taking in 1933 more resolute actions against illicit drug labs in Istanbul and the organizations behind them. Nevertheless, the smuggling operations from Anatolia to the Middle East, alongside legal exports of opium, continued apace throughout the interwar period, and beyond.[6] All these exports to and through the Middle East were not of negligible economic importance to Turkey, even if its overall trade volumes with the region or through it were much smaller than its trade with the major industrialized nations of Europe.[7]

The Kemalist leadership was evidently well aware that the potential economic benefit of Turkey's direct trade with the Middle East was limited. Ankara therefore saw much greater promise in attracting to its territory transit trade between Europe and the Middle East. Anatolia's historical role as a trade hub between East and West has diminished since its heydays in Byzantine and early Ottoman times, following the development of Eurasian maritime trade, particularly after the opening of the Suez Canal in 1869, and the opening of competing Eurasian trade and transportation land routes in Imperial Russia. Apart from its strategic and political significance, the Baghdad Railway project was partially aimed at rectifying that situation in late Ottoman times. After the end of World War I and the division of the Ottoman Empire, new plans for Eurasian transit routes to the Middle East and beyond were proposed by various governments and business interests. The republican government in Ankara was among them, believing that the modernization of transportation networks between Anatolia and the Middle East could offer a significant economic boon for Turkey if they would become a major conduit for Eurasian commerce and transportation. As in the past, the economic considerations were also linked to political and strategic concerns. Since the anticipated transportation networks to the Middle East were to run through Eastern and Southeastern Anatolia en route to Iran and Iraq, they were also intended to contribute to the pacification of these restive Kurdish-majority regions of the republic. The vision of Turkey as a major conduit for transcontinental trade and transportation appeared very promising to the Turkish government despite the significant financial, technical, and political obstacles that its successful realization was bound to face.

The ambitious goal of transforming Turkey into a major Eurasian transit route required building new roads, railways, and modern ports, all of which required capital, technical capabilities, and the cooperation of neighboring states. Existing roads in in Eastern Anatolia were neither paved nor suitable for year-round motorized traffic, in a region in which the winter conditions were harsh and the terrain mountainous and cut by many rivers and streams. As for trains, the completed parts of the Baghdad Railway connected Turkey to northern Syria, and a Russian-built narrow gauge line connected Erzurum to the Soviet border, but the rest of Eastern Anatolia had no railroads. Moreover, the old ports that were once pillars of the Eurasian trade, such as in Trabzon on the coasts of the Black Sea, were outdated and not equipped to handle modern shipping. Constructing and servicing roads and railroads that would connect Turkey to Iran and Iraq, and building ports that would serve their trade, required heavy capital investment which the Kemalist republic was lacking in the interwar period. Nevertheless, because of these projects' expected economic importance and strategic value, the Turkish government invested significant funds in their development. Preparing the proper infrastructure was obviously crucial for Turkey's efforts to restore Anatolia's importance as a major Eurasian trade and transportation route. However, for the vision to become reality, Ankara also needed to convince sometimes skeptical and oftentimes suspicious governments in neighboring countries that it was in their best interests to cooperate, particularly because of competition from other possible routes.

Alternative Eurasian trade routes already existed, or were envisioned, passing north and south of Anatolia through territories which were controlled by European powers. The Soviet Union inherited from Tsarist Russia Transcaucasian roads and railway network that connected Iranian Azerbaijan and other regions in northern Iran with the Black Sea port city of Batumi. This route thus bypassed the historic Tabriz-Trabzon route, which for many centuries was one of the most important segments in the network of silk roads that connected Europe and the Mediterranean world with Central and East Asia.[8] Britain and France, the new masters of much of the post–World War I Middle East, hoped to develop new trade and transportation routes that will help to revive and expand Eurasian trade, based on routes across territories located to the south of Anatolia. With rich petroleum deposits already known to exist in northern Iraq, the two colonial powers also sought to lay pipelines that would carry the crude oil to refineries and ports on the Levant coast, en route to European markets. The two European powers shared Turkey's anticipation that Eurasian transit routes through the Middle East would gain in importance and profitability, but hoped to channel it through territories under their control. Thanks to the less challenging terrain in the southern parts of the Middle East, their greater capability to finance large transportation projects, and their political clout in the early post-Ottoman period, the alternative routes that they planned posed a major challenge to the realization of the Turkish vision of transforming Anatolia into a major conduit for Eurasian trade.

The challenges for Turkey's quest to capitalize on its geostrategic position became more daunting in the 1930s, even as Ankara's resolve to overcome them grew firmer. Difficulties in financing, and international competition over trade, only escalated in the wake of the onset of the global economic crisis. But the dire consequences of financial crises in countries around the globe enhanced Ankara's appreciation of the importance of all its export markets, including in the Middle East. At the same time, Turkey hoped that once the crisis will pass and international trade levels increase again, it will benefit immensely from the infrastructure it would build during the years of crisis. At home, this task required national mobilization under the authoritarian power of the single-party regime, to overcome the financial and technical difficulties in realizing the major transportation projects. Abroad, it necessitated efforts to assuage concerns in neighboring countries about Turkey's purported hegemonic and expansionist goals, and effective use of Ankara's leverage and diplomatic relations to persuade neighboring governments that it would be in their best economic and strategic interests to cooperate with the Kemalist republic's ambitious international transportation projects and commercial goals.

I The Iranian Connection

The revival and modernization of the ancient Tabriz-Trabzon caravan route (Map 4.1) was a central component in Turkey's efforts to become a major conduit for Eurasian trade. The importance of this historical

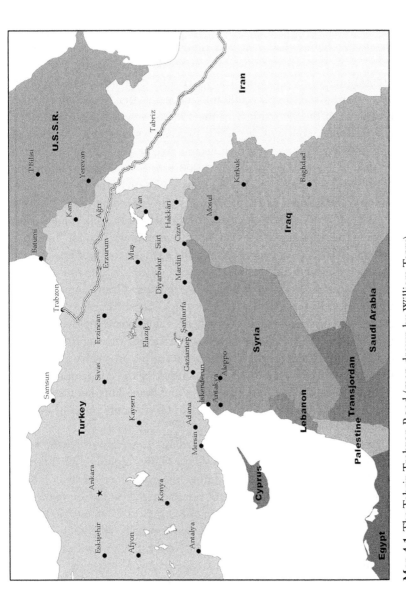

Map 4.1 The Tabriz-Trabzon Road (map drawn by William Terry).

route was diminished as a result of the general decline in Asian overland trade in the 1800s. It was dealt another blow with the completion
in 1900 of a Russian railway line from Jolfa on the Iranian border, to
Batumi on the coast of the Black Sea. With trade volumes already on
the decline before the Great War, they dwindled even more as a result
of the upheavals that followed its outbreak. Subsequently, the annual
10,000 tons of merchandize transported by caravans on that road in
1914 was halved to only 5,000 tons a decade later. Recurring Kurdish
rebellions in the second half of the 1920s, even as the Soviet regime
resumed the viability of the Transcaucasian route after a few years of
disruption, led to even further decline by the end of the decade. In
1930 it was estimated that only 1,000 tons were transported on the
Tabriz-Trabzon road, which was about one-tenth of the already diminishing trade volume in 1914. The once thriving route became only a
shadow of its glorious past as part of the network of silk roads across
Asia.[9] The prominent Turkish litterateur Ahmet Hamdi Tanpınar
lamented this decline between two visits he made to Erzurum, a major
commercial center on the Tabriz-Trabzon road, before and after the
Great War. He reminisced on how in the past "Iran's imports were
transported on the Trabzon-Tabriz caravan road." Every year 30,000
camels and perhaps twice that number of mules were employed on that
transit road. They would pass through Erzurum, arriving from Tabriz,
or returning from Trabzon, bringing with them prosperity and stabil-
ity. But after the Great War and as a result of the competition of the
Transcaucasian route, "the prosperous and flourishing Erzurum of old
which was once nurtured by the Iranian transit trade" became depopulated and impoverished by the 1920s.[10]

Statements of Turkish officials regarding the need to revive the route
abounded already from the early days of the republic. But nothing
much of substance was done during the period of the major Kurdish rebellions and the subsequent border dispute with Iran in the late
1920s. Iranian merchants who organized the caravans on the Tabriz-
Trabzon road complained of occasional raids by rebellious Kurdish
tribal groups on the one hand, and about difficulties with the Turkish military authorities who suspected them of smuggling weapons
and provisions for the rebels on the other. An early initiative for road
repair in 1925 was thus postponed indefinitely because of the insecu-
rity in the region, and the difficulties continued throughout the period
of the Second Ararat Rebellion in 1930 and the Turkish-Iranian border

dispute in its wake.[11] The volume of Turkish-Iranian trade on the route fell consistently and drastically during this period, from 3,500 tons in 1928 to 868 tons in 1931.[12] At this point, after the last major Kurdish rebellion in the Iranian frontier region was suppressed, and after the border between the two states was modified, steps could finally be taken toward reversing the alarming decrease in direct trade volumes between Turkey and Iran.

The conditions of the road itself were a major impediment to its recovery as a major trade and transportation route. A British report explained in 1930 that the "fortunes of the historic Trebizond-Tabriz transit route are at a low ebb owing to the bad condition of the road itself, the better facilities offered by the Batoum route and the difficulties imposed by the Turkish customs authorities. The road is blocked by snow for a considerable period each year and is not fit for heavy motor transport even under favourable conditions. The camel caravans take a minimum of six weeks to complete the journey from Tabriz to Trebizond as against a maximum of three weeks by the Batoum route."[13] The road conditions were indeed considered so unappealing and unsafe that until at least the mid-1930s, Turkish officials who were traveling to and from Iran usually opted for a northern route through the Soviet Caucasus, or in some cases, a southern route through Iraq. For example, in early 1932 Foreign Minister Aras traveled to Tehran by way of Soviet Batumi, and two years later, the Turkish ambassador to Iran traveled back to Turkey by way of Mosul in Iraq. By that time, Turkey was already devoting significant resources for the repair and modernization of parts of the road, and investing concerted efforts in convincing the Shah's government to lend its hand to the revival of the Tabriz-Trabzon route.[14] Indeed, when Reza Shah visited the Kemalist republic in summer 1934, the Turkish government insisted that the Iranian monarch travel to Turkey and back on the Tabriz-Trabzon road, despite initial Iranian concerns regarding the road's conditions. Ankara was hoping that the rapprochement between the two countries would convince Iran to cooperate in the restoration, modernization, and development of transportation networks between the two countries, beginning with the Tabriz-Trabzon route. Turkey was willing to risk the inconvenience experienced by the Shah in the hope that his personal observations would help convince him to cooperate in modernizing the road and restoring its viability and economic importance of yesteryear.[15]

The revival of what came to be known in the early 1930s as the Tabriz-Trabzon transit route became a main talking point in Kemalist propaganda in Eastern Anatolia. Mustafa Kemal himself set the tone during a tour of the region in early 1931. Speaking to the people of Trabzon, the president of the republic pledged that "the road to Tabriz, as far as the Turkish frontier, would be made fit for motor traffic, thus enabling merchandise to enter Northern Persia via Turkey instead of via Soviet Russia, as at present."[16] And when the republic celebrated its 10-year anniversary in 1933, a propaganda publication of Trabzon's Chamber of Commerce and Industry listed the funds allocated for the repair of the Trabzon-Tabriz Transit Road and the construction of Trabzon's Transit Warehouse at the top of the government's economic accomplishments that were destined to pay huge dividends in the near future. The Chamber indeed defined the road as the government's most important project in Eastern Anatolia.[17] Soon thereafter, Trabzon's daily newspaper, *Yeni Yol* (New Way, or New Road), adopted for its front page the motto "The harbor and transit trade are Trabzon's most important and vital concerns." In an editorial from the mid-1930s, the daily explained that once the Tabriz-Trabzon road will serve Europe's commerce with Iran and other Asian markets beyond it, that transit trade will bring immense economic benefits to Eastern Anatolia and help pacify and stabilize the region.[18] The daily *Varlık* of Erzurum opined in the same vein that "in the near future we will watch with satisfaction how the camel caravans that carried goods in the past are replaced with motorized convoys" going to and from the Iranian border.[19] Accordingly, the Turkish government began allocating funds for the construction of an all-weather road suitable for year-round motorized traffic of buses and trucks. In Tehran, meanwhile, the Turkish ambassador was instructed, shortly after the signing of the Turkish-Iranian border treaty in 1932, to urge Reza Shah to order similar efforts to be taken on the Iranian side of the border. The Iranian ruler was informed that once the road to Trabzon will be modernized and open for business, it would be much faster, more secure and convenient, and much more affordable for Iranian trade with Europe than the alternative routes through the Soviet Caucasus or Iraq. Reza Shah gave very positive yet noncommittal responses, even after Ankara all but compelled him in 1934 to travel to Turkey by this road in an effort to illustrate to him its merits.[20]

Turkey was hoping to benefit from Iran's desire to decrease its reliance on the Soviet route to Batumi, but it faced competition led by two other European powers. Persistent reports on French efforts to develop an alternative transit route from Iran to either Alexandretta in Syria or Beirut in Lebanon, and British schemes to do the same with Haifa in Mandate Palestine, worried Ankara. All these land routes from northern Iran through Iraq and to the Levant coast were much longer than the Tabriz-Trabzon route. But their terrain was much less mountainous and the winter climate conditions much less extreme than in Eastern Anatolia. The French authorities in Syria were particularly active in offering Iran storage facilities and promising lower customs rates. They first offered Alexandretta as the best outlet for the trade of north Iran, but concerns with Turkey's opposition finally led them to suggest Beirut instead. The fact that the Iranian ambassador to Baghdad was charged in 1933 with studying and recommending whether to pursue one of these options, and that an Iranian trade mission arrived in Syria in early 1934 only a few months before the Shah's visit to Turkey, were causes for concern in Ankara.[21] The Iraqi government was also invested in these negotiations, clearly preferring the development of a transit route from Iran through its territory to the Levant coast rather than by way of Turkey. The British colonial authorities shared that interest, only they hoped to channel the European-Iranian trade to Haifa. Until the mid-1930s, the British government was still contemplating the construction of a major highway and railway line from Iraq to Palestine, which aside from their strategic value were expected to serve as a conduit for much of the European trade with Iraq, Iran, and India. The British and French governments already negotiated successfully the construction of oil pipelines from Iraq to Mediterranean outlets under their control, and Turkey was worried that the transit routes that the two colonial powers envisioned would yet again bypass its territory and diminish its potential to serve as a major overland transit route for European trade with Iran, Iraq, and Asian markets farther to the east.[22]

After Reza Shah's travel on the Tabriz-Trabzon road and his visit to Turkey went very well, Ankara was expecting a greater commitment from the Iranian ruler for its planned transit route project. The Shah agreed that the modernization of transportation networks and the boosting of transit trade between Turkey and Iran was necessary and very promising, but he was unwilling to prioritize the development of this route over major construction projects already under way in Iran. The most important of these was the Trans-Iranian Railway, which was to cross the country from the Caspian Sea in the north to the Persian Gulf in the south. The Shah and other senior Iranian government officials made it very clear to Turkey that before the inauguration of that line, which was scheduled to 1938, Iran would not be able to allocate the necessary funds for any other major transportation project. Moreover, although willing to declare their belief in the great potential of the Tabriz-Trabzon route, Iranian officials stated quite plainly in early 1935 that Ankara would have to fulfill three conditions before Tehran could agree to invest heavily in its development. First, Turkey needed to prove that the road could be open year-round for motorized traffic, rather than its current closure for five to six months every year due to winter conditions. Second, the Turkish government was asked to guarantee that a transport company would maintain a regular service of buses and trucks between Trabzon and the Iranian border. Third, the Turkish government was told it would need to lower the costs of transit through Turkish territory by cutting customs rates, tariffs, and storage fees, and by eliminating unnecessary red tape. Furthermore, Iran was unwilling to commit to prioritizing the Turkish transit route over the development of alternative routes to Europe by way of Iraq and the Levant coast.[23] Persistent reports in the international press about Iranian negotiations with Britain and France on the development of transit routes, transportation systems, and storage facilities in the Levant for Iran's trade, drove home the point that Tehran was reluctant to fully commit to Ankara's project in the immediate aftermath of the Shah's visit to Turkey.[24]

The Turkish government remained unfazed, opting to continue in improving the route, with the hope that proven progress will induce Iran to channel much of its trade by way of Turkey. The local press in Eastern Anatolia and the ruling party's leaders in the region endorsed this position enthusiastically. When Prime Minister İnönü and Minister of Public Works Ali Çetinkaya traveled to the eastern provinces in 1935, they were received with calls to complete the work on the modernization of the road to the Iranian border in the fastest pace possible. The two leaders responded with promises that the old caravan route would soon be transformed into a thriving modern international highway that will have enormous economic impact on

Eastern Anatolia and on Turkey's economy as a whole. Minister Çetinkaya vowed to accelerate the work so that the road would be inaugurated by 1936. He pledged further that a government-owned and operated bus and truck company will run a regular passenger and freight services between Trabzon and the Iranian border.[25] Subsequently, the government's inspector-general of Eastern Anatolia, Tahsin Uzer, published in early 1936 a long and detailed article in which he sang the praises of the Tabriz-Trabzon route, which was presumably less than a year away from completion on the Turkish side of the border. Uzer emphasized in particular the road's superiority over alternative routes to either the Soviet coast of the Black Sea, or to the Levant coast of the Mediterranean by way of Iraq. He reiterated the argument that the modernized Tabriz-Trabzon transit road would be shorter, safer, and cheaper than any of the alternatives for the transportation of passengers and goods between Europe and Iran. Moreover, he reminded, once a new port is built in Trabzon, as promised by Prime Minister İnönü a few months earlier, the route will become even better suited for international trade. He concluded that since the benefits and superiority of this route were so obvious, the choice of any other alternative way could only be the result of political rather than economic calculations. He published this piece just as a high-ranking Turkish delegation was heading to Tehran in early 1936 for negotiations, including regarding cooperation in developing the trade route. The timing suggests that the article was aimed as a message to Iran that lack of cooperation would be interpreted in Turkey as a political affront. A similar idea was expressed by a Turkish daily in Eastern Anatolia when it argued that "just as two times two makes four, the interests of our neighbor and friend Iran necessitate the selection of the Trabzon route, which is undeniably the shortest and most affordable." And yet, Iran would not budge, with its Foreign Minister declaring in February 1936 that alternative routes to Syria and Palestine were still on the negotiating table too.[26]

The rapid completion of the road and the demonstration of its reliability became a priority for Turkey in 1936, despite serious challenges posed by Eastern Anatolia's climate and terrain. Heavy rains and snow storms in the rugged mountains of the region during wintertime resulted in landslides, slippery road conditions, and roadblocks for weeks on end between autumn and springtime. In these circumstances, finding a safe path and building a paved road that could be maintained open for year-round motorized traffic proved a difficult task. The Turkish government hired foreign experts and engineers to help overcome these difficulties. They oversaw the reinforcement or rebuilding of bridges, the rerouting of segments of the road that were prone to erosion and landslides, and the construction of service stations equipped with mechanized snow and ice removal equipment near vulnerable mountain passes along the route. The Ministry of Public Works hired 150 maintenance workers and built for them emergency shelters, garages, and storage facilities on various points on the road. The stated goal was to maintain the road open for traffic during the winter. The government promised that travel time from Tabriz to Trabzon would be shortened to six days, compared with the two to three months that the journey once took on camelback.[27] The work was declared completed in early 1937, but then suffered a setback shortly before its formal inauguration. A severe rainstorm led to flooding and landslides that carried parts of the road, which required in some areas the rerouting of the road through more stable terrain, and necessitated temporary detours through inconvenient roads. But Turkey did not retreat from its commitment to what Ankara believed was still a very promising project. New funds were allocated to repair and upgrade the affected parts of the route, and new pressure was brought to bear on Iran to reciprocate by equal investment in the road on its side of the border and by committing to channel much of its European trade through the Turkish route.[28]

The years-long concerted lobbying efforts finally netted results in spring 1937, when Turkey and Iran signed a number of bilateral agreements that allowed for the formal opening of the route for business. These agreements included a final small modification of the border between the two states, and authorization for cross-border traffic of passengers and goods on the Tabriz-Trabzon route. Accordingly, the border gates were opened for business in early May, two months before the signing of the Treaty of Saadabad. The Turkish press celebrated the formal opening of the road as a major event in the history of the republic, and predicted that it would soon handle a significant part of Europe's trade with Asia. The press in Trabzon was particularly euphoric about the potential opening of a new chapter of prosperity in the history of the city and the region. Even the usually levelheaded *Financial Times* opined that the new transit road might soon service much of Europe's trade not only with Iran but also with Afghanistan,

Soviet Turkestan, and China, on the one hand, and with the British Raj in India, on the other.[29] With these lofty expectations in mind, the Minister of Public Works, Ali Çetinkaya, declared in the National Assembly in Ankara that he could promise with confidence that all the substantial funds that have been allocated to the building and maintenance of the road from Trabzon to the Iranian border will soon prove insignificant in comparison with the economic benefits that Turkey was expected to reap. In the same vein, Turkish commentators predicted that "the Trabzon-Iran transit road is destined to become one of the greatest achievements of the republic."[30] Accordingly, only days after the treaties with Iran were ratified by parliament in early June 1937, including the transit trade agreement, none other than Mustafa Kemal himself traveled to Trabzon and Eastern Anatolia to participate in person in ceremonies and festivities that accompanied the official inauguration of the road in mid-June. Along with the much shorter road between Istanbul and the Bulgarian border, which connected Turkey to the European highway system, the new road to the Iranian border was now one of only two Turkish highways in the late 1930s which were built according to the most advanced standards of the day.[31]

The opening of the new road and the expectation that it would shortly "carry considerable amount of Iran's transit trade" proved slow to materialize despite the initial great hopes.[32] As promised, a newly established state-owned transportation company operated a regular passenger and freight service from Trabzon to the border gate. The main roads of principal towns along the way, such as Gömüşhane and Ağrı, were renamed Transit Yolu (Transit Road) or Transit Caddesi (Transit Street), but the rise in the volumes of trade with Iran on the route was more modest than initially expected by Ankara. The number of passengers more than doubled and custom revenues increased more than 100 percent, but the starting point was low. Issues such as Iran's refusal to allow Turkish vehicles to cross into its territory, requiring back to back unloading and uploading of freight, did not help either in this respect. The resulting modest economic impact of the road therefore did not produce any serious benefits to the national economy as was initially expected.[33] Turkish officials nevertheless remained bullish on the prospect of more dramatic contributions of the route to Turkey's economy in the near future. The building of a new port in Trabzon, they reasoned, would help boost the volume of trade on the road to Tabriz. Accordingly, the construction of a modern harbor in the city was included in the Five-Year Plan that was adopted by Turkey in 1938 and was mentioned as one of the major targets for investment and economic assistance that Ankara sought from the British government later that year.[34]

Ironically, Turkish optimism regarding the viability of the port and the route was largely informed by Ankara's anticipation that they would serve Nazi Germany's expanding trade with Iran. The volumes of trade between the two countries indeed grew rapidly from 1935 and the expectation was that the Shah's ambitious industrialization program would boost the commercial ties between Berlin and Tehran even more in the years to come.[35] The enmity between the Nazi regime and the Soviet government on the one hand, and Berlin's difficult relations with London and Paris on the other, suggested to Turkey that Germany would be disinclined to make use of either the Soviet route through the Caucasus or the British- and French-controlled routes through either the Suez Canal or overland from the coasts of the Levant and through Iraq. Turkish planners reached the conclusion that the Germans will prefer to make use of a route across Central Europe and down the Danube to the Romanian port city of Constanţa, and from there across the Black Sea to Trabzon and by road to Iran and other Asian markets beyond it. Optimism in Turkish government circles ran so high that the governor of Trabzon, Refik Koraltan, estimated in early 1939 that the volume of trade between the port city and Iran would increase in only two years from a modest 600 metric tons to the impressive 12,000 metric tons. Reports in mid-1939 on the soon to begin work on a new port in a matter of few months were construed in the Turkish press as a major step toward the realization of that fantastic prediction.[36]

The Tabriz-Trabzon road was expected to be part of a land-sea route that would serve primarily markets in Central Europe. But Ankara's ambitions to transform Anatolia into a major conduit of Eurasian trade was not limited to that route and these regions. Indeed, even as the modernization of the old caravan route was progressing in the late 1930s, Turkey was also pursuing an even more ambitious plan that envisioned the rapid expansion of its national railway system and its integration with the railway systems of Iran and Iraq, as part of a project to enhance international freight and passenger train services through Anatolia to Mediterranean ports of Turkey and to Istanbul, en route to Europe.

II On Track to Iraq

The 1930s have been at times portrayed as a golden age of railroading in Turkey. The Kemalist governments of the period took control over foreign-owned rail lines in Anatolia, and invested heavily in expanding lines inherited from Ottoman times to economically and strategically important regions, particularly in Eastern and Southeastern Anatolia.[37] Perhaps the two best-known railway projects of the period were the extension of the railway line from Ankara across the central Anatolian plateau to Erzurum in Eastern Anatolia, and the construction of a new line from Adana on the Mediterranean coast to Diyarbakır, the most important Kurdish urban center in Turkey. The line to Erzurum was planned to intersect with the Tabriz-Trabzon transit road which passed through the city. And the line to Diyarbakır was planned to run more or less parallel to the already completed and operating sections of the Baghdad Railway, which ran along the Syrian-Turkish border and were managed in cooperation between the Turkish government and the French mandatory authorities in Syria. Studies on the period have often highlighted this boom in railway construction in interwar Turkey as serving the cause of national and economic integration of remote and difficult to police and acculturate areas of Anatolia. This was certainly the case. But the international dimension of the railway construction boom has been almost universally overlooked in studies of the period, with the exception of the old route of the Baghdad Railway, which the republic inherited from Ottoman times. The Kemalist government's declared aim to establish direct railway links with Iran and Iraq as part of its strategic goal to transform Turkey into a major conduit for Eurasian trade has been mostly ignored in the historical literature on the period, perhaps because it did not fit the narrative of Kemalist efforts to detach Turkey from the Middle East. Yet the fact of the matter is that the construction of railway links from Turkey to Iran and Iraq was often emphasized by Turkish officials and commentators in the 1930s as a major national project of great economic and strategic significance.

Publications of Turkey's Ministry of Public Works and commentaries in the Turkish press explicated Ankara's evolving plans to link its railway system to Iran and Iraq. One plan which was ultimately put on hold and never implemented, suggested that once the Ankara-Erzurum line is completed, it would be extended to the Iranian border alongside the Tabriz-Trabzon road. Another plan, that was eventually adopted, called for the construction of railway lines from Diyarbakır to the Iranian border on the one hand, and to the Iraqi frontier on the other. The railway to Iran was projected to be connected on the other side of the border with a line leading to Tabriz, Tehran, and other destinations in Iran. The railway to Iraq was expected to be extended to Mosul and from there to Baghdad and Basra, thus establishing a direct link between the Turkish railway system and the head of the Persian Gulf en route to India.[38] The realization of such ambitious transportation projects hinged not only on overcoming financial and engineering obstacles, but also on securing the cooperation of Iran and Iraq. The American chargé d'affaires in Tehran expressed a common view in diplomatic and government circles in the region when he reported in 1937 that the Turkish government "had long been known to consider Turkey an important link between Europe and Asia, not only by virtue of her geographical position but also because of her vital interests on both continents."[39] The governments in Tehran and Baghdad, and in the latter case in London too, had to weigh carefully whether it would be in their best economic and political interest to allow Turkey to assume the role of vital commercial link to Europe, and perhaps thus acquire an instrument to extend its influence into Iranian Azerbaijan and northern Iraq. As was the case with the Tabriz-Trabzon road, Turkey opted to begin the construction of railway lines to its two neighbors even before securing their consent to build extensions to the Turkish lines inside their own territories.

Turkish lobbying for Iranian cooperation with its railway project began when the Shah visited Ankara in 1934, and remained consistent in the years that followed. Iran was willing to offer general statements of support but no immediate commitment for cooperation. As reported by an American diplomat, "the Shah has definitely promised that as soon as the [Trans-Iranian] railroad from the Caspian to the Persian Gulf has been constructed he would build a line to Tebriz which would ultimately link up with the Anatolian railways via Erzerum."[40] But since the completion of the Iranian railway project was scheduled for 1938, Turkey began exerting greater pressure on Iran in 1937 to commit itself more firmly to the construction of a railway line to Tabriz and from there to the Turkish border. When the issue was raised by a senior Turkish official directly with the Shah, the Iranian monarch responded favorably and even took out a map to point out the merits and drawbacks of several possible routes to the border. But he still avoided any commitment for a timetable. At this point, Ankara decided to press the issue by addressing a formal communication to the Iranian Foreign Ministry, in which a clearer commitment to the railway project was requested, including the anticipated timetable for the commencement and completion of work. The letter was sent at a time in which the two countries were already negotiating a slew of bilateral agreements in early 1937. Tehran's response therefore must have been quite disappointing to Ankara. The Iranian Foreign Ministry reasserted Iran's pledge to expand the Trans-Iranian Railway with a branch to the Turkish border, but cautioned that it might take a whole decade of studies and preparations before actual work on the line could commence in the late 1940s. Subsequently, the treaties signed between Turkey and Iran in spring 1937 included specific references only to the two countries' mutual commitment to developing the Tabriz-Trabzon road, but no mention of the construction of a direct railway line between them.[41]

Turkey did not fare much better in its efforts to sway the support of the Iraqi government to commit to the construction of a direct railway link between the two countries. In this case, the proposed Diyarbakır to Mosul line faced competition from alternative routes that were sponsored by Britain and France. The two European colonial powers neither shared economic or strategic interest with Turkey in this project, nor were they free of suspicion that Ankara might seek to exploit the proposed railway line to establish its hegemony over northern Iraq. The British government had a particular strong say in the matter because British interests continued to own the Iraq State Railways company for a few years after the country became formally independent in 1932. For a time, until the commission of the Kirkuk-Haifa oil pipeline in 1935, Britain considered the construction of an Iraq-Palestine railway line that would be built alongside the pipeline to the Mediterranean port city. The project was eventually deemed economically unfeasible, and finally became irrelevant when the Iraqi government assumed the full ownership of the Iraq State Railways in April 1936. But the sale agreement stipulated that British citizens will continue to hold senior managerial positions in the company for at least 20 years. These British officials were most skeptical of cooperating with Turkey on the

proposed Diyarbakır to Mosul line, based both on their political concerns with the purported Turkish expansionist intentions in northern
Iraq, and on doubts regarding the line's economic viability.[42] From
British and Iraqi perspectives, routes via Syria appeared to make better
political and economic sense. Britain already cooperated with France
in the construction of a second oil pipeline from Iraq to the Lebanese
port city of Tripoli. The two colonial powers also shared the conviction
that the completion of the Baghdad Railway would be sufficient to connect Iraq to the Mediterranean coast by way of Syria, and to Europe
by way of Syria and Turkey. The French authorities hoped that the
line will help attract Eurasian transit trade to their mandates in Syria
and Lebanon, largely bypassing Turkey. In that vein, the French government in Syria undertook to extend the old Ottoman railway from
al-Qamishli, on the Syrian-Turkish border, and across the Duck's Bill to
Tal Kushik (al-Ya'rubiya) on the Syrian-Iraqi border. The 45 mile long
tracks were commissioned in May 1935, thus completing the Baghdad
Railway line all the way from Istanbul to the Iraqi border, by way of
Aleppo. From the border crossing, a regular automobile service that
was operated by the Iraq State Railways ferried passengers to Mosul
and Kirkuk. But the Iraqi government vowed in 1936 to conclude the
construction of the uncompleted segments between Baghdad and the
Syrian border in order to finally complete the Baghdad Railway from
Mesopotamia to Istanbul and European destinations beyond it.[43]

The realization of that goal became interlinked for a time with the
discovery of new oilfields near Mosul, which yielded heavy crude oil
that could not be piped because of its high density. The new deposits
were discovered an owned by the British Oil Development Company
(BOD), which despite its name was in fact controlled in the mid-
1930s by Italian and German interests. Its main competitor, the Iraq
Petroleum Company (IPC), was controlled mainly by British, French,
and American interests. But whereas the well-funded IPC piped light
crude oil from its Kirkuk oilfields to Haifa and Tripoli, the only viable
solution for exporting the heavy crude oil discovered by BOD was to
transfer it by train. The company therefore proposed to the Iraqi government that it would construct a 70 mile railway line from its new
oilfields in Mosul to where the Syrian railway reached the border, so
that its oil could be transported to French-controlled export facilities in
Tripoli, Lebanon. The Iraqi government agreed, on condition that the
German-Italian owned company would also undertake to complete the

rest of the 180 mile long uncompleted sections of the Baghdad Railway between Mosul and the Iraqi capital city.[44]

With the proposed Diyarbakır to Mosul line still years in the offing, official Turkey and its press welcomed the prospect of the completion of the Baghdad Railway by BOD. When the French authorities in Syria inaugurated the short railway track from the Syrian-Turkish border to the Syrian-Iraqi border in May 1935, Turkish state officials participated in the ceremony, and the Turkish press praised this important step toward the completion of the Baghdad Railway. But the Turkish side was particularly thrilled that the new oil deposits in Mosul were discovered by an Italian-German owned company, which also undertook to construct the uncompleted segments of railways between the Syrian-Iraqi border and Baghdad. These views were expressed, for example, in an article established in late 1935 in the organ of the Turkish Ministry of Public Works, under the title "Mosul oil and the Baghdad Railway." The author predicted that BOD will import heavy machinery from Germany, both for the construction and operation of the oilfields, and for the extraction and transportation of the heavy crude oil to Europe. He concluded that Turkey will reap immense economic benefits from dues levied on the transportation of the equipment through its territory, and from a tremendous increase in the number of passengers and volumes of trade between Europe and Iraq by way of Anatolia, after the projected completion of the Baghdad Railway in 1938. Articles in the Turkish daily press featured similarly optimistic predictions. Commentaries in July 1935, for instance, suggested that "the linkage of the Iraqi railway to ours is very important from the perspectives of politics, the economy, culture, and tourism," and anticipated that the completion of the Baghdad Railway would help promote unity and cooperation between the "Eastern nations" of Turkey, Syria, and Iraq.[45]

At the same time, Turkey was not unaware that the successful operation of the Baghdad Railway risked undermining the economic premise and viability of direct railway links between Turkey, Iraq, and Iran. For one thing, it would make it easier for European trade with Iraq and Iran, and perhaps India too, to be transited through the Levant rather than overland by way of Anatolia. Iskenderun in the District of Alexandretta appeared as the most reasonable option to serve as a transit port for the Mediterranean-bound trade of Iran and Iraq. This was obviously unwelcome to Turkey, which maintained its own claim

to the city and its strategic environs, and which had no interest in seeing it becoming even more strongly integrated into the trade networks
of northern Syria and Iraq. For another, the expected rail-based heavy
crude oil export from the Mosul oilfields to the Levant coast was likely
to benefit French-controlled Syria financially and strategically, and at
the same time render Turkey dependent on importing oil from Iraq by
way of Syria. Such concerns increased Turkey's determination to deny
Syria any long-term claim to the strategic region of Alexandretta, even
as Ankara sought to push forward its goal to construct direct railway
lines to Iran and Iraq and thus develop an alternative to the Syrian
route.[46]

III Eastward Bound

The inauguration in November 1935 of the railway to Diyarbakır was
an occasion for national celebration in Turkey, and for reiteration of
the government's commitment to its extension eastwards. The keynote
speaker at the festivities, Minister of Public Works Ali Çetinkaya, proclaimed in no uncertain terms that "there is no doubt that the railway
line will not end in Diyarbakır. It will be extended to, and be integrated with, the railway systems of friendly and brotherly countries
in the east," thus restoring Diyarbakır's historical role as an important
junction of international trade and cultural exchange between East and
West. He pledged that the work on the railways to the east will commence in the near future, and predicted that the establishment of direct
rail links to Iran and Iraq will be considered in the future as some of
the greatest achievements of the presidency of Atatürk and the premiership of İnönü. Commentaries in the Turkish press of the day were as
optimistic regarding the great potential of this "new victory in our railways policy." The daily *Cumhuriyet*, for instance, anticipated that the
extension of the railway line from Diyarbakır to Iran and Iraq would
bring immense prosperity to Anatolia just like the silk roads once did,
and help create a "bond of steel" between Turkey and its two Middle Eastern neighbors.[47] The vision was grand, and its exploitation for
propaganda purposes evident, but financial and engineering challenges
and the ambiguity regarding the cooperation of Baghdad and Tehran
made the prospects for its realization much less than certain.

   Turkey's calculus became more complicated as a result of unexpected developments in Iraq in 1936. Previously, Ankara hoped that the

German-Italian majority-owned BOD will be reluctant to rely solely on the French-controlled railway system in Syria, and will thus cooperate in constructing another branch from Mosul to the Turkish border, en route to Diyarbakır. But financial difficulties hampered the company's operation and finally in August 1936 forced its majority share holders to sell their stakes to their main competitor, the Iraq Petroleum Company. The British-French-American majority-owned IPC inherited the responsibility to complete the unfinished segments of the Baghdad Railway, and the work commenced promptly in late 1936. However, because the IPC already had a significant stake in piping its light crude oil to Haifa in Mandate Palestine and Tripoli in Lebanon, it had much less incentive to export heavy crude oil aboard trains, let alone invest in the construction of a direct rail link from Mosul to the Turkish border.[48] This was bad news for Turkey. On the other hand, a military coup in Iraq in late October 1936, brought to power a new government that was perceived as very pro-Turkish, and thus could be expected to establish better relations of cooperation, that could extend to the proposed Diyarbakır to Mosul line. The route envisioned by Ankara was to bypass the territory of Syria, even though that meant a longer route through more challenging mountainous terrain. Whereas the shortest and most convenient route would have taken 220 mile and pass through Turkey's Mardin and Syria's al-Qamishli, the proposed route was 300 mile long, traversing a more mountainous region to Cizre on the banks of the Tigris River, before crossing into Iraq. The new government in Baghdad responded positively to Turkey's proposal for a direct railway link, but it was unwilling to commit to building a connection to the Turkish border until the expected inauguration of the Baghdad Railway in 1938. In the meanwhile, the Iraqi government allowed delegations of Turkish experts to conduct preliminary terrain studies in northern Iraq to determine the best potential route for a railway line from the Turkish border to Mosul. Ankara viewed that as a positive sign for the future of the project.[49]

Turkey therefore opted in 1937 to proceed with its plan to construct railways to the borders of Iran and Iraq even without firm pledges of cooperation from either Tehran or Baghdad. The signing of the Treaty of Saadabad in July increased the optimism in Ankara regarding the future of the proposed direct links to its two Middle Eastern neighbors. The Turkish government therefore allocated funds for immediate beginning of the work. A secondary but not less important consideration was that regions traversed by the planned route could be pacified and policed more efficiently. The major Kurdish rebellion in Dersim (Tunceli) in 1937–1938, which threatened to destabilize Ankara's hold over Eastern Anatolia, drove home the importance of constructing railways for the dispatch of military reinforcements, administrators, and various other means for the forced political submission and cultural assimilation of the local population. Atatürk was indeed reputed to have declared during that period that "the railway is a country's security weapon, which is more important than the rifle and the cannon."[50] The new railway project from Diyarbakır toward Tabriz on the one hand, and Mosul on the other, carried not only the promise of prosperity thanks to the transit trade of Iran and Iraq, respectively, but also the high likelihood of becoming a tool for the forced political, economic, and cultural integration of the restive Kurdish-majority regions in Eastern Anatolia.[51]

The groundbreaking ceremony for the beginning of work on the railways to Iran and Iraq was held in Diyarbakır in November 1937, with none other than Atatürk serving as the guest of honor. Accompanied by newly appointed Prime Minister Celal Bayar, a number of cabinet ministers, parliamentary deputies, high-level bureaucrats, and senior army officers, the president of the republic honored the festivities in person as a testimonial for the project's immense importance for the republic. A large sign over the tracks read "Toward Iraq and Iran" (Figure 4.3), and Atatürk, along with the Prime Minister and other dignitaries, signed a document that was to record the event for posterity. In a speech given by Minister of Public Works Ali Çetinkaya, he doubled down on a speech he gave in the same place two years earlier, promising that the railways that will connect the city to Iran and Iraq will restore its historical position as an international center of trade between East and West, and assume a new role as an important conduit for the transfer of modern arts, sciences, and trade from Europe to Asia. Prime Minister Bayar endorsed this message, adding that the railway line to Turkey's friends Iran and Iraq would bring progress and prosperity to the regions on the sides of the tracks. The required legislation, budget allocations, and initial terrain studies for the route was already completed by late 1937, and the work was expected to begin shortly after the end of the groundbreaking festivities.[52]

The railway line was to head from Diyarbakır eastward to the small Kurdish village of Misirc (renamed Kurtalan), where it would branch

Figure 4.3 "Toward Iraq and Iran" celebratory sign in Diyarbakır. From Kadri Kemal Kop, *Atatürk Diyarbakır'da* (Istanbul: Cumhuriyet Matbaası, 1938), 66.

southward toward Iraq, and northeastward toward Iran (Map 4.2). The route to Iraq was to follow the Tigris River to Cizre and from there to take an eastward course to the Iraqi border, near the present-day location of the Habur border gate. The route to Iran was to follow a northeastern course to Bitlis, turn eastward to Van and finally reach the Iranian border near the present-day Kapıköy border gate.[53] The work was estimated to be completed by late 1939, and articles in the Turkish and international press already predicted the "exceptional importance" of "the railway to the Iran frontier," and the certainty that the new railway will even serve India.[54] The following months witnessed the construction work progressing much slower than expected,

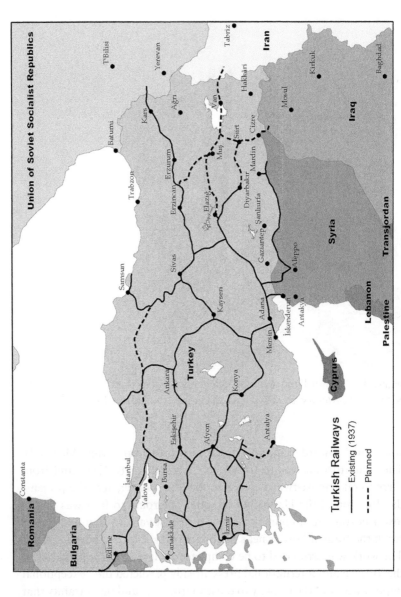

Map 4.2 Turkey's railroad system, 1937 (map drawn by William Terry).

however, even as public declarations continued apace regarding Turkey's determination "to proceed toward our borders and connect our railway system to those of our friends and neighbors Iraq and Iran." After the death of Atatürk and his succession by İnönü in November 1938, the government reemphasized its commitment to the policy, including by holding festivities in Diyarbakır in December 1938, in which the region's inspector-general drove the ceremonial first spike in the railway line to Iran and Iraq.[55]

The actual accomplishment of the feat soon proved to be more complicated than initially expected, particularly with regard to the planned route to the Iranian border. When initial studies were made in the mid-1930s, before the railway line even reached Diyarbakır from Elazığ (Elaziz), two options were considered. The first envisioned Elazığ as the railway junction from which one branch will go by way of Diyarbakır to the Iraqi border, and another branch will run toward Tatvan on the shores of Lake Van, en route to the Iranian border. The other option, which was eventually selected, suggested that the branching toward the Iranian and Iraqi border would take place after Diyarbakır. The latter route to the Iranian border was 45 miles shorter, and was deemed more affordable to construct. However, after more serious terrain studies were conducted in 1938, it became clear that this route to the Iranian border presented serious engineering problems because of elevation differences of 2,300 feet in the mountain range south of Lake Van, between Siirt and Tatvan. The completion of this route required the construction of dozens of tunnels, four massive bridges, and six viaducts, as well as overcoming recurring dangers of landslides and avalanches. Subsequently, a decision was finally made in early 1939 to revert to the first option of building a slightly longer, more expensive, but much less topographically challenging branch from Elazığ to the Iranian border. The route was to proceed eastward to Muş and then to Tatvan, on the shores of Lake Van. From there, a train ferry was to carry the train cars to the city of Van on the eastern shores of the lake, from where another railway line would lead to the Iranian border. The change in the route to Iran, to the more northerly option from Elazığ meant that Diyarbakır lost its planned role as a major hub of railway transportation for both Iran and Iraq, and now had to make do with the latter, which was still expected to make major impact on the city's economy by serving European transit trade with Iraq and India.[56]

The changes in the railway's planned route were in some cases taken very seriously by communities that were bypassed by the revised line. This was the case, for instance, with the town of Siirt, nestled 3,000 feet above sea level to the southwest of Lake Van. Like many other towns in Eastern Anatolia, the ravages of the Great War depopulated the city of its prewar Armenian and Assyrian communities, and the recurring Kurdish rebellions and their heavy-handed suppression by the government compounded its economic difficulties in the interwar period. Plans to route the planned railway line to Iran through the town were therefore seen by community leaders in Siirt as offering a great opportunity for economic relief and future prosperity for the townspeople. High expectations turned into a bitter disappointment, however, when more detailed terrain studies in 1938 led to the decision to change the route to Iran, and leave the station nearest to Siirt in the small village of Kurtalan, 20 miles to the west, from where the railway line was to bend southward toward Iraq. The town's community leaders petitioned the Ministry of Public Works in July 1938 to reconsider the decision, because it would deprive Siirt of the economic benefits that were promised it, and might bring it to economic ruin. But their protest did not net the results they desired. The government notified them that the topographical features of the terrain dictated the change. With the economic stakes believed to be very high, the town's community leaders did not make do with this disappointing response. In December 1938 they petitioned Prime Minister Bayar to request his personal intervention in the matter, but the decision stood nevertheless, and remained in force after Bayar was succeeded in office by Refik Saydam in January 1939.[57]

The good people of Siirt did not know it then, but the nondescript and little known village of Kurtalan was destined to be the final station in a railway line that never reached the Iraqi border. The new administration of President İnönü continued to trumpet the importance of Turkey's railway policies in general and the establishment of direct rail links to Iran and Iraq in particular. And Turkish propaganda outlets remained on message in 1939, with promises of great economic prosperity to Eastern Anatolia thanks to the expected transit trade and passenger traffic between Europe and Asian markets. Thus, one provincial daily declared in March 1939 that the completion of the project to link the national railway system to Iran and Iraq will display to the whole world the progress, unconditional economic independence, and absolute sovereignty of Turkey. And in late August 1939, only days before the German army launched its assault on Poland and ignited a new European war, the daily *Cumhuriyet* celebrated the progression of work on a large and impressive railway bridge over the Tigris River, which was intended to serve the new line between Europe and Iraq in the near future.[58] But the construction work moved much slower than anticipated, even before the beginning of hostilities in Europe, and was delayed even more after the outbreak of World War II. On the eve of the war, about 30 miles of the railway from Diyarbakır to Cizre en route to Iraq were in place, and the work on the line from Elazığ to Tatvan en route to Iran has only just begun.[59]

IV A Road Not Taken

The outbreak of World War II did not immediately deflate Ankara's hopes for turning Anatolia into a major conduit for transit trade between Europe and Asia. In the first stages of the global conflict, Turkey still maintained its assumptions regarding the potential of its grand transportation projects to be successful and have a transformative economic and strategic impact on the republic and its people. Thus, in mid-September 1939, just as advance German units were already reaching the outskirt of Warsaw, *Cumhuriyet* published an opinion piece in which the government was urged to expedite the construction of the railways to Iran and Iraq in order to posit Turkey as a major transit route for Europe's trade with Asia.[60] The Turkish government could not have afforded to accelerate the work, because of financial and logistical constraints, but it did not view the outbreak of war in Europe as justifying a stoppage in the rail construction either. Thus, in April 1940 a new law for the allocation of funds for the construction of the railways to Iran and Iraq was promulgated, even as the *Wehrmacht* was finalizing the invasion plans of France, Turkey's ally since October 1939.[61] The work in fact continued after the collapse of France, the entry of Italy into the war in June 1940, and the two Axis powers' invasion and occupation of the Balkans by June 1941. By that time, initial work on the railway toward Cizre and the Iraqi border had only begun near the village of Kurtalan, 100 miles east of Diyarbakır, and construction on the line from Elazığ to the east reached Genç, a small town about a quarter of the way to the Iranian border. Indeed, in early May 1941, only days before the British invasion of Iraq, and a few weeks before the joint British-Soviet occupation of Iran, the Turkish government proclaimed its determination to complete the work on the railway lines to the two countries as a sign of Turkey's great friendship with them.[62] The work on the tracks and supporting infrastructure such as bridges and tunnels continued in the latter war years, though on a much slower pace. Reports in the Turkish press between 1942 and 1945 continued to celebrate the progress in the work, but now mostly in the inside pages rather than on the front page. The only exception was the completion of the massive railway bridge over the Batman River, which was celebrated on the front pages of Turkey's newspapers and was honored with a special postal stamp in 1943. Ultimately, however, when the Second World War ended in 1945, the railway to Iraq reached what was destined to become its final terminus in the nondescript village of Kurtalan, still more than 150 mile north of the border, and the railway to the east was still hundreds of miles away from the Iranian border. Needless to say that none of these railways served any international transportation, as envisioned and expected only a few years earlier.[63]

World War II similarly derailed the rosy forecasts and optimistic expectations from the Tabriz-Trabzon route. That road was open and operable by the outbreak of hostilities in Europe, but it could not attract any significant international transit trade. The adverse economic effects of the conflict on the Turkish economy and on international commerce, particularly between Germany and markets outside of Europe, were rapid and profound. Following the signing of the Molotov-Ribbentrop agreement in August 1939, the Soviet and Nazi regimes became partners, which immediately undermined the need for an alternative route to the Transcaucasian railway line and roads from Soviet Batumi to northern Iran. In these circumstances, and because of financial and logistical considerations, the building of the new port in Trabzon, which was scheduled to begin in spring 1940, was immediately put on hold.[64] And when in June 1941 Germany launched Operation Barbarossa, the joint Soviet and British occupation of Iran eliminated any prospect of German-Iranian trade. At this juncture, however, Ankara was much more concerned with avoiding a fate in which the new road might serve as a transit route for invading foreign armies, than with the rapidly fading prospect of attracting foreign transit trade. World War II thus dashed any hopes for immediate and substantial economic impact of the Tabriz-Trabzon route on Turkey in general and on

Eastern Anatolia in particular. With Turkey becoming a de facto buffer state between German-dominated Europe and the Allied-controlled Middle East, any aspiration to serve as a vital link for Eurasian trade was taken off the table for the time being.

The same was true for another field in which the Kemalist leadership aspired to attract transcontinental transportation: the emerging industry of air travel. In 1936, the newly established State Airlines (*Devlet Hava Yolları*), the precursor of Turkish Airlines, declared its intention to open service to destinations in Syria, Iraq, and Iran. Shortly thereafter, even as the crisis over Hatay was still ongoing, Ankara initiated negotiations with Air France for cooperation in establishing a regular line from Europe to Syria by way of Turkey. The Turkish government suggested that the French company will manage the flights between European destinations and Istanbul, whereas the Turkish company will be in charge of flights over Turkish airspace and to airfields in the Syrian cities of Aleppo and Damascus. Concurrently, Turkish government officials held talks with their counterparts in Iraq and Iran in an effort to secure their agreement for Turkish flights between some of their major cities and Turkish airfields in Ankara and Istanbul, with European companies then servicing the segment between Istanbul and destinations in Europe.[65] Indeed, a publication of the Turkish Ministry of Public Works predicted in 1936 that in the near future Turkey would become a hub for international air travel between Europe, the Middle East, and destinations in Central and South Asia.[66] Reports on various schemes to advance this vision were published occasionally in the Turkish press and in the Middle East in 1938–1939. This included a plan for a Turkish air service to Iraq, a Turkish-French cooperation on a line from France to Syria by way of Turkey, and less than three months before the outbreak of war in Europe, a report on a planned German-Turkish line between Berlin, Istanbul, and Aleppo.[67] All these schemes were suspended after the outbreak of World War II. With the fires of war burning all around Turkey, and its wartime policy focused on keeping its airfields and airspace free of foreign military aircrafts,[68] the nonexistent prospect of attracting commercial air traffic between Europe and the Middle East became a moot point.

The Second World War indeed deflated the air of great expectations that informed Turkey's efforts in the 1930s to develop its transportation systems, and link them to the Middle East. The only railway line that was completed during that period was the Baghdad Railway. Once seen as a project of immense geostrategic and economic potential, the inauguration of the service to Baghdad in July 1940 was held with no fanfare or ceremony at all because of the inauspicious circumstances of the war conditions.[69] The alternative Turkish proposed direct line between Anatolia and Iraq and Iran was meanwhile not even close to completion. Circumstances beyond Turkey's control deemed the transformation of Anatolia into major hub of Eurasian transit trade unrealistic, if it ever were to begin with. Suffice it to say that Ankara was unable to even bring Baghdad and Tehran fully on board. Iran procrastinated for several years before cooperating in developing its part of the Tabriz-Trabzon route, while neither its government nor the Iraqi government began taking any meaningful step toward linking their railway systems to Turkey's by the beginning of World War II. The vision of a direct rail link to Iraq was in fact never realized. The rail link to Iran, on the other hand, was eventually completed along the route planned in the late 1930s, but only decades after the end of World War II. The failure of the great transportation projects of the 1930s to transform Turkey into a major hub of international transit trade was the combined result of global and regional circumstances beyond Ankara's control, and the limitations on Turkey's resources and capabilities. The great expectations attached to the development of Turkey as a major transit hub for Eurasian trade may appear in retrospect as unrealistic. At the same time, Turkey's willingness to invest so much efforts toward the realization of such fantastic plans serve as another attestation to the Kemalist leadership's awareness of the potential economic and strategic importance of Anatolia's geographic location between Europe and the Middle East, and as a testimonial to Ankara's hopes to capitalize economically on this geostrategic location by facilitating connections with the Middle East rather than turning Turkey's back on the region.

5 | *The Turkish Model*

Policies implemented by the Kemalist government in the interwar period in order to secure Turkey's political and economic independence, and transform its society, were keenly observed in the Middle East. For some in the region, Mustafa Kemal's leadership and accomplishments offered useful examples for emulation in their own societies, whether in order to secure complete liberation from foreign rule or to modernize them by doing away with restrictive local customs, traditions, and institutions. For others, Kemalist Turkey set an alarming precedence for other Muslim-majority countries, whether because of its secularizing and nationalist policies, or because of its non-democratic form of government. Either way, whether viewing the Kemalist republic as an inspiring model for other non-Western states and societies, or as a cautionary tale of developments to beware of, there was a widely held agreement that there were lessons to be learned from the Turkish experience and that the outcomes of the Kemalist reforms were relevant to the rest of the Middle East. Debates on the pros and cons of Kemalist Turkey and its internal policies therefore became part and parcel of larger conversations and controversies in many societies around the region regarding their own political, social, cultural, and economic realities, and the future course and orientation that they should follow. Reports and debates on Ankara's policies were featured regularly on the front pages of leading newspapers in the Middle East, and particularly in the flourishing and regionally influential press of Egypt.

Commentators in the Arab press discussed often and in some detail the merits and deficiencies of Kemalist social and legal reforms, economic programs, and nationalist and secularist policies. In 1932, for example, Turkey initiated preliminary steps toward the substitution of Turkish translations for the original Arabic texts in some aspects of the Muslim worship. This was widely interpreted as a likely first step toward the adoption of a Turkish translation of the Qur'an as the

139

basis for all forms of Islamic worship in the Kemalist republic.[1] Subsequently, the influential Egyptian daily *al-Ahram* devoted prime real
estate on its front pages for a long series of polemical articles by supporters and critics of Turkey's policies, under the title of "The Turks,
Islam, and the Noble Qur'an."[2] The argumentations in these articles,
and in many others related to the Kemalist government and its policies, were on one level about Turkey and the anticipated impact of
the Kemalist reforms on Turkish society, but on a deeper level were
essentially also about potential lessons and consequences for Egypt and
other Muslim-majority countries.

The Turkish government was not simply a passive observer on
debates and controversies concerning its policies, but was rather
actively involved in efforts to influence public opinion. One facet of
such activities involved straightforward propaganda. Turkish officials
and institutions distributed quite routinely pamphlets and booklets in
Arabic and French which celebrated the achievements of the Kemalist state and its reforms. For instance, when the republic celebrated its
fifteenth anniversary in 1938, a special photo album which lauded the
revolutionary changes in Turkey was translated to Arabic and printed
in Istanbul for distribution to Arab readers, exactly 10 years after the
language reform all but eliminated the use of the Arabic-based alphabet in Turkey.[3] Another facet of the propaganda efforts was informal, through surrogates in the Middle East. The Cairo-based Arabic-
Turkish bilingual weekly *Muhadenet/Mukhadana*(Amity), for instance,
was well known as an informal mouthpiece of the Turkish government. Hüseyin Remzi, the journal's proprietor and editor-in-chief, was
a staunch defender of Mustafa Kemal and his reforms, in articles on
the pages of his bilingual newspaper, in opinion pieces in the general
Arabic press, and through the publication of Kemalist propaganda
pamphlets and books in Arabic. In 1934, for instance, he published
a book containing Arabic translations of a collection of Prime Minister İnönü's speeches since the early 1920s.[4] A similar arrangement
existed with the Cairo-based news agency al-Anba' al-Sharqiya (The
Eastern News). This was a telegraphic service which was established in
the late 1920s by the Egypt correspondent for Turkey's government-
run Anadolu News Agency. It focused on translating flattering news
and opinion pieces from the Turkish press into Arabic and French,
and their distribution to media outlets around the Middle East. The
Turkish Ministry of Foreign Affairs secretly subsidized both of these

pro-Kemalist media operations, and a confidential report from 1937 suggested that Foreign Minister Tevfik Rüştü Aras viewed their services as very effective and valuable for Turkey.[5]

In the late 1930s Turkey added radio broadcasts to its arsenal of propaganda dissemination tools to the Middle East. The government-owned and -operated radio stations in Istanbul and Ankara began broadcasting in January 1937 news bulletins in Arabic several times a day. This service continued until the end of World War II. The news anchor was Abdul Salam al-Buseiri, a political refugee from Italian-ruled Libya, who in the mid-1950s would serve for a brief period as Libya's Foreign Minister. The very early radio broadcasts were received primarily in Syria, but with the purchase and installation of more powerful transmitters in late 1938, Arabic broadcasts from Turkey were also received in Egypt and Iraq, and according to a British report, even in as far as in Kuwait. Reports in the local Arabic press and in confidential British assessments suggest that the broadcasts found eager audiences in the Middle East. It is difficult to gauge how effective these broadcasts were in generating positive attitudes toward Turkey, but Ankara's efforts were noteworthy and were seen at least by the always vigilante British officials in the region as a potentially useful mode of influence on Arab public opinion.[6] Be that as it may, there is no question that the Turkish government and its press both followed closely on reports and commentaries regarding Turkey in the Arab press of the 1930s, and tried to influence it by compliment or rebuttal, as part of a broader effort to project a positive image of Turkey to the Middle East.[7]

One aspect of Turkey's public relations efforts involved refutation of various forms of criticisms, and another involved the presentation of Turkey as a shining model for emulation. Statements about historical bonds of fraternity with the peoples of the Middle East were made frequently, and any accusation of Turkish hostility toward Islam or the Arab peoples was denounced and rejected. Instead, the peoples of the region were invited to learn from Turkey's unique success in modernization, and implement the relevant lessons in their own societies. In a commentary on the congress of the Turkish ruling party in May 1935, a correspondent for the *London Times* reported that "although 'Kamalism' is the natural outcome of Turkey's struggle for independence and is designed first to meet purely Turkish conditions, a strong feeling exists in the minds of Turkish rulers that it contains valuable lessons for other countries whose political and economic independence is not assured. It is indeed believed that Persia and Afghanistan have already borrowed leaves from the Turkish book, and that other Asiatic or Moslem countries might profitably follow the example set them by Kamalist Turkey." Coincidentally or not, this commentary reflected almost to the word the content of a lecture on Turkey's foreign relations that was given only a year earlier by then Minister of Education Yusuf Hikmet Bayur.[8] Likewise, in a book published in 1936, the Kemalist ideologue Munis Tekinalp (Moiz Kohen) emphasized the importance of Turkey and Atatürk as inspirations for the liberation, social revival, emancipation of women, economic prosperity, and modernization of all the peoples in former Ottoman territories in the Middle East, as well as in other Eastern countries. He went on to suggest that the railway lines that were being built at the time toward the borders of Iraq and Iran would help spread the Kemalist influence in Eastern societies, with Turkey serving as a shining example for emulation.[9]

In debates in neighboring countries on whether Turkey should indeed serve as a role model, various aspects of the Kemalist republic and its policies were particularly scrutinized. One of these aspects was the gradual emancipation of women in Turkey under the auspices of the Kemalist state feminism. The encouragement of unveiling, the expansion of educational and employment opportunities for women, the substitution of European-based family and personal law codes for sharia-based ones, and the extension of more legal rights to female citizens of the republic, were seen by many commentators and women's rights activists in the Middle East as inspiring examples to follow, whereas critics viewed them as setting dangerous precedents that should be avoided. Another aspect under consideration was Atatürk's type of charismatic leadership, and his virtually unrestricted political authority. The crisis of democracy in 1930s Europe influenced debates in the Middle East on the type of leadership and political structure that would be best suited to secure political independence, social progress, and economic prosperity for the peoples of the region. Turkey and Mustafa Kemal were often featured in these polemics as either positive or negative examples for differing viewpoints.[10] The viability and desirability of the Turkish experience as a model for emulation for societies in the Middle East appeared increasingly relevant by the mid-1930s, with Britain and France facing growing pressures to allow greater measure of sovereignty to governments in the region, as a result of the combined effect of increasing constraints at home, challenges in Europe, and intensifying opposition and protests in the Middle East. Turkey and its policies faced many detractors in the region, particularly among pan-Islamists and pan-Arab nationalists. At the same time, there was no dearth of admirers and defenders of Atatürk and his reforms, particularly among the Arab educated elites. Indeed, writing in 1939, the American Turkey expert Donald Webster commented that in much of the Middle East, there is "a general awareness of the great progress and freedom attained in the only sovereign republic of that region," which produced "not only admiration and envy – especially in the countries without full autonomy – but also emulation." With Mustafa Kemal credited for Turkey's successes, he added, "many of the thoughtful in Arab lands and Iran have longed for such leadership."[11] Decades later, the eminent scholar of Arab intellectual history Albert Hourani would conclude similarly that until the late 1930s, the Kemalist republic "exercised a great influence over the political minds of the Arabs, not only because of the success of the Turks in beating back the encroachments of Europe, but because there still remained profound ties, of religion, a shared history and often a blood relationship between Arabs and Turks, and still more because of their uncompromising statement of the rights of the nation."[12] What has been often overlooked in studies on the period, however, is that Kemalist Turkey and its surrogates were actively engaged in public diplomacy in the Middle East, including by seeking to foster the idea that Turkey could and should serve as a model for emulation in the region.

I The Beautiful Face of Turkey

In July 1932, the unexpected victory of a Turkish contestant in an international beauty pageant offered the Turkish government a tremendous propaganda opportunity for its brand of state feminism. The competition, billed as one of the earliest Miss Universe pageants, included beauty queens from 28 mostly European countries. Miss Turkey, 19-year-old Keriman Halis, was elected as her country's representative in a competition sponsored annually since 1929 by the daily *Cumhuriyet*. Once news of her surprising election as Miss Universe reached Turkey, the popular newspaper celebrated her accomplishment as a major national victory. The government concurred and moved fast to take ownership of her success. With her photos and descriptions of her accomplishment gracing the pages of a wide variety of political and entertainment newspapers in Europe and North America, from French newspapers in Paris to a Yiddish daily in New York, the potential propaganda value of the Turkish teen's new title was not difficult to discern.[13] The Kemalist establishment hailed the new Miss Universe as a symbol of the great success of New Turkey in nurturing a new type of liberated and educated modern women, on par with the daughters of the most civilized nations on earth.[14] Reports in the Western press promoted the same line, regarding "a Turkish victory."[15] The *London Times*, for instance, published a long piece on "Feminism in Turkey," which reported that "the Turkish woman is moving rapidly toward complete emancipation. Already she has acquired one notable victory at the expense of women chosen from many Western countries. Keriman Halis Hanum, the Turkish beauty queen for 1932, was lately elected Miss Universe." The article went on to describe the great honor she won in Turkey "as a symbol of the new freedom which Turkish women have won, and a proof to the world that Turkey has finally shaken off the shackles which kept her for so long from taking her place among civilized nations." And driving the pro-Kemalist argument home, the author reported that after she was greeted personally by the president of the republic, the new Miss Universe made sure to declare her conviction that her achievement was "the result of the ideas inspired by [Mustafa Kemal] in the women of our country."[16]

With so much attention and fanfare in the Turkish and international press, the Arabic press did not stay far behind with reports on the Turkish Miss Universe, accompanied by her photos. The influential Egyptian daily *al-Ahram*, for example, adorned its front page with a large photo of Keriman Halis in an evening gown, along with a text that described her election and family background, and the profeminist Lebanese literary magazine *al-Ma'rid* published a large captioned photo of her.[17] The interest in the Arabic press in fact appeared intense enough to elicit in November 1932, while the beauty queen was in the midst of triumphant tour of Turkey's major cities, inaccurate reports that suggested she would soon be headed to Egypt and Syria for a victory tour in their major cities.[18]

After months of celebration in Turkey, Keriman Halis finally did travel to Egypt in early 1933, in what was planned as the first leg of a journey that was to end in a visit to the Chicago World's Fair. The Egyptian part of the tour was organized and publicized by Hüseyin Remzi, the proprietor and editor-in-chief of the bilingual Turkish-Arabic weekly *Muhadenet* and a paid surrogate of the Turkish Embassy, in cooperation with the Cairo-based Turkish Benevolent Society. Some reports in Turkey suggested that during her travels abroad Keriman Halis would help promote Turkish products.[19] But the organizers of the visit in fact viewed her trip to Egypt as an opportunity to foster positive publicity and good will that could help patch up the fallout from the Fez Incident, which was brought to an end only a few weeks earlier. A secondary goal was to help bolster ethnic pride and energize communal organizations among the Egypt-based Turkish community, which consisted of Muslim immigrants from Anatolia and the Balkans and their descendants. Many of them were still actively nurturing a Turkish identity, and some acquired Turkish citizenship, at a time in which Turkey was still demanding for them capitulatory privileges. The Egyptian press often denoted them "the Turkish colony" (al-Jaliya al-Turkiya), on par with the Greek, Italian, and Armenian colonies in the Land of the Nile. These self-identified ethnic Turks were most eagerly awaiting the visit of Miss Universe, but she was expected to appeal to all Egyptians as an ambassador of good will who embodied the modern, progressive, liberated, and beautiful face of Turkey (Figure 5.1).

An intensive publicity campaign preceded the Turkish beauty queen's visit to Egypt, but the level of curiosity and enthusiasm with which she was received still stunned her and her handlers. As it soon became clear that the visit was a resounding success, she and her father, who accompanied her on the trip, resolved to change their original travel plans. Rather than stay in Egypt for only two weeks before boarding a ship en route to Chicago, they decided to remain in the Land of the Nile a longer period, which eventually extended to almost four months. They never set sail to America. Instead, their schedule in Egypt was packed full with almost daily events in Cairo, Alexandria, and smaller towns in the Delta region, ranging from meetings with political leaders and journalists, to social activities, entertainment, and some tourism opportunities too. All these exploits were reported widely and in detail in the Egyptian press, and were followed by the Turkish press too. For a few months in early 1933, Keriman Halis was treated as one of the greatest celebrities in Egypt, being regarded as an international star and as an informal representative of Turkey, but oftentimes also hailed as a source of pride for all the peoples of the Middle East.

Figure 5.1 Miss Universe Keriman Halis on the cover of the Egyptian journal *al-Musawwar*, February 17, 1933.

The Turkish beauty queen got a taste of the enthusiasm and intense interest with which she was to be met already upon her arrival in Alexandria in early February 1933. The event was publicized on the front pages of Egypt's most popular newspapers. She was met at the docks by a welcoming committee made mainly of Egypt-based Turkish citizens, accompanied by Egyptian government officials, politicians, and local dignitaries, as well as throngs of Egyptian men and women who were curious to observe the newly minted international celebrity. After she was warmly received on shore, Keriman Halis and her father were led to a festive reception in her honor, which was attended by the Turkish consul in Alexandria, local Egyptian bigwigs, and wealthy Turkish citizens who lived in the city. On the following day, she boarded the train to Cairo.[20] Upon arrival in the Egyptian capital city, Miss Universe and her hosts were astounded to find the railway station clogged by hundreds of Egyptians, mostly males, who were eager to catch a glimpse of the famous visitor. Reports in the Egyptian press suggested that the crowd sought to convey to Keriman Halis their pride in the fact that a fellow Muslim and Easterner like the majority of the people of Egypt was elected Miss Universe. It took the local police half an hour to open for the Turkish visitor a path from her train car to an automobile that was waiting outside the station to whisk her off to her hotel.[21]

After this impromptu encounter with common Egyptians, the rest of Miss Universe's first day in Cairo included meetings and socializing with members of Egypt's high society. Dozens of curious Egyptian politicians, officials, dignitaries, and journalists hastened to greet her in her hotel's lounge. Among them stood out a delegation of the Egyptian Feminist Union, which congratulated Keriman Halis on her achievement, and for being such a positive role model for all Eastern women. She was therefore invited to attend a social event they were organizing a few days later. The beauty queen's hectic day continued with a visit to the royal palace, where she was "the first Eastern woman" to sign its official guestbook, at least according to reports in the Egyptian press. As evening fell, the long and eventful day culminated with a fancy ball at the mansion of Hüseyin Remzi, the owner of the weekly *Muhadenet* and one of the major driving forces behind the beauty queen's invitation to Egypt. His residence and the streets around it were decorated with dozens of Turkish and Egyptian flags, giving the social gathering an air of a friendly semiofficial event, less than a month after the end of the diplomatic crisis in the wake of the Fez Incident. The ball was held under the auspices of the Turkish Benevolent Society, which was a charitable organization of the Turkish community in Cairo, and was attended by the cream of the Egyptian capital city's high society. Dozens of onlookers lined the streets leading to the house, seeking to observe and greet the beauty queen as well as famous Egyptian figures on their way to the party. The attendees included Saiza Nabarawi, a feminist leader and the editor-in-chief of *l'Egyptienne*, the organ of the Egyptian Feminist Union. She was honored with giving a speech to the guest of honor and all other attendees. In it, Nabarawi welcomed Keriman Halis to the Land of the Nile on behalf of all the Egyptian women, and hailed her achievement as the first Muslim Miss

Universe as a great triumph not only for Turkish women, but rather for all the Eastern women. The following day, this particular speech, and the event as a whole, were featured in the Egyptian daily press, including photos of Miss Universe and other famous attendees.[22]

The immense level of public interest in Keriman Halis prompted the scheduling of many more public and social events in her honor, and informed her decision to stay in Egypt longer than planned. In the first month she attended different events on almost a daily basis, before the pace slowed down toward the end of her prolonged visit. Reports on her exploits were published frequently in the Egyptian press, accompanied by photos of her in tea parties, receptions, balls, and while visiting tourist attractions. Popular illustrated magazines splashed her photographs on their covers and pages.[23] For a few weeks, she was the toast of the town. In a reception in Parliament, she had an opportunity for meet and greet with senior politicians. The Minister of Education, Muhammad Hilmi 'Isa Pasha, was indeed so infatuated with her that some journals published mocking caricatures of his awkward behavior in her presence. In one cartoon, for example, he was presented as staring cross-eyed and star-struck at Keriman Halis, and in another as inviting the visiting beauty queen to deliver "a lecture on the science of... Beauty."[24] Her personal interactions were indeed primarily with the Egyptian elites and with members of the Turkish community in Egypt, but she also had some opportunities for public encounters with less privileged Egyptians as well. The advanced publicity given to the beauty queen's visit to Parliament, for example, attracted hundreds of Egyptian men and women, who lined the entrance to the building in order to catch a glimpse of the celebrated Turkish visitor. Some Egyptian royals were as interested in meeting the famous beauty queen in person. King Fuad's nephew Prince Muhammad Ali, for instance, arranged for himself a personal audience with Keriman Halis and her father.[25] The interest in her acquaintance extended to some respected intellectuals as well. For example, Muhammad Husayn Haykal, the editor-in-chief of the daily *al-Siyasa*, the organ of the Liberal Constitutional Party, organized a well-publicized reception in her honor, which was attended by senior journalists, intellectuals, and various members of the emerging urbanized and educated middle class known as "the new effendiyya" (Figure 5.2). The Istanbul born and bred Miss Universe was greeted as "the messenger of beauty from Ankara," and her visit was hailed as an expression of the strong bond and friendly

ملكه الجمال في دار « السياسة »

Figure 5.2 Keriman Halis hosted by the Egyptian daily *al-Siyasa*. From "Malikat al-Jamal fi Dar al-Siyasa," *al-Musawwar*, March 10, 1933, 3.

relations between Turkey and Egypt, pointing to the perception of her visit as being part of a semiofficial Turkish diplomatic outreach effort.[26] Indeed, just as the organizers of her visit to Egypt had hoped, reports in the Egyptian press described Keriman Halis time and again as an ambassador of goodwill on behalf of the Kemalist republic. That was the case when she was invited to attend soccer matches, a game which was fast growing in popularity in the interwar period. She was asked to hand out the trophy to the victorious team, which exposed her to a very different type of audience and resulted in references to her visit even in the sports sections of Egyptian newspapers.[27]

The representation of Keriman Halis as a symbol of the modernization and emancipation of Turkish women was embraced by the leading lights of the Egyptian feminist movement of the time. She was invited to a private meeting with Safiyya Zaghlul, the widow of the Egyptian national hero Saʿd Zaghlul, and a political activist in her own right, popularly known as Mother of the Egyptians (*Umm al-Misriyyin*). In the interwar period, she was "one of the most visible symbols and most powerful women of her time."[28] Avoiding entertainment establishments and parties since her husband's death in 1927, Zaghlul hosted the visiting Turkish beauty queen in her private mansion, popularly known as the House of the Nation (*Bayt al-Umma*), in honor of the important functions held in it during the events of the Egyptian Revolution of 1919. Another veteran feminist leader, Huda Shaʿrawi, did that and more. After a private meeting with the Turkish beauty queen, the leader of the Egyptian Feminist Union invited Keriman Halis to serve as the guest of honor in a party and a fund-raiser held by her organization in her private mansion.[29] Many Egyptian feminists in the 1930s viewed beauty contests as a symbol and expression of new opportunities and freedoms demanded and attained by modern women. Two years after Keriman Halis's visit, the young and fiery Egyptian feminist Doria Shafik made the headlines when she entered a beauty context in Egypt and was billed as the first Muslim Egyptian to do so. She came second, but she captured the heart of Ahmad al-Sawi Muhammad, a young but influential Egyptian journalist of *al-Ahram*, which helped land the photo of the sweethearts, and report on their romantic engagement, on the front page of Egypt's newspaper of record. During Keriman Halis's visit to Egypt, al-Sawi Muhammad wrote columns in which he confided that he was initially opposed to the idea of beauty contests and queens, but after observing the grace and dignity of Miss Universe, he was won over by her and warmed up to her title. This did not save his relations with Doria Shafik from flaming out shortly after their engagement, but it does testify to the Turkish beauty queen's success in presenting an image of a modern and dignified woman who should be seen as a praiseworthy pathbreaker and not as representing a vulgar and perhaps shallow and immoral venture.[30]

Engaging with wealthy and well-established feminist leaders helped boost the respectability of her title, but Keriman Halis did not shy away from also paying visits to popular entertainment haunts. Famous singers and dancers were often featured in benefit concerts that were sponsored by Huda Shaʿrawi for the Egyptian Feminist Union, but the atmosphere and the crowd there was often quite different than in Cairo's entertainment establishments. Keriman Halis's handlers arranged for her to be a guest of honor in concerts given by famous performers such as the singing sensation Umm Kulthum and well-known stars such as the singer Ibrahim Hamuda. Likewise, she was the featured guest in the weekly matinee for women only in Badi'a Masabni's popular music hall. The famous belly dancer and movie star established her successful entertainment business a few years earlier with money she had earned as an actress and dancer. Masabni was one of a number of women who made it big as entrepreneurs in Cairo's burgeoning entertainment industry, so the projection of the Turkish beauty queen as representing the new opportunities for Muslim women under the Kemalist republic appeared to mesh well with these businesswomen's efforts and achievements in interwar Egypt.[31] At the same time, Keriman Halis stated to the Egyptian press that her goal in life was to maintain a healthy lifestyle, get married, and raise a family. She added that she would have liked to promote a better diet and physical activity for the women of Egypt, because too many of them appeared to her to be overweight.[32]

The intense interest in Keriman Halis and the publicity that went along with it created commercial opportunities to capitalize on her fame, but also risked tarnishing her reputation. On the one hand, popular newspapers followed her exploits with flattering reports, and even published poems that applauded her looks, conduct, and praiseworthy accomplishment as the first Muslim and Eastern woman to be elected Miss Universe.[33] On the other hand, there were other voices that found in any hint of financial reward she might get, a proof that her visit to Egypt was all about monetizing her success. The weeklies *al-Kashkul* and *Ruz al-Yusuf*, for example, published satirical commentaries and caricatures that insinuated that the Egyptian public might have been fed with *Arabian Nights*–style stories about the Turkish visitor, who in reality might be nothing more than a glorified salesperson for the promotion of cosmetic products in Egypt.[34] It did not stop the same two periodicals from publishing many reports on her exploits in Egypt, but the suggestion that Keriman Halis was after economic rewards, and that it was an improper endeavor, lingered and put her on the defensive regarding the financial side of her visit. When the luxurious Heliopolis Palace Hotel lured her away from the Continental with the promise of free accommodation, it appeared innocent enough, because she did not actively advertise the hotel. The management expected the news itself to attract visitors to the hotel's dining room, cafeteria, and tea lounge. Or even when she went on a well-publicized tour of a cigarettes production facility of the small Mahmud Fahmi Company, which used imported Turkish tobacco, it appeared as an endorsement of her homeland's exports to Egypt rather than as a paid event.[35] But she did face criticism when reports began circulating that she sold signed photos of herself during a social event of the Egyptian Feminist Union. Keriman Halis later explained to a Turkish journalist that it was in fact the Egyptian feminist leader Huda Sha'rawi who initiated the sale as a fund-raiser for her organization, without the prior knowledge and against the will of the Turkish beauty queen. Miss Universe revealed that she could do nothing but shed some tears and accept promises made to her that the money will go toward good causes. She insisted that the only compensation she received was from Turkish benefactors in Egypt who covered the costs of travel, accommodation, and meals for herself and her father, and nothing more.[36]

Another debate, which was tinged with nationalism or at least Egyptian patriotism, revolved around the question of whether the Turkish visitor was indeed particularly beautiful. A commentary in the weekly *al-Kashkul*, for instance, opined that "there is no doubt that [Keriman Halis] is very graceful and likeable, and yet, she is not unique in her beauty, and those who visited San Stefano beach or Stanley Bay beach [in Alexandria] know that some of our own young women are more beautiful than her." In the same vein, the weekly *Ruz al-Yusuf* reported that after hosting Keriman Halis, the Egyptian feminist leader and nationalist activist Huda Sha'rawi commented to her friends that there are many more beautiful girls in Egypt. She reportedly went on to suggest that Egyptian female beauty should be put on display in a beauty pageant that would be organized by the Egyptian Feminist Union. Another commentary in *al-Kashkul* concurred, opining that Egyptian women, particularly those from the educated elites, were both beautiful and naturally equipped to succeed in international beauty contests.[37] Be that as it may, there must have been a sense of vindication when two years later an Egyptian named Charlotte Wassef won the title of Miss Egypt in a pageant organized by a newspaper in Alexandria before going on to win the title of Miss Universe in a competition in Brussels, Belgium. She was definitely a proud daughter of Egypt, but the fact that she was Christian meant that she could not be presented, as Keriman Halis was in 1933, as a symbol for the emancipation of Muslim women.[38] Interestingly, some Egyptian commentators were so impressed with Keriman Halis that they objected to impressionist appraisals that questioned her beauty. The well-known lawyer, intellectual, and political activist Fikri Abaza, for instance, rejected suggestions that her looks was average or that subjective judgments should be even accepted in the evaluation of any woman's appearance. He insisted that in this modern day and age, scientific factors, such as the proportion of the subject's facial parts and the relations between them, should be applied to measure female beauty, rather than personal tastes or sentimental considerations. He testified that after applying rigorous scientific standards to Keriman Halis, he can confirm with authority that she is indeed beautiful. He then added that after meeting and observing the Turkish beauty queen, he can also attest to her grace and dignified personal conduct, which could teach the women of Egypt a thing or two.[39]

The propaganda value of Keriman Halis's visit as an informal representative of Turkey was indeed expressed in one way or another quite often during her stay in Egypt. Turkish flags and cheers for the republic and its leader often greeted her on her visits to various locations. For example, when the beauty queen was invited by the Turkish community in Mansura to visit their provincial town in the Nile Delta region, she was received with chants of "Long Live the Gazi [Mustafa Kemal]! Long live Turkey! Long Live Miss Keriman!" (Figure 5.3).[40] Back in August 1932, shortly after her election as Miss Universe, Mustafa Kemal congratulated her for the title and for her representation of "the noble beauty of the Turkish race." He was very pleased that "with the endorsement of the international judges [in the beauty pageant], this beautiful Turkish girl of ours acquainted the world with the beauty that manifests itself naturally in the essence of her race."[41] That is exactly what Keriman Halis claimed to do in Egypt, in serving as an unofficial representative of her country and people. Generally speaking, it was not deemed a particular problem that she was partly of Circassian descent. That is, until rumors began circulating that in a meeting with Circassian residents of Egypt her father proclaimed his pride in his Circassian ethnic heritage. Such a statement would have run counter to the Kemalist republic's policies of Turkification and ethnic homogenization, and would have been particularly upsetting since Circassians in the Middle East were associated with various alleged plots against Mustafa Kemal in the interwar period. Father and

Figure 5.3 Keriman Halis hosted by the Turkish community in al-Mansura. From "Malikat al-Jamal fi al-Mansura," *al-Musawwar*, March 31, 1933, 24.

daughter therefore hastened to deny to Turkish reporters any truth in these rumors. Keriman Halis emphasized that all her family members were proud and loyal children of the Turkish nation and that throughout her visit, she emphasized time and again the importance of Mustafa Kemal as a great inspiration to her. She pointed to the great cheers of support for the president of the republic on many occasions during her visit, as a testimony to the great service she did to Turkey's image in Egypt, and she mentioned the great pride she brought to the Turkish community in the Land of the Nile.[42]

The visit was overall a great success, even if its impact was rather short-lived. It took place only a few weeks after the closure of the Fez Incident, the lowest point in Turkish-Egyptian diplomatic relations in the interwar period, and certainly succeeded in somewhat clearing the air of resentment against Turkey in Egypt. Both before and after her stay in Egypt, the Kemalist government and its policies had their fair share of critics in the Land of the Nile. But the reception of Keriman Halis, who was clearly perceived as an informal representative of the Turkish state and its social and legal reforms, indicates that there were many other Egyptians who were more than happy to put the Fez Incident behind them and afford respect and appreciation to the Kemalist republic, its symbols, and its leader. The Kemalist government thus did not only appropriate Keriman Halis as a propaganda tool in Turkey and Europe[43] but also made use of her for this public diplomacy initiative in Egypt. This was part of a broader effort of image management in the wake of the diplomatic crisis, aimed at displaying the beautiful face of Turkey to the Egyptian people. Keriman Halis's particular appeal to many in Egypt, and menace to some, had to do with the fact that she was at one and the same time foreign, being Turkish and Westernized in appearance, and broadly defined native of the region, and thus relatable for being Middle Eastern and Muslim.

This duality mirrored attitudes toward the Kemalist republic at large. Even after all the nationalist and secularist reforms of the late 1920s and early 1930s, and despite the Kemalist government's well-documented efforts to promote and enforce the adoption of European social norms and cultural tastes, there was no lack of people in the Middle East who still considered Turkey to be an Eastern country and society in transformation. Those who wished for similar reforms in their own societies, could thus find in the Kemalist republic a model for emulation, or at least for inspiration, albeit not necessarily in all aspects of social, economic, and political life. Some indeed did just that, with the encouragement of the Kemalist government. Ankara did not hesitate to make allusions to common "Eastern" bonds in its outreach endeavors in the Middle East, even as the Kemalist establishment was busy implementing in Turkey the ruling party's program of Turkification, secularization, and Westernization.

II State of Feminism

The Kemalist republic was consciously seeking to establish its international and regional credentials as the most progressive Muslim-majority country, particularly regarding women's rights. Ankara sought validation and praise first and foremost in Europe and North America, but also in the Middle East. Within this context, the Kemalist government invited the International Woman Suffrage Alliance (IWSA, later renamed the International Alliance of Women) to hold its international conference in Istanbul in April 1935.[44] All previous meetings of the feminist organization, since its establishment in 1904, were held in European cities, and the acceptance of the Turkish government's invitation was therefore seen as an endorsement of Turkey's Westernizing reforms and as reflective of the suffragist organization's efforts to appeal to non-European societies.[45] The Egyptian feminist leader Huda Sha'rawi and a few of her colleagues have already participated in earlier conferences of the organization. But in her memoirs, written in the mid-1940s, Sha'rawi relates that when she found out that Istanbul was selected as the location of the 1935 meeting, she resolved to organize a much larger Egyptian delegation than ever before, in order to emphasize the strong historical and sociocultural bonds between Egypt and Turkey. She appealed to the Turkish government for help in arranging the logistics of the visit of her 12-member delegation, and indeed the press attaché in the Turkish embassy in Cairo was instructed to accompany the Egyptian ladies to Istanbul, to arrange their itinerary and accommodation, and cover all the costs of their travel and stay in Turkey.[46] A sizable delegation also arrived from Syria and Lebanon, led by veteran women's rights activists such as Hayat al-Barazi, Julia Dimashqiya, Amina Khuri, and Huda Dumat, and including female members of some of Syria's most influential families, such as Su'ad Mardam Bey, Farlan Mardam Bey, and Ni'mat al-'Azm.[47] The conference highlighted the high regard in which Turkey and its state feminism were held by many Middle Eastern women's rights activists in the 1930s, as well as Ankara's conscious efforts to nurture an image of a progressive country that was trailblazing a path for other Muslim-majority societies.

Prominent Arab feminists depicted Turkey as a pathbreaker for other societies in the region already from the mid-1920s, when Ankara began implementing gradual steps toward the emancipation of women. In 1929, for instance, Huda Sha'rawi gave a public speech on methods and means to advance the liberation of women, in which she argued that in adopting steps toward full legal equality to Turkish women, the Kemalist government was setting important precedents for other societies in the region.[48] Likewise, the Syrian feminist leader Nur Hamada was similarly enthusiastic about the achievements of women in Turkey, suggesting that the Kemalist republic should serve as a role model for the rest of the Middle East on issues related to women's rights. She shared these views with delegates to two Eastern Women's Conferences which she helped organize, in Damascus in 1930 and in Tehran in 1932. In the meeting in Iran, Hamada asserted that the women of Turkey and Japan have secured the highest levels of progress

among Eastern women, and expressed her confident expectation that
their achievements will reverberate throughout other Eastern societies,
and stimulate progressive changes in them too. The Iraqi delegate
Tharwa Ahmad Halat shared a similar perspective in her address to the
congress in Tehran. She voiced her hopes that the reforms in Turkey
would help inspire a women's awakening in Mesopotamia as well.[49]
Indeed, it was generally assumed in the Middle East that the Turkish
policies on women's rights would likely influence potential reforms in
the region. Such assessments were made by both sympathetic observers
on the "women's awakening in Turkey," such as the Iraqi nationalist
daily *al-Istiqlal*, and by worried detractors of the Kemalist reforms,
such as the Egyptian conservative periodical *al-Risala*. A veteran Austrian diplomat thus concluded in 1937 that "Today many signs seem
to indicate that the success of the Women's Movement in Turkey will
serve as a model for, and greatly influence, the peoples and countries
of Asia."[50]

The Turkish government and press encouraged the depiction of
Turkey as a shining light for neighboring societies and amplified
expressions of praise and support from the Middle East. This was the
case in late 1934, for instance, when the Turkish government awarded
women the right to elect and stand for election in the parliamentary
elections of 1935. The decision, made only a few months before the
international suffragist meeting was scheduled to begin in Istanbul,
was received with enthusiasm and praise by Arab feminists in the Middle East. Huda Sha'rawi, for example, expressed her admiration for
the decision in an open letter to the Turkish ambassador in Cairo, in
which she depicted the Turkish women and their achievements as a
"role model for many Eastern women." The Turkish government-run
Anadolu News Agency duly reported her friendly gesture, which was
then given a pride of place in reports published in both the national
press in Ankara and Istanbul, and in the local press of provincial Turkish towns with substantial ethnic-Arab populations such as Urfa and
Adana.[51] Similarly, and oftentimes based on items distributed by the
Anadolu Agency, Turkish newspapers were more than happy to frame
reports on women's reforms in the Middle East, such as unveiling campaigns and development of female education, as inspired by precedents
set in Turkey.[52]

The suffragist conference in Istanbul in April 1935 presented a particularly enticing opportunity to present Turkey as a progressive and
inspiring pathbreaker for the rest of the Middle East. The Egyptian

delegation was bigger than to any previous IWSA conference, and for the first time in the suffragist organization's history, among the attendees were delegations representing Iran, Syria, and Lebanon, as well separate Arab and Jewish delegations from Mandate Palestine.[53] The correspondent of the Egyptian daily *al-Ahram* reported from Istanbul that the Turkish hosts displayed particular attentiveness and care for the delegates from "Eastern countries," more than to representatives of the other 40 countries in the conference. This hospitality may have been at least partly the result of an effort to refute false claims by the Syrian Prime Minister Taj al-Din al-Hasani and commentators in the Syrian press, according to which the Turkish authorities prohibited any use of Arabic at the conference. Turkish diplomats issued vehement denials, and the hosts in Istanbul went out of their way to dispel any notion of hostility or apathy toward the visiting Arab delegates.[54] For example, the Syrian feminist leader Hayat al-Barazi, who was the wife of the Syrian Minister of Education, was welcomed very warmly and her photo was featured prominently on the front page of the daily *Cumhuriyet*. Much respect was also given to the lone representative of Iran, although she was in fact a resident of Istanbul from a wealthy Turkey-based Iranian family.[55] But most attention and esteem was unquestionably focused on the veteran Egyptian women's rights activist Huda Sha'rawi and the delegation from Egypt (Figure 5.4). That was perhaps only to be expected, considering that Sha'rawi was by far the most famous feminist in the Middle East and because of her proven track record of public support for the Kemalist republic. Indeed, in the months preceding the suffragist conference, the mouthpiece of the Egyptian Feminist Union stepped up its praises of Turkey's feminist policies. The Turkish government reciprocated by giving the royal treatment to the Egyptian delegation, and by encouraging the publication of praiseful press reports on its members' experiences in Turkey, in both the Turkish and Egyptian press.[56]

   Sha'rawi and her colleagues were willing contributors to Turkey's efforts to project to the Middle East an image of progressive modernity and regional leadership on women's rights. En route from Alexandria to Istanbul, their steamship made a short stopover in Izmir, where they were greeted by the governor of the city and a cheering crowd. Sha'rawi thanked them with a speech in Turkish in which she hailed Turkey for its reforms in general and for its promotion of women's rights in particular. As will be the case throughout her stay in Turkey, the content of

Figure 5.4 Huda Sha'rawi traveling abroad. From *al-Musawwar*, July 6, 1934, 11.

the speech was shortly distributed to the press in Turkey and Egypt for publication in Turkish, Arabic, and French.[57] Upon arrival in Istanbul, the Egyptian delegation was led to the Republic Monument in Taksim, where Sha'rawi gave another well-publicized speech on the merits of the Kemalist reforms and the friendly relations between the peoples of Egypt and Turkey. Photos of the visit were taken, and were shortly published in the Turkish and Egyptian press.[58] The praises and photo opportunities continued in the days that followed. In a news conference in the famous Pera Palace Hotel, for example, the veteran Egyptian women's rights activist Saiza Nabarawi echoed her good friend Sha'rawi in singing the praises of the Kemalist republic. She declared that Turkey showed much greater hospitality to the suffragist delegates than all the European countries that hosted earlier IWSA conferences. She went on to commend the Kemalist republic for its inspiring and laudable love of progress in general, and its commitment to the emancipation of women in particular.[59] This was music to the ears of the Turkish hosts, as was Sha'rawi's speech to the conference. In it, the respected Egyptian feminist leader called for a greater degree of cooperation between Eastern and Western women and argued that the Turkish government's repositioning of the country as an essential bridge between East and West, and the awarding of full equality to Turkish women, transformed Turkey into a desirable model of emulation for all other non-Western societies. Sha'rawi delivered the speech in French, but its content was soon translated to Arabic and Turkish and published widely in Turkey and the Middle East.[60]

The delegates were indeed so effusive of the policies of state feminism in Turkey, and so praiseful of the government's hospitality, that they felt unable to criticize it even when it suppressed women's rights. That happened when, as the conference was drawing to a close, Ankara ordered the "voluntary" disbandment of the Turkish Women's Union (*Türk Kadınlar Birliği*). The reason given was that the awarding of full legal equality to women and the election of female delegates to parliament eliminated the need for such a gender-based organization. The reality was that this was a period in which the Kemalist government clamped down on many nongovernmental organizations in general, and that there was a certain concern in Ankara about the excessive independence of some of the women activists in the Union in particular.[61] The shocking news reached Istanbul just as most foreign delegates were heading home, while Sha'rawi, Hayat al-Barazi, and other members of IWSA's executive committee were preparing to travel to Ankara for meetings with Mustafa Kemal and other senior leaders of the republic. This blatant suppression of women activism was not taken well by the foreign suffragists. IWSA's President Margery Corbett Ashby informed the British Embassy in Turkey of the strong displeasure with which the decision was accepted by the visiting delegates. And a few weeks later, an Australian delegate divulged to an audience in London that the decision by the Turkish government "came as bombshell, and was naturally a great disappointment to the Conference."[62] But after issuing so many praiseful declarations about Turkey and its great potential to become a model for feminist progress in other non-Western societies, the foreign delegates opted to refrain from any forceful or meaningful public criticism of the decision, and IWSA's executive committee carried on with its scheduled visit to Ankara as if nothing has happened.[63]

Huda Sha'rawi and other members of the Egyptian delegation in fact did not let up with their enthusiastic endorsement of Turkey's policies of state feminism. Indeed, in a lecture she gave in Cairo in late 1935, only a few months after returning from the conference, Sha'rawi went as far as to actually justify the disbanding of the Turkish women's organization. In a booklet based on the lecture, which was entitled "The Role of Women in the Eastern Awakening," she contended that "Turkey has exceeded all the civilized nations in its positive attitude to women," and then went on to endorse Atatürk's assertion that after they have secured full equality before the law, there was no need any more for a separate and distinct women's organization.[64] In her memoirs, written a decade later, Sha'rawi explained that when she headed back to Egypt, she was more determined than before to dispel any negative notions about Turkey among the Egyptian people. In declarations to the Egyptian press upon her return from the conference, she indeed reiterated her admiration for Atatürk's benevolent and progressive policies in general, and his emancipation of Turkish women in particular. She emphasized yet again that Turkey should serve as an inspiration and model for emulation for Egypt and other Muslim-majority societies. The mouthpiece of the Egyptian Feminist Union, *l'Égyptienne*, followed suit with positive reminiscences from other delegates on their positive experiences and observations in Turkey. In mid-1936, the feminist periodical even published a special issue on the occasion of the one-year anniversary of the conference, in which it included articles that focused on the achievements and rights of women in the Kemal-ist republic. Saiza Nabarawi, the journal's editor-in-chief, reiterated yet again that Egypt should follow Turkey's example in implementing legal and social reforms that would benefit the Egyptian women and society in general. The Turkish press quoted at length these laudatory state-ments regarding Turkey's potential role as a model for emulation in other Muslim-majority societies.[65]

Egyptian and other Middle Eastern observers were particularly impressed with Turkey's investment in establishing modern educa-tional institutions for the daughters of the republic. The late 1920s and early 1930s witnessed the opening of various government-run schools for girls. The most celebrated of these was the İsmet Pasha Girls' Institute (*İsmet Paşa Kız Enstitüsü*) in Ankara, which was named after Prime Minister İnönü.[66] The school's stated goal, as expressed by the Turkish government in 1936, was to nurture model middle-class women who would become "future house-wives with all the mod-ern knowledge and technique of house-keeping," but would also be equipped with competencies that would "enable them to earn their own living." The Kemalist authorities proudly declared the school to be "a perfect model of its kind, not only in Turkey, but also in the whole of the Near East," and insisted therefore that it should be seen as being "of immense educational importance, not only to Ankara, and Turkey, but also to all the countries of the Near East."[67] Subse-quently, whenever foreign leaders and dignitaries visited Ankara, the school became an essential stop in their tour of the Turkish capital city. Among the visitors were Emir Faisal of Saudi Arabia in 1932, the Shah of Iran in 1934, the Emir of Transjordan in 1937, and a represen-tative from the Jewish Agency for Palestine in 1938. Similarly, Huda Sha'rawi and Hayat al-Barazi visited the institution along with other fellow feminist delegates when visiting Ankara in 1935, and so did the Lebanese author and women's rights activist Salma Sayigh and the influential Egyptian journalist Fuad Sarruf, among other visitors from the Middle East.[68] The foreign visitors were shown how "at the Ismet Inonu Institute the girls are initiated into all branches of modern fem-inine education: hygiene, infant welfare and kindergarten, housekeep-ing and home-making, cooking, sewing and millinery, everything they will need to run a modern household in a sensible, practical way."[69] In short, following the example of many European countries of the interwar period, this type of modern education for women meant a

 معهد عصمت باشا للبنات في انقرة وهو عبارة عن مدرسة فنون بنية

Figure 5.5 The İsmet Pasha Girls' Institute in Ankara. From Muhammad Fadhil al-Jamali, *Al-Tarbiya wa-al-Ta'alim fi Turkiya al-Haditha* (Baghdad: Matba'at al-Hukuma, 1938).

strong emphasis on drilling maternalism into young female students, with the aim of teaching them how to become modern mothers, wives, and homemakers (Figures 5.5 and 5.6).[70]

The educational philosophy of the school and the way it operated were impressive enough for some visitors from the Middle East that they believed they should be emulated in their own countries. The decision to establish in Tehran an all-girls boarding school, the *Honarestan-e Dokhtaran*, was reportedly made after the Shah's visit to Ankara. Its administrative structure and curriculum were based on the İsmet Pasha Girls' Institute.[71] A few years later, an official in the Lebanese Ministry of Education named Sa'id Sannu traveled to Turkey to study its modernization, and reported in a book he published in 1938 that he found the curriculum of the girls' school to be very impressive and very adequate for the education of modern women. He therefore recommended its emulation in the Middle East.[72]

Dans la cuisine.

Figure 5.6 Cooking lesson in the İsmet Pasha Girls' Institute. From La Direction générale de la Presse au Ministère de l'Intérieur, *La Turquie Contemporaine* (Ankara, 1935), 249.

Huda Sha'rawi reached the exact same conclusion after visiting the school. Upon her return from Turkey in 1935, she expressed in public speeches and in interviews with the Egyptian press her desire to see the establishment of similar girls' schools in Egypt. However, as this could not be achieved in the short term, she also approached the Turkish Embassy in Cairo to inquire whether the Turkish government would be willing to sponsor the enrollment of Egyptian girls in the Ankara school. The response was swift and enthusiastic. The Turkish Ministry of Culture made the decision to offer two comprehensive scholarships which covered all costs and expenses for two Egyptian students, including tuition, room, and board. The decision elicited positive reporting in the Egyptian press. Turkish commentaries praised the public relations achievement, and opined that not only would the two young Egyptian girls receive great education, they will also be transformed into life-long advocates of Kemalist modernist ideas and reformist philosophy, and serve as valuable ambassadors of good will on Turkey's behalf.[73] They were not the only Middle Eastern girls enrolled in the girls' school. When the Lebanese educator Saʿid Sannu visited Ankara in 1938 he encountered among the students two Iraqi girls and quite a few more Egyptian girls.[74] It is not clear who they were, whether they were able to complete their education before or during World War II, and how supportive they became of Kemalism. But the motivation of the Kemalist government to project a positive image to the Middle East and promote its reputation as a bastion of modernity and progressive womanhood is plainly clear from Turkish statements and actions in the 1930s. Indeed, in a book he originally published in 1936, the Kemalist ideologue Tekinalp presented a vision according to which hundreds of students from neighboring countries would be studying in Turkey, and then upon their graduation and return home they would help spread in their societies the progressive Kemalist agenda, including on women's rights.[75]

The fact that state feminism in the Kemalist republic was implemented under a paternalistic and non-democratic regime did not affect Turkey's positive image in the eyes of many feminists. Even otherwise liberal and pro-democracy women's rights activists prioritized the tangible results they observed, over the authoritarian political circumstances within which they were implemented. Ankara could boast of fully enfranchising women in 1935, years before France, Italy, Greece, or Switzerland. And the Turkish government opened new opportunities for education and employment for women, which were more extensive than in any other part of the Middle East. At the same time, Kemalist Turkey also relaxed many legal and social restrictions on women, albeit mainly in the major urban centers. From this perspective, many feminists in the Middle East shared the assessment of the Iranian academic and women's rights activist Fatimah Sayyah, when she declared in 1945 that Turkey was the "gold standard for the East" when it came to rights and opportunities available to women. The Egyptian journalist and suffragist Munira Thabit indeed admonished her countrymen in 1945 that even though Egypt claimed to be a democracy, Egyptian women were not afforded equality before the law, whereas "the women of Turkey – Turkey in which there is a regime of national dictatorship – enjoy full political and social equality with the men."[76] Foreign observers, including from democratic countries, indeed often insinuated that the rapid and comprehensive social and legal changes introduced by the Kemalist regime, more than compensated for the lack of political freedoms in Turkey, at least for the time being. Not a few foreign observers were in fact convinced that a strong leadership was absolutely necessary in order to affect essential societal reforms in conservative Muslim societies, including regarding women's rights. In Turkey's case, admirers of the transformative policies of the government took their cue from the Kemalist regime in giving overwhelming credit for the changes to Mustafa Kemal, his vision, and his will-power. The Turkish government actively sought to promote Atatürk's image and elevate his stature abroad, including in the Middle East. Critics of the Kemalist republic and its policies in the region were obviously not very receptive to this message. But there were many others, including women's rights activists in the Middle East, who were positively impressed with the Turkish leader. Supporters of Mustafa Kemal, the model of leadership that he appeared to represent, and its applicability as an inspiring type of leadership to their own societies, helped disseminate aspects of his cult of personality in the Middle East of the 1930s, oftentimes with assistance from the Turkish authorities.

III Father of the East

The non-democratic character of the Turkish government and its leader were internationally well known in the interwar period, even as official Turkey felt ill at ease with its designation as undemocratic. In Germany of the interwar period, Mustafa Kemal became a source of inspiration for nationalist parties in general, and for Hitler and his National-Socialist Party in particular. There were no gripes in Ankara when Adolf Hitler told the editor of the semiofficial *Hakimiyet-i Milliye*, in a special interview shortly after he came to power in 1933, that he considered Mustafa Kemal to be the greatest man of the modern period and that his movement was following in the footsteps of the Turkish national movement.[77] But in Western Europe and North America, where democratic systems continued to function despite the traumatic effects of the global economic crisis, the popular designation of the Turkish leader as a dictator appeared to Ankara to be much less flattering and as potentially damaging. It did not matter that Mustafa Kemal was often depicted by scholars and commentators in the democratic countries of Western Europe and North America as a "good dictator," a "dictateur modern," or even a "democratic dictator."[78] The Turkish government cringed when the *Washington Post* informed its readers in 1933 that "Turkish Schooling was to be Brought Up to Date by

Dictator," when the *Times* of London referred to the country's leader in 1937 as "a famous dictator," or when the Parisian *Le Petit Journal* described him in 1938 as "the first European dictator after the Great War."[79] The Turkish press criticized these designations in the Western press, both before and after the death of Atatürk, and the Turkish government at times complained to Western journals against the use of the term, but to no avail. For example, when the Turkish Press Ministry protested to the popular American illustrated magazine *Life* about its use of the phrase "Turkey's dictator, Kamal Atatürk," all it received in response was a statement of willingness to reconsider the "applicability" of the designation at an unspecified time in the future.[80] Kemalist Turkey was indeed one of only very few non-democratic regimes in the interwar period that sought to present itself to Western audiences as democratic, or at least as a work in progress toward democracy. At a time in which many other one-party states of the 1930s were openly scornful of democracy, Turkish propagandists insisted in publications in English and French that "present-day Turkey is a democratic republic," as put in 1939 by the prominent Turkish legal scholar Ali Fuad Başgil.[81] Nevertheless, the authoritarianism and paternalism of the single-party regime during the interwar period was evident to most foreign sympathizers and critics of Kemalism alike.

Observers in the Middle East were similarly aware of the non-democratic political system in Turkey, but opinions differed sharply on whether the Turkish government liberated the people or oppressed them. Admirers of Mustafa Kemal made their position clear when they cheered the decision of the Grand National Assembly of Turkey in 1934 to confer on him the last name Atatürk, "Father of the Turks." The chosen surname sought to immortalize the Eternal Leader (*Ebedi Şef*) of the republic not only as the celebrated commander, leader, and guide of the Turkish people but also as their great patriarch.[82] Admirers of Kemalism in the Middle East did not take issue with this paternalistic premise. In fact, none other than the Egyptian feminist Huda Sha'rawi declared in Atatürk's presence, when meeting him after the suffragist conference in 1935, that the appellation was too restrictive. She later explained to the Turkish and Egyptian press that in her mind, as well in the eyes of his many admirers in the Middle East, the Turkish leader should be considered as "Father of the East." At times she used the pre–language reform appellation Ataşark/Atasharq, which was more legible to Arabic speakers, and at other times the newer

Turkish term of Atadoğu. "We Egyptians love Atatürk very much," she explained to the Turkish press in 1935, "and we consider it a great honor to follow the path he pioneered. That is why, whereas you call him Atatürk, we call him *Atasharq*, because we see him not only as the father and leader of Turkey, but also [as the father] of the East in general, and of brotherly Egypt in particular."[83] She reiterated the same ideas in interviews with the Egyptian press, and in her memoirs, which were written few years after the death of the Turkish leader in late 1938.[84] Her countryman Aziz Khanki, a prominent attorney of Syrian origin, a paid surrogate of Turkey since the early 1930s, and a regular contributor to popular Egyptian dailies, happily integrated Sha'rawi's term and observations into his pro-Kemalist writings. He also featured them and similar adoring statements by Arab observers in a hagiography of Atatürk which he published in 1938, and which was excerpted in installations in *al-Ahram*, Egypt's newspaper of record.[85] The Turkish press and Kemalist propagandists were more than happy to publicize and amplify such statements. This was the case, for instance, with the sycophantic statement by the Emir Abdallah during his visit to Ankara in 1937, according to which Atatürk was a gift from God to all the peoples of the East, to serve as their guide and role model. The Kemalist ideologue and propagandist Tekinalp duly recorded Abdallah's patently insincere statement in the French edition of his book *Kemalism*, along with similarly adoring statements from famous Arab personalities, as a purported testimonial to the Turkish leader's clout in the Middle East.[86]

The reality was that quite a few people in the region obviously opposed Atatürk, his regime, and his policies, and took to task those who described the Turkish leader as a positive role model. One such rebuttal came from 'Abd al-Wahhab 'Azzam, an academic of pan-Islamic proclivities, who after World War II would become a long-serving diplomat in the Egyptian foreign service, and much later also be known as the maternal grandfather of al-Qaeda leader Ayman al-Zawahiri.[87] In a commentary he published in July 1935, shortly after Sha'rawi returned from Turkey and coined the term *Atasharq*, he took umbrage with her appellation of Mustafa Kemal as "Father of the East" and with her suggestion that Kemalist Turkey was widely admired among the Arabs. He insisted that the praises heaped by her and other likeminded Arabs on "the recent awakening in Turkey" were misplaced. He accused Mustafa Kemal of acts of betrayal against his people's Turkish and Muslim heritages by deceitfully introducing to Turkey depraved European norms and standards of immorality, under the guise of the "liberation of women." Most Egyptians and Arabs, he insisted, were well aware of that ugly reality, and therefore they despised Mustafa Kemal and did not share the views of Sha'rawi and likeminded admirers of Turkey and its leader.[88]

'Azzam displayed in this criticism his intellectual affiliation with "Eastern-inclined intellectuals" in Egypt, who criticized what they denounced as "the indiscriminate Westernization attempted by Turkey" and thus rejected "Turkey as a model" for modernity in Muslim-majority societies.[89] The Europe-based Syrian intellectual and political activist Shakib Arslan may have been the most determined and vociferous of these critics in the 1930s. He made quite a stir in 1937, for example, when claiming that during a League of Nations meeting in Geneva, the Turkish Foreign Minister Tevfik Rüştü Aras commented with pride that his countrymen were recently able to finally throw off the yoke of "the Arab religion of Islam." The allegation won such traction in the Arabic press in the Middle East that the Turkish Foreign Ministry felt compelled to issue an official denial of the story. Turkish diplomats in the region were instructed to reiterate to the Arab public and press that the Turkish leader and his government held the Arab peoples with the greatest respect and admiration. This was neither the first or last time in which official Turkey issued public denials of accusations in the Arab press about the Kemalist republic's purported hostility to the Arabs and Islam.[90] Indeed, by the mid-1930s, the radical nationalist and secularist policies of the Kemalist regime, compounded with suspicions about Ankara's territorial ambitions at Syria's expense, converged to produce recurring criticisms of Turkey and Atatürk by pan-Islamists, pan-Arab activists, and in a few cases also by liberal advocates of democracy.[91]

At the same time, throughout much of the 1930s, there was no dearth of admirers of Atatürk in the Middle East, and particularly of his leadership style. In their core, debates on the Kemalist republic and its leader were largely informed by differing visions on the future of societies in the region, and not necessarily by interest in Turkey per se. At times, critics and admirers could in fact share similar assessments on certain aspects of the Kemalist republic but disagree whether these characteristics were objectionable or worthy of emulation. For example, even as Turkey sought to reject its depiction as a dictatorship and its association with the Fascist regime in Italy and the Nazi government in Germany, many observers in the Middle East nevertheless did make the connection quite frequently, at times in a disapproving tone, and at others with appreciation. Arab commentators indeed made their recurrent comparisons between the European dictators and Atatürk, and at times Reza Shah too, so ubiquitous, that it has been argued that in Iraq of the 1930s the "names of Hitler and Mussolini appeared simultaneously with Atatürk and Reza Shah most of the time."[92]

Arab journalists and intellectuals indeed made analogies between Atatürk and European dictators very frequently, sometimes matter-of-factly, and at others judgmentally. The highbrow Egyptian monthly *al-Muqtataf*, for example, pointed to parallels already shortly after the Nazis came to power in 1933, comparing the similarities and differences between Fascism, Nazism, and Kemalism, without either commending or denouncing any of them.[93] On the other hand, the Egyptian conservative and Islamist-leaning *al-Risala* employed the comparison to lambast Kemalist Turkey. In 1936, for example, an article under the title "Language Fanaticism Following Racial Fanaticism" criticized the Kemalist efforts to "purify" the Turkish language and culture from "foreign" influences, which in effect oftentimes meant Arabic vocabulary and Middle Eastern and Islamic customs, norms, and institutions. The journal argued that these and other nationalist reforms in Turkey were informed by the same kind of reprehensibly racialist and extremist nationalist policies of Fascist Italy and Nazi Germany. The author took Reza Shah to task too, for ostensibly following in the footsteps of Atatürk in adopting detestable and fanatical anti-Arab and anti-Islam policies, which were purportedly racist in essence and as aggressive as the actions of the Italian and German dictators.[94] A few months before the publication of this disparaging article, the Iraqi nationalist newspaper *al-Istiqlal* published an article entitled "The Gazi Atatürk Emulates Herr Hitler," which reported on purported efforts to organize a visit of Atatürk to Nazi Germany and on Turkish ostensible intention to militarize the population based on Nazi models. In this case the author commended Turkey for purportedly following the German example in mobilizing women too for military service and hypothesized that the ideological affinities between the Nazi and Kemalist regimes might soon lead the two countries to establish close political cooperation.[95] The political analysis was obviously faulty, but the tone of the article was of appreciation with a tinge of envy. The Iraqi daily was not always in agreement with Turkish policies, but in this and in other articles, it described Turkey as presenting a model of successful leadership on par with the vigorous and potent regimes in Italy and Germany.[96] Although official Turkey certainly did not condone such analogies, there is no indication that Ankara demurred when they were made within the context of explicit or implied praise for Atatürk. This was par for the course in other instances outside the Middle East as well. For example, when the former American ambassador to Turkey published in 1936 a book which praised Mustafa Kemal, Mussolini, and Franklin Delano Roosevelt as sharing similar leadership traits, it was translated within a year to Turkish and published in Istanbul.[97]

The 1930s indeed witnessed the publication of a significant number of Arabic books, pamphlets, and articles that were very praiseful of Turkey and its leader. Some of these publications focused on his role as a national savior against European colonial schemes to partition Turkey, whereas others focused on his reforms and policies, such as in education, economic life, the military, or social customs. The underlying message of them all, which was at times stated explicitly and at times implied, was that if the Arab peoples wish to secure independence and prosperity, they would do well to take inspiration from the Kemalist republic and its leader. The popularity of translated biographies by Western authors in the early 1930s gives clear indication to the continued fascination of educated Arabs with Atatürk and his reforms. In 1933, for instance, Kamil Masiha published in Beirut an Arabic translation of Dagobert von Mikusch's popular biography of Mustafa Kemal. The hagiographical book was originally published in 1929 in German and in less than three years was translated to English, French, Italian, Swedish, Danish, Finnish, Turkish, Hebrew, and a host of other languages. After the Nazis rose to power in his homeland, Mikusch suggested that the main lesson of his book was that in order to achieve their country's national goals, the people should follow their great national savior without questioning.[98] The Arabic translation of the reverential tome sold out all the 5,000 printed copies shortly after its publication. The translator Masiha therefore decided to translate another admiring Western biography of Mustafa Kemal, this time by Charles Sherrill, the former American ambassador to Turkey in 1932–1933. Shortly after leaving office, this admirer of Mussolini and Hitler published a very reverential biography of Mustafa Kemal and his accomplishments. Masiha immediately translated it to Arabic and

published it in 1934 in book form, and a year later also in installments in Arabic newspapers such as the Palestinian daily *al-Jami'a
al-Islamiya*.[99]

The evident demand for books on Mustafa Kemal and modern
Turkey encouraged some Arab intellectuals to produce their own
biographies of the Turkish leader. These products were all very uncrit-
ical of his career and policies, whether out of conviction or because of
the authors' assessment of the market demands. The Egyptian Muhammad Muhammad Tawfiq, for example, published in 1936 a detailed
biography of Mustafa Kemal, which soon thereafter was published in
Persian translation as well. The author's dedication reveals the book's
tone quite clearly: "To the man who created Turkey, awakened the
East, and tormented the West; to the statesman and soldier: Kemal
Atatürk. From an Egyptian who sees in him the greatest example of
the ideal holy warrior and the perfect statesman." Going against the
grain, Tawfiq hailed the Turkish leader as an inspiration for hundreds
of millions of Muslims around the world, who purportedly viewed him
as their hero and as "the sword of Islam." These colonized Muslims
purportedly accepted him as a guide toward "a holy struggle on the
path of freedom, the path of the East, the path of Islam." The introduction to the book was written by Fikri Abaza, a well-known Egyptian nationalist intellectual. In the 1920s he was very critical of Turkey,
but by the early 1930s he became a huge admirer of Mustafa Kemal
and his regime. Abaza explained in the book's introduction that the
story of Atatürk should be read by the Egyptian political elite and
the general public as an operation manual for modernization, which
should subsequently be implemented in the modernization of Egypt's
national culture and intellectual life.[100] Descriptions of Mustafa Kemal
as a proud Eastern leader that should serve as a role model for both
modernizing reforms, national regeneration, and resistance to European colonialism were shared by other Arab authors in the late 1930s.
The Maronite Lebanese writer Fuad Shimali, for example, defined the
essential goal of his book on modern Turkey, which he published in
1939, to be the correction of misplaced criticisms and defamations of
Turkey in the Arab press of Syria and Lebanon. Shimali was a socialist activist who in the 1920s was one of the founders of the Syrian-
Lebanese Communist Party. His book reads almost like a propaganda
piece on Turkey's behalf. In fact, his endorsement of the official Turkish
narrative was so complete that he even insisted that the Kemalist government was indeed ruling over a democratic republic that respected

the free will of all its citizens. Similarly, Shimali endorsed each and every one of the Kemalist reforms, as well as emphasized Turkey's record of friendship with the Arab people, both under Atatürk and under his newly minted successor İsmet İnönü.[101] As a determined opponent of French colonialism and a socialist advocate of revolutionary changes in his society, he may have been genuinely impressed by the Turkish leaders despite the suppression of Communism under their rule.[102]

No such potential qualms bothered the Egypt-based intellectual Aziz Khanki, who in the 1930s became one of the best-known and most consistent surrogates of the Kemalist government in the Middle East. He published dozens of adoring opinion pieces on Turkey and its leader and was oftentimes the go-to person to write refutations against critics of Kemalism in Egypt, such as the exiled former Sheikh ul-Islam Mustafa Sabri Efendi.[103] Khanki's propagandist work culminated in 1938 with the publication of his book *The Turks and Atatürk*, a few months before the death of the Turkish leader, with long excerpts of it published in columns on the front page of *al-Ahram*, Egypt's newspaper of record.[104] The book was a vigorous defense of Mustafa Kemal, Kemalism, and Turkey, in complete adherence to the official Turkish propaganda of the time. Khanki insisted that Turkey was administered by a democratic and populist government rather than by a despotic and oppressive regime, as was purportedly the case in Ottoman times. Not only were Islam and Islamic institutions not suppressed in Turkey, he contended, but the separation of religion and politics in fact allowed them to flourish and thrive in modern Turkey. He proclaimed, therefore, that the Kemalist republic has instituted "complete freedom to all, men and women, in every matter. Freedom of religion and freedom of thought. Freedom of speech. Freedom of the press . . . Freedom of assembly. Freedom of association." These statements did not stop Khanki from lauding Turkey's single-party regime or from making approving analogies to Fascist Italy and Nazi Germany. He suggested that the elimination of party politics helped keep the country united and peaceful, meshing the party and state successfully in similar vein to the achievements of Mussolini and Hitler. In other words, he contended that the Kemalists were able to combine the virtues of both democratic and authoritarian regimes. He acknowledged, however, that Turkey's reputation among many people in the Middle East was less than stellar. Yet he insisted that the criticisms and negative views in the Arab lands were the result of ignorance and vile propaganda that should be corrected by reading informative and educating books like his, and through the attainment of firsthand impressions by visiting Turkey. He implored his readers to pursue greater familiarity, understanding, and cooperation between the peoples of Turkey and the Middle East. To reach a wider audience, the book was published in French translation in 1939, with only slight changes due to Atatürk's death and his succession by İnönü.[105]

The number and quality of the endorsements garnered by Khanki's books illustrate that Turkey still had its fair share of admirers in the Middle East even in the late 1930s. Indeed, some of Egypt's most respected and well-known leaders and intellectuals recommended the propagandist book to the Egyptian and Arab publics. The daily *al-Ahram* both commended the author and the text, and printed approving remarks on the book's qualities by important figures from various walks of Egyptian public life, including former Prime Minister Isma'il Sidqi Pasha, the Coptic Pope John XIX, the litterateur Salih Jawdat, the veteran women's rights activist Huda Sha'rawi, and the young up-and-coming female author and academic Bint al-Shati (pen name of 'Aisha 'Abd al-Rahman). In their published remarks they praised the leadership qualities of Atatürk and the "awakening" he stimulated in Turkey, and some of them reiterated the contention that Kemalist Turkey could and should serve as a model for emulation for the peoples of the East.[106]

The most praiseworthy quality virtually all biographers recognized in Atatürk was his ability to lead his people from despair to liberation, from occupation to independence. Among such admirers of the Turkish leader and his reforms were even some pan-Arab activists who otherwise were opposed to Turkey's territorial claims on Alexandretta. In Mandate Palestine and Iraq of the 1930s, for instance, some Arab nationalists presented the Atatürk-led defense of Anatolia as an inspiring example for a popular struggle against foreign occupiers. Mustafa Kemal's reputed success in mobilizing the downtrodden population of the land and in leading it to victory over the territorial schemes of major European powers and local non-Muslim populations, appeared to his Arab admirers to be offering insightful lessons for their struggle against the British colonial rule and the Jewish designs on the land. The Palestinian pan-Arab political activist Akram Zu'aytir, for instance, recalled in his memoirs how during campaigning and mobilization efforts in Palestine of the early 1930s, he used to feature in his lectures highlights from Mustafa Kemal's biography, presenting the Turkish leader's career as an inspirational story of patriotic resistance against his nation's enemies.[107] Similar motives convinced Ra'fat al-Dajani, an attorney and member of one of the most prominent Arab families in Palestine, to publish in 1935 his Arabic translation of a Turkish booklet entitled *Mustafa Kemal and His Four Horsemen*. The text described in very emotional terms the heroic struggle of Mustafa Kemal and the nationalist forces under his command against the French and Armenian efforts to occupy Southeastern Anatolia. Ironically, this was a region that quite a few Arab nationalists viewed as being rightfully part of natural Syria and the Arab homeland. The translator explained that rather than dwell on the specifics of the Turkish experience, his purpose in making the book accessible to Arab readers was to emphasize the importance of a great national leader for an effective struggle against foreign rule. In his preface, al-Dajani indeed made a direct analogy between the plight of the Turks during the war over Anatolia and the dire straits in which the Arab nation has found itself since the Great War, as a result of the perfidy and oppression of the European colonial powers. He therefore called upon the sons of the Arab nation to be inspired by the successful Turkish salvation of their homeland and to follow in the footstep of Mustafa Kemal and his supporters in an uncompromising struggle for the liberation of the Arab homeland, including Palestine. His book was recommended by several Palestinian Arab newspapers, and excerpts from it were published in installments in the daily *al-Jami'a al-Islamiya*.[108] A similar perspective encouraged an Iraqi army officer to publish in 1934 an Arabic translation of a Turkish book entitled *Mustafa Kemal and the Last Turkish-Greek War* only a year after its publication in Turkey. In the introduction to the book, which was dedicated to the Iraqi Chief of Staff Taha al-Hashimi, the translator explains that the book contains valuable military information, but more importantly, it offers a very inspiring example for the Iraqi people on what it takes to conduct a successful struggle for national liberation against enslavement by colonial powers (Figure 5.7).[109]

But whereas many Arab commentators highlighted Mustafa Kemal's role as a warrior-leader, others focused on his function as the educator-in-chief in independent Turkey. Two books that were published in Iraq and Lebanon in 1938, for instance, suggested that Arab societies would do well to follow his example by following the Turkish template for

صورة هزلية رمزية نمثل طرد الكماليين ابو ذييب من الاناضل

Figure 5.7 An Arab caricature of the Kemalists booting the Greeks out of Anatolia. From Husayn Ramzi al-Qabtan, *Mustafa Kamal wa-al-Harb al-Turkiya al-Yunaniya al-Akhira, aw Kayfa Jara' al-Hujum al-'Am* (Baghdad: Matba'at al-Furat, 1934), 184.

a very resolute implementation of wide-ranging reforms in national education. The book *Education and Schooling in Modern Turkey* was published by Muhammad Fadil al-Jamali. He was an Iraqi Shiite Arab who graduated from the American University in Beirut and earned his doctorate in Columbia University, before assuming senior positions in the Iraqi Ministry of Education from the early 1930s. Jamali was a committed Arab nationalist but also a great admirer of Mustafa Kemal and his educational reforms. Therefore, when he was commissioned by his government in 1937 to travel to Europe to study the best educational systems in the continent in order to suggest needed reforms in Iraqi education, he insisted on including Turkey in his tour of study. He spent six weeks in the Kemalist republic, and several months after his return to Baghdad, the Iraqi government published a book on his particular findings and impressions in Turkey. The study hailed the dynamism and educational reforms under the leadership of Mustafa Kemal and credited them for stimulating the recent national awakening in Turkey. The author surveyed in some detail the various policies and educational institutions in the Kemalist republic, with an approving emphasis on the incorporation of military ideals, standards, and discipline into the state schools, and on the fusion of Eastern and Western influences under the indispensable leadership of the educator-in-chief Atatürk.[110] The Lebanese educator Sa'id Sannu reached similar conclusions after visiting Turkey several times to collect material for a book entitled *Kemalist Turkey*. The author, an inspector in the Lebanese Ministry of Education, lauded Mustafa Kemal's effective educational policies and contrasted them sharply with the perfidious and allegedly incompetent by-design programs implemented by the colonial authorities in the Arab lands. Even as the dispute over Alexandretta was increasingly poisoning Turkey's relations with Syria in the late 1930s, Sannu called on the peoples of Syria, Lebanon, and neighboring Arab countries to vie for closer ties with Kemalist Turkey and to embrace it as a model for emulation toward national liberation and modernity.[111]

Turkey's reputation and prestige in the Middle East receded significantly in the late 1930s, but even then, the Kemalist republic was neither universally reviled nor devoid of any proponents. Indeed, when Atatürk died in November 1938, the obituaries in important Arab newspapers were for the most part very reverential, and his legacy of national struggle and transformational reforms was still admired by many intellectuals and political leaders in the Middle East. Commentaries in important dailies such as *al-Ahram* argued that he left a lasting impact on all the peoples of the East and a powerful legacy of many successful policies and reforms that could serve as models for emulation in the Middle East.[112] Only the most committed detractors of Kemalist Turkey, such as the Egyptian Islamist-leaning periodical *al-Risala*, took the opportunity to denounce him and his impact on Turkey. The journal had to concede that Atatürk did have impressive leadership skills, but denounced him for using them negatively in a manner allegedly similar to pernicious leaders such as Mussolini and Hitler.[113]

As the 1930s were coming to a close, the Kemalist republic lost much of its previous appeal in the wake of the conflict over Hatay, the warming relations between Ankara and the two major European colonial powers, the death of its charismatic leader and his replacement by the much less captivating İnönü, and the gradual coming of age of the radical first post-Ottoman generation in the Middle East. The seeds of these processes may be traced to earlier years in the interwar period, but their convergence began taking place only on the eve of World War II, and not as a result of Turkish disinterest in the Middle East or apathy toward Turkey's image in the region. In fact, official Turkey and its surrogates invested efforts throughout the 1930s to generate positive public image in the Middle East, with the cooperation and support of important figures in public and intellectual life in the region, who believed that various aspects of the Kemalist reforms could serve as a beneficial model for emulation in their own societies.

6 | *Strolling Through Istanbul*

Turkey's interest in capitalizing economically on its geographical proximity and historical ties to the Middle East, and its aspiration to improve its image in the region, converged in the field of tourism. The Turkish government and various business interests began investing greater efforts in attracting foreign tourists to Turkey in the wake of the global economic crisis in 1929, with the main motive being economic, but a secondary consideration also being the improvement of Turkey's image abroad. The foreign tourists were expected to contribute much needed hard currency to the Turkish economy, acquire appreciation for the Kemalist republic and its reforms, and perhaps become informal ambassadors of goodwill on Turkey's behalf.[1] The new appreciation of the importance of tourism prompted the government to organize in Istanbul in May 1930 a five-day international conference aimed at increasing tourism to Turkey. New visa regulations and a law that reduces the extent of military no-go zones were promulgated a few weeks before its opening, to facilitate the travel and vacationing of foreigners in Turkey.[2] Although the main focus of these efforts was on Europe, and to a lesser extent on North America too, the Turkish government and private stakeholders in its main tourist destinations were no less interested in attracting tourists from the Middle East. Historically, the old imperial capital and a number of other cultural and natural attractions in its vicinity and in Western Anatolia drew the largest numbers of visitors and vacationers. But the emergence of Ankara as the modernist face of Kemalist Turkey transformed this otherwise inconspicuous central Anatolian city, only a few hours train-ride from Istanbul, into another intriguing destination for foreign visitors who were interested in exploring the vibrant center of Kemalism in the 1930s.

Visitors from Egypt and the Levant were very conspicuous in Istanbul and other parts of Anatolia in late Ottoman times, but their numbers dropped significantly after the outbreak of the Great War. The

decade of violent conflict, death, and devastation that followed, over-
rode the appeal of the weather, natural beauty, and historical treasures
of various destinations in Anatolia. Only after the establishment of the
republic in 1923 and the restoration of public order did Turkey see a
small and gradual recovery in the number of visitors from the Middle East. In Ottoman times, well-to-do travelers from Egypt and from
neighboring countries were in the habit of spending the hot summer
months in the temprate climates of Istanbul, Izmir, and other destinations in their vicinity. Other visitors sought remedy for various health-
related issues in the hot springs of Yalova or Bursa. The wealthier visitors oftentimes owned summer houses on the shores of the Bosporus,
in the Prince Islands or elsewhere, whereas most others rented lodg-
ings for vacations that could range from a few days to a few months.
No visa was required and no residency or currency restriction was in
force, because until 1914 both Egypt and the Levant were formally
parts of the Ottoman Empire. The situation changed drastically in the
wake of the Treaty of Lausanne. New international borders, citizenship status, currency and customs regimes, and other factors made the
travel between Turkey and the Middle East more complicated, even as
changes in cultural tastes and social orientations precipitated the emergence of alternative destinations in Europe and Lebanon as greater
draws for vacationers from Egypt, Greater Syria, and Iraq.[3]

The relative stabilization of the political situation in Turkey and the
Middle East in the late 1920s led to a certain recovery in travel and
tourism to Anatolia, but still left much to be desired. For instance,
Egyptian royals and senior officials, oftentimes with family ties to Anatolia, began making their way back to Istanbul and its vicinity for
summer vacations in the late 1920s. But the overall number of travelers from Egypt to Turkey was still a far cry from the prewar figures.[4] The Turkish government and various business interests hoped
that better transportation options to the Middle East would help
reverse this downward trend. Turkey's first and most important private travel agency during the interwar period, the National Turkish
Tourist Agency (NATTA), indeed opened two of its first foreign offices
in the late 1920s in Cairo and Beirut.[5] And when the government-
run Touring and Automobile Club of Turkey opened offices abroad in
the interwar period, they included bureaus in Cairo, Alexandria, and
Jerusalem.[6]

The Turkish government and businesspeople in the tourism industry expected to capitalize on the inauguration of new transportation

services between Turkey and the Middle East. In 1926, an agreement was reached with the Simplon Orient Express to add to its European train service to Istanbul, a new leg from Haydarpaşa on the Asian side of the former imperial city to Aleppo in Syria and Tripoli in Lebanon, with connection services to Baghdad and Tehran on the one hand, and Damascus, Beirut, and Cairo on the other. In 1930 this Asian extension of the Orient Express was named the Taurus Express (*Toros Ekspresi*).[7] European-owned maritime lines between the Turkish ports of Mersin, Izmir, and Istanbul and ports in the Levant and Egypt also operated in the late 1920s, but their operators did not have any particular stake in serving Turkey's interests. In spring 1930 the Turkish government inaugurated its own direct steamship line between Istanbul and Alexandria, with the aim of supporting its own commercial interests. The regular service, with stops in Izmir and Piraeus, was seen as having a great potential for solidifying the trade, social, and political ties between Turkey and Egypt.[8] As of 1930, the Taurus Express and the Istanbul-Alexandria line each carried only about 10,000 passengers annually between Turkey and the Middle East. But the hopes and expectations in Turkey were that with proper advertisement and propaganda, this number could be increased to many tens of thousands annually. Particular importance was attached to influencing the younger generation of Middle Eastern people, who had little or no memory of Ottoman times, and thus no particular nostalgia or attachment to Anatolian destinations. In a report issued by the Turkish Ministry of National Economy in 1935, the necessity of promoting maritime tourism from Egypt and train-based tourism from the rest of the Middle East, was indeed emphasized.[9] Business interests, particularly in Istanbul and Izmir, were very invested in these efforts, at times much more than the government in Ankara, because the ties with the Middle East affected their economic interests more directly. The Turkish government was nevertheless also interested in the expansion of travel and commerce between Turkey and the Middle East, both for the anticipated economic benefits, and for the hope and expectation that the visitors would become ambassadors of goodwill on Turkey's behalf and help burnish its image and reputation in the region.

I The State That the Gazi Built

The prominent Egyptian journalist Mahmud Abu al-Fath was given in October 1931 the rare honor of a personal interview with Mustafa

Kemal, popularly known as the Gazi, the victorious war hero. The interview was timed by the Turkish government to take place a few weeks before Turkey and Egypt were scheduled to begin negotiations on a bilateral treaty of friendship. The Turkish President dedicated four hours to the meeting with the former editor-in-chief of the daily *al-Ahram*. The visiting journalist was also given access to Prime Minister İnönü and Foreign Minister Aras. All three Turkish leaders emphasized the fraternal bonds of friendship between the two nations, their personal admiration for the Egyptian people and their king, and their determination to overcome recent misunderstandings and restore the close relations of old for the benefit of the two nations.[10] But Ankara was interested in more than sending a message of amity and creating a positive atmosphere for the upcoming talks. The visiting Egyptian journalist was hosted by the Turkish government for five weeks, during which he was given the opportunity to observe both the vibrancy of the Kemalist republic and the attractiveness of the land as a travel and vacation destination. Ankara's expectation was that in his reporting on his experiences in Turkey, Abu al-Fath will intersperse positive commentary on the effects of the Kemalist reforms with exuberant impressions from the sights and sites of Turkey. His hosts must have been happy with the return on their investment. The prominent journalist's articles were full of admiration for the Kemalist success in transforming Turkey from being considered "the sick man of Europe" into a vibrant nation state with an exciting present and a bright future. His visit was the first of a series of sponsored tours in the years that followed in which Egyptian journalists and other shapers of public opinion were invited to Turkey by the government and other stakeholders for similar purposes.

The Egyptian newspaper of record published Abu al-Fath's reporting in a series of columns which were featured on its front page in December 1931, under the title "al-Ahram in Turkey." The articles included wide-ranging commentaries on the characteristics of the Turkish government and the effects of its reforms but also featured descriptions of some of its main tourist attractions in Western Anatolia. Abu al-Fath was given the opportunity to observe some of the deliberations of the Second Balkan Conference, which he used as a starting point for a discussion of Turkey's influential position in international affairs, particularly in southeast Europe. On another occasion, he was taken to the site of large military maneuvers of the Turkish army, which he detailed in awe, as part of a more general description of the

Turkish armed forces' proven track record in the war over Anatolia and their readiness to defend their country valiantly against any external threat. He contrasted the enviable position of Turkey, which, despite meager resources at its disposable, succeeded in building a modern military that was respected by friends and foes alike, with the situation of Egypt and other countries in the Middle East, which were weak and occupied despite having much greater resources at their disposal. After securing its sovereignty, the Turkish state could break the domination of foreigners over its economy and social life, as purportedly existed in Ottoman times, and lamentably was still the case in interwar Egypt. He explained that the establishment of a secular republic (*Jumhuriya 'Ilmaniya*), the steps taken toward the full emancipation of women, and the implementation of legal equality between all religious communities by no means turned Turkey into a European country. Instead, thanks to its bona fide independence and beneficial reforms, the government in Ankara could suppress the harmful activities of missionaries and to enforce the permeation of the national culture into every aspect of life in the republic, from requiring all store signs to be in Turkish to the imparting of a strong patriotic sentiment to the population. Besides these commentaries, which must have been music to the ears of the Turkish government, Abu al-Fath described his very positive impressions from the city of Istanbul, its historic treasures, and its natural beauty as well as the pleasant experiences he had in Bursa, Izmir, and a number of other vacation spots in Western Anatolia. His remarks on the efficiency and convenience of the Turkish shipping line between Alexandria and Istanbul drove home the implicit invitation to his readers to visit Turkey for its historical, cultural, and natural attractions as well as for observing its transformation into a modern state and society.[11]

Abu al-Fath was correct in his remarks on the Kemalist hostility toward Christian missionaries,[12] but the authorities were apparently willing to make some exceptions to help their bid for foreign tourists. In July 1932, an all-male group of 40 vacationers joined a tour organized by the Cairo YMCA and led by Donald Atwell, an American missionary and the secretary of the organization's branch in the Egyptian capital. The group included mostly Muslim and Christian Egyptians, among them lawyers, merchants, physicians, teachers, and journalists from the dailies *al-Ahram* and *al-Jihad*. One of these journalists, Tawfiq Habib, a young Egyptian Copt and a regularly featured columnist in *al-Ahram* (under his peculiar pen name "The Old Journalist"), mailed to Cairo reports on their experiences, which were published in Egypt's newspaper of record.[13] These columns were received well enough that after the group's return from its three-week vacation in Turkey, he published a book in which he described his exploits in and around Istanbul. As fate would have it, the group's first exciting experience happened aboard the steamer from Alexandria to the old imperial city. After the ship made its regular stop in Izmir, none others than Prime Minister İnönü and Foreign Minister Aras chanced to board the ship for the last leg of its voyage to Istanbul. They happened to be in the Aegean port city for the unveiling ceremony of a celebrated bronze statue of Mustafa Kemal on horseback, which took place on the occasion of the 10-year anniversary of the liberation of Izmir. When informed on the presence of the Egyptian group on board, the Turkish leaders immediately asked that the tourists be brought into their presence to personally welcome them to Turkey. They congratulated the Egyptians, wished them well, and expressed the Turkish people's great friendship and admiration toward their Egyptian brethren. In impromptu interviews each gave to Habib, both the Turkish Prime Minister and his Foreign Minister emphasized that they would like to warmly invite the Egyptian people to visit Turkey, promising that they would feel right at home, as if they were in their own homeland. Undoubtedly on cue from the Turkish government, when the ship arrived at the docks in Istanbul, the Egyptian visitors were pleasantly surprised to be welcomed very warmly by well-wishers and to see the Turkish newspapers of the following day reporting at length on their encounter with the Turkish leaders and their arrival in the city. Not surprisingly, the Istanbul press omitted any mention of the group's affiliation with the YMCA or of the presence of Christians among its members. Indeed, the daily *Cumhuriyet* referred to the group with the term "our coreligionists" in its reports on the visit and on how their arrival purportedly symbolized the unbreakable bonds of friendship and brotherhood between the Turkish and Egyptian peoples. The group's first day in Istanbul indeed took the form of a semiofficial visit rather than of a leisurely vacation. The Egyptian visitors met with Turkish officials and with members of professional organizations. The Egyptian reporters, for instance, were hosted by local Turkish journalists who welcomed them and shared with them Turkey's great expectations from its relations with Egypt, including in the field of tourism. Most of the rest of the Egyptian group's stay in Turkey was indeed dedicated to sightseeing and leisure activities.[14]

The group began its vacation with an extensive tour of the cultural and historical treasures on the European side, before settling for a leisurely stay in a YMCA summer camp on the Asian side. During the first week, the group devoted the daytime to visits of palaces, museums, mosques, and other historical and cultural sites but also attended lectures on the past successes and future goals of the Turkish republic. At night, they spent their time in some of the city's finest restaurants and night clubs. Habib shared with his readers his impressions from many of these places and establishments. For example, he reported that one of the main draws of some of the more popular taverns and cabarets was the fact that many of their waitresses and entertainers were young and beautiful girls from the city's substantial community of White Russian refugees. He thus presented the European side of Istanbul as offering visitors the opportunity to acquaint themselves with the Byzantine and Ottoman treasures of the past, the Kemalist achievements of the present, and various types of traditional and modern entertainment. The second half of the group's vacation was mostly spent in relaxation on a fashionable beach in Suadiye, on the Asian side of Istanbul, and in short excursions to the Prince Islands and to the thermal hot springs in Yalova. Habib reported that on the beach his group interacted with Turkish citizens of various ethnic and religious backgrounds, including Armenians, Greeks, and Jews, as well as with some foreign vacationers, including Bulgarian, Russian, British, and American tourists. They communicated with one another with a mix of Arabic, French, and English, which suggests that the Egyptian visitors were not conversant in Turkish. His enthusiastic reports on the trip, and his warm recommendation for all Egyptians and "Easterners" to visit the Kemalist republic were greatly appreciated in Turkey and by its surrogates in Egypt.[15]

The writings of Habib were in fact seen as such a great advertisement for tourism to Turkey that Ankara and various Turkish business interests sought to amplify and extend their effect. Descriptions of the Kemalist state often emphasized its strict disciplinarian attitude, and for a good reason. Habib, on the other hand, depicted it as a fun place for leisurely vacation. Turkish business interests in Egypt therefore hastened to sponsor the republication of his columns in a book form, headlined with the statement that "Turkey is the best summer destination for Egyptians" and with the first pages occupied by advertisements for Turkish tourism-related businesses. Among them were ads for the Turkish-owned Alexandria-Istanbul steamship line, the thermal hot springs in Yalova and their health benefits, the Alexandria branch of the Turkish government-owned *İş Bankası*, and the weekly *Muhadenet*, "the organ of the Turkish colony in Egypt."[16] The booklet had the misfortune of coming out just as the Fez Incident was souring Turkey's relations with Egypt. But the end of the controversy in January 1933 and the enthusiastic reception of Keriman Halis a few weeks later, helped convince the promoters of Turkish tourism to request Habib to publish a new testimonial on Turkey's attractiveness as a travel destination. He was offered the opportunity to spend a second vacation in Istanbul, all expenses paid by the host country, in return for the publication of his impressions in a new book. He already had vacation plans to spend the summer in a cruise to Greece and along the coasts of the Adriatic, but he simply could not pass on the generous Turkish offer. He thus spent 11 days in Istanbul in summer 1933, before proceeding from Turkey to Greece, to carry on with his earlier vacation plans. In the book he published after returning to Egypt, he again commended the allure of the old imperial city and the hospitability of its Turkish residents, while also sharing anecdotes on his encounters with other Egyptian vacationers in the city. This time around, however, there was much less leisurely lying on the beach for him and much more propagandistic tours of Kemalist institutions, such as a recently established People's House. He was also taken on a tour of a modern textile factory, shown around a new library, met Turkish women's rights activists, and was given lectures on the Kemalist reforms and system of government, and more particularly on the merits of the single-party regime. In his book, Habib duly contrasted the national unity in Turkey with the political divisiveness of the multiparty system in Egypt and commended the Kemalist regime for its nationalist economic policies, which he yet again contrasted with his own country's lack of significant government involvement in the economy. He further commented that to see the true beating heart of Kemalism he should have traveled to Ankara, but alas, there was not enough time for that. In short, Habib's second book was much shorter on leisure and fun than his earlier one, but its Turkish sponsors got what they paid for in terms of its run-of-the-mill Kemalist propaganda.[17]

Turkey's efforts to dim the memory of the Fez Incident and promote its brand was endorsed by the well-known lawyer and intellectual Fikri Abaza. He would remain a fixture of Egyptian public life for decades to come and later in life be known as the Dean of Journalists. He wrote a laudatory preface for Habib's book, based on his own impressions of a visit to Turkey, and argued that other Middle Eastern societies would do well to emulate many of the Kemalist reforms.[18] Abaza elaborated on this theme in a series of columns in the Egyptian press on his experiences in Turkey in summer 1933. In a column entitled "Long Live the Turks," for instance, Abaza shared how impressed he was with the everyday expression of patriotism and economic nationalism among the Turkish people. He sought to illustrate the point with several examples. One instance was when his group dined in a restaurant in Istanbul and ordered a whisky bottle. They were astonished, but very impressed, when the patriotic waiter refused to fulfill their request, explaining to them that he is willing to serve them only with local products, be they rakı, beer, or wine. In another instance, when Abaza returned to his hotel after an excursion outside Istanbul, he was surprised to discover that the hotel attendant disposed of his foreign cigarettes while he was out of town. The employee proudly admitted the deed, proclaimed it to be a patriotic act to promote local products, and offered to supply the visitor with Turkish brand matches and cigarettes. Rather than viewing such behaviors as unprofessional and scandalous, Abaza in fact described them as worthy of admiration and as illustrative of the voluntary patriotism and dedication of ordinary Turkish citizens to their national interests. He contrasted that praiseworthy approach with the apathy of the Egyptians, and the Turkish proud sovereignty with the economic domination of foreigners in Egypt. He testified that after spending time in Istanbul, he realized how libelous were accusations of Turkey as being "atheistic, unbelieving, and licentious." He attested that the mosques of the old imperial capital were in fact full of worshippers who performed their religious duties as of old, save for the fact that they were dressed differently and have ridden themselves of many superstitions and false practices. Abaza made his newly acquired emotional attachment to the Kemalist republic very evident when he declared in one of his columns in August 1933: "Greetings to you, oh Great Gazi, offered to your eminence from the bottom of my heart, mixed with my tears of emotion... Long live your homeland!... All the others can drop dead!"[19] Official Turkey certainly liked the sentiment, if not the exact rhetoric and the somewhat peculiar examples presented to illustrate the Turkish hospitality to foreign visitors.

Figure 6.1 The Egyptian friendship delegation. From "Wafd al-Wadad," *al-Musawwar*, August 25, 1933, 9.

The good track record of winning the admiration of visitors led Turkey to shift gears and organize a carefully picked group of Egyptian opinion setters for a visit in summer 1933. A 15-member delegation consisting of journalists and senior physicians was offered an opportunity to travel free of any expense to both Istanbul and its vicinity and to Ankara, the architectural and institutional face of New Turkey. The group, informally dubbed "the friendship delegation," was headed by Dr. Ali Ibrahim Pasha, vice-rector of Cairo University and the Dean of its Medical School, who also served as the head of the Egyptian Medical Association. The members included senior officials from Egypt's Ministry of Health and a number of other government agencies, as well as several prominent journalists from popular periodicals such as *al-Ahram* and *al-Muqtataf*. As in past Turkish outreach activities in Egypt, Hüseyin Remzi, the proprietor of the Cairo-based Turkish-Arabic weekly *Muhadenet*, helped organize and coordinate the endeavor, and this time around also chaperoned the Egyptian delegation (Figure 6.1).[20] The Turkish hosts went out of their

way to make the visit informative and enjoyable. The visitors were welcomed warmly and reports on their exploits appeared daily in the press.
These included meetings with members of professional associations,
visits to various Kemalist institutions, and lectures on the progress and
successes of Turkey. They were also shown around the city and were
given the opportunity to visit its historical and cultural treasures, as
well to sail the Bosporus and take a trip to the Prince Islands. At the
end of this part of the visit they were taken to Yalova, famous for its
thermal hot springs, which made it a favorite vacation destination for
Mustafa Kemal. Since the Turkish leader indeed happened to be in the
spa town at the time, it was arranged for the Egyptian delegation to
meet with him there rather than in Ankara. He congratulated the visitors very warmly as unofficial representatives of a brotherly nation,
wished them well, and called on them to share with their fellow Egyptians the great affection of Turkey to them, and its desire to invite them
to visit. The group was then taken to Bursa, before finally traveling to
Ankara. In the capital city they were received in the railway station
by government officials, and were lodged for the duration of their stay
in the Ankara Palace, the capital city's fanciest hotel in the 1930s. All
in all, during the Egyptian group's 20-day stay in Turkey, its members were given the VIP treatment that was usually reserved to foreign
diplomats and officials. Their experiences in visiting various institutions, establishments, and sites were covered widely and prominently
by both the Turkish and the Egyptian press, yet again signifying the
high visibility of the visit and the importance attached to it, at least
from Ankara's standpoint.[21]

Turkey's investment in hosting the "friendship delegation" paid
immediate dividends in positive coverage of the Kemalist republic in
the Egyptian press in late 1933. The journalists on the delegation wrote
articles in some of Egypt's most popular newspapers in which they
praised the Kemalist reforms, suggested that Turkey should serve as a
role model for reforms in Egypt and the Middle East, and advocated
the strengthening of ties between the Turkish and Egyptian peoples
and their governments. In some cases, the change in tone in the writing of some of these journalist was very striking, in comparison with
their harsh criticism of Turkey during the Fez Incident crisis less than
a year before. For example, Ahmad al-Sawi Muhammad of *al-Ahram*
was very critical of Turkey and its leader during the diplomatic crisis
in late 1932, but after spending more than two weeks in Turkey as

the government's guest, his tune changed significantly. In his post-visit columns he praised the leadership qualities of Mustafa Kemal and the success of an "Eastern" land such as Turkey to transform itself in such a short time from a backward society into a youthful and forward-looking country. He called on his countrymen in no uncertain terms to adopt Turkey as a model of a reform program that involves the adoption of European influence, on the one hand, and the building and nourishment of a unique nationalist culture and economic independence, on the other. Another member in the delegation, Fuad Sarruf, who was the editor-in-chief of the influential monthly *al-Muqtataf*, stroke a similar tone. In a series of articles in his journal he praised his hosts, their government, and their country. Sarruf, in his series of articles on his journey "From Cairo to Ankara," and al-Sawi Muhammad, in his "On the Road to Ankara," shared with their readers both general information on the Kemalist republic, its institutions, and reforms and anecdotes on their personal experiences in Turkey.[22]

Their reporting on Istanbul included not only the regular commentary on its historic structures and cultural institutions but also extensive references to entertainment options in the former imperial city. In one instance, al-Sawi Muhammad wrote about his visit to a Turkish movie theater and described in vivid detail how the audience became very emotionally and loudly involved in the plot. In another instance, the two Egyptian journalists described their impressions from the night clubs of Istanbul. They reported that the waitresses and female entertainers were mostly immigrants from Europe and that the clientele was overwhelmingly male, not unlike the situation in most Egyptian night clubs. The two in fact made direct comparisons between nightlife choices in Istanbul and in Cairo's famous entertainment district in Qasr al-Nil and suggested impressionistically that the Turkish night scene was three times as big. They therefore concluded that "the city of the caliphs" maintained much of its past ways. But whereas Sarruf described the old imperial city as magnificent and charming, al-Sawi Muhammad denounced it in very Kemalist-like terms as a painful reminder to both long-lost glory and a more recent detestable and corrupt past.

A year later, in 1934, the Turkish government indeed launched a campaign aimed at transforming popular entertainment and shifting it away from traditional forms associated with Ottoman times. The initiative involved efforts to suppress traditional Anatolian and Middle

Eastern music, which was very prevalent in Istanbul's popular enter-tainment joints, and replace it with European-inspired modern Turkish music. Subsequently, traditional songs and tunes were banned from the radio stations of Ankara and Istanbul, and the importation of gramo-phone records of Middle Eastern music was prohibited. To the utter frustration of the Kemalist authorities, various forms of the so-called *alaturka* music remained very popular nevertheless. After the inaugu-ration of the Egyptian State Radio in mid-1934, one form of subverting the campaign in Istanbul's cafes and entertainment establishments was tuning in to Arabic songs broadcasted from across the Mediterranean. Writing in 1936, the well-known Turkish journalist and music critic Peyami Safa, who was supportive of a stylized form of *alaturka* but not the more popular "tavern style," in fact complained that Egyp-tian music has become so popular in Istanbul because of the Egyptian radio broadcasts that misinformed Turkish listeners began viewing it as their own.[23] Once the formal ban on traditional forms of music was lifted in 1936, popular night clubs in Istanbul indeed began immedi-ately to offer shows featuring traditional Anatolian and Arab music and dances. Some of the most popular joints, such as the Belvü Garden in Harbiye or the London Beer House in Beyoğlu, employed Egyptian and Syrian singers and dancers in frequent "Arab revue" shows in the latter 1930s. Advertisements for these shows displayed musicians who were at times identified specifically as either Egyptian or Syrian and at others were depicted wearing a tarbush as a proximate signifier of their Middle Eastern background, or at least their form of music. Star per-formers in many shows throughout the late 1930s included the visiting "Egyptian film star and dancer" Tahiya Muhammad, better known as Tahiya Karioka, and the "dancing queen" and "Syrian star" Malika Jamal (Melika Cemal).[24] Istanbul, then, maintained many of the hall-marks of its pre-Kemalist past, which some visitors like Sarruf found refreshing and others like al-Sawi found depressing.

Both Egyptian journalists agreed that it was in Ankara that the true essence of New Turkey is revealed to the visitor in all its impressive magnificence. After Huda Sha'rawi visited Turkey in 1935, she shared with an Egyptian newspaper an anecdote about her meeting with a young Turkish boy aboard a train to the city of Bursa. She asked the youth what city he liked better, Ankara or Istanbul, and he immediately replied "Ankara," explaining that this is because it was where the Gazi resides and where his reforms originate. The Turkish government must have approved of the sentiment because the article was translated from Arabic to Turkish for dissemination as propaganda.[25] Sarruf and even more so al-Sawi Muhammad felt similarly about where the genuine essence of the Kemalist republic could be observed and experienced. Sarruf described in some detail his impressions from various institutions in the republic's capital, interspersing details on architecture and urban planning with long passages on the virtues of Mustafa Kemal and on the praiseful rule of the Republican People's Party. He commented approvingly that the RPP in Turkey displays "a combination of some aspects of the [Italian] Fascist Party, in that it represents the will of the nation, and of the Communist Party in Russia, in that it has monopoly on governance." At the same time, both Sarruf and al-Sawi Muhammad endorsed the Kemalist insistence that Turkey was not a dictatorship. But whereas al-Sawi Muhammad claimed that Turkey was in fact a democracy, Sarruf upheld the more defensible explanation that the Turkish government had laid strong foundations for a future democracy.

Judging by these commentaries, and in the case of al-Sawi Muhammad also later writings on Turkey, the sponsoring of the "friendship delegation" resulted in exactly the type of publications that Ankara desired.[26] Thanks in no small part to the efforts of official Turkey and its surrogates, Arab journalists thus helped counter negative imageries of the Kemalist republic with their positive testimonials. The popular illustrated weekly *al-Musawwar* continued the positive trend with a full-page article on "modern Turkey" in September 1933. The piece included captioned photos from Ankara, Istanbul, and Izmir. Some were photos focused on Kemalist institutions and symbols, whereas others were concerned with Turkey's historical and natural attractions. The former included photos of the İsmet Pasha Girls' Institute in Ankara and the recently installed statue of Mustafa Kemal facing the sea on horseback in Izmir. The latter involved tourist destinations such as the fortress of Rumelihisarı, a Bosporus scenery, and one of the Prince Islands. The photos and their accompanying text were framed as an invitation for Egyptians and other Arabs to visit both old and new Turkey and its natural and manmade attractions.[27]

One potential hindrance for Arab travelers was the legal inhibitions and strong prejudice of the Kemalist authorities against Middle Eastern clothes and headgears. The sensitivity of the issue was accentuated as a result of the Fez Incident of late 1932. Examination of written reports and of photos of the groups of Egyptian visitors to Turkey suggest that Arab travelers were likely expected to adhere to the Turkish law and refrain from wearing their *tarbush*, the fez-like red tasseled hat that was still the headgear of choice among the educated middle and upper classes in Egypt and Greater Syria of the 1930s. A Turkish journalist who traveled to Syria aboard a train in 1936 described a scene that may be representative of the practice of many Arab travelers to Turkey. He relates that as soon as the train crossed into Syria, male Arab passengers who returned from Turkey immediately opened their luggage to change from European-style clothes and hats into the types of clothes and headgears that were prevalent in their homelands since at least the nineteenth century.[28] In the case of the "friendship delegation," a photo taken on the docks in Alexandria, and published in the Egyptian press, shows the men wearing their tarbushes just before boarding the Turkish steamer to Istanbul. However, later photos, taken upon their arrival in Izmir and then in Istanbul, and published in the Turkish press, show them all either wearing fedoras or with no headgear at all.[29] It appears, however, that restrictions on the use of traditional articles of clothing by Arab visitors were not strictly enforced without exception. For example, in summer 1933, only a short time after the departure of the high-profile Egyptian delegation, a 30-member group of Syrian Boy Scouts visited Istanbul, en route to Europe. In photos taken at the foot of the Republic Monument in Taksim, and which were published in both the Turkish and Arabic press, they are waving the Syrian flag and wearing the kufiyahs that were part of their uniform (Figure 6.2).[30] In other instances in the latter 1930s, which are discussed later in the chapter, photos of Arab visitors to Istanbul show them very clearly wearing their tarbushes on Turkish soil. This, however, seem to have been the exception to the rule. For the most part, Arab visitors to Turkey likely changed their clothes, or at least their headgear, in accordance with official Turkey's demands, as many of them would have done while visiting European countries. None of the visitors in the delegations to Turkey expressed any public reservation regarding the implementation of Turkey's dress laws on visitors from the Middle East, which may be either a reflection of their own preferences or of understanding of Turkish sensitivities. Or perhaps they viewed the expectation to change their headgear as a minor annoyance and a sacrifice worthy of making in order to enjoy the natural and historical treasures of Turkey, and gain a firsthand impression on the state that the Gazi built.

Figure 6.2 Syrian scouts in Istanbul. From "al-Kashafa al-Suriyun fi Turkiya," *al-Musawwar*, September 8, 1933, 8.

II Setting Sail to Istanbul

Egyptian travelers to Turkey in the early 1930s crossed the Mediterranean almost invariably aboard Turkish steamships. The regular twice-weekly maritime service, with stops in Izmir and Piraeus, was opened in July 1930 with the aim of boosting passenger traffic and trade between the two countries. The new Turkish line signified the first time since the formation of the republic that the government-owned Turkish Navigation Company (*Seyrisefain*) established a steamship line to any foreign destination.[31] The decision to establish it was prompted by the suspension in early 1930 of an earlier direct Alexandria-Istanbul line which was operated until then by the British-owned Khedivial Mail

Line Company. With the global economic crisis that began in 1929 hitting hard the profitability of Turkish exports, the new Turkish service was expected to boost trade and passenger traffic between Turkey, Greece, and Egypt. Yet, the maintenance of the economic viability of the line proved very challenging. After a promising beginning in 1930, the number of passengers and the volume of freight appeared to be on the decline by 1932. The loss of business was so steep that by the first half of 1933 the revenues from the line were reportedly lower than the costs of its operation. The fact that the volume of agricultural exports from the Aegean region to Egypt fell by 70 percent between 1929 and 1933 didn't help the cause of the Alexandria line either. A major reorganization in the Turkish Navigation Company in 1933, which placed the line under the administration of the State Maritime Lines (*Devlet Deniz Yolları*), led the new management to ponder whether it might be an economically sounder decision to cancel the line to Alexandria. The ships that serviced it would then be reassigned to internal Turkish lines along the coasts of Anatolia.[32] Subsequently, just as the summer tourist season was approaching, a decision was taken in Ankara in June 1933 to abolish the regular Turkish steamship line to Alexandria. The surprising cancellation of the three-year-old line was not taken lightly in Istanbul, however. The decision ignited a firestorm of public controversy in the Turkish press, which reflected the degree to which some Turkish stakeholders were invested in Turkey's ties with Egypt.

The charge against the cancellation of the steamship line was led by the daily *Cumhuriyet* and its proprietor and editor-in-chief Yunus Nadi, who was also a member of parliament. As soon as the decision was made public in early June 1933, the newspaper began publishing a heavy dose of editorials and articles in support of maintaining the line operative. The aim was to generate enough public support to pressure the government-run company to reconsider its decision. The journal presented a slew of arguments to undercut the assertion that the service was economically unviable. One general point made was that the continued operation of the line was vital for the preservation and further expansion of the historical and valuable ties between Turkey and Egypt, and for the reassertion of the Kemalist republic's claim for regional importance in the Eastern Mediterranean. More specific points were made regarding the current and future profitability of the line. One recurrent argument asserted that the disappointing revenues were the result of the global economic crisis and that Turkey should weather that storm and protect its market share in Egypt in anticipation of the boom that would surely follow the current bust. Another argument contended that if the customs and taxes that were collected on the freight are factored in, the line was in fact profitable. Pointing out to the Italian, Greek, and Romanian policies of subsidizing their steamship lines to Alexandria, commentators in *Cumhuriyet* insisted that the Turkish government should do the same for strategic reasons and out of long-term economic considerations. As the public campaign against the cancellation heated, the government was pressed to respond. The official in charge was Celal Bayar, the Minister of National Economy, who was at the time in Europe on state business. After more than a week of intense campaign in the press of Istanbul, and a day before the cancellation of the line was to come into effect, he finally telegraphed from London a public directive to suspend the decision until a further review will be held shortly. Subsequently, the line was saved for the time being and its operation was guaranteed until further evaluation. *Cumhuriyet* celebrated the decision with screaming headlines and extensive reporting, crediting the reversal to its own public campaign, and vowing to keep harping on the importance of the steamship line to Alexandria until a determination is made to maintain it permanently.[33]

With the fate of the maritime service still hung in the balance, supporters of its continuation kept the high intensity of their public campaign against its cancellation. *Cumhuriyet* continued leading the way, with *Muhadenet* in Cairo also weighing in to express the interest of the Turkish colony in Egypt in the preservation of the service. The Istanbul daily meanwhile published on its front page an appeal to Prime Minister İnönü to personally intervene in the matter, and for more than two weeks printed daily editorials and reports on the political, social, and economic importance of the steamship line. This was not a consensual view in the Turkish press, however. Mehmet Asım Us of the daily *Vakit*, for example, argued that the unprofitability of the line and the pressing need for more steamships to handle traffic between Turkish ports made the maintenance of the service to Egypt a luxury that Turkey simply could not afford. *Cumhuriyet* countered that the financial losses were much smaller than claimed, that the timing of the planned cancellation just before the beginning of the summer tourist season was inconceivable, and that the vast majority of Turks and Egyptians

Gazetemizin bir hizmeti

İskenderiye hattının ilgasından vazgeçildi

Celâl Bey, seferlere devam edilmesini bildirdi, mesele yeniden tetkik edilecek

Figure 6.3 *Cumhuriyet*'s headline celebrating the continuation of the Istanbul-Alexandria maritime line. From "Gazetemizin bir Hizmeti: İskenderiye hattının ilgasından vazgeçildi," *Cumhuriyet*, June 25, 1933, 1.

were supportive of the continued operation of the service. The public debates continued until finally, after long weeks of uncertainty, the government made its determination in early July, and *Cumhuriyet* could declare triumphantly: "We have won our case: the decision to cancel the Alexandria Line has been rescinded." The influential daily reported that the decision was received with great relief on both sides of the Mediterranean, because the majority of Turks and Egyptians understood the importance of the maritime service for bolstering the fraternal bonds of friendship between the two nations (Figure 6.3).[34]

Cumhuriyet could bask in the glory of its success in helping to save the line, but public campaigns could not substitute for a real improvement in the service's financial situation. Initial indications appeared to suggest a successful summer season in 1933. But by early fall it became clear that the number of passengers, and to a lesser degree the volume of freight too, continued to drop for the second year in a row. The consequent growing losses led at the end of the year to a decision to decrease the frequency of the service from weekly to biweekly.[35] But Turkey did not yet give up on the line. In early April 1934, Mehmet Sadettin Serim, the director of State Maritime Lines, traveled to Alexandria to discuss with Egyptian officials, merchants, businesspeople, and other stakeholders ways to increase the traffic aboard the Turkish ships. Serim was encouraged enough by the talks to increase the frequency of the line again to a weekly service during the upcoming summer season of 1934. As part of the effort to put the service's finances in the black, the company began promoting in late May discounted tickets for 11-day cruises and tours of Izmir, Athens, and Alexandria. In Cairo, meanwhile, the journal *Muhadenet* invested significant real estate on its pages for the promotion of Turkey as a desirable tourist destination. Its proprietor even pledged to publish free of charge advertisements for any Turkish hotel, rental property, or tourism-oriented business which was interested in attracting Egyptian visitors. On its part, the Turkish government adopted in June 1934 new regulations that lowered the custom dues and tariffs on travelers arriving from Alexandria and Piraeus aboard the Turkish steamships. With all these new measures in place, *Cumhuriyet* reported very optimistically that the stage was set for the arrival of many groups of Egyptian travelers and for a very successful tourist season.[36]

One of the most unusual group of Egyptian visitors in summer 1934 was of boy scouts affiliated with the Young Muslim Rover Scouts (*Jawalat al-Shuban al-Muslimin*) in Alexandria. They were led by Abd al-Wahhab al-Najjar, an Islamic scholar and author of popular books on the early caliphs and on the prophets of Islam. Since the late 1920s, he won some renown in Egypt as a founding member of the pan-Islamic organization of the Young Men's Muslim Association (*Jam'iyyat al-Shuban al-Muslimin*). The organization's main aim was to shield the Muslim youth in Egypt and beyond from the influence of Christian missionaries and non-Muslims more generally, as well as from the impact of harmful European ideological and cultural influences. Abd al-Wahhab al-Najjar was well traveled in the Middle East. In summer 1933, for example, he led a group of young members of the

الشبان المسلمون فى تركيا

Figure 6.4 The Young Men's Muslim Association delegation in Istanbul. From *al-Musawwar*, August 31, 1934, 25.

organization on a tour of Palestine.[37] Considering his organization's focus and goals, the decision to lead another group of 22 members on a tour of Kemalist Turkey was far from an obvious choice. The fact that the visit was reported on quite extensively in both the Turkish and Egyptian press, along with photos and commentaries, suggests that it might have been part of the Turkish outreach efforts in Egypt. Indeed, when the group was still in Alexandria before boarding the ship to Istanbul, its members gave an interview to Turkish reporters in which they expressed their great admiration and appreciation for "Turkey, the land of heroes." A photo of the group in Istanbul, a few days later, shows al-Najjar wearing a traditional Islamic religious garb and turban, while some members of his group were donning tarbushes on Turkish soil (Figure 6.4). Taken together, it appears that both sides of this unusual engagement were willing to do their part to make it a successful visit. The travelers began their tour of Istanbul with a visit to the Republic Monument in Taksim, where they listened to a lecture on Turkey's heroic struggle for independence, before laying a wreath and observing three minutes of silence in honor of the fallen. In the next three weeks the group visited mosques, palaces, and museums in Istanbul, traveled to the Prince Islands and sailed along the shores of Bosporus, was led on excursions to Bursa and Yalova, and visited the beating heart of Kemalism in Ankara. In short, they were taken on a tour that combined history, culture, nature, and contemporary politics, which was by then the usual package marketed by Turkey to prospective tourists from the Middle East.[38]

Cumhuriyet trumpeted the arrival of this group and of other visitors from Egypt through much of the summer, but ultimately even that greatest supporter of the steamship line had to admit its difficulties. The number of passengers simply did not meet the expectations, despite occasional jubilant headlines such as "350 Egyptian travelers arrived in our city." In order to change the fortunes of the Alexandria-Istanbul line the figures needed to be consistently in the thousands, not in the hundreds. Moreover, much greater numbers of Egyptians appeared to be interested in visiting Greece than Turkey, including many who sailed aboard the Turkish steamships but disembarked in Piraeus rather than continued to Izmir or Istanbul. *Cumhuriyet* called on the government to ease various financial and customs restrictions on travelers and increase the advertisement efforts in Egypt in order to reverse this trend.[39]

The Turkish government indeed invested new efforts to promote the line in 1935, even as the mounting financial losses strengthened the hand of the advocates of its cancellation. A small office of the Touring and Automobile Club of Turkey already operated since 1933 on the premises of the Alexandria branch of the government-owned İş Bank. In early 1935 a decision was taken to boost this modest presence by the opening of two new Turkish tourism offices, in Cairo and Alexandria. These branches were entrusted with promoting Turkey as a desirable travel destination and served as the agents of Turkey's State Maritime Line, State Railway Administration, and the Touring and Automobile Club. In a related move, the presidents of the Turkish and Egyptian touring clubs announced the establishment of a Turkish-Egyptian Friendship Association, with its stated aims being to stimulate trade and tourism between the two countries and strengthen the social and cultural bonds between the two peoples.[40] As in the previous years, however, it became clear by late 1935 that the goal of increasing the traffic on the Alexandria-Istanbul line was easier said than done. The numbers continued to disappoint and the losses continued to pile. Turkey could not compete effectively with the much greater investments in tourism advertisement by European countries, could not reverse changing cultural tastes that made European destinations more appealing to many Egyptians and could not overcome its well-deserved image as disciplinarian and restrictive rather than a place of leisure and entertainment. Subsequently, after another tourism season ended in disappointment, a decision was made in late 1935 to cancel the Istanbul-Alexandria steamship line after five years of regular service. Having learned the lesson of the public campaign two years earlier, the line was formally suspended indefinitely rather than abolished, but the ramifications of the decision were clear enough.[41]

Supporters of the continued operation of the steamship line again riled against the decision, but this time around the economic realities of its operation trumped their protests and arguments. The renewed campaign for the line was yet again led by the daily *Cumhuriyet*, although with somewhat less gusto than two years earlier, and with a powerful pushback in favor of the line's cancellation from the Ankara-based semiofficial daily *Ulus*.[42] Still, in the period between the cancellation decision in December 1935 and the eve of the summer tourist season in May 1936, *Cumhuriyet* and other Istanbul-based periodicals published dozens of columns and articles in support of the line's restoration. Yunus Nadi, the daily's proprietor and influential editor-in-chief, who was by the mid-1930s known for his pro-Nazi sympathies, argued that the line was indispensable in order to preserve Turkey's ties with Egypt in general and with the "many Egyptians who share racial bonds" with the Turkish people in particular. Previous arguments regarding defending Turkey's international position in the Eastern Mediterranean, protecting its market share in Egypt's economy in anticipation of better economic times, and tending to the interests of Turkish exporters and tourism-dependent businesses, were also aired yet again. The daily indicated that senior officials in Türkofis, the government agency charged with boosting Turkey's exports, shared this perspective too. Nevertheless, the indefinite suspension stood.[43] The Istanbul-Alexandria line was never restored until after World War II, despite occasional reports on its planned reopening in the late 1930s. Maritime transportation between Istanbul and Alexandria was carried after 1935 by foreign steamship lines, most important of which was the Romanian service from the port city of Constanţa to Alexandria with a stop in Istanbul.[44]

The cancellation of the steamship line did not mean that the Kemalist authorities and other Turkish stakeholders gave up completely on their outreach efforts to Egyptian travelers. In summer 1936, for example, a very high profile Egyptian delegation was enticed to visit Turkey on their way to the Summer Olympic Games in Berlin. The group consisted of 94 university students, and was led by 10 professors. The Kemalist authorities did not want to pass on the opportunity to secure favorable coverage and publicity in Egypt and perhaps win some hearts and minds among the members of the large delegation of young educated people on a path of upward mobility. Turkey was particularly interested in outreach to Egypt at the time, as the visit took place shortly after King Farouk's succession to the throne, the establishment of a new majority cabinet led by the popular Wafd party, and the opening of British-Egyptian negotiations toward formal independence to Egypt. The high public profile of the group was attested to by the fact that Prime Minister al-Nahhas took the time to bid its members farewell in person, and to wish them success as Egypt's informal ambassadors of goodwill.[45] The Turkish government resolved to make the planned 10-day stay of the group in Turkey as impressive and memorable as possible, both for the short-term impact it might have in Egypt, and for the long-term effect it may have on this group of likely future academics, intellectuals, professionals, businesspeople, and government officials.

The propaganda efforts began immediately upon the entry into Turkish waters of the Romanian steamer that transported the Egyptian group from Alexandria. As the ship approached Çanakkale, opposite the site of the Battle of Gallipoli, it was boarded by the governor of the province, who came to greet the Egyptian visitors in person. They were then given a lecture on the heroic defense of the Straits during the Great War, purportedly under the magnificent command of Mustafa Kemal, to which the Egyptians reportedly responded with cries of "Long live Mustafa Kemal Atatürk" and "Long live independent Turkey," before throwing into the water a wreath in honor of the fallen. Upon arrival in Istanbul, the Egyptian visitors were received warmly at the docks. Since they happened to arrive in Turkey just as the Montreux Convention was being signed, they also had the opportunity to observe massive public demonstrations in support of the Kemalist regime's achievement in securing the right to remilitarize the Straits. The hosting of the large Egyptian group was shared by various entities, including the governor of Istanbul, the University, and the Touring and Automobile Club. According to a report in the Egyptian daily *al-Ahram*, the group's leaders were pleasantly surprised to learn that the Turkish hosts decided to cover all their travel, lodging, and dining expenses while in Turkey. They were more generally impressed with the kindness and hospitality they encountered. Published photos of members in the group show Professor Zaki Umar with his tarbush safely on his head in Istanbul, which yet again suggests that the desire to refrain from unpleasant tensions led the Turkish authorities to not make a fuss about that issue. The group's weeklong stay in the old imperial city included a combination of visits to Istanbul's famous historic and natural attractions and tours of modern institutions such as the university, hospitals, and People Houses. The Egyptian visitors were also taken on short excursions to Yalova, to bathe in its famous hot springs, and to Bursa, for a hike on Uludağ Mountain, before proceeding to Ankara to observe the modern achievements of the Kemalist government. Par for their course, the Turkish authorities sought to thus expose the visitors both to Turkey's traditional tourist attractions and to its modern institutions. The propaganda value of these events was obvious. The Turkish and Egyptian press reported that at the end of their 10-day stay in Turkey, the grateful members of the large delegation were full of appreciation for their hosting by their "eastern brothers" and their leader "the Father of the East."[46]

The escalation of the conflict over Hatay in late 1936 and through 1937 put the Turkish outreach to Egyptian visitors on a temporary hold until summer 1938. Warming up in Turkish-Egyptian bilateral relations in the face of the perceived common Italian threat, and Ankara's desire to dispel accusations that its demands on Hatay were fueled by anti-Arab sentiments, informed the decision to sponsor the visit of another large group of students and professors from Cairo University. The visit came about shortly after Foreign Minister Aras's official visit to Egypt in spring 1938, and only weeks before the Egyptian royal yacht *al-Mahrusa*, visited Istanbul with the commander of the Egyptian fleet on board, which was followed shortly by a visit to the city by Aziz Ali al-Masri, the Inspector-General of the Egyptian army, who once played a pivotal role in the Arab Revolt during the Great War.[47] All the expenses of the 30-member group and the professors who led it were covered by the Turkish government. At a time when the Turkish press was complaining that "the aim of the Syrian press is to provoke the Arab world against Turkey," this and a few other initiatives were part of an effort to present a friendly face of Turkey to Egypt and other Arab countries in the region. Within that context, the Egyptian student group's stay in Istanbul happened to coincide with a visit by Egyptian athletes for a friendly competition with local athletes. The Egyptian students indeed were invited to watch the sporting events. They were part of a large crowd of thousands of spectators who flocked to the stadium, among them hundreds of Egyptian nationals on their summer vacation in Istanbul, as well as senior Turkish officials and the ambassadors of Egypt and Iraq. The remainder of the group's time in Turkey was devoted to the by then usual mix of historical, cultural, and natural sites of traditional touristic value and propagandistic lectures and visits to modern institutions of the Kemalist republic.[48]

The Turkish outreach to Egyptian visitors remained steady throughout the 1930s, but the initial hopes that substantial number of Egyptian tourist could be attracted to Turkey mostly faded by the end of the decade. The indefinite suspension of the Alexandria-Istanbul steamship line in 1935, and the decision not to recommence it in the years that followed, attest to that reality. Indeed, in his venerating book on Turkey and Atatürk, which was published in Egypt in 1938, the only topic for which Aziz Khanki took the Kemalist republic to task was its purported insufficient efforts to attract Egyptian visitors to Turkey. He lamented the fact that European advertising budgets for their tourist attractions were much larger and therefore more effective in attracting Egyptian travelers to their countries. He implored the Turkish government to intensify its efforts in this respect, because the arrival of more Egyptian travelers to Turkey would help "boost the political, economic, social, familial, educational, and intellectual bonds" between the two important Eastern Mediterranean neighbors.[49] By that point in time on the eve of World War II, however, any prospect for significant increase in Egyptian traffic to Turkey, or via its territory to Europe, appeared to be less likely linked to maritime transportation between Alexandria and Istanbul, and more to the development of overland routes through the Levant. On its way back home, the 30-member Egyptian student group that visited Turkey in summer 1938 indeed boarded the Taurus Express in Ankara for the short ride to Aleppo in Syria en route to Cairo. With both economic gains and propaganda benefits in mind, this was indeed the most important means of transportation that the Turkish government was hopeful would carry many more visitors from the Middle East, either to vacation in Turkey or to travel through it to Europe.

III Making Tracks for Ankara

Agatha Christie published her hugely successful detective novel *Murder on the Orient Express* in 1934, at a time when transcontinental train travel appeared to be very promising for the future. Although the most important parts of the plot take place as the fictitious passengers travel from Istanbul across southeast Europe toward European destinations, the novel in fact begins in Aleppo, Syria, where the reader first meets the main protagonist and two other important characters. They are waiting in the railway station to board the Taurus Express to Istanbul. The main protagonist is a Belgian, returning from Syria, and the other two characters are said to be a British woman who arrived from Baghdad by way of Kirkuk and Mosul and an English colonel from India. The three Western passengers ride the train "through the magnificent scenery of the Taurus" and look down "toward the Cilician Gates," before having a stopover in the city of Konya, and finally arriving in Haydarpaşa, on the Asian side of Istanbul. The main protagonist plans to spend a few days in the former imperial city before proceeding to Europe, while the other two express the desire to do the same.[50] In the interwar period, Turkish officials were very much hopeful and expectant that, just like in Christie's story, a growing number of travelers between Europe, the Middle East, and India will ride the train through its territory, make stopovers in its cities, and make significant economic contributions to Turkey's economy. But whereas Christie's story was focused primarily on Western travelers, Ankara expected that Middle Eastern visitors too would take advantage of the service, enrich its coffers, and perhaps return home with greater appreciation and affection for the Kemalist republic and its reforms.

The Istanbul-Aleppo line began service in the mid-1920s, but the history of the line and its planning as a transcontinental service stretched back to late Ottoman times. The Orient Express line first reached Istanbul in 1889, with a more southerly route of the Simplon Orient Express inaugurated in 1919. The idea to establish a separate service from Berlin to Istanbul, and then across Anatolia and to Mesopotamia, was

also first hatched in the late 1800s. After various political complications were overcome in the early 1900s, the work on the line began
in earnest, but it was yet to be completed by the outbreak of World
War I. After the establishment of the republic, Turkey negotiated with
the Compagnie Internationale des Wagons-Lits, which operated the
Simplon-Orient Express, an agreement to run a complementary service
from Istanbul to Aleppo, on the existing tracks of completed sections
of the Baghdad Railway. The European company began operating the
line in 1927, with a connecting service to Tripoli in Lebanon. It was initially a twice-weekly service but was expanded to three times a week in
the early 1930s. Automobile transportation services connected Aleppo
with Mosul in Iraq and with various destinations in Greater Syria,
but the long-term plan was to extend one branch of the railway from
Aleppo to Baghdad and to the head of the Persian Gulf and another
branch to Cairo in Egypt by way of Beirut and Haifa.[51] New tracks in
Syria extended the line in 1933 all the way to the Iraqi border. Work
on continuing it to Baghdad was well under way by the late 1930s,
but the service was not yet operable at the beginning of World War II.
Inside Turkey, the Turkish government effected a major change in its
route in 1935, following the completion of the Ankara-Adana line. The
service was then rerouted to a longer path by way of Ankara, rather
than passing through the original shorter route by way of Konya. The
declared goal of the change was that "this way the foreign passengers
on the Taurus Express will have the opportunity to fulfill their desire to
visit Ankara while traveling through Turkey."[52] The Kemalist government was indeed more interested in attracting foreign travelers to the
modern republican capital than to the conservative central Anatolian
city.

The Taurus Express proved quite popular with passengers who traveled between Turkey, Syria, and Iraq in the 1930s (Map 6.1). In 1935
it was estimated that about 15,000 foreigners rode aboard the Taurus Express annually, with several thousands of them being from Iraq,
Greater Syria, and Egypt. It is less clear how many of them only transited to Europe by way of Turkey, and how many traveled to Turkey for
business or vacation. The Turkish government was occasionally offering discounts and deals in an effort to lure more passengers from the
Middle East. For instance, in 1935 the Turkish State Railways offered
a special discount rate to Iraqi passengers, in an effort to convince
the estimated 2,000 well-to-do Iraqi families who spent their summer

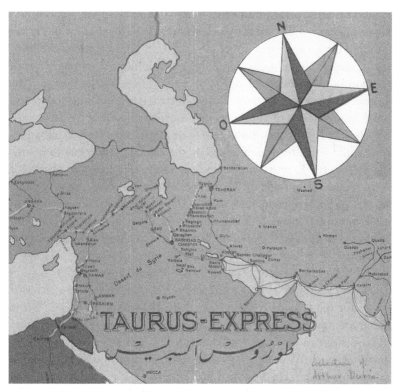

Map 6.1 The Taurus Express. From Compagnie Internationale des Wagons-Lits, *Taurus-Express* (Paris, 1938), cover.

vacations in Lebanon to reconsider Turkey as an attractive alternative. Likewise, significant discounts were offered to Middle Eastern travelers who rode the Taurus Express to visit the annual Izmir International Fair. Just like in the case with Egyptian tourism, some Turkish dailies, led by *Cumhuriyet*, took it upon themselves to raise public awareness to the importance of Middle Eastern tourism and lobby the government for initiatives to encourage its growth. The influential daily celebrated the arrival of groups of tourists from the Middle East with reports and photos and reminded the authorities how important these visitors were, both from an economic standpoint and from the perspective of winning hearts and minds in the region.[53] At least once, in 1938, the Turkish government did try to organize a visit of a large group of journalists from Syria and Lebanon aboard the Taurus Express, in a similar fashion to its initiatives in Egypt. But a flare-up in Hatay led to an abrupt cancellation of the visit.[54] Indeed, with the shadow of Turkey looming large over Syria in the late 1930s, it became pretty challenging to present the Kemalist republic as a hospitable neighbor. Visits of journalists and intellectuals who arrived to Turkey overland aboard the Taurus Express were usually individualized, with no sponsorship and much less oversight of Turkish government handlers. For the most part, travelers to Turkey who published their experiences were usually persons who were already impressed by the Kemalist state before boarding the Taurus Express and were therefore predisposed to observe it through rose-tinted glasses. There were a few exceptions, however. The reports of two commentators who arrived in Turkey aboard the Taurus Express in the mid-1930s epitomize the range of attitudes and deep polarization in Arab societies in the region regarding the Kemalist government and its reforms.

The Iraqi law student Husayn Ali al-A'zami traveled to Turkey in 1935, and his impressions served as the basis for a series of articles he wrote for the Baghdadi nationalist daily *al-Istiqlal*. He was 28 years old at the time and in the final stages of his studies in the Iraqi Faculty of Law (*Kulliyat al-Huquq*) in Baghdad. This was his first step in a long and distinguished career as a prominent intellectual and legal scholar in monarchic Iraq.[55] He described his impressions and experiences from the time he boarded the Taurus Express and through his stay in the Kemalist republic in a long series of more than 20 articles under the title of "What I have witnessed in Turkey." His reports include a mix of remarks on the train service, personal anecdotes during his visit, and general commentaries on the Kemalist government and its reforms and their applicability as examples for emulation in Iraq. The general tone of his eyewitness account was of admiration toward the achievements of the Kemalist government under the capable leadership of Atatürk. He assured his readers that neither the Turkish state nor its leader were hostile to Islam or supportive of atheism in any way or shape. After visiting the mosques of Istanbul he concluded that malicious accusations that Turkey was suppressing or subverting Islam were unsubstantiated. He insisted that the mosques of the old imperial city were full of devout worshippers without any hindrance from the authorities, which purportedly proved that neither the transformation of Hagia Sophia into a museum, nor the use of translated Turkish texts in some aspects of the worship, justified the libeling of the government as antireligious.

He likewise found the economic rationale for having Sunday as the day of rest to be sound, and in no way anti-Islamic. Proceeding with his vigorous defense of the Kemalist government, he went on to reassure his readers that the various Kemalist social reforms, and in particular the emancipation of women, did not lead to any breakdown in social order or morality. The opposite was the truth, he insisted. As mothers, wives, and professionals under the new conditions, educated Turkish women could now contribute to the collective interests of the nation much more than before. He suggested that prior to his visit, he was skeptical about Kemalism. But after spending time in Turkey, he became convinced that the Iraqi people in general, and the educated elites in particular, would do well to study the Kemalist reforms and take example from them, particularly on how to get rid of foreign rule and establish a powerful state and robust society.[56]

In his ode to the Kemalist state, however, al-A'zami also illustrated, perhaps inadvertently, at least one major aspect that made it difficult for Turkey to attract leisure tourism from the Middle East. The Iraqi visitor, like some Egyptian travelers before him, wrote with admiration about the permeation of nationalist thought and practice into every aspect of public and private life in the Kemalist state. He commended Turkey's economic nationalism and applauded Ankara's encouragement of the militarization and securitization of society. He reported approvingly on the insistence of business owners, service providers, and the population as a whole on the consumption of only Turkish goods and products. He was as impressed with the military-style training and discipline of the Turkish youth, which he claimed was easily observed by visitors to the country. Furthermore, he remarked favorably that from the moment the Taurus Express crossed the border from Syria into Turkey and until he left the Kemalist republic, he felt that he was being under constant surveillance by the authorities and by ordinary people alike. In several instances he noticed that Turkish citizens were looking at him with suspicion, and in a few cases these concerned individuals indeed reported on him to Turkish law enforcement agencies. He was not physically harassed, however, nor was he offended. In fact, he viewed these experiences not as inhospitable, xenophobic, and intimidating, but rather as impressive displays of the serious commitment of the Turkish government and its people to the security of their state and society. He contrasted this praiseworthy national mobilization against potential foreign threats and subversive activities with the free hand purportedly given to Zionist agents in Iraq to engage unscathed in all sorts of nefarious activities. The Iraqi commentator understood all these manifestations of committed Turkish patriotism, and the like-mindedness and cooperation between people and government, as the result of a system defined by the wholehearted acceptance of the doctrine of "one leader, one party, one nation." He concluded that this was the most important explanation for the difference between the powerful and unified Turkey and the socially divided and politically unstable Iraq. In short, he made direct analogies between Kemalist Turkey, Fascist Italy, and Nazi Germany and identified what he believed were admirable and emulable characteristics of Iraq's powerful neighbor to the north.[57] Although al-A'zami's ideas sat well with an influential current of militarist nationalism in Iraq of the 1930s, albeit not a consensual one,[58] the way he depicted Turkey was certainly not as an ideal or particularly attractive vacation destination.

And yet, quite a few senior Iraqi and other Middle Eastern statesmen did occasionally travel aboard the Taurus Express by way of Turkey and enjoyed taking vacations in Istanbul. In most instances a few days of leisure in the imperial city or on the shores of the Bosporus were part of a trip to Europe. In 1936, for example, Sheikh Hamad bin 'Isa Al Khalifa of Bahrain preferred the overland railway service through Anatolia over the alternative land and sea routes through Beirut, Haifa, or Port Said. Like many Middle Eastern leaders in the 1930s, he did not pass on the opportunity of spending a few days in Istanbul, before boarding the Taurus Express to Syria on his way back to Bahrain. Senior Syrian statesmen, such as Prime Minister Jamil Mardam, made similar choices in the mid-1930s, before the escalation of the conflict over Hatay in 1938 made such preferences politically untenable.[59] In a few cases, Turkey was the specific destination of Middle Eastern leaders, who enjoyed taking vacations in Istanbul and visiting the haunts of their youth in the former Ottoman capital. This was particularly evident with some Iraqi leaders, who sometimes spent time in Turkey out of their choice, and at others as a convenient place for their political exile. Stopovers in Ankara, in contrast, were virtually always strictly for official state business, and their duration was kept to the necessary minimum. Nuri al-Said in particular, whether as Foreign Minister or Prime Minister of Iraq, enjoyed taking a few days off in Istanbul during his many travels aboard the Taurus Express to or from Europe in the 1930s. Like most other senior Iraqi officials of the interwar period, he was very well conversed in Turkish and very familiar with the old imperial capital from his days in the service of the Ottoman Empire.[60] Taha al-Hashimi, the Iraqi Chief of Staff and brother of Prime Minister Yasin al-Hashimi, also spent several days of vacation in Istanbul in October 1936, on his way back from Europe. He planned to end the vacation with a short visit to the Turkish capital for talks with his Turkish counterparts before riding the Taurus Express to Aleppo on his way back to Baghdad. But while in Ankara, his brother was overthrown in the first military coup in the history of Iraq and was forced to leave the country for exile. Taha too opted to take a prolonged vacation in Turkey rather than risk trying to return to Iraq. During this period of exile he traveled occasionally to Syria and Lebanon, but he was finally able to return to Iraq only after the assassination of the coup leader in August 1937. In an ironic reversal of fortunes, the abrupt end of the coup regime forced another senior Iraqi leader to seek political refuge in Turkey. Hikmat Sulayman, who served as Prime Minister under the coup regime from October 1936 to August 1937, was even more intimately familiar with the old imperial capital. He was the brother of Mahmud Shevket Pasha, one of the most famous Grand Viziers of the late Ottoman period and a respected martyr of the Young Turk period. In 1933, when he served as Iraq's Minister of the Interior, Sulayman spent a month-long summer vacation in a mansion on the shores of the Bosporus. Four years later, when he was forced into exile after the fall of the coup regime, he chose to again board the Taurus Express to Istanbul to spend a political cooldown period in Turkey. Shortly after taking temporary residence in the old Ottoman capital, he may have crossed paths with Abd al-Illah, the brother-in-law of king Ghazi of Iraq, who spent weeks-long vacation on the shores of the Bosporus in October 1937. Less than two years later, after the young king's death, Abd al-Illah would become in April 1939 the regent to the throne of Iraq.[61] These dignitaries, who belonged to the last Ottoman generation in Iraq, may have adopted the ideology of Arab nationalism in the closing years of the empire, but their ideological and political choices did not erase the allure of the old imperial city, which was much easier to reach since the late 1920s thanks to the Taurus Express.

With only a few exceptions, most published reports by Arab visitors to Turkey in the 1930s were written by admirers of the Kemalist regime. Most Arab critics of Turkey in the interwar period opted to keep away from Anatolia. The Egyptian 'Abd al-Wahhab 'Azzam was the rare exception. By the time he boarded the Taurus Express in July 1937 to travel from Aleppo to Istanbul, the scholar, journalist, and future Egyptian diplomat was a veteran contributor to the Islamist-leaning journal *al-Risala*. The weekly was widely read in Egypt, Iraq, and the Levant and was well documented for its contention that "Kemalist Turkey is a non-religious state," using the Islamist-preferred term *la-diniya*, which implied atheism rather than merely secularism.[62] 'Azzam spent almost two months in Turkey in summer 1937. He published some of his impressions from the trip in a series of articles in *al-Risala*, under the title "Between Cairo and Istanbul." Two years later, he added more information on his travels to other cities in Anatolia, in a book he wrote on his travels in Turkey and many other countries. The Islamist-leaning author was neither an admirer of ethnic nationalism nor of the dictatorial regimes that were spreading in Europe and winning hearts and minds in the Middle East. He reported that he visited Istanbul twice before, most lately in 1929, but that following the acceleration and radicalization of the nationalist and secularist policies of the Kemalist government he decided to stay away from Anatolia thereafter. What convinced this well-traveled writer to board the Taurus Express and travel to Istanbul in 1937 is not explained, but the fact that nothing he saw changed his negative views on Turkey is very apparent. Indeed, only a few months after his return from Turkey, he was the driving force behind the establishment in spring 1938 of the "Association of Islamic Brotherhood," as an ecumenical organization aimed at promoting Islamic solidarity and unity.[63]

'Azzam's journalistic reports on his experiences in Turkey were very peculiar in that he oftentimes opted to send a message to his readers through silences rather than statements. In fact, he did not include any explicit criticism of Turkey in his published reports, perhaps in order to leave the door open for future visits. Instead, in his journalistic reports he mostly simply disregarded the current government and present political conditions in Turkey, and instead focused in a very deliberate manner on the land's pre-Islamic past and Islamic history. For example, he entitled the specific piece on his journey from Syria to Turkey "From Damascus to Constantinople" (*Qustantiniya*), before describing the first city as the capital of the great Umayyad Caliphate and using the increasingly obsolete name of the latter to focus on its past as the city of the Christian Roman emperors. To drive the message home, he writes that as the train was approaching the famous

Cilician Gates in the Taurus Mountains, he was reminded that this pass must have been where the frontier lines used to lie for so many centuries between the Abode of Islam to the south and the lands of the infidels to the north. Incidentally, or not, the Taurus Mountains range was also where many Arab nationalists argued that the borders between Turkey and Syria should have been marked. After setting this historical tone, 'Azzam has nothing to say in his journalistic report about his impressions of Ankara and instead proceeds to immediately discuss his arrival in Istanbul and its glorious history as the capital of the Ottoman Empire. Even though his hotel was near Taksim, the most modern and vibrant part of the city, he says virtually nothing about modern aspects of city life and on the impact of the Kemalist reforms. His reports were quite explicitly pointing at what was lost to the Turks and other Muslims because of Ankara's policies, without even the slightest allusion to anything that might have been gained.[64] The readers of *al-Risala*, who were fed for years a steady diet of articles that were very critical of the purported distancing of Turkey from Islam and from the peoples of the East, were likely well attuned to the implicit messages of 'Azzam's articles. Two years later, when he published his book, 'Azzam did include additional information on his visits to Ankara, Bursa, Konya, and Adana. Here he only made passing references to the Kemalist government, while reporting time and again on the deep religiosity of the ordinary Turks and suggesting that they were very friendly toward Egyptians and Iraqis, which made him hopeful for a future of a more Islamic Turkey. 'Azzam's book clearly attests to that he did not return from Turkey any more appreciative of its government and its policies than he was when boarding the Taurus Express in Aleppo to begin his journey.[65]

The expectations that the train service between Turkey and the Middle East may offer major contributions to Turkey's economy and to its image in the region were likewise proven to be overstated. The number of travelers between Turkey and the Middle East, and through Turkey to Europe or back, remained relatively stable. In his book, 'Azzam does refer matter-of-factly to chance meetings in Istanbul and on the train with fellow Egyptians, Iraqis, and Syrians.[66] But hopes that the extension of the railway line to Baghdad would boost the traffic significantly proved unfulfilled. When the Taurus Express service to Baghdad was finally inaugurated in July 1940, World War II was already affecting much of Europe, and its shadow was already looming large over the

Middle East. After the Axis powers' invasion of the Balkans in 1941, on the one hand, and the British occupation of Syria and Iraq, on the other, the Taurus Express and the Simplon-Orient Express operated as virtually the only functional transportation service between German-occupied Europe and the Allied-dominated Middle East. The Taurus Express carried diplomats, spies, businesspeople, refugees, and ordinary folks between Turkey and the Middle East during the war, but probably hardly any tourists and vacationers as was originally hoped and expected.[67] Maritime transportation to Turkey was completely disrupted during the war years, as the waters of the Mediterranean, and after 1941 of the Black Sea too, became arenas for maritime battles between the Axis and Allied navies. Immediately upon the end of hostilities in 1945, and a decade after suspending the line due to financial losses, Turkey moved to reinaugurate the steamship line between Istanbul and Alexandria.[68] Neither then, nor at no point during the interwar period, did any ideological consideration prescribed a concerted Turkish effort to turn Turkey's back on the Middle East, either metaphorically or practically. It is true that the travel of Turkish citizens to the Middle East was not encouraged, as it was bound to siphon away needed foreign currency and risked exposing the travelers to anti-Kemalist influences. Visits to the region were therefore condoned only for absolutely necessary reasons, usually on state affairs or for business. For example, Mustafa Kemal's own adopted daughter Afet (İnan) visited Egypt in October 1933, including tours of the pyramids and Cairo's historic mosques, but that was for the specific purpose of expanding her knowledge and horizons as a budding historian.[69] But Turkey was certainly not averse to hosting visitors from the Middle East in the interwar period, in view of their expected economic contributions and because of the hope that they would become informal ambassadors of goodwill on Turkey's behalf.[70] In short, Kemalist Turkey of the interwar period sought controlled interactions on Ankara's terms rather than severance of ties and building metaphorical and real barriers between Turkey and the Middle East. Most of the expectations from these ties were frustrated not as a result of a deliberate ideological choice but because they were not close to the top of Ankara's long list of priorities and because of circumstances beyond Turkey's control.

7 | *A Distant Neighbor*

The relations between the Kemalist republic and the Middle East in the interwar period have been commented on quite extensively but studied very insufficiently in the historiography of modern Turkey. The main reason for that was the all but consensual assumption that these relations either amounted to very little or were virtually nonexistent. One popular textbook on Turkish foreign policy, for instance, suggests that the British and French dominance of much of the region during the interwar period "had the fortunate effect for Turkey of virtually removing the Middle East from its list of foreign policy concerns until 1941."[1] Another prominent scholar of the modern history of Turkey argues along similar lines that from the mid-1920s, "Ankara turned away from the Arab Middle East, not because Turkey was hostile to the Arabs or to Islam, as conventional wisdom would have us believe, but because the Arab world had lost its independence to Britain and France and was incapable of acting independently."[2] Interwar Turkey was thus purportedly sending a strong message to the world, as explained by an expert on Turkish foreign policy, stating that "we are satisfied to live within our borders and have no wish to interfere in matters beyond our frontiers."[3]

This book has sought to suggest otherwise, both in terms of Turkey's actual policies and their perception by contemporaries during the interwar period. Turkey's interests and involvement in the Middle East during the 1930s may not have been Ankara's top priority. They were obviously much more limited in scope and importance than in Ottoman times. But Turkey certainly did not turn its back on the Middle East during the early republic, nor were its interests and involvement in the region insignificant or nonexistent, as has been suggested in many studies on modern Turkey and its foreign policy.

As the 1930s were coming to an end and the winds of war were beginning to blow over Europe, Turkey appeared to be anything but resolved to detach itself from the Middle East. Hatay was formally annexed to Turkey in July 1939, despite loud protests in many Syrian cities. This apparent instance of Turkish revisionism was obviously not overlooked by scholars of the period, but it was generally presented as sui generis, or "an exceptional case of irredentism, consisting of the use of 'pressure' with a military power hovering in the background combined with some heavy 'bargaining' with the French."[4] The border modifications with Iran in the early 1930s were in fact secured through similar means, albeit with much lower regional and international stakes. Moreover, it was far from clear to contemporaries in 1939 that with the rapidly changing international situation, Turkey might not seek to annex other parts of northern Syria, and perhaps of Iraq too. Kemalist Turkey was certainly not an aggressive revisionist power in the mold of Nazi Germany or Fascist Italy by any stretch, but it is safe to say that in all the important capitals of Europe, and in the Middle East too, it was generally assumed on the eve of World War II that Ankara would be more than willing to push its Middle Eastern borders southward if a good opportunity presented itself. This widely held assumption was largely informed by Turkey's very active diplomacy in the Middle East in the late 1930s, its very evident interest in extending its transportation systems into the region, and persistent suspicions that it was not fully resigned to the loss of territories in northern Syria and Iraq that were claimed by the National Pact. Ankara's engagement in various forms of outreach and public diplomacy in the Middle East did not appear to indicate disinterest in the region either. As the world was entering a period of severe instability and uncertainty with the outbreak of war in Europe, the future relations of Turkey and the Middle East were far from predetermined, and certainly not set since the 1920s on a course of deliberate disengagement and detachment. The actual distancing of Turkey and the Middle East in fact took place within the context of the specific circumstances of World War II and the early Cold War.

Many of the developments that eventually played a major role in distancing Turkey from the Middle East of course did have their roots in the interwar period. Among these, one can count the nationalist and pan-Arab radicalization of much of the youth in countries such as Syria, Iraq, and Egypt; the instilling of a strong sentiment of ethnic distinction and superiority among the young generation of the Kemalist elite in Turkey; the festering controversy over the annexation of Hatay; the emergence of the Palestine question as a focus of regional politics;

and the early steps taken toward the emergence of a regional Arab state system. Yet, all these processes were still in their early phases in the 1930s, and none reached a critical stage by the outbreak of World War II. Their seeds were sown in the interwar period and began to germinate as the 1930s were coming to a close, but it was the circumstances and developments in the following decades that supplied them with the conditions and nutrients that ensured their rapid growth and prevalence over other possible choices, which eventually culminated in the long-term and deliberate detachment and mutual distancing between Turkey and the Middle East.

I A Status Quo State

The outbreak of World War II precipitated dramatic changes in Turkey's geopolitical situation in general, and in its engagement with the Middle East in particular. The signing of the Molotov-Ribbentrop Pact in August 1939, only days before the beginning of the German invasion of Poland, opened a period of uncertainty that shook the Kemalist republic's foreign policy to the core. Despite cooling off in its relations with Moscow since 1936, Ankara still operated in the late 1930s under the assumption of general Soviet support for its policies in the Middle East, as has been the case since the early days of the republic. When Turkey, Britain, and France declared in mid-1939 their intention to negotiate a strategic defense agreement, Ankara assumed that separate treaties between the two Western European powers and the Soviet Union would complement what was essentially conceived as an instrument to check Italian aggression in the Balkan and Mediterranean arenas. But once the Soviet Union switched sides so surprisingly, and invaded the eastern part of Poland in coordination with Germany, Turkey's calculus changed rapidly and dramatically. After high-level talks in Moscow failed to achieve Soviet reassurances to Turkey's territorial integrity in general, and its sovereignty in the Straits in particular, Ankara opted to finalize the negotiations and sign a defensive treaty with Britain and France in mid-October 1939, despite Soviet and German advices not to do so. At this point in time, Turkey viewed the new treaty as necessary measure against potential Soviet aggression, as much as Italian.[5] The subsequent Soviet invasion and occupation of Finland, the Baltic states, and parts of Romania by late 1940, even as the French army suffered a shockingly rapid defeat to the Wehrmacht by late June, while Italian and German armies were marching into the Balkan states, only increased Ankara's fears that it might be targeted for territorial demands and threats of invasion.[6] These unsettling developments in 1939–1940, particularly regarding the Soviet position, cut Turkey to size. Gone were any aspirations to serve as a leading actor in southeast Europe through the Balkan Pact, or in the Middle East through the Treaty of Saadabad. The defense of Turkey's existing borders became Ankara's first priority, as the government was seeking to navigate in the uncertain waters of the early years of World War II (Map 7.1).

Dramatic developments in 1941 prompted Turkey to shortly explore deserting its position of nonbelligerence and its commitment to the preservation of its Middle Eastern borders. In the first half of 1941, the British government was engaged in negotiations with Turkey about the prospects of Ankara's entry into the war on Britain's side. The talks involved discussions on the possibility of a Turkish military contribution to a British advance on the Vichy France–controlled territories of Syria and Lebanon. Throughout these negotiations, Britain weighed its options under the assumption that Turkey would likely demand a territorial compensation in northern Syria in return for its cooperation, perhaps including the city of Aleppo. Suspicions about such Turkish designs on Syrian lands were spreading far and wide among the Arab political elites as well. Britain eventually acted on its own, occupying Iraq in May 1941, and Syria and Lebanon in June, thus establishing effective control over the Middle Eastern territories south of Turkey's borders. In the second half of 1941, after the Axis forces completed the occupation of the Balkans, and in the wake of the German surprise attack on the Soviet Union in late June, it was the Nazi government's turn to consider luring Turkey to join their side, partly by dangling the award of territories in northern Syria and perhaps in northern Iraq too as bait. Both British officials and statesmen, all the way up to Prime Minister Winston Churchill, and German negotiators and leaders, all the way to Adolf Hitler himself, were indeed convinced that Turkey maintained a strong interest in revising its Middle Eastern borders. That is because, despite public declarations to the contrary, in secret negotiations with both London and Berlin, Turkish officials indicated Ankara's likely interest in pushing its borders to the south. All these talks eventually came to naught, as the German failure to defeat the Soviet Union and the United States's entry to the war convinced Turkey

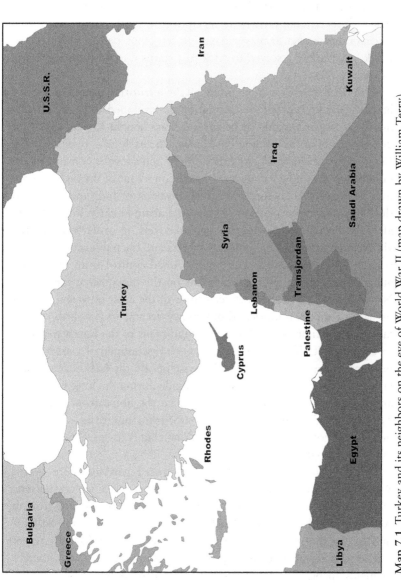

Map 7.1 Turkey and its neighbors on the eve of World War II (map drawn by William Terry).

to maintain its nonbelligerent position and continue hedging its bets until the outcome of the war became clearer. With the Axis forces and their allies controlling the Balkan states to its west, Allied armies occupying all its Middle Eastern frontiers to the south and east, and the German and Soviet armies engaged in ferocious battles north of the Black Sea, Turkey resolved to stick to a status quo position regarding its own borders.[7]

With the flames of war engulfing all the territories around it, Turkey had little use for the diplomatic relations it developed in the region during the interwar period. To be sure, Ankara sought to keep a tab on developments in the Middle East during the early war years. Feridun Cemal Erkin, a senior foreign office official and a former consul-general in Beirut in the mid-1930s, was thus sent on a tour of the region's capitals in early 1941, before the British invasion of Iraq and Syria and the Anglo-Soviet occupation of Iran, and again in early 1942, shortly after the British and Soviet military takeovers, in order to gauge the views and moods of local political leaders and the public at large.[8] But with most of the Middle East under Allied control from mid-1941, and the fate of the region dependent on the outcome of the war in North Africa and Europe between some of the most powerful nations on earth, regional politics and diplomacy became of very little importance for the time being. Ankara's grand plans of the interwar period to carve for itself a major role in the transcontinental transit trade between Europe and Asia were likewise put on the backburner. Similarly, as Turkey entered into survival mode during the long war years, addressing the dire economic situation in the home front, including by heavy-handed treatment of the non-Muslim minorities, took precedence over continued reforms or making claims to serve as a shining model for progressive modernity.

Turkey's commitment to a status quo stance regarding its pre–World War II borders hardened further as the Allied eventual victory became increasingly evident from 1943. With Soviet armies occupying Iranian Azerbaijan in the east since 1941, and driving south into the Balkans in the west in 1944, Turkey was increasingly concerned with Soviet threats to its sovereignty. Arab political elites in the region continued to be highly suspicious of possible Turkish territorial demands on Syria's territory well into 1943.[9] By then, however, Turkey was in fact focused on resisting Soviet revisionism in Eastern Anatolia and the Straits and lost any leverage it might have had to pursue revisionist claims on any neighboring country. Subsequently, in the last two years of the war, Ankara adopted a defensive mode that was increasingly dependent on diplomatic, military, economic, and technical assistance from Britain and the United States, particularly after breaking off trade and diplomatic relations with Germany in August 1944 and declaring war on the rapidly crumbling Nazi regime in February 1945. This increasing reliance on the Western allies was not welcome by all veteran Kemalist statesmen of the interwar period. Indeed, none other than former Foreign Minister Tevfik Rüştü Aras, who served as Turkey's chief diplomat from 1923 and until shortly after Atatürk's death in 1938, warned against any step that might be interpreted in Moscow as unfriendly. In a series of newspaper articles in early 1945, Aras advised the Turkish government to resort to the prewar policy of maintaining equal distance and equally friendly relations with both "our great neighbor and friend" the Soviet Union and Great Britain and their American allies. He explained that in the interwar period, this moderate policy was essential for Turkey's ability to protect its interests and exert regional influence, including in the Middle East.[10] The decision makers in Ankara and an emerging consensus in the Turkish political elite of the late 1940s dictated otherwise. President İnönü and the ruling party were in fact so determined to secure the protection and economic assistance of the emerging Western alliance that they were willing to approve of the gradual transformation of their non-democratic single-party regime into a competitive multiparty parliamentary system and posit Turkey as a truly status quo power more than ever before.

II On the Outside Looking In

The late 1940s and early 1950s witnessed the gradual incorporation of Turkey into the American-led Atlantic alliance, which influenced its position vis-à-vis the Middle East. Beginning in 1947, the Truman doctrine secured for Turkey the promise of American military support in case of Soviet aggression, and the Marshall Plan helped prop up its struggling economy. The gradual transition to democracy, culminating in a peaceful shift of power to the main opposition party in 1950, and the subsequent dispatch of a Turkish brigade to Korea to fight on the side of the American-led UN forces helped cement Turkey's position within the emerging bipolar world of the early Cold War. Its acceptance into North Atlantic Treaty Organization in 1952 sealed Turkey's formal position as a member of the western alliance. Turkey was expected to serve as a major bulwark against Soviet penetration of the Middle East. Within this context, Ankara was involved since the late 1940s in various political, military, and economic plans for the establishment of pro-Western regional groupings and alliances. Turkey indeed signed in 1947 treaties of friendship with Iraq and Transjordan, and King Abdallah of Transjordan traveled to Turkey on an official visit as a head of state, exactly a decade after his previous informal visit in 1937. His hope to secure Turkish support for his ambitions in Greater Syria in return for his recognition of the annexation of Hatay remained unfulfilled. At the same time, Turkish decision makers were considering the merits of the establishment of a customs union with Iraq, which would later be extended to other countries in the region. A detailed study was produced by a senior Turkish government official in support of the project, but it never reached a policy-making stage.[11] Political instability in Iraq, the war in Palestine and its regional effects, Ankara's recognition of the state of Israel, and the political uncertainty in Turkey after the transition to democracy, all combined to limit the Turkish involvement in Middle Eastern affairs at the close of the 1940s.[12]

The surprising electoral victory of the Democrat Party in the parliamentary election of 1950 precipitated a period of renewed Turkish activism in the Middle East on a level not seen since the 1930s. In the early 1950s, Prime Minister Adnan Menderes and President Celal Bayar paid official visits to Iraq, Jordan, and Lebanon as part of their efforts to establish a pro-Western regional defensive alliance, despite stiff Egyptian, Syrian, and Saudi opposition. Turkey appeared to achieve a breakthrough with the signing of a strategic treaty with Pakistan in 1954, which precipitated the conclusion of a military agreement with Iraq in 1955 and the establishment in the same year of a military alliance that came to be known as the Baghdad Pact, which included Turkey, Iraq, Iran, Pakistan, and Britain. Although Turkish efforts to pressure Jordan and Lebanon to join the pact failed, Ankara's involvement in regional affairs appeared on the rise in the mid-1950, similar to appearances in the late 1930s. Indeed, the Treaty of Saadabad was presented by many observers at the time as a precursor to the Baghdad Pact, despite the very different regional and global circumstances of these two eras.

Turkey's engagement with the Middle East in the early Cold War was managed under very different conditions than during the interwar period. In the multipolar world of Atatürk's time, the Kemalist republic presented itself as fiercely and proudly independent from foreign dictates. It was perceived neither as subservient to Soviet Union in the 1920s nor as under the sway of Britain and France in the late 1930s. That was not the situation after World War II. In the bipolar world of the early Cold War, Turkey was resigned to accept the role of a junior ally of the United States and became dependent on Washington for its security and economic recovery. Subsequently, whereas during Atatürk's time, Ankara's involvement in the Middle East was generally understood by friends and foes to represent its own interests and policy goals, during the early Cold War, its regional initiatives could be easily construed, fairly or not, as serving first and foremost American and British policies and interests. Soviet propaganda and pan-Arab media outlets, particularly in Egypt after the revolution of 1952 and in Syria after the coup of 1954, indeed sought to present Turkey as a regional subcontractor on behalf of the Western imperialist powers and their exploitative capitalist interests. Turkey's evident economic reliance on the United States during a period of economic liberalization under the Democrat Party rule increased the believability of such damning appraisals. This was very different situation than in the 1930s, when Turkey projected to the Middle East an image of a rapidly industrializing country that was implementing policies of economic nationalism to secure its long-term prosperity and independence from earlier dependency on foreign capital and investments. This façade began to dissipate on the eve of World War II and crumbled completely in its wake. Along with it, Turkey's image as a modernist, progressive, and reformist country dissolved too. Many of the interwar policies of the single-party government were diluted or eliminated in the late 1940s and early 1950s after the transition to a democratic multiparty regime, and the new government allowed the reappearance in the public sphere of various forms of conservatism. In these circumstances, Western propaganda efforts to present Turkey as a model for emulation in recently decolonized states rang hollow in much of the Middle East, certainly in comparison with the Kemalist republic's image as a genuine pathbreaker during the interwar period. The change in perceptions and imageries of Turkey were gradual but very evident in Arabic publications in the post–World War II Middle East.

A book which was published in 1946 by the Palestinian intellectual Muhammad 'Izzat Darwaza reveals that some imageries of the prewar period still held sway in the mid-1940s. Darwaza, who was a prominent pan-Arab activist in the interwar period, was forced to take refuge in Damascus during the Arab Revolt in Palestine in the late 1930s. When the British forces occupied Syria in 1941, he and fellow pan-Arab activists escaped arrest by crossing the border to Turkey and then requesting and receiving political asylum from the Turkish government. He stayed in Turkey until the end of the war, where in 1945 he wrote a book entitled *Modern Turkey*. He published the book a year later, in Lebanon, just as he was about to join the Arab Higher Committee, which was the recognized leadership of the Palestinian struggle for the establishment of full Arab sovereignty over the whole territory of Mandate Palestine. In his book, Darwaza explores the history of Turkey since the early republic in a very laudatory tone and with particular appreciation of the Kemalist reforms of the interwar period. He does state in the preface that the Arab reader should find the work as a useful introduction to both Kemalist policies worthy of Arab emulation, and others that the Arabs should beware of adopting. But the text itself is almost invariably very enthusiastically praiseful when discussing Turkey's political, social, economic, and cultural policies and reforms during the interwar period. Depicting Atatürk as instrumental for the success of the transformation of his country, Darwaza suggests that the Turkish example should inspire the Arabs in general and their youth in particular, as to how a strong and capable leadership coupled with a resolute national will could help them emulate Turkey's success to rid the homeland of foreign dominance and launch a series of highly successful reforms to solve similar problems as faced by Arab societies.[13]

A book published in Beirut only a year later shows how perceptions of Turkey were changing rapidly in the bipolar world of the late 1940s. Fittingly entitled *Turkey between Two Superpowers*, the book came out in 1947, a few months after France evacuated its last troops from Syria and Lebanon, and even as Turkey was increasingly seeking American assurances for its security. The author, Basil Daqqaq, offers a generally favorable description of the Turkish nationalist policies and reforms of the 1930s, albeit with the exception of Hatay, but is generally critical of Ankara's diplomatic engagement with the newly independent Arab governments in the region in the immediate aftermath of World War II. The book argues that the annexation of Hatay exposed the hollowness of Turkey's claim during the interwar period to being content with its Lausanne borders. The result was tense Turkish-Syrian relations, as newly independent Syria demanded the restoration of its sovereignty in Alexandretta and the return of refugees that were forced to leave their homes and seek shelter in Syria and Lebanon. Daqqaq argues that the concurrent "professed rapprochement between the Turks and Arabs" in 1946–1947, which found expression in high-level talks between Turkey and Lebanon, Jordan, and Iraq, and in the signing of friendship agreements with the two Hashemite kingdoms, "was accomplished under the auspices of the British and Americans." He in fact insists that Turkey was involved in these diplomatic negotiations halfheartedly, simply to satisfy American demands because of Ankara's complete military, economic, and diplomatic dependence on Washington. In sum, the author still describes the Kemalist policies of the interwar period as effective and impressive, but postwar Turkey is belittled as a subservient tool of American power.[14]

The same sort of criticism of Ankara as submissive instrument of foreign powers increased in volume and intensified in its tone after the Egyptian Revolution of 1952. A book published in Cairo in 1954 under the auspices of the new regime of Gamal Abdel Nasser, illustrates the depiction of Turkey by the most powerful Arab state and under the most popular pan-Arab leader of the 1950s and 1960s. Entitled *Turkey and Arab Politics*, the book was cowritten by Amin Shakir, a member of the Free Officers movement, and two government employees who were also part-time historians. The preface was credited to none other but Nasser himself, still as Prime Minister of Egypt. Published two years after Turkey joined NATO and five years after it recognized Israel, the book was part of a series of publications that included titles such as *Leaders of the Gangs of Colonialism* and *This Is Zionism*. It was written at a time when relations between Cairo and Ankara were still very tense, but not as hostile as they would become in 1955 in the wake of the establishment of the Baghdad Pact, on the one hand, and the Soviet-sponsored Egyptian-Czechoslovak arms deal, on the other. In the preface to the book, Nasser opted to point out possible reasons for cooperation between the Turkish and Arab peoples. He mentioned that they share a long history of good relations and that they all were the victims of the same imperialist powers that in the wake of the Great War–occupied Izmir, Damascus, and Cairo. He suggested that the Arabs and Turks should not be divided by the scheming of the foreign enemies that seek to dominate them but rather should unite in resistance against the forces of imperialism and in a common struggle to secure their complete independence.[15] The main body of the text, however, is much more directly critical of Turkey, both in its purported earlier manifestation as the Ottoman Empire, and in its newer republican form. The Ottoman Turks are accused not only of establishing a destructive imperialist rule over the Arab lands, but also of deliberately preparing the ground for their colonization by the European powers. Mustafa Kemal is credited with breaking this mold in the early 1920s and fighting against the foreign imperialists, which purportedly won him the wholehearted support of the Arabs. But he is bitterly criticized for then turning his back on the Arabs in the Treaty of Lausanne, in which he accepted the European colonization of the Arab lands. He then compounded this sin by initiating a series of reforms that were intended to destroy the historical, religious, social, and cultural ties between Arabs and Turks, in order to facilitate the detachment of Turkey from the Arab and Muslim East and its attachment instead to the European West. The authors acknowledge that Mustafa Kemal saved Turkey from falling under foreign rule but insist that the excessive price for that was the loss of freedoms for all citizens of Turkey and the particularly cruel suppression of the Kurdish uprisings. The current leadership of Turkey in the 1950s was invited to atone for Turkey's past sins by returning Alexandretta to Syrian sovereignty, ending Ankara's spurious association with the oppressive West, and restoring Turkey's authentic affiliation to the peoples of the East.[16] Portions of this narrative were already in place during the interwar period, but it was only after 1952 that it was embraced so powerfully outside of Syria and soon adopted as the predominant narrative in the Arab Middle East in the decades that followed.

Not surprisingly, the main effort at presenting a counternarrative on Turkish-Arab relations was produced in Iraq, Turkey's ally in the Baghdad Pact. Colonel Shakir Sabir's *History of Turco-Iraqi Friendship*, which was published in early 1955 with endorsements by Prime Minister Nuri al-Said and the Iraqi Chief of Staff Muhammad Rafiq 'Arif, offered a very positive perspective on Turkey. The two senior government officials, and the Iraqi historian Mustafa Jawad, wrote the book endorsements that lauded the author's success in presenting a true picture of the historical friendship and cooperation between the Arab and Turkish peoples, thus dispelling the false propaganda that deceitfully suggested otherwise.[17] Sabir argued that Turkish-Iraqi friendship was centuries old and was based on genuine amity and cooperation rather than on conquest and subjugation. He insisted therefore that the recent military alliance between Turkey and Iraq was not based merely on the convergence of national interests but rather was the result of this historical fraternity and camaraderie. He accused those who were trying to spread false propaganda aimed at driving a wedge between the Arabs and Turks of taking their cue from the nefarious British propaganda during World War I. None others than Atatürk and King Faisal realized how damaging and false was this effort to spread discord and therefore purportedly led the way in restoring the historical friendship between Turkey and Iraq. The two national heroes reportedly shared much in their biographies, in that both liberated their respective nation from centuries of Ottoman oppression, which was allegedly as burdensome and ruinous for the Turkish people as it was for the Arabs. The recent military alliance between Turkey and Iraq, the author concluded, was therefore the natural outcome of the realization by the Turkish and Iraqi people that they do not only share a common past of friendship but also a future destiny of amity, brotherly bonds, and prosperity.[18]

This type of propaganda that emphasized commonalities and shared interests between Arabs and Turks also had its origins in the interwar period, but by the 1950s it was running its course even in Iraq. A booklet published in 1954 by the Iraqi radical pan-Arab writer and activist Abd al-Majid al-Wandawi illustrates the growing perception of Turkey as a tool of the imperialist West among radical nationalists in Iraq of the 1950s. Wandawi wrote the pamphlet shortly after the signing of the Turkish-Pakistani treaty of friendship and cooperation, as an implicit if ultimately futile warning to the Iraqi government not to join this new alignment. The title of the publication, *The Turkish-Pakistani Alliance and the Colonialist Schemes in the Middle East*, encapsulates the author's stance. Looking back at the interwar period, Wandawi makes the revisionist argument that Turkey became a willful partner in Britain's imperialist plots in the region already in the 1930s, before becoming an outright dependency and instrument of American imperialism in the wake of World War II. He accuses Turkey of supporting international enemies of the Arabs such as Britain and regional foes such as Israel and of being generally hostile to the cause of Arab liberation and unity. The author therefore calls on the Arabs to be cognizant of how Turkey's territory has become a bridgehead for American and NATO endeavors for imperialist subjugation of the Middle East and to unite in resistance to Turkey and its foreign masters in order to secure freedom and prosperity for all the Arab lands.[19]

A series of regional events beginning with the Suez Crisis in 1956 and culminating in the overthrow of the monarchy in Iraq in 1958 finally curtailed Turkey's involvement in the region. Following the failure of the tripartite Israeli-French-British attack on Egypt, which was aimed at bringing about the downfall of Nasser, the Egyptian leader in fact won unprecedented popularity as a national hero in many Arab societies, including south of Turkey's borders. Syria became a particular matter of concern for Ankara in 1957, when its regime was teetering and it appeared on the verge of falling under communist rule. Increasing tensions with Damascus led Ankara to amass military forces on its side of the border in a threatening show of force, while the United States engaged in instigating subversive activities inside Syria. But a stern Soviet warning and American unwillingness to back any Turkish military intervention in Syria forced Turkey to stand down. The lesson was learned. That was the last time Turkey would try to pull such a maneuver until the end of the Cold War. Shortly after the receding of the Turkish-Syrian crisis, Ankara could only watch helplessly when in early 1958 Nasser was invited by Syrian officers to expand his regional influence by uniting Egypt and Syria and becoming the leader of the new United Arab Republic (UAR). Less than six months later, a bloody military coup against the monarchy led to the establishment of a radical regime in Iraq and to profound changes in the country's domestic and international policies. The revolution in Iraq was the coup de grace to Ankara's drive for regional influence in the Middle East in the 1950s. The Baghdad Pact was formally disbanded in 1959 and was replaced by the Central Treaty Organization (CENTO), in which Turkey was a member alongside with the non-Arab states of Iran and Pakistan.[20] A few months earlier, in late 1958, Turkey reached a secret agreement for strategic cooperation with Israel, primarily aimed at establishing a common front against Nasser's drive for regional prominence, which was a major concern for both countries until the breakup of the UAR in 1961 and the reemergence of political divisions and rivalries between Cairo and Damascus. The Turkish setbacks in the Middle East of the late 1950s, and the political upheavals in Turkey before and after the military coup that ended the Democrat Party rule in 1960, led Turkey to abruptly end its previous efforts since the early 1950s to secure a position of influence in the region.[21]

The rapid distancing of Turkey from involvement in regional politics in the late 1950s coincided with, and was influenced by, the generational change of guard in leadership throughout the region. Until the late 1940s, virtually all the heads of states and many major figures in the political elites in Egypt, Greater Syria, and Iraq were members of the last Ottoman generation, who were oftentimes conversant in Turkish and could hardly view Anatolia as geopolitically detached from the Middle East. By 1959, the Israeli Prime Minister David Ben-Gurion, known in his country as "the Old Man," was probably the last of this dying breed of Turkish-speaking statesmen in the Middle East. Gone were the days when the Iraqi Minister of Finance Rustam Haydar could be described by a Turkish newspaper in 1931 as someone who speaks Turkish like a native son of Istanbul and has fond memories of his days as a former classmate of the Turkish Minister of Finance Şükrü Saracoğlu.[22] By 1960, the first post-Ottoman generation in both Turkey and the Middle East had mostly replaced the leadership generation of the interwar period oftentimes through succession or military coups, and in rarer cases through elections. This younger generation in the major Arab countries of the region came of age during a period of nationalist radicalization in the 1930s that included great emphasis on the Arabic language and culture, and increasing disinterest in the Turkish language and cultural production, with the exception of primarily rural Turkmen communities in the region.[23] Thus, when, in 1938, Turkey dispatched the Ankara Municipal Theater to Baghdad as part of its outreach efforts to Arab societies at the time, the actors and organizers of the tour were shocked and dismayed to discover that only the older generation understood Turkish, while the younger generation of Baghdadi Arabs showed no knowledge in the language or interest in the show.[24] By the 1950s, that younger generation of the interwar period gradually came to dominate most positions of power and influence in the region, and the younger post–World War II generations in Turkey and the Arab lands became even more distant and ignorant of one another. Thus, When the Lebanese author Muhammad Jamil Bayhum visited Istanbul in the late 1950s, he was stunned and appalled to discover that Turkish university students knew so little about the Middle East that they confused his native Lebanon with Libya.[25]

The changing regional and global realities in the wake of World War II also impacted the fate of Turkey's aspiration to become a major transcontinental hub for Eurasian trade. The Tabriz-Trabzon transit road project was revived immediately after the end of World War II, when a British firm was awarded in 1945 a contract to build a modern port in Trabzon. It was initially scheduled to be completed by 1949, but various difficulties led to its eventual completion only in 1954.[26] By that time, however, the premises on which the whole project was based proved unrealistic. First was the Soviet occupation of Iranian Azerbaijan until 1946, then years of internal political upheavals in Iran until the coup of 1953 placed power firmly in the hands of Muhammad Reza Shah, and finally, with much of Eastern and Southeastern Europe within the Soviet sphere, the Tabriz-Trabzon route had no economically viable route to markets in Central and Western Europe. American funds were invested in upgrading the road nevertheless, but more for strategic then economic reasons. The same calculus informed the American-funded construction of a modern road from the Iranian border to Diyarbakır, en route to the Mediterranean port city of Iskenderun in Hatay. Plans were made in Washington and Ankara to build modern roads to Iraq too, but they were neglected after the coup in 1958. Separately, a decision was made in 1956 to complete the 1930s project of the Iran-Turkey railway line. It was funded with American grants and smaller British subventions, initially under the auspices of the Baghdad Pact and from 1959 of CENTO. The Iran-Turkey railway was constructed over the same route that was planned in the late 1930s but it was finally opened for full service only in the early 1970s. The Taurus Express service to Syria and Iraq meanwhile maintained its service throughout all these long years of political upheavals and deterioration in regional relations. Neither of these international railway lines lived up to the lofty expectations of the 1930s during the long decades of the Cold War.[27]

Of all the transit projects, however, the most promising and ultimately disappointing was Turkey's failure to become a major conduit for the export of Middle Eastern oil to the West. In the 1950s, the significant rise in the demand for Middle Eastern oil, on the one hand, and recurring disruptions of existing export routes, on the other, appeared to warrant the construction of pipelines from Iraq and Iran to Turkey's

Mediterranean coast. During the Arab-Israeli war of 1948, Iraq cut the flow of oil in the Kirkuk-Haifa pipeline after the Mediterranean port city became part of Israel. Instead, Iraqi oil continued to be piped through Syrian territory to Tripoli in Lebanon, and another pipeline was inaugurated in 1952 to the Syrian port city of Baniyas. During the Suez Crisis of 1956, however, the piping of oil through Syrian territory was disrupted by Damascus as a show of solidarity with Egypt, even as the passage of oil tankers through the Suez Canal was blocked. In these precarious circumstances, plans were hatched by Western oil interests to construct oil pipelines from Iraq to Turkey's Mediterranean coast near Iskenderun, with possible extension to Iranian and Kuwaiti oil fields as well. By early 1957 the American and British governments were contemplating giving the project not only financial support but also international security assurances. Talks with Iraq and Iran regarding the feasibility of this international oil pipeline project continued into mid-1958. Iran and Turkey even declared that they have reached a preliminary agreement for the construction of a pipeline from Iran's oil fields near Qom to Anatolia, which would be later connected to the planned Iraqi-Turkish pipeline from Kirkuk to the Gulf of Iskenderun. These projects had the potential of providing Turkey with significant transit fees, energy security, and other economic benefits. Yet, the bloody coup in Iraq in July 1958 prompted the cancellation of the plans for the Iraq-Turkey oil pipeline.[28]

Turkey's diminished involvement in Middle Eastern politics after 1958 certainly did not mean either disinterest in the region or complete dissociation from it. Rather, it meant a more risk-averse approach, lower profile, efforts to guard against entanglements in regional conflicts, and greater focus on bilateral relations than on regional alignments. The ties with Iran remained cordial, albeit not particularly warm, until the end of the monarchy in 1979. For a time in the late 1960s, in the wake of the closure of the Suez Canal after the Arab-Israeli War of 1967, talks were reopened with Tehran about the construction of an oil pipeline from Iran to the vicinity of Iskenderun. Prohibitive costs and security and engineering challenges convinced Iran to opt instead for more economically viable options to bypass the post-1967 blocked Suez Canal through Israeli or Egyptian territories. The fall of the Shah and the establishment of the Islamic Republic in 1979, shortly before Turkey was rocked by a military coup in 1980, did not lead to any major crisis between the two neighboring states as expected by some observers. Turkey's trade volumes with Iran in fact grew significantly in the 1980s, as Turkish transit routes were used by the two neighboring countries to circumvent international sanctions on Tehran, including on its oil exports. During this period Iran even resurrected the idea of constructing an oil pipeline to Turkey, but the project never materialized as long as the Iran-Iraq War was raging on.[29] Meanwhile, the project of a Turkish-Iraqi oil pipeline, first conceived in the 1930s, was finally actualized in the early 1970s. After the Baath Party led a successful coup in 1968, Iraq's tense relations with Syria prompted it to negotiate the construction of a direct oil pipeline to Turkey. The Kirkuk-Dörtyol pipeline opened for business in 1976, bypassing Syria completely along the route envisioned in the 1930s for a Turkish-Iraqi railway, and ending in a terminus on the Gulf of Iskenderun.[30] The important economic stakes in the relations with both Iran and Iraq played a crucial role in Ankara's decision to maintain a generally neutral stance during the Iran-Iraq War (1980–1988). Relations with Syria, on the other hand, remained tense and unfriendly throughout the long decades of the Cold War, as they have been since the 1930s. The ties with Cairo did thaw somewhat in the late 1960s and improved significantly after Nasser's death in 1970, although they became only cordial and never very warm.[31] In sum, after 1958 and during the closing decades of the Cold War, Turkey strived to maintain its distance from the stormy waters of the Middle East's regional politics, although it was not averse to take advantage of opportunities to secure its energy supply. By the last years of the Cold War, this rather passive and generally aloof stance was often wrongly attributed to decisions taken by Atatürk during the interwar period in order to set Turkey on a course off ever-growing detachment and dissociation from the Middle East.

III Back to the Future?

The end of the twentieth century and the beginning of the new millennium witnessed important global, regional, and local changes in Turkey that had profound impact on its engagement with the Middle East. The end of the Cold War and the dissolution of the Soviet Union eliminated the greatest deterrent for Turkish intervention in the Middle East since the late 1930s. Signs of greater Turkish political activism and economic aspirations in the region were evident already in the 1990s. In the previous decade, the Iraqi government authorized several Turkish strikes in its territory against the separatist Kurdistan Workers' Party (PKK) during the Iran-Iraq War, but after the Gulf War (1990–1991) Ankara began launching recurrent attacks on PKK bases in Iraq without prior approval from Baghdad. As the battle against the PKK insurgency intensified in the late 1990s, Turkey established strategic cooperation with Israel, at least partly in order to increase the pressure on Syria, the PKK's major regional backer at the time. With the Soviet power not shackling its freedom of action anymore, Ankara was able to amass forces on Syria's border in 1998 and force Damascus to order the PKK leader Abdullah Ocalan to leave its territory. Meanwhile, with little heed to its southern neighbors' concerns, Turkey engaged in major damming and water management projects in the upstream of the Tigris-Euphrates River Basin, which created further irritation in its relations with Syria. At the same time, the 1990s also witnessed early initiatives for greater economic cooperation between rapidly industrializing and economically liberalizing Turkey and new markets in the Middle East. Political volatility in Turkey, however, as well as the international sanctions regime against Iraq, the tense relations with Syria, and the mutual suspicions with Iran, restricted the level of economic cooperation between Ankara and its immediate Middle Eastern neighbors, even as economic ties with Israel and the Gulf States were expanding in the late 1990s.[32]

The early twenty-first century has witnessed significant changes in Turkey, its global position and aspirations, and its relations with the Middle East. These topics have all been discussed at length in scholarly books, academic articles, and journalistic accounts. The main contours of change are therefore well documented. In Turkey, the Islamist-rooted Justice and Development Party (AKP) was able to establish consecutive single-party governments, since it first won little less than 35 percent of the popular vote in the parliamentary elections of 2002. Its leader Recep Tayyip Erdoğan, first as Prime Minister until 2014, and as the President thereafter, has become the most powerful Turkish political leader since the days of the single-party regimes of Mustafa Kemal Atatürk and İsmet İnönü. After appearing to fulfill his promise of political liberalization in the early years of his rule, Erdoğan began moving in an increasingly more non-democratic direction after subordinating to his authority the military and the so-called Deep State, and crushing in 2016 a military coup attempt that the AKP-government attributed to the followers of Fethullah Gülen, the ruling party's erstwhile ally. Turkey's tremendous economic growth under the AKP rule played a crucial role in the party's political success in Turkey and in Erdoğan's development of aspirations for regional leadership and global influence. The succession of Bashar al-Assad to power in Syria in 2000, which helped accelerate the budding rapprochement between Damascus and Ankara, and improving relations with Iran, particularly after Turkey's refusal to support the American invasion of Iraq in 2003, facilitated a rapid increase in Turkey's trade with the Middle East, and in its political stature in the region. The AKP's pivot to the Middle East was accompanied by a heavy reemphasis of Turkey's Islamic identity and Ottoman heritage, as part of an endeavor to culturally reorient and socially transform Turkish society, and within the context of outreach efforts to Muslim-majority societies in the region and beyond.

Commentaries on Erdoğan's policies have often tended to emphasize, for obvious reasons, the shift he affected from previous governments' policies, ideological motivations, and endgames. The literature is quite extensive and thorough. But since this book offers a reassessment of the Kemalist republic's engagement with the Middle East during the interwar period, it may be worthwhile to briefly point out some continuities and commonalities, as well as divergences and differences, between Kemalist Turkey's policies in the multipolar world of the 1930s, and the more recent policies of the AKP government during a period of transition from the seemingly unipolar world of the 1990s to the increasingly multipolar world of the 2010s.

In the early years of the twenty-first century, Turkey has moved rapidly to become a major exporter to the Middle East, and position itself as a major transit hub across Eurasia. It was thus able to take significant strides toward fulfilling a vision that was explicated but could not be realized in the interwar period. The Kemalist government aspired to industrialize Turkey and develop in the Middle East markets for its agricultural exports and manufactured goods. Turkey's actual industrial output in the interwar period was very limited, however, and even miniscule in comparison with the economy inherited and further grown by the AKP. The size and purchasing power of most Middle Eastern markets meanwhile grew exponentially since the 1930s. Under Erdoğan's leadership, Turkey became an industrial powerhouse, with its mostly industrial exports growing from $27 billion in 2002, with 9 percent of it going to the Middle East, to $134 billion by 2011, with 20 percent of it accredited to the region.[33]

Turkey was able at the same time to also realize in the early twenty-first century some of the major transportation and transit projects that the early Kemalist republic aspired to develop in the interwar period, although now on a much larger scale. The early 2000s witnessed the completion of several major natural gas and oil pipeline projects. Natural gas pipeline from northern Iran to Turkey was completed in 2001, and was linked in 2006 to a similar pipeline from Azerbaijan. Plans were drawn in the wake of the American invasion of Iraq in 2003 to link this line to natural gas fields in Iraq, and perhaps even as far south as Qatar, but instability in Iraq and various political complications hindered that project. Meanwhile, despite grimacing from Baghdad, an oil pipeline was completed from the Kurdish autonomous region in north Iraq to a terminus in the Gulf of Iskenderun. This oil pipeline opened for business in 2014, a little less than a decade after the completion of a major oil pipeline from Azerbaijan to the same Mediterranean export terminal.[34] At the same time, Turkey embraced various schemes for the building of transcontinental railway lines, aimed at connecting China and Central Asia to Europe, as first envisioned in late Ottoman times and as promoted during the interwar period. In the 1990s and early 2000s, UN bodies and the European Union played a major role in sponsoring the construction of a Eurasian rail link, with planned branches to India and the Middle East. In recent years, however, the Chinese government took the leading role in efforts to establish a modern high-speed rail link between China and Europe, via Iran and Turkey. Add to this the impressive expansion of Istanbul-centered Turkish Airlines services to destinations all over the Middle East and the rest of Eurasia, and Turkey may well be under way toward fulfilling the great expectations of the interwar period to see Anatolia resume its historic role as a major conduit for transcontinental passenger traffic and international trade across Euroasia.[35]

The AKP governments of the early 2000s sought quite successfully to tether economic success to the expansion of Turkey's diplomatic and cultural footprint in the Middle East. This included the transformation of Turkey into a major draw for Middle Eastern tourists as much as for businesspeople from the region. One of the most important accomplishments in that respect was a Turkish-Syrian rapprochement, which by 2009 led to the signing of a strategic cooperation agreement between the two countries. Kemalist diplomats of the early republic failed to achieve that feat, as the Hatay crisis and fears of Turkish revisionism were still fresh. In a book published in 1959, the veteran

Turkish diplomat and influential author Aptülahat Akşin indeed argued that Turkey must overcome the mutual distrust and seek a rapprochement with the Arab peoples and governments. He explained that the long border with Syria and Iraq dictates the necessity of friendship and cooperation in order to maintain frontier security, prevent subversive activities, utilize cross-border transportation networks, and enjoy mutually fruitful economic relations.[36] Erdoğan's government appeared by 2011 to have achieved all of the above with Syria. As minefields between the two states were being cleared and border gates opened for commercial and tourist traffic, Syria appeared to becoming not only a new market for Turkey, but also a major gateway for burgeoning trade relations with countries beyond it. As tractor-trailer with Turkish exports were going south, Syrian and other Middle Eastern tourists were flocking north to enjoy the services of Turkey's growing tourist industry. Whereas the Kemalist state of the 1930s found it difficult to attract significant numbers of Middle Eastern tourists to Turkey, EU candidate and purportedly liberalizing Turkey of the early 2000s faced no such challenge. Turkey's improving image in the region was also conspicuously evident in the popularity of Turkish soap operas in much of the Middle East. One of the Kemalist republic's greatest propagandists in Egypt of the 1930s claimed that during the interwar period, Turkish films were also very popular in Syria, Iraq, and Iran.[37] If that indeed was the case, this must have been a short-term success, and certainly not anything close to the type of exposure to Turkish television series in the early 2000s. All in all, by the end of the first decade of the twenty-first century, many observers believed that Erdoğan's Turkey's influence is rising and rising in the region, thanks to the AKP government's astute use of diplomacy and soft power.[38]

The cards dealt to the AKP government were certainly much more promising than what the Kemalist government had to contend with, but Erdoğan's Turkey soon overplayed its hand. Once the wave of Arab revolutions began spreading in the Middle East in 2011, Ankara expected regime changes in much of the region and believed it was in a position to capitalize on the public protests. In a clear deviation from any precedent set since the establishment of the republic, including the period of greatest Turkish activism in the region in the 1930s and 1950s, Erdoğan allowed his ideological preferences and personal desire for regional domination to trump over his formerly impressive political pragmatism and any careful assessments of the risks inherent in entangling Turkey in regional rivalries and internal affairs of Middle Eastern states. Sneering at the cautiousness and reactiveness of previous Turkish governments, Erdoğan's Turkey sought to shape regional circumstances and realities, not only in disregard of the potential costs because of opposition from regional stakeholders but without sufficient attention to possible blowback from global powers. The result was a short period of euphoria in 2011 but a longer-term destruction of many of the achievements of the early years of Erdoğan's rule. By 2017, Syria was again a bitter enemy, ties with Iraq were far from friendly, and relations with Egypt became hostile. With the frenemy relations with Iran becoming even more fraught with mutual suspicions, a crisis in the relations with Israel ongoing, and tensions with Saudi Arabia ebbing and flowing, the cooperation with tiny albeit influential Qatar remained one of the few constants in Turkey's increasingly isolated position in the region. The regional upheavals south of its borders had a direct impact on Turkey's economy and society. Disruptions in transportation systems to Middle Eastern markets, and crises in relations with some governments in the region, combined to produce a steady decline in Turkey's exports to the region, from a high of $49 billion in 2012 down to $37 billion in 2015.[39] Meanwhile, reports from 2011 on how "High-Spending Arab Tourists Flock to Turkey" gave way by 2016 to stories on "Steep Drop in Middle Eastern Tourists to Turkey."[40] Instead of vacationers, Turkey became the recipient of hundreds of thousands of Middle Eastern refugees, mostly from devastated Syria, and the effects of Islamic militancy and terrorism, on the one hand, and Kurdish nationalism and separatism, on the other, were increasingly spilling from Syria and Iraq into Turkey. In short, what initially appeared in 2011 as a tempting opportunity to expand Turkey's footprint in the Middle East turned by 2017 into a major diplomatic, economic, and security debacle for Ankara.

The euphoria and hopes of 2011 gave way by 2017 to aggressive policies and fear, driven by Erdoğan's ambitions and by the rekindling by AKP surrogates of the so-called Sèvres syndrome. The establishment of a PKK-affiliated and American-supported political entity in northern Syria, and the reignition and intensification of the war against the PKK inside Turkey, led to the resurfacing of decades-old lingering suspicions about Western schemes to effect the division of Turkey. In a book on Turkish foreign policy, it has been argued convincingly that the war over Anatolia was the single most "full-fledged act of revisionism" in the history of modern Turkey, since it challenged and successfully defied the borders set for Turkey in the post–World War I Versailles order.[41] More than 90 years after a new regional order was negotiated in Lausanne in 1923, President Erdoğan took in 2016 to defining the struggle against the PKK, its affiliates in Syria and Iraq, plotters and traitors in Turkey, and their alleged foreign sponsors as Turkey's new War of Independence, like in the pre-Lausanne situation in the early 1920s. The Turkish leader followed through with public attacks on the injustices of the Lausanne borders. His spokespersons hastened to issue rebuttals to any suggestion his statements amounted to any practical revisionist challenge to Turkey's decades-old Aegean and Middle Eastern borders. Longtime AKP surrogates in the Turkish press, however, took what they understood to be the genuine meaning of their leader's announcements at face value, insisting that Turkey should thwart all the foreign conspiracies against it by invading and annexing frontier regions in northern Syria and Iraq. These are regions that the National Pact assigned to Turkey during the original Turkish War of Independence in the early 1920s and that Turkish ultranationalists never fully gave up on. Erdoğan's insistence that he was leading his country yet again through a new War of Independence aroused concerns in neighboring countries that he might be pursuing revisionist goals, in particular because the Turkish army was indeed moving to occupy parts of northern Syria in order to derail Kurdish territorial achievements south of Turkey's borders, and since Ankara already stationed military units on Iraqi soil north of Mosul, despite Baghdad's vehement protests.[42] How these tension-filled situations will be resolved is impossible to predict, but as of late 2017, there is no peaceful solution in sight.

The early republic's acceptance of the terms of Lausanne, which entailed forgoing certain territories claimed by the National Pact, has been justified in the past in pragmatic terms. Aptülahat Akşin, a veteran Turkish diplomat and influential scholar of Turkish foreign policy, explained in the early 1960s in a book entitled *The Principles of Atatürk's Foreign Policy and Diplomacy* that the founder of the republic accepted the painful loss of lands claimed by the National Pact as a heroic national sacrifice in order to secure favorable conditions for necessary internal reforms, establish constructive relations with powerful foreign powers, and secure the friendship of the Arab peoples.[43] This book has suggested that the early republic was perceived by contemporaries in the interwar period as much less committed to a status quo position than was implied by its public statements and those of Akşin and many other scholars in the decades that followed, and that its engagement with the Middle East was not defined only by tensions or aloofness, as has often been assumed. Writing in 1932, a German expert on Turkey and a future advisor to the Nazi government stated matter-of-factly the common assumption outside of Turkey at the time, according to which the Turks "have not yet abandoned their hope of securing further concessions from France, notably at Aleppo," and that although "Kemalist Turkey has reconciled herself to the loss of the Arabian portion of the former Ottoman Empire, she nevertheless refuses to regard the northern frontier of the State of Iraq as finally settled."[44] Seven years later, only weeks before the outbreak of World War II, an anti-Nazi German expert still concurred that for some time there has been anticipation that "Turkey will now be tempted to follow a policy of imperialist expansion" at Syria's expense.[45]

It is patently clear, however, that interwar Turkey was acutely aware of the limitations on its powers, resources, and abilities to shape circumstances beyond its own borders. Ankara was not averse to looking for opportunities to take advantage of changing global and regional circumstances for its own political, diplomatic, and economic ends. But it did that generally with measured moves and with attention to isolate adversaries as much as possible in the regional and international arena before making any move. A particularly big no-no were public revisionist challenges to the existing borders, even when pressuring Iran or France to change them, along with a clear aversion for undeniable intervention in the internal affairs of any neighboring state in the region. Thus, although there are many reports on Turkish intelligence activities in Syria and Iraq of the 1930s, which the European colonial powers deemed subversive, Ankara refrained from any appearance of open intervention in the political process in either of the countries. For example, political realism dictated responding to events rather than trying to shape or transform them when Iraq underwent a coup in 1936 and when the coup leader, who was considered to be very pro-Turkish, was assassinated a year later. Likewise, Turkey was careful not to cross red lines in its relations with France even when it suspected that the French authorities in Syria either helped foment, or at the least abetted, the Dersim Rebellion of 1937–1938, in order to weaken Turkey's claims on Hatay.[46] Conversely, when it did adopt a very threatening stance on Hatay, Ankara made sure to secure the acquiescence of Britain and the Soviet Union and to prevent its regional isolation by improving its relations with Egypt and Iraq. Political pragmatism indeed trumped time and again in the 1930s ideological considerations and adventurism.

The policies of the early republic indeed appear very self-restrained and cautious in comparison with their successors to power in Ankara in the early twenty-first century. At the same time, this book has demonstrated that prevalent assertions that "Under Atatürk Turkey had wanted to distance itself from the Middle East," or that he and his supporters implemented policies that dictated that they "would turn their backs on the Middle East and the emerging Arab world," are a textbook case of a serious overstatement of the realities of Turkey's policies in the interwar period.[47] Any juxtaposition between Kemalist Turkey of the interwar period and the current policies of Erdoğan's Turkey ought not to be focused on contrasting the supposed drive to sever ties with the Middle East under the early republic as opposed to recent efforts at reconnection and reengagement but rather on parallels and dissimilarities in motivations, endgames, and degrees of political pragmatism in their Middle Eastern policies.

Notes

Chapter 1 Not-So-Distant Neighbor

1 "Filistinde garib bir haydudluk vak'ası," *Cumhuriyet*, April 9, 1936, 8; "Maziden intikam!," *Cumhuriyet*, April 13, 1936, 3; "Arzı Mevudda," *Cumhuriyet*, April 25, 1936, 3.

2 Başbakanlık Cumhuriyet Arşivi [BCA]: 30.18.1.2–63/24/6, March 31, 1936; "Türkofis Reisinin Kahiredeki tetkikatı," *Cumhuriyet*, April 25, 1936, 3; "Şam sergisi," *Yeni Mersin*, April 5, 1936, 1; "Şam sergisindeki Türk paviyonu," *Cumhuriyet*, June 24, 1936, 6; "Şam sergisindeki Türk komiseri çıkarıldı," *Cumhuriyet*, June 27, 1936, 1; "Şam sergisinde yeni Türk paviyonu," *Cumhuriyet*, July 29, 1936, 5; Feridun Cemal Erkin, *Dışişlerinde 34 Yıl: Anılar Yorumlar* (Ankara: Türk Tarih Kurumu, 1980), 1:80.

3 "al-Ghazi yuhdi 'Akka al-Sha'ra al-Nabawiya al-Sharifa," *Filastin*, February 4, 1931, 3; "Mısırlı bir prenses geldi," *Cumhuriyet*, June 24, 1933, 2; Yaşar Demir, *Fransa'nın Yakındoğu Politikaları Suriye ve Hatay* (Istanbul: Mostar, 2013), 195.

4 August Ritter von Kral, *Kamal Atatürk's Land* (Vienna: Wilhelm Braumüller, 1938), 273.

5 Lilo Linke, "Turkey," in *Hitler's Route to Bagdad* (London: George Allen & Unwin, 1939), 331.

6 Suad Davaz in Gérard Tongas, *La Turquie: Centre de Gravité des Balkans et du Proche-Orient* (Paris: Librairie Orientaliste Paul Geuthner, 1939), 7–8.

7 David Fromkin, *A Peace to End All Peace* (New York: Holt, 1989), 552.

8 Yaroslav Trofimov, "Turkey's Autocratic Turn," *Wall Street Journal*, December 10, 2016, c1.

9 Erik J. Zürcher, *Turkey: A Modern History* (New York: I. B. Tauris, 2004), 234.

10 Ali Karaosmanoğlu, "The Evolution of the National Security Culture and the Military in Turkey," *Journal of International Affairs*, Vol. 54, No. 1 (2000), 208.

11 Sabri Sayari, "Turkish Foreign Policy in the Post–Cold War Era: The Challenges of Multi-Regionalism," *Journal of International Affairs*, Vol. 54, No. 1 (2000), 170.

12 Bülent Aras and Aylin Görener, "National Role Conceptions and Foreign Policy Orientation: The Ideational Bases of the Justice and Development Party's Foreign Policy Activism in the Middle East," *Journal of Balkan and Near Eastern Studies*, Vol. 12, No. 1 (2010), 73, 78.

13 Lenore G. Martin, "Turkey's Middle East Foreign Policy," in Lenore G. Martin and Dimitris Keridis, eds., *The Future of Turkish Foreign Policy* (Cambridge, MA: MIT Press, 2004), 159.

14 Baskın Oran, ed., *Turkish Foreign Policy, 1919–2006* (Salt Lake City: University of Utah Press, 2010), 216–222.

15 Oran, *Turkish Foreign Policy*, 154–161; Peter Sluglett, *Britain in Iraq: Contriving King and Country, 1914–1932* (New York: Columbia University Press, 2007), 71–86; Keith David Watenpaugh, *Being Modern in the Middle East* (Princeton, NJ: Princeton University Press, 2006), 160–173.

16 Joseph M. Levy, "3 Powers Reach Accord," *New York Times*, June 20, 1938, 7.

17 Zürcher, *Turkey*, 199; Z. Y. Hershlag, *Introduction to the Modern Economic History of the Middle East* (Leiden: Brill, 1964), 195; Ervand Abrahamian, *A History of Modern Iran* (Cambridge: Cambridge University Press, 2008), 68; Charles Tripp, *A History of Iraq*, 3rd ed. (Cambridge: Cambridge University Press, 2007), 45, 76.

18 William Hale, *Turkish Foreign Policy since 1774*, 3rd ed. (New York: Routledge, 2013), 41–53.

19 Gerold Ambrosius and William H. Hubbard, *A Social and Economic History of Twentieth-Century Europe* (Cambridge, MA: Harvard University Press, 1989), 7; League of Nations, *Statistical Year-book of the League of Nations, 1933–34* (Geneva, 1934), 18, 21–22; Julian Bharier, "A Note on the Population of Iran, 1900–1966," *Population Studies*, Vol. 22ii (1968), 275.

20 Zürcher, *Turkey*, 181.

21 "Mısırlı dostlarımız," *Ulus*, July 23, 1936, 2; Central Zionist Archives (CZA), KH4/1972.

22 Falih Rıfkı, *Zeytindağı* (Ankara: Hakimiyeti Milliye Matbaası, 1932); Atilla Özkırımlı, *Çağdaş Türk Edebiyatı*, ed. Turhan Baraz (Eskişehir: Anadolu Üniversitesi, 1993), 171–172; Altan Öymen, "Erdoğan gençlere 'Zeytindağı'nı okuyun' dedi ama …," http://Radikal.com.tr, June 19, 2014 [retrieved February 25, 2015]. For more details on the book, see Geoffrey Lewis, "An Ottoman Officer in Palestine, 1914–1918," in David Kushner, ed., *Palestine in the Late Ottoman Period* (Jerusalem: Yad Izhak Ben-Zvi Press, 1986), 402–415.

23 For a recent example of this long-standing argument, see Bülent Aras, "Turkey's Rise in the Greater Middle East: Peace-Building in the Periphery," *Journal of Balkan and Near Eastern Studies*, Vol. 11i (2009), 31.

24 CZA, L22\97.

25 "İzmir panayırını gezen ecnebiler," *Cumhuriyet*, November 11, 1936, 7; "Bedava ilân," *Cumhuriyet*, March 25, 1934, 3; "Mısır Hariciye Nazırı ve Gazetemiz," *Cumhuriyet*, June 19, 1939, 3; "Hamidiye İskenderiyede," *Cumhuriyet*, June 14, 1938, 3; "Mısır Kralı," *Cumhuriyet*, June 15, 1938, 3.

26 Umut Uzer, *Identity and Turkish Foreign Policy* (New York: I. B. Tauris, 2011), 67.

Chapter 2 Degrees of Separation

1 Feroz Ahmad, *Turkey: The Quest for Identity* (Oxford: Oneworld, 2003), 92.

2 Tevfik Rustu Aras, "Turkey's Domestic and Foreign Policies of Tranquility and Security," *Financial Times*, special supplement on Turkey, February 1, 1937, 11.

3 For a thorough discussion of the Sèvres syndrome, see Fatma Müge Göçek, *The Transformation of Turkey* (London: I. B. Tauris, 2011), 98–184.

4 Daniel Silverfarb, *Britain's Informal Empire in the Middle East* (New York: Oxford University Press, 1986), 33–35. For more information on developments during World War I in eastern Anatolia in general and regarding the Assyrians in particular, see Michael Reynolds, *Shattering Empires: The Clash and Collapse of the Ottoman and Russian Empires 1908–1918* (New York: Cambridge University Press, 2011), 115–119ff.; League of Nations, *Question of the Frontier between Turkey and Iraq* (1924).

5 League of Nations, *Question of the Frontier between Turkey and Iraq* (1924), 20–21; David McDowall, *A Modern History of the Kurds*, 3rd ed. (New York: I. B. Tauris, 2005), 144–146.

6 Nevin Yazıcı, *Petrol Çerçevesinde Musul Sorunu (1926–1955)* (Istanbul: Ötüken, 2010), 65–69.

7 "Bize göre Musul meselesi," *Cumhuriyet*, May 13, 1934, 1, 6.

8 The National Archives [TNA]: FO 141/768/27, Humphrys to Simon, December 21, 1932.

9 Silverfarb, *Britain's Informal Empire*, 27, 74; Liora Lukitz, *Iraq: The Search for National Identity* (London: Frank Cass, 1995), 37.

10 Silverfarb, *Britain's Informal Empire*, 35–40; Lukitz, *Iraq*, 25; McDowall, *The Kurds*, 178.

11 BCA: 30.10.0.0-230/548/7, January 22, 1930; 30.10.0.0-230/548/8, July 24, 1930.

12 Bilal N. Şimşir, *Atatürk ve Yabancı Devlet Başkanları* (Ankara: Türk Tarih Kurumu Basımevi, 2001), Vol. 2, 250; TNA: FO 195/2490; BCA: 30.10.0.0-113/768/6, December 26, 1931.

13 TNA: FO 371/16916/733, Humphrys to Simon, January 25, 1933; TNA: FO 371/16916/733, Humphrys to Simon, April 6, 1933.

14 TNA: FO 371/16889/7, memorandum by Sterndale Bennett, September 4, 1933.

15 TNA: FO 371/16889/7, Ogilvie-Forbes to Simon, August 23, 1933; TNA: FO 371/16889/7, Humphrys to Foreign Office, September 4, 1933.

16 "Irak isyanının iç yüzü," *Yeni Mersin*, August 15, 1933, 1; "Asuri İsyanını İngiliz mi Çıkartı? Lavrens yine sahnede," *Yeni Mersin*, August 31, 1933, 1.

17 Silverfarb, *Britain's Informal Empire*, 41–42, 47; Soner Cagaptay, *Islam, Secularism and Nationalism in Modern Turkey: Who Is a Turk?* (New York: Routledge, 2006), 129–130.

18 TNA: FO 371/16916/733, Ogilvie-Forbes to Simon, June 28, 1933; BCA: 30.10.0.0-259/741/11, July 18, 1932; 30.10.0.0-259/741/25, January 4, 1933; McDowall, *The Kurds*, 178–180.

19 "Quwat al-Hukumatayn al-'Iraqiya wa-al-Turkiya," *al-Istiqlal*, July 12, 1935, 2; "Türk-Irak sınırında," *Cumhuriyet*, September 28, 1935, 5; Yazıcı, *Petrol Çerçevesinde Musul Sorunu*, 188–189.

20 "Bayna al-'Iraq wa-Turkiya," *Filastin*, March 4, 1938, 2.

21 TNA: AIR 23/666.

22 Sabri Ateş, *Ottoman-Iranian Borderlands: Making a Boundary, 1843–1914* (New York: Cambridge University Press, 2013), 229–315.

23 Touraj Atabaki, "Going East: The Ottomans' Secret Service Activities in Iran," in Touraj Atabaki, ed., *Iran and the First World War* (New York: I. B. Tauris, 2006), 29–42.

24 Mochaver-ol-Memalek, *Claims of Persia before the Conference of the Preliminaries of Peace at Paris* (Paris: Georges Cadet, 1919), 1–14.

25 Jacob Landau, *Pan-Turkism: From Irredentism to Cooperation*, 2nd ed. (Bloomington: Indiana University Press, 1995), 74–97.

26 Touraj Atabaki, *Azerbaijan: Ethnicity and the Struggle for Power in Iran* (New York: I. B. Tauris, 2000), 55–58; Brenda Shaffer, *Borders and Brethren: Iran and the Challenge of Azerbaijani Identity* (Cambridge, MA: MIT Press, 2002), 47–48.

27 Gökhan Çetinsaya, "Atatürk Dönemi Türkiye-İran İlişkileri, 1926–1938," *Avrasya Dosyası*, Vol. 5iii (1999), 150–151; BCA: 30.18.1.2-31/68/10, November 2, 1932; 30.18.1.2-31/70/3, November 16, 1932.

28 Memduh Şevket Esendal, *Tahran Anıları ve Düşsel Yazılar* (Ankara: Bilgi Yayınevi, 1999), 82.

29 McDowall, *The Kurds*, 214–221.

30 BCA: 30.10.0.0-112/753/14, September 3, 1929; 30.10.0.0-112/755/8, June 31, 1931; 30.10.0.0-81/530/19, November 28, 1931.

31 Barış Çin, *Türkiye-İran Siyasi İlişkileri (1923–1938)* (Istanbul: IQ Kültür Sanat Yayıncılık, 2007), 90–97; Çetinsaya, "Atatürk Dönemi," 154–165; Hüsrev Gerede, *Siyasi Hatıralarım I: Iran* (Istanbul: Vakit, 1952), 15–25, 70; BCA: 30.10.0.0-128/915/43, August 20, 1929.

32 NARA: Charles C. Hart (Istanbul) to Secretary of State, September 20, 1930, Central Files, 867.154/11.

33 BCA: 30.18.1.2-12/45/18, June 25, 1930; 30.10.0.0-83/549/3, July 8, 1930; "Ağrı Hadisesi," *Hakimiyet-i Milliye*, June 29, 1930, 1; "İranın notası geldi," *Cumhuriyet*, August 11, 1930, 1; "Mount Ararat: Turkish Offer to Persia," *Times*, August 25, 1930, 10; "Bayna Turkiya wa-Iran," *al-Ahram*, November 14, 1932, 5; Gerede, *Siyasi Hatıralarım*, 152–153, 193–198; McDowall, *The Kurds*, 205–206.

34 "Şarktaki Aşiretlerin Hareketleri Hakkında Ajans Yeni Haberler Aldı," *Hakimiyet-i Milliye*, July 4, 1930, 1; BCA: 30.10.0.0-81/530/19, November 28, 1931; 30.18.1.2-23/69/8, October 4, 1931; TNA: FO 371/15369/68, Clerk to Reading, October 7, 1931.

35 BCA: 30.10.0.0-230/547/9, January 25, 1932; "The Exchange of Ararat," *Times*, January 22, 1932, 9; TNA: FO 371/16062/33, Hoare to Simon, January 27, 1932.

36 Çetinsaya, "Atatürk Dönemi," 167; "Türkiye-İranla Hudut İşi Halledildi," *Yeni Mersin*, June 13, 1934, 1; BCA: 30.10.0.0-261/759/7, June 9, 1934; 30.10.0.0-261/759/13, August 4, 1934; 30.18.1.2-64/36/15, April 30, 1936; 30.18.1.2-83/53/18, June 20, 1938.

37 "Arap sayıklıyor," *Yeni Mersin*, September 27, 1936, 1; "Mardin Türktür ve Türk kalacaktır!," *Cumhuriyet*, October 3, 1936, 8; "Eşşebab Gazetesine cevap," *Ulus Sesi*, October 5, 1936, 1; "Bir Suriye gazetesinin saçmaları: Suriyenin tabii hududu Toros dağları imiş!," *Cumhuriyet*, October 18, 1936, 3.

38 NARA: Joseph C. Grew (Istanbul) to Secretary of State, October 3, 1928, Central Files, 676.90d15/14; Joseph C. Grew (Ankara) to Secretary of State, June 3, 1929, Central Files, 767.90d15/21.

39 "Syrian Frontier," *Times*, June 24, 1929, 13; "Franco-Turkish Treaty," *Times*, February 21, 1930, 13; BCA: 30.10.0.0-230/549/3, December 22, 1929.

40 BCA: 30.10.0.0-230/549/2, May 11, 1929; "Berut Baş Şehbenderimiz Muhitdin Raşit Beyin Yeni Mersin Muhabirine Muhtelif Mes'eleler Hakkında Beyanatı," *Yeni Mersin*, February 9, 1931, 1; Müftüzade Ziya,

"Fransa Suriye mandasını bize devredecekmiş," *Cumhuriyet*, January 30, 1934, 1; "Bir Arap gasetsi," *Türk Sözü*, December 13, 1934, 1.

41 BCA: 30.10.0.0-193/321/10, November 25, 1928; 30.10.0.0-193/325/9, May 30, 1930; 30.10.0.0-262/769/4, March 11, 1930; "Abide: Şehit tayyare zabitleri için Şam'da abide," *Cumhuriyet*, January 19, 1930, 1; "Suriyede Şehitler Abidesi," *Yeni Mersin*, August 6, 1933, 1; "Suriyede Türk Şehitlikleri," *Yeni Mersin*, June 11, 1934, 1.

42 Tetz Rooke, "Tracing the Boundaries: From Colonial Dream to National Propaganda," in Inga Brandell, ed., *State Frontiers: Borders and Boundaries in the Middle East* (London: I. B. Tauris, 2006), 123–139.

43 BCA: 30.10.0.0-262/769/9, May 18, 1930; "Kilis hududunda Soyğunculuk," *Yeni Mersin*, February 15, 1931, 1.

44 BCA: 30.10.0.0-112/758/3, June 18, 1928; 30.10.0.0-128/917/37, November 23, 1929; "Hudut Kongrası," *Yeni Mersin*, February 24, 1931, 1; Benjamin Thomas White, *The Emergence of Minorities in the Middle East: The Politics of Community in French Mandate Syria* (Edinburgh: Edinburgh University Press, 2011), 104–105, 108–115.

45 McDowall, *The Kurds*, 202–203; Sureya Bedr Kan, *The Case of Kurdistan Against Turkey* (Stockholm: Sara, 1995 [originally published in Philadelphia in 1928]), 55–56; Watenpaugh, *Being Modern*, 219–220; Nikola B. Schahgaldian, "The Political Integration of an Immigrant Community into a Composite Society," unpublished PhD diss., Columbia University, 1979, 152–162.

46 Jam'iyat Khoybun al-Wataniya al-Kurdiya, *al-Kurd Iza' al-'Afw al-'Am al-Turki* (N.P., 1933). Turkish title: Kürd Hoybun Cemiyeti, *Türk Afv-ı Umumisi Karşısında Kürdler*.

47 Rohat Alakom, *Hoybun Örgütü ve Ağrı Ayaklanması* (Istanbul Avesta Yayınları, 1998), 65–94; Martin Strohmeier, *Crucial Images in the Presentation of Kurdish National Identity* (Leiden: Brill, 2003), 95–99; BCA: 30.10.0.0-113/771/1, April 4, 1929; 30.10.0.0 -113/771/2, April 12, 1929; 30.10.0.0-113/771/3, April 10, 1929; 30.10.0.0-113/771/7, August 22, 1929; McDowall, *History of the Kurds*, 203; Ekrem Cemil Paşa, *Muhtasar Hayatım* (Ankara: Beybun Yayınları, 1992), 61–71; Yavuz Selim, ed., *Taşnak-Hoybun* (Istanbul: İleri Yayıncılık, 2005 [originally published in Istanbul in 1931]), 17–18.

48 Cagaptay, *Islam, Secularism, and Nationalism*, 131–133; "Taşnaklar Faaliyette," *Yeni Mersin*, August 13, 1933, 1; "Suriye Bir Fesat Ocağı Oldu: Hoyboncular Aleyhimize Çalışıyor," *Yeni Mersin*, August 29, 1933, 1; "Kürt dağında yakalanan çetenin Hoybunculara çeliştiği anlaşıldı," *Yeni Mersin*, April 16, 1936, 1; BCA: 30.18.1.2-48/64/12, September 20, 1934; 30.10.0.0-115/803/22, December 16, 1934; 30.10.0.0-115/799/15, November 16, 1935.

49 BCA: 30.10.0.0-107/697/1, December 2, 1929; 30.18.1.2-12/42/9, June 21, 1930; 30.18.1.2-29/43/13, May 30, 1932; "Yasak edilen gazette," *Yeni Mersin*, September 18, 1933, 1.

50 BCA: 30.10.0.0-106/695/30, July 7, 1925; 30.10.0.0-106/695/38, August 12, 1925; 30.10.0.0-110/740/11, March 7, 1927; Cagaptay, *Islam, Secularism, and Nationalism*, 113–114; "Plot on Kemal's Life Traced to Amman," *Palestine Post*, October 24, 1935, 1; "Amman Police Free Circassian Leaders," *Palestine Post*, October 30, 1935, 1; "Deny Syrians Plotted Murder," *Palestine Post*, November 8, 1935, 2; "Atatürke suikasd teşebbüsü," *Cumhuriyet*, January 1, 1936, 7; "Tarihi ehemmiyeti haiz iddianamenin tam metnini aynen neşrediyoruz," *Cumhuriyet*, January 8, 1936, 7–13; "Türkiye aleyhinde bulunan Hilmi Hudut harici edildi," *Ulus Sesi*, September 27, 1936, 3.

51 Erkin, *Dışişlerinde 34 Yıl*, 1:40, 74–76, 100.

52 "al-Di'aya al-Turkiya fi Suriya," *al-Ahram*, April 30, 1937, 4.

53 BCA: 30.10.0.0-111/748/7, August 9, 1938; 30.10.0.0-264/781/19, August 3, 1938; 30.10.0.0-111/751/20, October 19, 1938; 30.10.0.0-107/698/7, July 31, 1939.

54 B.L., "La menace turque sur la Syrie," *Correspondance d'Orient*, No. 473 (May 1937), 225.

55 NARA: George L. Brandt (Beirut) to Secretary of State, Washington, May 31, 1929, Central Files, 767.90d/14.

56 "Atatürk Çanakkaleyi bir defa daha kurtardı," *Cumhuriyet*, July 20, 1936, 1; "13 yıllık bir ayrılıktan sonra ebediyete kadar sürecek bir kavuşma," *Cumhuriyet*, July 21, 1936, 1.

57 "Turkiya wa-Almanya fi Sabil Wahid," *al-Jami'a al-Islamiya*, April 14, 1936, 6.

58 Sarah D. Shields, *Fezzes in the River* (New York: Oxford University Press, 2011), 99; Cagaptay, *Islam, Secularism, and Nationalism*, 117–118.

59 TNA: FO 371/16086/226, Clerk to Simon, January 8, 1932.

60 "Matami' al-Atrak fi Shimal Suriya," *al-Jami'a al-'Arabiya*, March 10, 1933, 6; "al-Amir Shakib Arslan Hadaf li-Hamlat ghayr Sharifa," *al-Jami'a al-'Arabiya*, March 10, 1933, 1.

61 "İskenderun ile Antakya bize iade mi ediliyor?," *Cumhuriyet*, April 20, 1934, 1, 8; İskenderunlu Tayfar, "Antakya havalisinden bir ses …," *Cumhuriyet*, May 6, 1934, 3; "Iskenderun Bize Verilecekmiş …," *Yeni Mersin*, November 7, 1934, 1.

62 "Turkiya Tuhtafiz bi-Huquqiha fi Liwa' Iskandarun," *al-Istiqlal*, April 17, 1936, 1.

63 "Marahil al-Anshalus al-Turki," *al-Istiqlal*, June 12, 1938, 1; "Mu'amirat al-Musta'mrin 'ala' Bilad al-'Arab," *al-Istiqlal*, June 14, 1938, 1.

64 TNA: FO 371/21915/1120, Phipps to Halifax, November 17, 1938; FO
    371/20853/83, minutes of the Eastern Department, March 2, 1937.

65 Oran, *Turkish Foreign Policy*, 20.

66 Seda Altuğ, "Secterianism in the Syrian Jazira: Community, Land and
    Violence in the Memories of World War I and the French Mandate
    (1915–1939)," unpublished PhD diss., University of Utrecht, 2011,
    251–252; White, *The Emergence of Minorities*, 12, 76–82, 113; BCA:
    490.1.0.0-607/102/7, March 18, 1934; "Hoybuncular faaliyete geçtiler,"
    Urfada Milli Gazete, September 17, 1934, 1–2.

67 TNA: FO 371/16889/7, memorandum by Sterndale Bennett, September
    4, 1933; "Derzor-Halep Mıntakasının Türkiyeye verileceği şayıaları,"
    Urfada Milli Gazete, March 4, 1935, 2.

68 Philip S. Khoury, *Syria and the French Mandate* (Princeton, NJ: Princeton
    University Press, 1987), 525–534; Martin Thomas, *Empires of Intelli-
    gence* (Berkeley: University of California Press, 2008), 277; "al-Di'aya
    al-Turkiya fi Suriya al-Shimaliya," *al-Ahram*, February 10, 1937, 4;
    Suriyede şiddetli çarpışmalar," *Ulus Sesi*, August 12, 1937, 1; "Suriyeden
    hudutlarımıza iltica edenler 1000 kişiye yaklaşıyor," *Ulus Sesi*, August
    16, 1937, 1; "Suriyede isyan bütün şiddetile devam ediyor," *Ulus Sesi*,
    August 25, 1937, 1; "Kamışlıda kanlı vakalar ...," *Ulus Sesi*, January
    4, 1938, 1; Altuğ, "Secterianism in the Syrian Jazira," 254–257; "Nishat
    Turkiya al-'Askariya," *al-Istiqlal*, March 10, 1938, 2; "Min Dimashq,"
    Filastin, June 15, 1938, 6.

69 "Alexandretta, Mosul and Pan-Arabism," *Palestine Post*, January 12,
    1937, 8; "Hal taghazu Turkiya Suriya idha waqa'at al-Harb fi Uruba," *al-
    Istiqlal*, January 30, 1938, 1; "Hal Hunak Mu'amara li-Tajzi'at Suriya,"
    al-Istiqlal, June 12, 1938, 1; "Suriya wa-Turkiya," *al-Jami'a al-Islamiyya*,
    January 10, 1939, 2; "Turkiya tunfi isha'at matami'ha fi Suriya," *al-
    Jami'a al-Islamiyya*, January 18, 1939, 2; Erkin, *Dışişlerinde 34 Yıl:
    Anılar Yorumlar*, 1:77.

70 BCA: 30.10.0.0-222/495/1, June 26, 1939; "Hatayla beraber Halep'te
    Türkiyeye iade edilecek," *Ulus Sesi*, June 2, 1939, 1; "Suriye ve Filistin
    Türkiyeye verilmelidir," *Ulus Sesi*, July 1, 1939, 1.

71 David Ben-Gurion, *Zikhronot min Ha-'Izavon* (Tel Aviv: 'Am 'Oved,
    1987), 6:448–449; Ben-Gurion Archives Online [BGAO]: item nos.
    211196, 213437, and 213546.

72 Silverfarb, *Britain's Informal Empire*, 57; Shields, *Fezzes in the River*,
    235; Ben-Gurion, *Zikhronot*, 6:445; Barnet Litvinoff, ed., *The Let-
    ters and Papers of Chaim Weizmann* (New Brunswick, NJ: Transaction
    Books, 1984), 2:301.

73 TNA: FO 371/23212/554, Knatchbull-Hugessen to Foreign Ministry,
    October 16, 1939.

74 Oran, *Turkish Foreign Policy*, 19.

Chapter 3 Ties That Bind

1 M. Talha Çiçek, "Erken Cumhuriyet Dönemi Ders Kitapları Çerçevesinde Türk Ulus Kimliği İnşası ve 'Arap İhaneti,'" *Divan*, Vol. 17, No. 32 (2012), 179–187.

2 Feroz Ahmad, "The Historical Background of Turkey's Foreign Policy," in Lenore G. Martin and Dimitris Keridis, eds., *The Future of Turkish Foreign Policy* (Cambridge, MA: MIT Press, 2004), 18–19; M. Şükrü Hanioğlu, *Atatürk: An Intellectual Biography* (Princeton, NJ: Princeton University Press, 2011), 199–225.

3 Charles H. Sherrill (Ankara) to Secretary of State, December 13, 1932, *NARA*, Central Files, 767.83/3.

4 Bilal N. Şimşir, *Doğunun Kahramanı Atatürk* (Ankara: Bilgi Yayınevi, 1999), 257–261, 323–324; "al-Ghazi Mustafa Kamal Basha wa-al-Tarbush," *al-Ahram*, November 12, 1932, 4.

5 "Aqwal al-Suhuf," *al-Ahram*, November 13, 1932, 2; "Aqwal al-Suhuf al-'Arabiya wa-al-Ifrikiya," *al-Ahram*, November 14, 1932, 11; "Mas'alat al-Tarbush," *al-Ahram*, November 17, 1932, 6; Şimşir, *Doğunun Kahramanı*, 266–267.

6 Abdallah Husayn, "Masa'il fi al-Diblumasiya," *al-Ahram*, December 15, 1932, 1; Abdallah Husayn, "al-'Alaqat bayna Misr wa-Turkiya," *al-Ahram*, December 18, 1932, 1; TNA: FO 141/764/1, Morgan to Simon, January 2, 1933.

7 Şimşir, *Doğunun Kahramanı*, 265, 270–294, 300–316, 325–327; Şimşir, *Atatürk ve Yabancı*, 3:354–363; "Kardeş Mısır ve Türk Milletleri," *Cumhuriyet*, January 9, 1933, 1; "Taswiyat Hadithat al-Tarbush bayna Misr wa-Turkiya," *al-Ahram*, January 16, 1933, 7.

8 "Apologize!," *Time*, December 19, 1932.

9 Yusuf Turan Çetiner, *Turkey and the West: From Neutrality to Commitment* (Lenham, MD: University Press of America, 2014), 336–338.

10 The Turkish envoy to Turkey held the rank of minister, which is formally one lower than ambassador. TNA: FO 141/764/1, Morgan to Simon, March 30, 1933; Clerk to Simon, May 13, 1933; Loraine to Simon, November 4, 1933; Şimşir, *Doğunun Kahramanı*, 315–316.

11 TNA: FO 371/15376/913, Turkey: annual report for 1930, February 18, 1931; FO 141/764/1, Clerk to Simon, May 13, 1933.

12 TNA: FO 371/17029/904, Campbell to Simon, April 1, 1933.

13 TNA: FO 141/751/16, Clerk to Henderson, July 22, 1931.

14 "Egypt," *Times*, May 9, 1898, 8; "Telegrams in Brief," *Times*, September 24, 1925, 11; "Le Beau-Frère du Roi Fuad," *Le Journal*, September 2, 1925, 1, 3; "Le prince Seifeddin veut se marier," *L'Homme Libre*, October 1, 1925, 2.

15 "The Affairs of Prince Seif-Ed-Din," *Times*, November 3, 1928, 11; Afaf Lutfi Sayyid-Marsot, *Egypt's Liberal Experiment, 1922–1936* (Berkeley: University of California Press, 1977), 110, 124; Lord Lloyd, *Egypt since Cromer* (London: Macmillan, 1934), 2:275; TNA: FO 141/760/8, Loraine to Simon, December 13, 1933.

16 "İbrahim Tali Bey Kahire'ye gitti," *Cumhuriyet*, January 9, 1933, 1; "Bayna Turkiya wa-Misr," *al-Ahram*, February 19, 1933, 6; TNA: FO 371/18013/554, Lampson to Simon, February 21, 1934; FO 371/18013/554, Lampson to Simon, June 8, 1934; FO 371/18013/554, Loraine to Foreign Office, August 3, 1934; FO 371/18013/554, Loraine to Foreign Office, August 15, 1934; "Mısır hükumetilede anlaşıyoruz," *Yeni Mersin*, September 6, 1934, 1.

17 TNA: FO 371/18013/554, Peterson to Simon, September 11, 1934.

18 BCA: 30.10.0.0-258/740/3, April 2, 1931.

19 BCA: 30.10.0.0-258/740/6, June 4, 1931; 30.10.0.0-258/740/7, July 5, 1931; 30.10.0.0-258/740/11, July 25, 1931; Şimşir, *Atatürk ve Yabancı*, 2:247–252; "The King of Iraq," *Times*, June 6, 1931, 11; "Türkiye ve Irak," *Cumhuriyet*, July 7, 1931, 2.

20 Şimşir, *Atatürk ve Yabancı*, 2:253–258; "Rihlat al-Malik Faysal ila Uruba," *al-Ahram*, July 10, 1931, 5; "Irak Kıralı Faysel Hz. Geldi," *Hakimiyet-i Milliye*, July 7, 1931, 1; "Gazi Hazretlerinin Kıralı Hz. Şerefine Verdiği Ziyarette Samimi Nutuklar Söylendi," *Hakimiyet-i Milliye*, July 8, 1931, 1, 5.

21 TNA: FO 371/15323/3137, Clerk to Henderson, July 8, 1931; BT 11/286, Clerk to Henderson, July 14, 1931; "Faysel Hazretleri Şehri Dolaşıyor," *Son Posta*, July 11, 1931, 1.

22 "Kral Faysal Suriye'ye de mi, Kral oluyor?," *Cumhuriyet*, October 16, 1931, 5; "Suriye ve Irak ittihadı," *Cumhuriyet*, November 9, 1931, 1; "Suriye tahtı ve kral Faysal," *Cumhuriyet*, November 18, 1931, 3; "The Outlook for Syria," *Times*, November 20, 1931, 13; Ali A. Allawi, *Faisal I of Iraq* (New Haven, CT: Yale University Press, 2014), 545.

23 TNA: CO 32/47/7, Kirkbride to Acting High Commissioner, Jerusalem, October 6, 1931; FO 371/15376/718, Clerk to Reading, November 2, 1931; BCA: 30.10.0.0-258/740/21, November 28, 1931.

24 Karl Krüger, *Kemalist Turkey and the Middle East* (London: Allen & Unwin, 1932), 42–43; Israel Gershoni and James P. Jankowski, *Egypt, Islam, and the Arabs* (New York: Oxford University Press, 1986), 52; "The Throne of Egypt," *Times*, May 13, 1931, 15; "Sumu 'Abbas Hilmi Pasha," *al-Ma'rid*, No. 32 (May–July 1931), 14.

25 "Yeni bir mücadele," *Cumhuriyet*, January 19, 1930, 1; "Eski Hidiv Mısır Kıralı mı olmak istiyor?," *Cumhuriyet*, August 1, 1930, 3; "Sabık Hidiv," *Cumhuriyet*, July 22, 1931, 3.

26 "Gazi Hz. Abbas Hilmi Pş. yı kabul ettiler," *Cumhuriyet*, December 10, 1931, 3; "Abbas Hilmi Pş. Beyrut'tan Kudüs'e hareket etti," *Cumhuriyet*, December 28, 1931, 3; "Abbas Hilmi Pş.," *Cumhuriyet*, January 8, 1932, 1; Yehoshua Porath, *In Search of Arab Unity, 1930–1945* (London: Frank Cass, 1986), 20.

27 TNA: CO 732/54/4, Loraine to Foreign Office, December 21, 1931; FO 371/16086/226, Clerk to Simon, January 6, 1932; FO 371/16086/226, Loraine to Simon, January 20, 1932; FO 371/16086/226, Loraine to Simon, March 5, 1932; Mahmud 'Azmi, *Khabaya Siyasiya* (Cairo: Jaridat al-Masri, 1939), 96–98.

28 "Türkiye-Irak Muahedesi İmzalandı," *Cumhuriyet*, January 11, 1932, 1; BCA: 30.10.0.0-258/740/20, November 24, 1931; 30.10.0.0-259/741/8, June 12, 1932; TNA: FO 371/16086/226, Clerk to Simon, January 15, 1932; FO 371/17959/1, Turkey: annual report for 1933, January 20, 1934; FO 371/16916/733, Humphrys to Simon, April 6, 1933; Ellen Marie Lust-Okar, "Failure of Collaboration: Armenian Refugees in Syria," *Middle Eastern Studies*, Vol. 32i (1996), 56, 62–63; Porath, *In Search of Arab Unity*, 3.

29 TNA: FO 1011/61, Loraine to Simon, March 16, 1934.

30 Gerede, *Siyasi Hatıralarım*, 263–269; BCA: 30.10.0.0-261/758/2, January 21, 1933; 30.10.0.0-261/757/26, September 18, 1932; 30.18.1.2-31/66/17, October 24, 1932; 30.10.0.0-261/758/17, November 23, 1933; Şimşir, *Atatürk ve Yabancı*, 2:474–482; "İran'la Muahede İmzaladık," *Hakimiyet-i Milliye*, November 6, 1932, 1.

31 TNA: FO 371/17905/776, clip from the *Daily Express* of June 20, 1934; FO 371/17905/776, Hoare to Foreign Office, June 2, 1934; FO 371/19037/854, Turkey: annual report for 1934, January 31, 1935; "İran gazeteleri diyor ki: Bugün Türkiye ve İran, iki kardeş gibi elele ilerlemektedirler," *Türk Sözü*, July 5, 1934, 1, 2; Afshin Marashi, "Performing the Nation: The Shah's Official State Visit to Kemalist Turkey, June to July 1934," in Stephanie Cronin, ed., *The Making of Modern Iran* (New York: Routledge, 2003), 99–119.

32 BCA: 30.10.0.0-69/457/19, April 17, 1934; 30.10.0.0-200/367/3, June 12, 1934; 30.10.0.0-259/742/19, August 5, 1934; Gerede, *Siyasi Hatıralarım*, 269–271, 283–284; Şimşir, *Atatürk ve Yabancı*, 487–489, 512–515; "Un ordre nouveau s'élabore en Orient," *Le Petit Journal*, June 5, 1934, 1; "al-Shah Bahlawi," *al-Jami'a al-'Arabiya*, June 11, 1934, 2; "Mawqif 'Iraq min al-'Alaqat al-Iraniya al-Turkiya," *al-Jami'a al-'Arabiya*, July 24, 1934, 4.

33 "Bütün haşmetlular gibi …," *Cumhuriyet*, May 4, 1936, 3; "Şehinşah Pehlevi," *Cumhuriyet*, November 6, 1936, 2; TNA: FO 371/18987/292, Tabriz Diary for October; November 1934, January 14, 1935; Christoph

Werner, "Drama and Operetta at the Red Lion and Sun: Theatre in
Tabriz 1927–1941," in Bianca Devos and Christoph Werner, eds., *Culture and Cultural Politics under Reza Shah* (London: Routledge, 2013),
219–222; Alidad Mafinezam and Aria Mehrabi, *Iran and Its Place
among Nations* (Westport, CT: Praeger, 2008), 55–57.

34 "İran-Efgan ihtilafı," *Yeni Mersin*, October 7, 1934, 1; BCA: 30.10.0.0-
258/733/16, August 8, 1935; Pirouz Mojtahed-Zadeh, *Boundary Politics
and International Boundaries of Iran* (Boca Raton, FL: Universal, 2006),
194–197.

35 TNA: FO 371/20045/356, Butler to Eden, March 28, 1936;
FO 371/20835/1117, Seymour to Eden, January 26, 1937; FO
371/20835/1117, Seymour to Eden, April 9, 1937; "Türkiye-İran
arasında yeni anlaşma," *Ulus Sesi*, April 24, 1937, 1.

36 TNA: FO 371/15323/3137, Clerk to Henderson, July 14, 1931;
FO 371/17830/400, Foreign Office Memorandum, January 17, 1934;
FO 371/17830/400, Simon to Munir Bey, January 20, 1934; FO
371/17830/400, Loraine to Foreign Office, February 20, 1934; FO
371/17830/400, Maconachie to Simon, September 26, 1934; Ogilvie-
Forbes to Foreign Office, October 27, 1934; İsmail Soysal, "1937 Saadabad Pact," *Studies on Turkish-Arab Relations*, Vol. 3 (1988), 133–136.

37 TNA: FO 371/19032/36, Loraine to Foreign Office, January 1, 1935;
FO 371/19032/36, conversation with Nuri Pasha, February 2, 1935; FO
371/19032/36, conversation with the Turkish chargé d'affaires, February
13, 1935.

38 TNA: FO 371/18976/32, Bateman to Foreign Office, October 3, 1935; D.
Cameron Watt, "The Saadabad Pact of 8 July 1937," in Uriel Dann, ed.,
The Great Powers in the Middle East, 1919–1939 (New York: Holmes
& Meier, 1988), 337–338; Soysal, "1937 Saadabad Pact," 137.

39 "Mithaq al-Sharq al-Adna," *Filastin*, January 4, 1936, 1; "Ataturk Sahib
Fikrat al-Mithaq al-Sharqi," *Filastin*, January 25, 1936, 3; "Mu'ahadat
'Adm Ta'adi," *al-Istiqlal*, October 4, 1935, 2; "A'zam Inqilab Khatir fi
Siyasat al-Umam al-Sharqiya," *al-Istiqlal*, January 13, 1936, 1; "New
Four-Power Pact," *Times*, January 13, 1936, 11.

40 "Dört devlet arasında bir misak yapılacak," *Cumhuriyet*, May 31, 1936,
1, 7; "Irak hariciye nazırı," *Yeni Mersin*, July 25, 1936, 1; "Dala'il
al-Sadaqa bayna al-'Iraq wa-Turkiya," *al-Istiqlal*, July 29, 1936, 1;
"Nuri Pş. nın beyanatı," *Cumhuriyet*, September 13, 1936, 1; "Can-
lanan Türkiye: Balkanlarda da, Asyada da siyasi nüfuza sahibdir!,"
Cumhuriyet, September 29, 1936, 7.

41 BCA: 30.10.0.0-259/744/13, December 13, 1935; 30.10.0.0-
259/745/10, November 23, 1936; 30.10.0.0-259/746/6, June 8,
1937; 30.10.0.0-200/363/9, July 8, 1937; TNA: FO 371/20015/1419,

Morgan to Eden, November 7, 1936; FO 371/20015/1419, Morgan to Eden, November 17, 1936; "Misafirimiz," *Ulus*, April 26, 1937, 1; "al-Mubahathat bayna Turkiya wa'l-'Iraq," *al-Ahram*, April 29, 1937, 4; "Dr. Rushdi Aras Vague on Negotiations for Pact," *Palestine Post*, June 22, 1937, 1; "al-Wafd al-Turki fi Baghdad," *al-Ahram*, June 25, 1937, 5; "Irak ve Afğan Hariciye Nazırları Tahrana hareket ettiler," *Ulus Sesi*, June 30, 1937, 1; "Türkiye-İran-Irak-Afgan paktı tahranda imzalandı," *Yeni Yol*, July 10, 1937, 1.

42 Soysal, "1937 Saadabad Pact," 146–148.

43 TNA: FO 371/23301/1214, Turkey: annual report for 1938, February 11, 1939.

44 Şimşir, *Atatürk ve Yabancı*, 4:225–230.

45 Lajnat al-Difaʿ ʿan al-Iskandaruna, *al-Iskandaruna ʿArabiya Raghm Kul Quwwa* (Damascus: Matbaʿat Ibn-Zabdun, [1937]), 4–5.

46 "The Turkish Consul," *Palestine Post*, February 9, 1937, 8.

47 BCA: 30.10.0.0-200/367/18, May 29, 1937; TNA: CO 831/44/12, Wauchope to Ormsby-Gore, June 12, 1937; "Maverayi şeria emiri bugün Ankaraya geliyor," *Ulus*, May 31, 1937, 1, 5.

48 TNA: CO 831/44/12, Morgan to Eden, June 5, 1937; CO 831/44/12, Wauchope to Ormsby-Gore, June 12, 1937.

49 "Le projet d'Empire arabe," *Correspondance d'Orient*, No. 475 (July 1937), 324.

50 TNA: CO 831/44/12, Wauchope to Ormsby-Gore, June 9, 1937; "Emir Abdallah gitti," *Ulus Sesi*, June 10, 1937, 1; Moshe Sharett, *Yoman Medini* (Tel Aviv: Am Oved, 1971), 2:200; "A Visit in Arab Interests: Emir Abdallah in Turkey," *Palestine Post*, August 11, 1937, 2; Mary C. Wilson, *King Abdallah, Britain and the Making of Jordan* (New York: Cambridge University Press, 1987), 121–122.

51 "Tahiyyat al-wafd al-Suri fi Anqara," *Filastin*, February 5, 1937, 12; "Başbakanımızla Suriye Başvekili Cemil Mürdam görüştüler," *Ulus Sesi*, June 28, 1937, 1; "al-Iskandaruna bayna Turkiya wa-Suriya," *al-Ahram*, June 28, 1937, 4; "Suriye Başvekili Büyük Şefe takdim edildi," *Ulus Sesi*, December 24, 1937, 1; "al-ʿalaqat bayna Turkiya wa-Suriya," *al-Ahram*, December 24, 1937, 4; TNA: FO 371/21914/88, Loraine to Eden, December 30, 1937; HW 12/222, No. 70141, December 11, 1937; "al-Mufawadat al-Suriya al-Turkiya," *al-Istiqlal*, April 4, 1938, 1; "al-Amir ʿAdil Yutahadith li-Murasil Filastin," *Filastin*, May 5, 1938, 1, 4; FO 371/21914/88, Morgan to Foreign Office, July 8, 1938; "Syria and the Sanjak Accord," *Palestine Post*, July 10, 1938, 1.

52 TNA: FO 371/21935/4033, Cox to High Commissioner (Jerusalem), June 23, 1938; CO 831/50/6, Baxter to Undersecretary of State, Colonial Office, July 21, 1938.

53 Wilson, *King Abdallah*, 93; TNA: FO 371/23251/8138, MacMichael to Secretary of State for the Colonies, October 30, 1939.

54 TNA: FO 371/23302/2612, Abdallah to Kirkbride, March 23, 1939; FO 371/23302/2612, MacMichael to Shuckburgh, March 28, 1939; "Emir Naif Leaves for Ankara," *Palestine Post*, April 30, 1939, 2; "Emir Abdallahın oğlu Şamda tezahüratla karşılandı," *Ulus Sesi*, April 29, 1939, 1; "Emir Naif Reisicumhur fahri yaveri," *Yeni Yol*, May 3, 1939, 2; "Telegrams in Brief," *The Times*, September 27, 1939, 7.

55 Selim Nuh, "Türk-Mısır dostluk muahedesi yapılıyor," *Cumhuriyet*, April 20, 1936, 1; "Qadayat al-Jumhuriya al-Turkiya dida Wizarat al-Awqaf," *al-Ahram*, April 23, 1936, 10; "Türkiye ve Mısır münasebetleri," *Cumhuriyet*, April 28, 1936, 3; "Türkiye-Mısır yakınlığı," *Cumhuriyet*, July 18, 1936, 5; "Türkiye-Mısır münasebatı," *Yeni Mersin*, July 21, 1936, 2; "al-Mu'ahada al-Misriya al-Turkiya," *al-Ahram*, July 22, 1936, 8; "Mısır Meclis-i Meb'usan reisinin beyenatı," *Cumhuriyet*, December 10, 1936, 3.

56 "al-Ihtifal bi-'id al-Jumhuriya al-Turkiya ams," *al-Ahram*, October 30, 1936, 1.

57 James Jankowski, "Egyptian Regional Policy in the Wake of the Anglo-Egyptian Treaty of 1936: Arab Alliance or Islamic Caliphate?," in Michael J. Cohen and Martin Kolinsky, eds., *Britain and the Middle East in the 1930s* (New York: St. Martin's Press, 1992), 84–86.

58 BCA: 30.18.1.2-73/25/11, March 31, 1937; TNA: FO 141/445, Loraine to Lampson, April 5, 1937; FO 141/445, Loraine to Eden, April 7, 1937; FO 371/21935/2214, annual report for 1937.

59 "Wazir Harijiyat Turkiya," *al-Ahram*, February 18, 1938, 8; "Egypt and Moslem Powers' Pact," *Times*, April 7, 1938, 16; "Awal wazir kharijiya yazur Misr rasmiyan," *al-Ahram*, April 10, 1938, 1; "Hariciye Vekilimiz İskenderiye ve Kahirede halk tarafından çoşkun tezahüratla karşılandı," *Ulus Sesi*, April 11, 1937, 1; TNA: FO 371/22003/601, Lampson to Halifax, April 14, 1938; "Türk-Mısır Muahedesi," *Yeni Yol*, April 20, 1938, 1; "L'Activite diplomatique dans le Proche Orient," *Correspondance d'Orient*, No. 485 (May 1938), 210.

60 "Hamidiye İskenderiyede," *Cumhuriyet*, June 14, 1938, 3; "al-Safina al-Madrasiya 'Hamidiya' fi al-Iskandariya," *al-Ahram*, June 14, 1938, 1.

61 "King Farouk Invited to Visit Turkey," *Times*, April 14, 1938, 12; "Mısır Kralı Türkiyeye gelecek," *Ulus Sesi*, August 2, 1938, 1; "League vs. Husseinis in London," *Palestine Post*, September 9, 1938, 1; TNA: FO 371/23301/1214, Turkey: annual report for 1938, February 11, 1939; HW 12/235/073448, January 25, 1939; FO 371/23361/364, Loraine to Halifax, January 29, 1939; Israel Gershoni and James Jankowski,

Redefining the Egyptian Nation, 1930–1945 (New York: Cambridge University Press, 1995), 162–163.

62 "Egyptian Relations with Turkey: Security in the Eastern Mediterranean," *Times*, June 19, 1939, 13; "Le ministre égyptien des affaires étrangères rend officiellement visite à la Turquie," *L'Echo d'Alger*, June 16, 1939, 3.

63 "Misr wa-al-indhimam li-mithaq al-hilf al-sharqi," *al-Jami'a al-Islamiya*, January 20, 1939, 5; "Suudiye ve Mısır hükumetleri de Saadabad paktına giriyorlar," *Ulus Sesi*, June 15, 1939, 1; "Mısır Hariciye Nazırı Abdülfettah Yahya Paşa Ankarada, Majeste Kral Faruk yakında Türkiyeye gelecek," *Ulus Sesi*, June 19, 1939, 1; "Wazir Kharijiyat Misr fi Anqara," *al-Ahram*, June 20, 1939, 1; "A'da' wafd Misr fi al-sahafun al-Turkiya," *al-Ahram*, June 23, 1939, 1, 15; "Abdülfettah Yahya Paşa Ebedi Şef Atatürkün muvakkat kabrini ziyaret ederek bir çelenk koydu," *Ulus Sesi*, June 20, 1939, 1; "al-Wazir ala darih Ataturk," *al-Ahram*, June 25, 1939, 9; Gershoni and Jankowski, *Redefining the Egyptian Nation*, 157–158.

64 Israel Gershoni and James Jankowski, *Confronting Fascism in Egypt* (Stanford, CA: Stanford University Press, 2010), 193.

65 "L'Egypte dans la politique méditerranéenne," *Correspondance d'Orient*, No. 498 (June 1939), 251–252.

66 TNA: FO 371/23366/2182, Lampson to Foreign Office, June 15, 1939; FO 371/23366/2182, Knatchbull-Hugessen to Halifax, June 22, 1939; FO 371/23366/2182, Lampson to Foreign Office, July 5, 1939; FO 371/23367/2182, Army Council to Undersecretary of State, Foreign Office, July 18, 1939; FO 371/23367/2182, Lampson to Foreign Office, July 25, 1939.

67 TNA: FO 371/23367/2182, Sterndale-Bennett to Foreign Office, July 29, 1939; FO 371/23367/2182, Sterndale-Bennett to Foreign Office, August 10, 1939; "Mısır askeri heyeti geliyor," *Cumhuriyet*, August 10, 1939, 3.

68 "Mısır askeri heyeti dün şehrimize geldi," *Cumhuriyet*, 1; "Mısır askeri heyeti reisinin mühim beyanatı," *Cumhuriyet*, August 23, 1939, 1; TNA: FO 371/23367/2182, British Embassy, Egypt to Halifax, August 14, 1939; FO 371/23367/2182, Arnold to Knutchbull-Hugessen, September 3, 1939; "Mısır askeri heyeti," *Cumhuriyet*, September 5, 1939, 4; FO 371/23367/2182, Lampson to Foreign Office, September 11, 1939.

69 Brock Millman, *The Ill-Made Alliance: Anglo-Turkish Relations 1939–1940* (Montreal: McGill-Queen's University Press, 1998), 213–219; Gershoni and Jankowski, *Confronting Fascism*, 26; Gershoni and Jankowski, *Redefining the Egyptian Nation*, 193–194.

70 TNA: FO 371/21923/67, Minute by Loraine, August 31, 1938; FO 371/23297/297, Campbell to Baxter, January 7, 1939; FO

371/23297/297, Baxter to Cawthorn, August 2, 1939; HW 12/238, No.
74325, April 15, 1939.
71 TNA: HW 12/239, No. 74612, May 5, 1939; HW 12/239, No. 74672,
May 7, 1939; FO 371/23297/297, Cawthorn to Baxter, July 5, 1939; FO
371/23297/297, Baxter to Cawthorn, August 2, 1939; Khoury, *Syria and
the French Mandate*, 600–601.
72 TNA: HW 12/240, No. 74772, May 23, 1939; FO 371/23287/43, MacK-
ereth to Foreign Office, June 22, 1939; FO 371/23300/1142, Newton to
Foreign Office, July 3, 1939; FO 371/23300/1142, Davis to Halifax, July
4, 1939; FO 371/23297/297, Baxter to Cawthorn, August 2, 1939; FO
371/23286/43, High Commissioner for Tran-Jordan to Minister of State
for the Colonies, May 13, 1939.

Chapter 4 Great Expectations

1 Roger Owen and Şevket Pamuk, *A History of Middle East Economies
in the Twentieth Century* (Cambridge, MA: Harvard University Press,
1999), 16–17; Zürcher, *Turkey*, 195–200.
2 Press Department of the Ministry of Interior, *The Development of
National Banking in Turkey* (Ankara, 1938), 73.
3 "Masalih Turkiya fi Misr," *al-Ahram*, April 11, 1932, 6; "İş Bankasının
İskenderiye şubesi," *Cumhuriyet*, April 6, 1932, 1; "Türkofis teşkilatı
genişletiliyor," *Cumhuriyet*, April 26, 1935, 2; "Türkofis Reisinin
Kahiredeki tetkikatı," *Cumhuriyet*, April 25, 1936, 3; "İskenderiye'ye
Gönderilecek Taze Meyvelerimiz," *Yeni Mersin*, June 7, 1933, 2; "Mersin
Kereste ihracatı," *Yeni Mersin*, June 9, 1933, 1.
4 "al-Sajayir al-Turkiya al-Asliya," *Filastin*, February 11, 1936, 8; "Smoke
and Enjoy," *Palestine Post*, November 17, 1935, 4; "Ashnu et ha-Sigaryot
me-ha-Tabaq ha-Turki ha-Amiti," *Davar*, April 3, 1933, 4; Relli Shechter,
Smoking, Culture and Economy in the Middle East (London: I. B. Tauris,
2006), 75.
5 "Kahire tütün fabrikası," *Cumhuriyet*, April 24, 1935, 4; "Mısırda
Türk tütünleri aleyhine yapılan reklam," *Cumhuriyet*, July 26, 1935, 5;
"Kahirede büyük bir ziraat ve sanayi sarayı açıldı," *Cumhuriyet*, March
15, 1936, 5.
6 Özgür Burçak Gürsoy, "Losing Wealth or Restricting the Poison? Changing Opium Policies in Early Republican Turkey, 1923–1945," *Historia Agraria*, Vol. 61 (2013), 115–143; Alan A. Block, "European Drug
Traffic and Traffickers between the Wars," *Journal of Social History*,
Vol. 23ii (1989), 320–322, 326–329; Ryan Gingeras, *Heroin, Organized
Crime, and the Making of Modern Turkey* (New York: Oxford University

Press, 2014), 65–81, 105–119; "Afyon, Eroin ve Morfin," *Cumhuriyet*, March 30, 1932, 3; "Turkey and Opium Conventions," *Times*, April 29, 1932, 13; "Hukumat Turkiya wa-al-Mukhaddarat," *al-Ahram*, January 17, 1933, 1; "A Dangerous Cargo," *Palestine Post*, January 27, 1933, 2.

7 Max Weston Thornburg et al., *Turkey: An Economic Appraisal* (New York: Twentieth Century Fund, 1949), 282.

8 For Ottoman efforts to revive this route in the nineteenth century, see Fulya Özkan, "The Role of the Trabzon-Erzurum-Bayezid Road in Regional Politics and Ottoman Diplomacy, 1850s–1910s," in Yaşar Cora et al., eds., *The Ottoman East in the Nineteenth Century* (New York: I. B. Tauris, 2016), 19–41.

9 Trabzon Ticaret ve Sanayı Odası, *Cumhuriyet'in 10 Yılında İktisat Meydanında Trabzon* (Trabzon: Şark Matbaası, 1933), 17–21.

10 Ahmet Hamdi Tanpınar, *Beş Şehir* (Ankara: Ülkü, 1946), 25, 30–31.

11 Esendal, *Tahran Anıları*, 38–40; "A la frontière turco-persane," *Le Temps*, October 25, 1927, 2; "Trabzon-Erzurum-Beyazıt ve Devamı Karayolunun Motorize Edilmesi için Yapılan Teşebbüsler ve Meselenin Bugünkü Durumu," *Bayandırlık İşleri Dergisi*, Vol. 3v (October 1936), 183–184; BCA: 30.10.0.0-219/477/7, April 20, 1927; Michael Vyvyan, "Teheran to Trebizond," *Times*, May 8, 1930, 17; "The Exchange of Ararat," *Times*, January 22, 1932, 9.

12 Trabzon Ticaret ve Sanayı Odası, *Cumhuriyet'in 10 Yılında* (1933), 23.

13 Department of Overseas Trade, *Economic Conditions in Turkey* (London: His Majesty's Stationary Office, 1930), 27.

14 Esendal, *Tahran Anıları*, 9; Gerede, *Siyasi Hatıralarım* I, 26–27, 206; Department of Overseas Trade, *Economic Conditions in Turkey* (London: His Majesty's Stationary Office, 1932), 23; Department of Overseas Trade, *Economic Conditions in Turkey* (London: His Majesty's Stationary Office, 1934), 34.

15 Şimşir, *Atatürk ve Yabancı*, Vol. 2, 476–479, 495.

16 "Turkey To-Day: The Ghazi's Tour of Discovery," *Times*, January 19, 1931, 11.

17 Trabzon Ticaret ve Sanayı Odası, *Cumhuriyet'in 10 Yılında*, 27–28.

18 Beker Tumay, "Ökonomik Durum...," *Yeni Yol*, February 28, 1935, 1.

19 "İran Transit yolu," *Varlık*, April 2, 1936, 2.

20 BCA: 30.10.0.0-261/757/26, September 18, 1932; Gerede, *Siyasi Hatıralarım I*, 215–216; Şimşir, *Atatürk ve Yabancı*, Vol. 2, 495; "Liman ne zaman yapılacak," *Yeni Mersin*, June 26, 1934, 1.

21 "Beyrouth port franc pour la Perse," *Correspondance d'Orient*, No. 421 (January 1933), 35; Gaudin (Beirut) to State Department, July 9, 1934, *NARA*, Central Files, 667.90d23/1.

22 "İran, Berut ve İskenderun Limanlarında Tesisat Yapacak," *Yeni Mersin*,
    August 7, 1933, 2; "İranın transit merkezi: Kabine değişikliği transit ihti-
    mallarını kuvvetlendirdi," *Yeni Mersin*, September 29, 1933, 1; "İran
    transiti: depoları kiralamak için heyet Beruta geldi," *Yeni Mersin*, Febru-
    ary 14, 1934, 1; FO 371/17905/776, Hoare to Foreign Office, June 2,
    1934; FO 371/17905/776, Foreign Office Minute, June 4, 1934.

23 "İran-Irak ihtilafı hallediliyor," *Cumhuriyet*, January 5, 1935, 5; "Trab-
    zon transit yolu için İranlılar üç şartın teminini istiyorlar," *Cumhuriyet*,
    February 11, 1935, 5.

24 "Iran in Search of Sea Outlet: Delegation on Way Here," *Palestine Post*,
    April 4, 1935, 9; "İran ticaret yolu," *Cumhuriyet*, November 18, 1935,
    4; "İran transit ticareti," *Cumhuriyet*, November 23, 1935, 6.

25 "Erzurum-Karaköse Transit Yolu," *Varlık*, August 20, 1934, 2; Bekir
    Süküti Beker, "Tabzonun Ekonomik Dikim ve Kalkınması," *Yeni Yol*,
    September 25, 1935, 1; "İran Yolunu da Açacağız," *Yeni Mersin*, Septem-
    ber 7, 1935, 2; "'Doğu Anadolu ihya edilecek!' Bayındırlık Bakanının
    Cumhurıyet'e diyevi," *Cumhuriyet*, September 20, 1935, 1, 5.

26 "İrana bir murahhas heyetimiz gidiyor," *Cumhuriyet*, February 27, 1936,
    5; "İran transiti," *Cumhuriyet*, February 14, 1936, 8; T.U., "İran Tran-
    sit yolunda Mevkiimiz," *Cumhuriyet*, March 4, 1936, 1, 2; "Trabzon
    Limanının ilk olarak yapılması kararlaştırıldı," *Yeni Yol*, March 28,
    1936, 1; "İran Transit yolu," *Varlık*, April 2, 1936, 2.

27 "Trabzon-İran transit yolu üzerinde bulunan Zıgana, Vavuk ve Kop
    dağlarının kış durumu hakkında rapor," *Bayındırlık İşleri Dergisi*, Vol.
    2xi (April 1936), 65–70; Kadir Kurt O., "Gümüşane İlinde Yol Bakımı ve
    Transit Yolunun Kış Durumu," *Bayındırlık İşleri Dergisi*, Vol. 2xii (May
    1936), 35–43; "İran transit yolu hazırlanıyor," *Cumhuriyet*, September
    28, 1936, 2.

28 "Trabzon-İran Transit Yolunda Sel Tahribatına Karşı Yapılacak Tert-
    ibat Hakkında Gümüşhane Nafıa Müdürünün Raporu," *Bayındırlık
    İşleri Dergisi*, Vol. 3ix (February 1937), 31–35; "Trabzon-İran Transit
    Yolunda Tesadüf Edilen Mevzii Bir Heyelana Karşı Alınan Tedbirler,"
    Bayındırlık İşleri Dergisi, Vol. 4ii (July 1937), 121–123.

29 "Trabzon-İran yolunda otobüs servisi açılıyor," *Cumhuriyet*, January
    29, 1937, 5; "Türkiye-İran," *Yeni Yol*, April 24, 1937, 1; "Türk-İran
    dostluğu," *Cumhuriyet*, April 25, 1937, 1; "Turkey's Link with Persia,"
    Financial Times, April 12, 1937, 4; "Kardeş İranla yapılan yeni mua-
    hedeler," *Cumhuriyet*, May 25, 1937, 1.

30 "Trabzon transit yolundan neler kazanacağız," *Ulus*, April 30, 1937, 2;
    "Türkiye-İran transit yolu," *Yeni Yol*, May 11, 1937, 1.

31 "Türk-İran Dostluğu," *Cumhuriyet*, June 7, 1937, 1; "Atatürk Seyaha-
    tinin ilk Merhalesinde," *Cumhuriyet*, June 11, 1937, 1; Bekir Süküti

Kulaksızoğlu, "Transit yolu," *Yeni Yol*, June 19, 1937, 1; Veysel Usta, *Atatürk ve Trabzon* (Trabzon: Serander, 2011), 180.

32 Department of Overseas Trade, *Report on the Economic and Commercial Conditions in Turkey* (London: His Majesty's Stationary Office, 1939), 36.

33 "Trabzon-Erzurum-Beyazıt ve Devamı Karayolunun Motorize Edilmesi için Yapılan Teşebbüsler ve Meselenin Bugünkü Durumu," *Bayandırlık İşleri Dergisi*, Vol. 3v (October 1936), 183–184; "Devlet Demiryollarının (Avrupa hattı hariç) Temmuz 1937 yolcu nakliyat gelirini takribi olarak gösterir mukayeseli cetvel," *Bayandırlık İşleri Dergisi*, Vol. 4iv (September 1937), 64; "Devlet-İran yolu üzerinde Devlet Demiryolları ve Limanları İşletme Umum Müdürlüğünce otobüs, kamyon ve otomobil işletmesi hakkında nizamname," *Bayandırlık İşleri Dergisi*, Vol. 4viii (January 1938), 22–30; "Transit kamyon Ve otobüsleri," *Yeni Yol*, June 7, 1939, 1.

34 "Turkish Bankers in London," *Times*, February 22, 1938, 13.

35 Rashid Khatib-Shahidi, *German Foreign Policy toward Iran before World War II* (New York: I. B. Tauris, 2012), 161–173; Antoine Fleury, *La penetration allemande au Moyen Orient, 1919–1939* (Leiden: A. W. Sijthoff, 1977), 245–248.

36 "Başvekilin Beyanatı: Dört senelik iktisadi plan . . . ," *Yeni Yol*, September 21, 1938, 1; "Trabzonun iktisadi hayatında da inkişaf başlamıştır," *Yeni Yol*, January 12, 1939, 1; "Limanımızın inşası Yakında Başlıyor," *Yeni Yol*, April 26, 1939, 1.

37 Zeynep Kezer, *Building Modern Turkey* (Pittsburgh, PA: University of Pittsburgh Press, 2015), 160–166.

38 M. Arslan, "Münakalat Bakımından İran ve Türkiye-İran Münasebatı," *Bayındırlık İşleri Dergisi*, Vol. 2xii (May 1936), 20–30; M. Arslan, "İranın transit yolları: İranla Mersin limanını bağlıyacak demiryolu," *Cumhuriyet*, November 11, 1936, 2.

39 NARA: C. Van H. Engert (Tehran) to Secretary of State, July 10, 1937, Central Files, 767.91/92.

40 NARA: C. Van H. Engert (Tehran) to Secretary of State, July 10, 1937, Central Files, 767.91/92.

41 BCA: 30.10.0.0-261/761/10, November 5, 1936; 30.10.0.0-151/71/15, July 6, 1937.

42 "Transfer of Railways in Iraq," *Times*, April 4, 1936, 13; TNA: CAB 24/202; Philip Willard Ireland, "Berlin to Baghdad Up-to-Date," *Foreign Affairs*, Vol. 19iii (1941), 667.

43 "Calais to Baghdad by Rail," *Times*, November 21, 1936, 11.

44 "al-Ihtifal bi-Tadshin al-Khat al-Hadidi," *al-Istiqlal*, May 6, 1935, 1; "Sikka Hadidiya min Tal Kutshik ila' Huqul al-Naft," *al-Istiqlal*, June

17, 1935, 1; "New Railway for Iraq," *Times*, June 19, 1935, 13; BCA: 30.10.0.0-263/771/20, June 6, 1935; Joseph Sasson, *Economic Policy in Iraq, 1932–1950* (New York: Frank Cass, 1987), 243.

45 A. Bazoğlu, "Musul Petrolları ve Bağdad Demiryolu," *Bayındırlık İşleri Dergisi*, Vol. 2iv (September 1935), 13–15; "Bağdadı İstanbula bağlıyacak demiryolu," *Cumhuriyet*, July 27, 1935, 1; "İstanbul-Bağdad demiryolu," *Cumhuriyet*, July 27, 1935, 2.

46 "Irakta bir Türk heyeti tetkikat yapıyor," *Cumhuriyet*, January 13, 1935, 3.

47 "Demiryolu siyasetimizde yeni bir zafer," *Cumhuriyet*, November 22, 1935, 1, 4; "Saadet yolu," *Cumhuriyet*, November 22, 1935, 3; "Bayındırlık Bakanının dün verdiği söylev," *Cumhuriyet*, November 23, 1935, 1; "İlk Tren Diyarbekire Giderken," *Bayındırlık İşleri Dergisi*, Vol. 2vii (December 1935), 42–50.

48 Muharrem Feyzi Togay, "Musul Petrolları," *Cumhuriyet*, August 7, 1936, 2; "Mosul Oil Fields," *Times*, August 11, 1936, 12.

49 "Turkiya Tuzahim Khat Tal Kushik," *al-Istiqlal*, April 21, 1936, 2; "Türkiye-Nusaybin: Demiryolu Musul petrolun bağlanıyor," *Yeni Mersin*, October 14, 1936, 1; "Khat Hadidi bayna al-'Iraq wa-Turkiya," *al-Istiqlal*, October 22, 1936, 2; "Komşu Hükumetler Demiryolları," *Bayındırlık İşleri Dergisi*, Vol. 3ix (February 1937), 57.

50 "Cumhuriyetin Demiryol politikası," *Ulus Sesi*, October 28, 1938, 2.

51 Joost Jongerden, *The Settlement Issue in Turkey and the Kurds* (Leiden: Brill, 2007), 175–177.

52 Kadri Kemal Kop, *Atatürk Diyarbakır'da* (Istanbul: Cumhuriyet Matbaası, 1938), 61–81; "Diyarbekir-Cizre Demir Hattının Hazırlıklarına başlandi," *Ulus Sesi*, May 7, 1937, 1, 2; "Diyarbekir-Cizre Demiryolu yapılıyor," *Ulus Sesi*, May 26, 1937, 1; "Sancak muahedesi ile Diyarbekir-Irak-İran Demiryolu kanunları Kabul edildi," *Ulus Sesi*, June 16, 1937, 1; "Diyarbekir-Irak Demiryolunun inşaatına başlandı," *Ulus Sesi*, July 10, 1937, 1; BCA: 30. 18.1.2-72/18/8, March 15, 1937; "Diyarbekir İstasyonundan Irak ve İran hududlarına kadar yapılacak demiryolları hakkında kanun," *Bayındırlık İşleri Dergisi*, Vol. 4ii (July 1937), 24.

53 Department of Overseas Trade, *Report on the Economic and Commercial Conditions in Turkey* (London: His Majesty's Stationary Office, 1939), 35.

54 "Diyarbakır Irak hattı," *Ulus Sesi*, December 28, 1937, 1; "İki yeni hattımız," *Cumhuriyet*, February 23, 1938, 5; "The Way to India through Turkey," *Great Britain and the East*, April 7, 1938, 383; "La liaison ferroviaire entre la Turquie, l'Irak et l'Iran," *Le Temps*, March 5, 1938, 2; "Roads and Railways," *Times*, August 9, 1938, 54.

55 "Cumhuriyetin Demiryol politikası," *Ulus Sesi*, October 28, 1938, 2; "Diyarbakır-Cizre-Van Demiryolunda Ray ferşiyatına başlandı," *Ulus Sesi*, December 14, 1938, 1.

56 "Demiryolunun Vana uzatılması," *Cumhuriyet*, September 28, 1936, 7; Yıldırım, *Cumhuriyet Döneminde Demiryolları*, 106–107; "Diyarbakır-Cizre hattında faaliyet," *Cumhuriyet*, January 23, 1939, 2.

57 BCA: 30.18.1.2-73/29/6, April 12, 1937; 30.10.0.0-151/72/1, January 12, 1939.

58 "Cumhuriyetin Demiryol Politikası ve örülen demirağlarımızın bir plançosu," *Ulus Sesi*, March 22, 1939, 2; "D.Bakır-Cizre hattında inşa edilen büyük köprü," *Cumhuriyet*, August 24, 1939, 3.

59 BCA: 30.18.1.2-87/44/13, May 18, 1939; "Cizre-Diyarbakır demiryolu," *Ulus Sesi*, July 21, 1939, 1.

60 "Demiryollarımız," *Cumhuriyet*, September 11, 1939, 2.

61 "Irak ve İrana gidecek hatlar," *Cumhuriyet*, April 13, 1940, 1.

62 BCA: 30.18.1.2-94/22/11, March 19, 1941; "Yeniden yapılmakta olan demiryollarımız," *Cumhuriyet*, August 15, 1941, 3; "Demiryolu inşaat faaliyeti," *Cumhuriyet*, September 10, 1941, 3; "Un chemin de fer va relier la Turquie à l'Irak et à l'Iran," *Paris-Soir*, May 20, 1941, 3.

63 "Diyarbakır-Irak hudud demiryolu," *Cumhuriyet*, October 28, 1942, 3; "Batman hattı açılırken," *Cumhuriyet*, July 2, 1943, 1; "Yeni posta pulları," *Cumhuriyet*, October 30, 1943, 2; "Bayındırlık alanındaki başarılar," *Cumhuriyet*, October 29, 1945, 5.

64 Trabzonun En Büyük Derdi: Liman!," *Yeni Yol*, July 22, 1939, 1; "Yeniyol, Trabzon Limanının ilkbaharda Yapılacağını Kat'i Bir ifade ile Müjdeler," *Yeni Yol*, July 26, 1939, 1.

65 "Türk Hava Yolları," *Cumhuriyet*, February 26, 1936, 1; "Insha Khat Jawi bayna al-'Iraq wa-Turkiya wa-Iran," *al-Istiqlal*, April 17, 1936, 2; Department of Overseas Trade, *Report on the Economic and Commercial Conditions in Turkey* (London: His Majesty's Stationary Office, 1937), 14.

66 M. Arslan, "Münakalat Bakımından İran ve Türkiye-İran Münasebatı," *Bayındırlık İşleri Dergisi*, Vol. 2xii (May 1936), 30.

67 "French Permission for Turkish Airline," *Palestine Post*, February 15, 1938, 8; "Bayna al-'Iraq wa-Turkiya," *Filastin*, March 27, 1938, 1; "Berlin-İstanbul-Halep hava seferleri," *Ulus Sesi*, June 5, 1939, 1.

68 Selim Deringil, *Turkish Foreign Policy during the Second World War* (New York: Cambridge University Press, 1989), 118, 148–150.

69 "Opening of the Baghdad Railway," *Times*, July 17, 1940, 3; Ireland, "Berlin to Baghdad Up-to-Date," *Foreign Affairs*, Vol. 19iii (1941), 667.

Chapter 5 The Turkish Model

1 For information about the quest to produce a Turkish Qur'an and controversies surrounding its possible uses, see M. Brett Wilson, *Translating the Qur'an in an Age of Nationalism* (New York: Oxford University Press, 2014), 221–247.

2 For a small sample of these articles, see Muhammad Farid Wajdi, "al-Turk wa-al-Qur'an wa-al-Islam, I," *al-Ahram*, February 6, 1932, 1; Muhammad al-Ghanimi al-Taftazani, "al-Turk wa-al-Islam wa-al-Qur'an al-Karim, II," *al-Ahram*, February 13, 1932, 1; Husayn Ramzi, "al-Turk wa-al-Islam wa-al-Qur'an al-Karim," *al-Ahram*, February 14, 1932, 1.

3 *Turkiya fi 1938* (Istanbul: al-Jumhuriya, 1938).

4 Maktabat al-Mukhadana, *'Ismat Basha: Khutba wa-Aqwaluhu al-Siyasiyya wa-al-Ijtima'iyya, 1920–1933*, trans. 'Abd al-'Aziz Amin al-Khanji (Cairo: Matba'at al-Sa'ada, 1934).

5 BCA: 30.10.0.0-84/557/5, December 10, 1937.

6 "İstanbul ve Ankara radyolarında Yapılan Arapça neşriyat Suriyede Büyük bir memnuniyet uyandırdı," *Ulus Sesi*, January 22, 1937, 1; BCA: 30.18.1.2-67/65/7, July 29, 1936; Vedat Nedim Tör, *Yıllar Böyle Geçti* (Istanbul: Milliyet Yayınları, 1976), 29–30; Muhammad 'Izzat Darwaza, *Turkiya al-Haditha* (Beirut: Matba'at al-Kashaf, 1946), 275; TNA: FO 371/23298/493, annual report on Turkey for 1938, April 29, 1939 and FO 371/23195/7767, Weightman to Prior, November 6, 1939.

7 "Irakta ecnebi düşmanlığın başladı: İngiliz müesseselerine şiddetli hücumlar yapılıyor araplar milli varlıklarını tanıtmak için Türkleri örnek Tutuyorlar," *Yeni Mersin*, January 12, 1934, 1; "Türkiyenin emsalsiz kalkınması," *Cumhuriyet*, January 22, 1936, 5; "Dışarıdan bakınca Türkiye," *Cumhuriyet*, August 13, 1936, 3; Siret Bayar, "Suriyeden yükselen sesler ... Atatürk bütün şarkın kurtarıcısıdır," *Ulus Sesi*, February 10, 1937, 1.

8 "Kamalism in Turkey," *Times*, May 17, 1935, 15; Yusuf Hikmet, *Yeni Türkiye Devletinin Harici Siyaseti* (Istanbul: Akşam Matbaası, [1934]), 162.

9 Tekinalp, *Kemalizm* (Istanbul: Toplumsal Dönüşüm, 1998 [originally 1936]), 308–315.

10 For the debates in Egypt, for example, see Zakariya Sulayman al-Bayyumi, *Mawqif Misr min al-Mutaghayyirat fi Turkiya bayna al-Harbayn al-'Alimiyatayn* (Cairo: Dar al-Kitab al-Jami'i, 1989), 120–131.

11 Donald Everett Webster, *The Turkey of Atatürk* (Philadelphia: The American Academy of Political and Social Sciences, 1939), 123.

12 Albert Hourani, *Arabic Thought in the Liberal Age* (New York: Cambridge University Press, 1983), 296.

13 "Mlle Keriman Halis, Miss Univers," *L'Intransigeant*, August 2, 1932, 5; "Une Miss Univers qui n'est pas coquette!," *Paris-Soir*, August 22, 1932, 2; "Le Championnat de la Beauté," *Le Semaine à Paris*, September 2, 1932, 2–4; "A World of Beauty," *Forward*, August 14, 1932, 15.

14 Ada Holland Shissler, "Beauty Is Nothing to Be Ashamed Of: Beauty Contests as Tools of Women's Liberation in Early Republican Turkey," *Comparative Studies of South Asia, Africa and the Middle East*, Vol. 24iv (2004), 112.

15 "Une victoire turque," *Correspondance d'Orient*, No. 416 (August 1932), 91.

16 "Feminism in Turkey," *Times*, November 12, 1932, 11.

17 "Malikat al-Jamal fi Turkiya untuhibat Malika li'l-Jamal fi al-'Alam," *al-Ahram*, August 6, 1932, 1; "Miss Turkiya Malikat al-Jamal fi Uruba l'il-'amm 1932," *al-Ma'rid*, No. 36 (May–August 1932), 22.

18 Malikat al-Jamal fi Turkiya," *al-Ahram*, November 17, 1932, 4; "Keriman Hanımın İzmir seyahati intibaları ...," *Cumhuriyet*, November 26, 1932, 1.

19 "Dünya Güzeli Keriman H. bu sabah Mısır'a hareket ediyor," *Cumhuriyet*, February 7, 1933, 5; "Dünya güzeli dün gitti. Keriman H. Mısır ve Amerika seyahatinde milli mahsullere propaganda yapacak," *Cumhuriyet*, February 8, 1933, 1.

20 "Malikat al-Jamal al-Turkiya fi Misr," *al-Ahram*, February 12, 1933, 1.

21 "Malikat al-Jamal al-Turkiya!," *al-Kashkul*, February 17, 1933, 4; "Ba-Munasabat Ziyarat Malikat al-Jamal," *al-Kashkul*, February 17, 1933, 14; "Usbu' al-Mar'a," *al-Kashkul*, February 17, 1933, 22.

22 "Malikat al-Jamal al-Turkiya fi Misr," *al-Ahram*, February 13, 1933, 1.

23 "Dünya Güzeli Mısır'da!," *Cumhuriyet*, February 23, 1933, 1.

24 "Wazir al-Ma'arif ... wa-al-Jamal!," *Ruz al-Yusuf*, No. 262, February 20, 1933, 3; *Ruz al-Yusuf*, No. 264, March 6, 1933, 2.

25 "Fi Majlis al-Nuwwab: Malikat al-Jamal fi al-Majlis," *al-Ahram*, February 16, 1933, 2; "Dünya Güzeli Mısır'da!," *Cumhuriyet*, February 23, 1933, 1–2.

26 "Takrim Malikat al-Jamal fi Dar al-Siyasa," *al-Ahram*, March 3, 1933, 7.

27 "al-Al'ab al-Riyadiya," *al-Ahram*, February 13, 1933, 10; "al-Al'ab al-Riyadiya," *Ruz al-Yusuf*, No. 263, February 27, 1933, 41.

28 On Zaghlul's life and activism, see Beth Baron, *Egypt as a Woman* (Berkeley: University of California Press, 2005), 135–161. Quote from page 161.

29 "Malikat al-jamal fi Dar al-Ittihad al-Nisa'i," *al-Ahram*, February 14, 1933, 7; "Dünya Güzelinin Mısır seyahatı," *Cumhuriyet*, March 20, 1933, 5.

30 al-Sawi, "Qala wa-Dala," *al-Ahram*, March 17, 1933, 1; al-Sawi, "Ma Qala wa-Dala," *al-Ahram*, February 20, 1933, 7; "al-Ustadh al-Sawi wa-'Arusuhu," *al-Ahram*, September 6, 1935, 1; Cynthia Nelson, *Doria Shafik, Egyptian Feminist: A Woman Apart* (Gainesville: University of Florida Press, 1996), 60–64.

31 "Malikat al-Jamal Tasma'u Umm Kulthum," *al-Ahram*, March 1, 1933, 7; "Takrim Malikat al-Jamal fi Dar al-Siyasa," *al-Ahram*, March 3, 1933, 7; *al-Ahram*, March 11, 1933, 12. On Masabni and her music hall, see Virginia Danielson, *The Voice of Egypt* (Chicago: University of Chicago Press, 1997), 48. On employment of dancers and singers in events of the Egyptian Feminist union, see Sania Sharawi Lanfranchi, *Casting Off the Veil* (London: I. B. Tauris, 2012), 193–194.

32 "Dünya Güzelinin Mısır seyahatı," *Cumhuriyet*, March 20, 1933, 5.

33 "Tahiyat Misr ila' Malikat al-Jamal," *al-Ahram*, February 16, 1933, 7; "Malikat al-Jamal," *al-Ahram*, February 18, 1933, 7; "Ila' Malikat al-Jamal," *al-Ahram*, March 6, 1933, 7; "Ila' Malikat al-Jamal," *al-Ahram*, March 14, 1933, 1.

34 *al-Kashkul*, February 17, 1933, 13; "Bayna al-Suhuf wa-al-Majalat," *Ruz al-Yusuf*, No. 263, February 27, 1933, 39.

35 "Malikat al-Jamal," *al-Ahram*, February 20, 1933, 7; "Malikat al-Jamal," *Filastin*, February 17, 1933, 2.

36 Mekki Sait, "Dedikodulu Mısır Seferi: Keriman Ece Gördüklerini Anlatıyor ...," *Yedi Gün*, No. 12, May 31, 1933, 14.

37 "Malikat al-Jamal al-Turkiya!," *al-Kashkul*, February 17, 1933, 4; "Akhbar Raqiya wa-Ghayra Raqiya," *Ruz al-Yusuf*, No. 262, February 20, 1933, 13; "Hal Tuqam Mubarat li'l-Jamal fi Misr ... !," *al-Kashkul*, March 3, 1933, 14.

38 "Untuhiba Miss Misr Malika li'l-Jamal fi al-'Alam," *al-Ahram*, October 1, 1935, 1; "La colonie égyptienne fête Miss Egypte 1935," *Le Journal*, September 24, 1935, 7; "Une foule immense assiégé la salle où eut lieu l'élection de Miss Univers," *Paris-soir*, October 1, 1935, 1.

39 Fikri Abaza, "Jamal Malikat al-Jamal?!," *al-Musawwar*, February 24, 1933, 2.

40 "Mansure bayram yaptı," *Cumhuriyet*, March 30, 1933, 1–2.

41 *Atatürk'ün Söylev ve Demeçleri* (Ankara: Türk Tarih Kurumu Basımevi, 1961), 3:92.

42 "Keriman Hanım Mısırdan avdet etti," *Cumhuriyet*, May 20, 1933, 3; Mekki Sait, "Dedikodulu Mısır Seferi: Keriman Ece Gördüklerini Anlatıyor...," *Yedi Gün*, No. 12, May 31, 1933, 14.

43 Alev Çınar, *Modernity, Islam, and Secularism in Turkey* (Minneapolis: University of Minnesota Press, 2005), 70–73.

44 "Ra'isat al-Ittihad al-Nisa'i al-Dawli tatahadith ila al-Ma'rid," *al-Ma'rid*, No. 41 (February–April 1935), 20.

45 For information on the attitudes of the International Woman Suffrage Alliance regarding the Middle East, see Charlotte Weber, "Unveiling Scheherazade: Feminist Orientalism in the International Alliance of Women, 1911–1950," *Feminist Studies*, Vol. 27 (2001), 125–157.

46 Huda Sha'rawi, *Mudhakirat Huda Sha'rawi: Ra'idat al-Mar'a al-'Arabiya al-Haditha* (Cairo: Dar al-Hilal, 1981), 450.

47 "al-Sayida Barazi tahadathna 'an al-Mu'atamar al-Nisa'i," *al-Ma'rid*, No. 42 (May–June 1935), 20.

48 Huda Sha'rawi, *Dawr al-Mar'a fi Harakat al-Tatawwur al-'Alami* (Cairo: N.P., 1929), 18.

49 Charlotte Weber, "Between Nationalism and Feminism: The Eastern Women's Congresses of 1930 and 1932," *Journal of Middle East Women's Studies*, Vol. 4 (2008), 94; Gholamreza Salami and Afsaneh Najmabadi, *Nahzat-e Nisvan-e Sharq* (Tehran: Shirazeh, 2005), 53, 59, 70, 82, 255; Sabiha al-Shaykh Daud, *Awwal al-Tariq* (Baghdad, 1958), 163.

50 "Nahdat al-Mar'a fi Turkiya," *al-Istiqlal*, December 11, 1935, 1; Abd al-Wahhab Azzam, "6 – al-Nahdha al-Turkiya al-Akhira," *al-Risala*, July 29, 1935, 1210; Kral, *Kamal Atatürk's Land*, 42–43.

51 "Mısır kadınlarının büyük sevinci," *Cumhuriyet*, January 29, 1935, 1; "Kadınlar başkanı: Türk kadınlarının birçok doğu kadınlarına örnek olduğunu söylüyor," *Türk Sözü*, January 30, 1935, 1; "Mısır Kadınların Tebriki," *Urfada Milli Gazete*, February 4, 1935, 1.

52 "İranda inkılablar," *Cumhuriyet*, June 20, 1935, 1; "İran kadınları tekamül yolunda, hayret edilecek bir hızla ilerliyorlar," *Cumhuriyet*, November 25, 1935, 8.

53 Ellen Fleischmann, *The Nation and Its "New" Women* (Berkeley: University of California Press, 2003), 297n56; Sarah Azaryahu, "Ha-Qongres ha-Beyn-Leumi shel Nashim le-Shivuy Zkhuyot," *Davar*, April 30, 1935, 27; "İstanbul kongresi ve İran kadınlığı," *Cumhuriyet*, April 22, 1935, 5.

54 Elizabeth Thompson, *Colonial Citizens* (New York: Columbia University Press, 2000), 139; "al-Lugha al-'Arabiya fi Turkiya," *al-Ahram*, April 19, 1935, 6.

55 "Iftitah al-Mu'atamar al-nisa'i fi Istanbul," *al-Ahram*, April 19, 1935, 4; "Misr fi al-Mu'atamar al-nisa'i," *al-Ahram*, April 21, 1935, 4; Sha'rawi, *Dawr al-Mar'a*, 11; "İstiyoruz ki erkeklerin bile asker olmasına lüzum kalmasın!," *Cumhuriyet*, April 17, 1935, 1; Salami and Najmabadi,

Nahzat-e Nisvan-e Sharq, 341, 345–348; Salma Sayegh, *Suwar wa-Dhikrayat* (Beirut: Dar al-Hadara, 1964), 175–178.

56 "Mısırlı kadınlar İstanbulda Cumhuriyet abidesine bir Çelenk koydular," *Yeni Mersin*, April 18, 1935, 1–2; "L'Hommage des Deleguees Egyptiennes," *Ankara*, April 20, 1935, 1; "al-Wafd al-Nisa'i al-Masri," *al-Ahram*, April 21, 1935, 6.

57 "Kadının kurtuluşunu Atatürke borçluyuz," *Cumhuriyet*, April 13, 1935, 1; "Le Congrès de l'Union Internationale des Femmes," *Ankara*, April 20, 1935, 1; Sha'rawi, *Mudhakirat*, 450.

58 "Biz Türkiyeye hayran olamağa geldik," *Cumhuriyet*, April 16, 1935, 1.

59 "Discours de Mlle Ceza Nabaraoui au offert a la presse a l'Hotel Pera Palace, le 15 Avril," *L'Égyptienne*, Vol. 11, No. 113 (May 1935), 36–37.

60 "Dün Şark ve Garb kadınlarının aynı prensipler etrafında birleşmilerine dair bir karar kabul edildi," *Cumhuriyet*, April 20, 1935, 1; "al-Mu'atamar al-Nisa'i al-Dawli," *al-Ahram*, May 3, 1935, 1–2; "Discours de Mme Charaoui Pacha (19 Avril 1935)," *L'Égyptienne*, Vol. 11, No. 113 (May 1935), 35–36; Sha'rawi, *Mudhakirat*, 452.

61 Kathryn Libal, "Staging Turkish Women's Emancipation: Istanbul, 1935," *Journal of Middle East Women's Studies*, Vol. 4 (2008), 33, 42–45.

62 TNA: FO 371/19041/2765, Loraine to Simon, April 27, 1935; "The Women's International Conference," *Journal of the Royal Central Asian Society*, Vol. 22iii (May 1935), 366.

63 "Le Congrès d'Istanbul," *Bulletin Périodique de la presse Turque*, No. 107 (April–May 1935), 6.

64 Sha'rawi, *Dawr al-Mar'a*, 13–14, 26.

65 Sha'rawi, *Mudhakirat*, 454–455; "Sitti Şaravinin Mısır gazetelerine beyanatı," *Cumhuriyet*, May 29, 1935, 4; Fatma Nimet Rachid, "Mon enquête en Turquie," *l'Égyptienne*, Vol. 11, No. 117 (November 1935), 28–29; "Mısırda Türkiye için güzel bir eser," *Cumhuriyet*, May 21, 1936, 6.

66 For information on the Girls' Institutes in Turkey of the interwar period, see Kezer, *Building Modern Turkey*, 208–225.

67 Press Department of the Ministry of the Interior, *Public Instruction in the Republic of Turkey* (Ankara, 1936), 45.

68 "Emir Faysal Hz.," *Cumhuriyet*, June 15, 1932, 1; "Emir Abdullah ile," *Cumhuriyet*, June 5, 1937, 7; Richard Lichtheim, "The New Turkey," *Palestine Post*, June 12, 1938, 8; Fuad Sarruf, "Min al-Qahira ila' Anqara," *al-Muqtataf*, October 1933, 349–350; "Lübnanlı bir kadın yazıcı geldi," *Cumhuriyet*, July 18, 1935, 2.

69 Stephan Ronart, *Turkey To-day* (London: Robert Hale, 1938), 149.

70 Mark Mazower, *Dark Continent: Europe's Twentieth Century* (New York: Vintage, 2000), 83–84; Sibel Bozdoğan, *Modernism and Nation Building: Turkish Architectural Culture in the Early Republic* (Seattle: University of Washington Press, 2001), 85–87.

71 Pelin Gürol, "Building for Women's Education during the Early Republican Period in Turkey: İsmet Paşa Girls' Institute in Ankara in the 1930s," unpublished MA thesis, Middle East Technical University, 2003, 175; David Menashri, *Education and the Making of Modern Iran* (Ithaca, NY: Cornell University Press, 1992), 108.

72 Sa'id Sannu, *Turkiya al-Kamaliya* (Beirut: Maktab al-Ashah wa-al-Nashr, 1938), 91–93.

73 "Sitti Şaravinin Mısır gazetelerine beyanatı," *Cumhuriyet*, May 29 1935, 4; Sha'rawi, *Dawr al-Mar'a*, 12–13; Selim Nuh, "Ankarada okutulacak Mısırlı iki genç kız," *Cumhuriyet*, March 29, 1936, 5.

74 Sannu, *Turkiya al-Kamaliya*, 91–93.

75 Tekinalp, *Kemalizm*, 311–312.

76 Camron Michael Amin, "Globalizing Iranian Feminism, 1910–1950," *Journal of Middle East Women's Studies*, Vol. 4i (2008), 22–23; Munira Thabit, *Thawra fi . . . al-Burj al-'Aji* (Cairo: Dar al-Ma'arif lil-Tiba'a wa-al-Nashr, 1946), 88.

77 "Hitler, son œuvre et ses collaborateurs," *Bulletin Périodique de la presse Turque*, No. 98 (July–October 1933), 12. For a detailed study of the topic, see Stephan Ihrig, *Atatürk in the Nazi Imagination* (Cambridge, MA: Harvard University Press, 2014).

78 For a French example, see Jacques Bainville, *Les Dictateurs* (Paris: Les Éditions Denoël et Steele, 1935), 220–221; for a British example, see Diana Spearman, *Modern Dictatorship* (New York: Columbia University Press, 1939), 16, 262; for an American example, see Guy Stanton Ford, *Dictatorship in the Modern World* (Minneapolis: University of Minnesota Press, 1935), 152–153.

79 "La vie mouvementée de Ataturk," *Le Petit Journal*, November 11, 1938, 3; "Kemal Orders Modernization of University," *Washington Post*, July 30, 1933, 7; "Turkish Policy," *Times*, November 10, 1937, 15.

80 "La funérailles de Ataturk," *Bulletin Périodique de la presse Turque*, No. 127 (November 1938–January 1939), 4; "Mustafa Kamâl Atatürk Maneuvers His Army in Turkey," *Life*, September 13, 1937, 93; "Atatürk's comeback," *Life*, November 1, 1937, 8. See also Pınar Dost-Niyego, *Le Bon Dictateur: L'image de Mustafa Kemal Atatürk en France (1919–1938)* (Istanbul: Libra Yayınevi, 2014), 204–228.

81 Ali Fuad Başgil, "La Constitution et le Régime politique," in *La Vie Juridique des Peuples: Turquie* (Paris: Librairie Delagrave, 1939), 9. Ironically, with Turkey's passage to actual democracy after World War II, Başgil emerged in the 1950s as one of the staunchest critics of the authoritarianism of President İnönü and the early republic.

82 Mustafa Kemal was known since the early 1920s as the Gazi (Great Warrior-Savior), since the early 1930s as *Büyük Şef* (Great National Leader), and after his death in 1938 as the Eternal Leader, while his successor İnönü took the title of *Milli Şef* (National Leader).

83 "Mısır kadınları ve Atatürk," *Cumhuriyet*, April 28, 1935, 1, 6.

84 "Sitti Şaravinin Mısır gazetelerine beyanatı," *Cumhuriyet*, May 29, 1935, 4; Margot Badran, *Feminists, Islam, and Nation* (Princeton, NJ: Princeton University Press, 1995), 213.

85 Aziz Khanki Bey, *Turk wa-Ataturk* (Cairo: al-Matba'a al-Misriya, [1938]), 100.

86 Tekin Alp, *Le Kemalisme* (Paris: Alcan, 1937), 278–279.

87 Arthur Goldschmidt, "'Azzam, Dr. 'Abd al-Wahhab," in *Biographical Dictionary of Modern Egypt* (Boulder, CO: Lynne Reiner, 2000), 29–30; Sayed Khatab, *Understanding Islamic Fundamentalism* (Cairo: American University in Cairo Press, 2011), 212.

88 'Abd al-Wahhab 'Azzam, "6 – al-Nahda al-Turkiya al-Akhira," *al-Risala*, July 29, 1935, 1210–1211.

89 Gershoni and Jankowski, *Redefining the Egyptian Nation*, 42–43.

90 "Ma Qawl al-Atrak?," *Filastin*, February 26, 1937, 10; "Tasrih Madsus 'ala Wazir Turki," *Filastin*, March 3, 1937, 1; "Nazara fi Siyasat al-Turk al-Qawmiya: al-Sharq wa-al-Inqilab al-Turki," *al-Istiqlal*, April 10, 1935, 1.

91 al-Bayyumi, *Mawqif Misr min al-Mutaghayyirat*, 120–131.

92 Peter Wien, *Iraqi Arab Nationalism: Authoritarian, Totalitarian, and Pro-Fascist Inclinations, 1923–1941* (London: Routledge, 2006), 113.

93 "Ma'rid al-Madhahib al-Siyasiya: al-Fashistiya wa-al-Naziya wa-al-Kamaliya," *al-Muqtataf*, December 1933, 510–515.

94 "al-Ta'asub al-Laghwi ba'd al-Ta'asub al-Jinsi," *al-Risala*, February 3, 1936, 195.

95 "Harakat 'Askariya Khatira fi Turkiya: al-Ghazi Ataturk yuqalid al-Herr Hitler," *al-Istiqlal*, June 11, 1935, 1; "Hal Tattafiq Turkiya ma'a Almanya qariban?! Al-Ghazi yazur al-Fuhrir Hitler!," *al-Istiqlal*, July 15, 1935, 1.

96 Wien, *Iraqi Arab Nationalism*, 67–68.

97 Charles H. Sherrill, *Kamal – Roosevelt-Mussolini* (Bologna: Zanichelli, 1936); *Üç Adam: Kemal Atatürk, Roosevelt, Mussolini* (Istanbul: Cumhuriyet Matbaası, 1937).

98 Dagobert von Mikusch, *Mustafa Kamal: al-Mathal al-A'la'* (Beirut: Matba'at al-Wafa,' 1933); "Sifriya Hadasha shel Hevra: Pras le-Menuyey Davar," *Davar*, May 11, 1933, 4. On the use of Mikusch's book in Nazi propaganda, see Ihrig, *Atatürk in Nazi Imagination*, 168.

99 Sharls Shiril, "Sana ma'a Mustafa Kamal," *al-Jami'a al-Islamiya*, February 27, 1935, 3. Original: Charles H. Sherrill, *A Year's Embassy to Mustafa Kemal* (New York: Charles Scribner's Sons, 1934); "Leadership Called Biggest World Need," *New York Times*, June 4, 1933, 5.

100 Muhammad Muhammad Tawfiq, *Kamal Ataturk* (Cairo: Dar al-Hilal, 1936), 3–7, 111–112. On Abaza's views on Turkey in 1925, see Wilson Chacko Jacob, *Working Out Egypt: Effendi Masculinity and Subject Formation in Colonial Modernity, 1870–1940* (Durham, NC: Duke University Press, 2011), 203–205.

101 Fu'ad Shimali, *Turkiya al-Haditha* (Beirut: Dar al-Maktaba al-Ahliya, 1939), 7–8, 51, 98–103, 166–176.

102 He is sometimes referred to as Fu'ad Shamali or Fouad Chemali. "M. de Jouvenel fait mettre au secret le leader du Parti ouvrier de Beyrouth," *L'Humanité*, February 9, 1926, 1; Samir Kassir, *Beirut* (Berkeley: University of California Press, 2010), 337–338; Taline Ter Minassian, *Colporteurs du Komintern: l'Union soviétique et les minorités au Moyen-Orient* (Paris: Presses de Sciences Po, 1997), 164–166.

103 Mustafa Sabri, "Madinat al-Qustantiniya, li-Munasibat murur 500 Sana Hijriya ala Fathiha," *al-Ahram*, August 17, 1938, 1, 11; Aziz Khanki, "Madinat al-Qustantiniya, li-Munasibat murur 500 Sana Hijriya ala Nish'atiha," *al-Ahram*, August 19, 1938, 1, 14.

104 Aziz Khanki Bey, "Turk wa-Ataturk," *al-Ahram*, April 9, 1938, 1–2; Aziz Khanki Bey, "Turk wa-Ataturk," *al-Ahram*, April 10, 1938, 1–2.

105 Khanki Bey, *Turk wa-Ataturk*, 3–5, 30–35, 49–56, 142–143; Aziz Hanki Bey, *Turcs et Atatürk* (Cairo: F. E. Noury, 1939).

106 "Turk wa-Ataturk," *al-Ahram*, October 29, 1938, 3.

107 Akram Zu'aytir, *Min Mudhakkirat Akram Zu'aytir* (Beirut: al-Mu'assasa al-'Arabiya lil-Dirasat wa-al-Nashr, 1994), 1:440, 609.

108 Burhan Jahid, *Al-Ghazi Mustafa Kamal wa-fursanuhu al-Arba'a 1918*, trans. Ra'fat al-Dajani (Jafa: Matba'at al-Kamal, 1935), translator's note. Original: Bürhan Cahit, *Gazinin 4 Süvarisi* (Istanbul: Kanaat Kütüphanesi, 1932); "al-Ghazi Mustafa Kamal wa-Fursanuhu al-Arba'a," *al-Jami'a al-Islamiya*, March 11, 1936, 7; "Mustafa Kamal wa-Fursanuhu al-Arba'a," *Filastin*, March 22, 1936, 3.

109 Husayn Ramzi al-Qabtan, *Mustafa Kamal wa-al-Harb al-Turkiya al-Yunaniya al-Akhira, aw Kayfa Jara' al-Hujum al-'Am* (Baghdad: Matba'at al-Furat, 1934), 2–4. Original: M. Şevki, *Büyük Taaruz Nasıl Oldu?* (Istanbul: Akşam Kitaphanesi, 1933).

110 Muhammad Fadil al-Jamali, *al-Tarbiya wa-al-Ta'lim fi Turkiya al-Haditha* (Baghdad: Matba'at al-Hukuma, 1938), 1–5, 105–106; Reeva Spector Simon, *Iraq between the Two World Wars: The Militarist Origins of Tyranny*, updated ed. (New York: Columbia University Press, 2004), 72–80.

111 Sannu, *Turkiya al-Kamaliyah*, 185–194.

112 "Mata Ataturk," *al-Ahram*, November 11, 1938, 1; al-Sawi, "Ma Qalla wa-Dalla," *al-Ahram*, November 11, 1938, 1; "Nahdat Turkiya wa-Nahdat Misr," *al-Ahram*, November 15, 1938, 1–2; "Marathi al-Shu'ara," *al-Ahram*, November 21, 1938, 3; "Thawrat Ataturk," *Filastin*, November 22, 1938, 4.

113 "al-Ghazi Kamal Ataturk," *al-Risala*, November 14, 1938, 1841–1842; Mahmud Ghanim, "Ataturk," *al-Risala*, November 21, 1938, 1883–1885.

Chapter 6 Strolling through Istanbul

1 Burhan Belge, "Mısırlı dostlarımız," *Ulus*, July 23, 1936, 2; Tekinalp, *Kemalizm*, 208–315.

2 "Le tourisme," *Bulletin Périodique de la presse Turque*, No. 77 (April–June 1930), 10; "Turizm Kongresi Dün Açıldı," *Cumhuriyet*, June 1, 1930, 1; US Department of Commerce, *The Promotion of Tourist Travel by Foreign Countries* (Washington, DC: Government Printing Office, 1931), 56.

3 "Ila' ayna yusafir sukkan Misr," *al-Musawwar*, October 7, 1932, 9.

4 "Mısırlı bir prenses geldi," *Cumhuriyet*, June 24, 1933, 2; "Mısır Adliye Nazırı Yalovada," *Cummhuriyet*, August 19, 1933, 6; "al-Ustadh al-Taftazani fi Istambul," *al-Musawwar*, July 27, 1934, 12; "Mısırlı seyyahlar azaldı," *Cumhuriyet*, August 30, 1933, 2.

5 Gökhan Akçura, *Turizm Yıl Sıfır* (Istanbul: Om Yayınevi, 2002), 46.

6 "À l'Étranger," *Türkiye Turing ve Otomobil Klöbü Belleteni*, February 1939, 31.

7 "Travaux Publics: Chemins de Fer," *Correspondance d'Orient*, February 1933, 84; "Europe-Asie par le Simplon-Orient-Express et le Taurus Express," *Comœdia*, May 13, 1933, 4; Irene Anastasiadou, *Constructing Iron Europe* (Amsterdam: University of Amsterdam Press, 2011), 161.

8 "La navigation," *Bulletin Périodique de la presse Turque*, No. 78 (June–August 1930), 12.

9 Akçura, *Turizm Yıl Sıfır*, 206–207.

10 "Mandub al-Ahram fi 'Asimat Turkiya," *al-Ahram*, November 1, 1931, 4; "Mu'ahadat al-Sadaqa bayna Misr wa-Turkiya," *al-Ahram*, November 3, 1931, 4; "Türkiye ve Mısır," *Cumhuriyet*, October 24, 1931, 3; Goldschmidt, *Biographical Dictionary*, 12.

11 Mahmud Abu al-Fath, "*al-Ahram* fi Turkiya," *al-Ahram*, December 8, 1931, 1; Mahmud Abu al-Fath, "*al-Ahram* fi Turkiya," *al-Ahram*, December 10, 1931, 1, 12; Mahmud Abu al-Fath, "*al-Ahram* fi Turkiya," *al-Ahram*, December 19, 1931, 1; Mahmud Abu al-Fath, "*al-Ahram* fi Turkiya," *al-Ahram*, December 22, 1931, 1, 2; Mahmud Abu al-Fath, "*al-Ahram* fi Turkiya," *al-Ahram*, December 24, 1931, 1–2.

12 Cagaptay, *Islam, Secularism and Nationalism*, 137–139.

13 For biographical information on Tawfiq Habib and his column in *al-Ahram*, see Yunan Labib Rizk, "Story-telling," *al-Ahram Weekly Online*, No. 797 (June 1–7, 2006), http://weekly.ahram.org.eg/Archive/2006/797/chrncls.htm.

14 "Gazi heykeli açıldı ve İsmet Paşa 50,000 kişi huzurunda nutkunu söyledi," *Cumhuriyet*, July 28, 1932, 1; "Mısır'lı Seyyahlar geldi. Elehram muhabiri İsmet Pş. İle görüştü," *Cumhuriyet*, July 30, 1932, 1; "Mısır'lı misafirler idarehanemizde," *Cumhuriyet*, August 5, 1932, 2; "al-Sayyah al-Misriyun fi al-Asitana," *al-Ahram*, August 2, 1932, 4; "Şehrimizdeki Mısır'lı misafirler," *Cumhuriyet*, August 12, 1932, 2; Yunus Nadi, "Bir kardeşlik tezahürü: Türk'ler ve Mısırlı'lar," *Cumhuriyet*, August 15, 1932, 1; al-Sihafi al-'Ajuz, *Ala' al-Hamish: Rihlat Iksbris bayna Iskandariya wa-Istanbul* (Cairo: Matba'at Fu'ad, 1932), 8–9, 26–30.

15 al-Sihafi al-'Ajuz, *Ala' al-Hamish*, 38–64, 75–77.

16 al-Sihafi al-'Ajuz, *Ala' al-Hamish*, unnumbered first pages.

17 al-Sihafi al-'Ajuz, *Rihlat Sayf ila' Turkiya wa-al-Yunan wa-Yujuslafiya wa-Italiya* (Cairo: Maktabat al-Fajala al-Misriya, 1933), 24–75.

18 al-Sahafi al-'Ajuz, *Rihlat Sayf ila' Turkiya*, v–vi; Goldschmidt, *Biographical Dictionary*, 1.

19 Fikri Abaza, "Yasha! Yasha! … Yashasin Turklar," *al-Ahram*, July 31, 1933, 7; Fikri Abaza, "Yawm al-Jum'a! …," *al-Ahram*, August 2, 1933, 7.

20 "Da'wat ba'dh Kibar al-utaba' li-Ziyarat al-Bilad al-Turkiya," *al-Ahram*, August 11, 1933, 6; "Bayna Misr wa-Turkiya," *al-Ahram*, August 11, 1933, 4; Husayn Ramzi, "Li-Ziyarat Turkiya," *al-Ahram*, August 12, 1933, 7; "Mısır heyeti cumaya geliyor," *Cumhuriyet*, August 16, 1933, 2; "al-Utaba' wa-al-Sahafiyun al-Misriyun fi Turkiya," *al-Ahram*, August 18, 1933.

21 "Mısırlı misafirlerin gezintileri," *Cumhuriyet*, August 20, 1933, 1; "Wafd al-Widad fi Turkiya," *al-Ahram*, August 21, 1933, 6; "Mısırlı misafirler şerefine dün verilen ziyafetler," *Cumhuriyet*, August 21 1933, 2; "Mısırlı misafirler," *Cumhuriyet*, August 23, 1933, 2; "Mısırlı misafirler Ankarada," *Cumhuriyet*, August 27, 1933, 5; "Mısırlı misafirlerimiz geliyorlar," *Cumhuriyet*, August 28, 1933, 2; "Mısırlı misafirler," *Cumhuriyet*, August 29, 1933, 5.

22 All references to al-Sawi and Sarruf in the following pages are based on al-Sawi, "Ma Qala wa-Dala," *al-Ahram*, December 9, 1932, 1; al-Sawi, "Ma Qala wa-Dala," *al-Ahram*, December 10, 1932, 1; "Wafd al-Sahafiyin wa-al-Utaba'al-Misriyin fi Turkiya," *al-Ahram*, August 24, 1933, 4; al-Sawi, "Ma Qala wa-Dala," *al-Ahram*, September 3, 1933, 1; al-Sawi, "Ma Qala wa-Dala," *al-Ahram*, September 5, 1933, 1; al-Sawi, "Ma Qala wa-Dala," *al-Ahram*, September 6, 1933, 1; al-Sawi, "Ma Qala wa-Dala," *al-Ahram*, September 7, 1933, 1; A.S.M., "Fi al-Tariq ila' Anqara (4)," *al-Ahram*, September 16, 1933, 1, 13; A.S.M., "Fi al-Tariq ila' Anqara (5)," *al-Ahram*, September 30, 1933, 1, 11; Fuad Sarruf, "Min al-Qahira ila' Anqara," *al-Muqtataf*, October 1933, 336–350; Fuad Sarruf, "Min al-Qahira ila' Anqara," *al-Muqtataf*, November 1933, 439–453.

23 Orhan Tekelioğlu, "The Rise of a Spontaneous Synthesis: The Historical Background of Turkish Popular Music," *Middle Eastern Studies*, Vol. 32II (1996), 205; "Man' al-Istiwanat al-'Arabiya min Dukhul Turkiya," *al-Jami'a al-'Arabiya*, December 31, 1934, 1; "La musique," *Bulletin Périodique de la Presse Turque*, No. 106 (January–February 1935), 7–8; Peyami Safa, "Mısır Radyosu," *Cumhuriyet*, August 6, 1936, 3; John Morgan O'Connell, *Alaturka: Style in Turkish Music (1923–1938)* (Burlington, VT: Ashgate, 2013), 200–201.

24 "Harbiyede Belvü Bahçesinde," *Cumhuriyet*, June 19, 1936, 8; "Her akşam Beyoğlunda Londra Birahanesinde," *Cumhuriyet*, October 15, 1936, 9; "Ferah Sinemada," *Cumhuriyet*, November 26, 1936, 4; "Her akşam: Harbiyede Belvü," *Cumhuriyet*, August 21, 1937, 10; "Suadiye plajında," *Cumhuriyet*, September 17, 1937, 4; "Bu akşam Harbiyede Belvü Bahçesi," *Cumhuriyet*, May 19, 1939, 12; "İnci Gazinosunda," *Cumhuriyet*, September 7, 1939, 8.

25 Reproduced in a Turkish translation from the daily *al-Balagh* in *Yabancı Gözüyle Cumhuriyet Türkiyesi* (Ankara: Dahiliye Vekaleti Matbuat Umum Müdürlüğü Neşriyatı, 1938), 134.

26 "Mısırda Türkiye," *Cumhuriyet*, March 30, 1935, 3; al-Sawi, "Ma Qala wa-Dala," *al-Ahram*, November 11, 1938, 1.

27 "Turkiya al-Haditha," *al-Musawwar*, September 15, 1933, 13.

28 Akverdi, "Suriyede kısa tetkikler: Türkiye hasreti," *Cumhuriyet*, October 12, 1936, 5.

29 "Mısırlı misafirlerimiz," *Cumhuriyet*, August 19, 1933, 1; "Wafd al-Wadad," *al-Musawwar*, August 25, 1933, 9; A.S.M., "Fi al-Tariq ila' Anqara (3)," *al-Ahram*, September 10, 1933, 1.

30 "Dün Taksim abidesine çelenk koydular," *Cumhuriyet*, August 20, 1933, 5; "al-Kashafa al-Suriyun fi Turkiya," *al-Musawwar*, September 8, 1933, 8.

31 "Milli vapurcular Mısır'a sefer tertibini düşünüyorlar," *Cumhuriyet*, April 16, 1930, 2; "Mısır'a!," *Cumhuriyet*, May 14, 1930, 2.

32 Efdal As, *Cumhuriyet Dönemi Ulaşım Politikaları* (Ankara: Atatürk Araştırma Merkezi Yayınları, 2013), 393–394.

33 Yunus Nadi, "Seyrisefainin İskenderiye Seferleri," *Cumhuriyet*, June 22, 1933, 1; Mısır seferlerinin ilgası zararlı olacaktır," *Cumhuriyet*, June 24, 1933, 1, 6; "Gazetemizin bir Hizmeti: İskenderiye hattının ilgasından vazgeçildi," *Cumhuriyet*, June 25, 1933, 1, 3; "Mısır hattını karla işletmek mümkündür," *Cumhuriyet*, June 28, 1933, 1, 3.

34 "İskenderiye Seferleri," *Cumhuriyet*, June 22, 1933, 1, 5; "İskenderiye seferlerinin karı 1,5 milyon liradır," *Cumhuriyet*, June 26, 1933, 1, 5; "260.000 lira kar için 4.000.000 lira zarar!," *Cumhuriyet*, June 27, 1933, 1; "Başvekil Paşa Hz. nden rica ediyoruz İskenderiye seferleri devam etmelidir," *Cumhuriyet*, June 30, 1933, 1–2; "Her Mısırlı merakla Soruyor!," *Cumhuriyet*, July 1, 1933, 1; "Yaz ve ihracat mevsiminde hiç ilga edilemez," *Cumhuriyet*, July 4, 1933, 1; "Davamızı Kazandık. İskenderiye seferlerinin ilgasından vazgeçildi," *Cumhuriyet*, July 7, 1933, 1; "Bir Mısır gazetecinin dedikleri," *Cumhuriyet*, July 8, 1933, 5; Sahafi 'Ajuz, "'Ala' al-Hamish," *al-Ahram*, July 21, 1933, 7–8.

35 "Gazeteciliğin mükafatı!," *Cumhuriyet*, July 8, 1933, 8; "Mısırlı seyyahlar azaldı," *Cumhuriyet*, August 30, 1933, 2; "İskenderiye seferleri gene arttılacak mı?,"*Cumhuriyet*, December 27, 1933, 2.

36 "Mısır seferleri," *Cumhuriyet*, April 3, 1934, 2; Z.D., "İskenderiye vapur seferlerinin faydası," *Cumhuriyet*, May 10, 1934, 3; "İskenderiye hattı," *Cumhuriyet*, May 14, 1934, 2; "Mısırda iktısadî vaziyet gün geçtikçe iyileşiyor," *Cumhuriyet*, December 31, 1933, 4; "Ucuz Mısır seyahatı," *Cumhuriyet*, May 29, 1934, 2; "Bedava ilân," *Cumhuriyet*, March 25, 1934, 3; "Mısırdan 150 kişilik bir seyyah kafilesi gelecek," *Cumhuriyet*, June 7, 1934, 2; "Mısırlılar grup halinde memleketimize gelecekler," *Cumhuriyet*, June 8, 1934, 2; "Mısırlı seyyahlar geliyor," *Cumhuriyet*, June 20, 1934, 2.

37 'Abd al-Wahhab al-Najjar, *al-Ayyam al-Hamra*,' ed. Ahmad Zakariyya al-Shilaq (Cairo: Matba'at Dar-Kutub wa'l-Watha'iq al-Qawmiyya, 2010), 8; Jacob, *Working Out Egypt*, 316n125; Selma Botman, *Egypt from Independence to Revolution, 1919–1952* (Syracuse, NY: Syracuse University Press, 1991), 116–117.

38 "Mısırlı izciler geliyor," *Cumhuriyet*, July 21, 1934, 2; "Mısırlı bir kafile," *Cumhuriyet*, August 4, 1934, 1; "Mısırlı kafilesi," *Cumhuriyet*, August 5, 1934, 3; "Firqat al-Kashafa al-Misriya fi Istanbul," *al-Ahram*, August 7, 1934, 4; "Firqat al-Kashafa al-Misriya fi Istanbul," *al-Ahram*, August 8, 1934, 4; "Rihlat al-Shuban al-Muslimin ila Turkiya," *al-Ahram*, August 13, 1934, 11; "Kahramanlar diyarı

Türkiyeye can atarız," *Cumhuriyet*, August 14, 1934, 2; "al-Shuban al-Muslimin fi Turkiya," *al-Musawwar*, August 31, 1934, 25. For information on the Boy Scouts movement in Egypt until the mid-1930s, see Shafiq Naqash and 'Ali Khalifa, *al-Haraka al-Kashfiyya fi al-Aqtar al-'Arabiyya* (Beirut: Mataba'at al-Kashaf, 1936), 99–120.

39 "Şehrimize 350 Mısırlı seyyah geldi," *Cumhuriyet*, July 18, 1934, 2; "Mısır niçin Atinayı tercih ediyor?," *Cumhuriyet*, July 19, 1934, 5.

40 "İskenderiye'de bir büro açıldı," *Cumhuriyet*, January 9, 1933, 6; "Mısır'da bir Türkiye turizm bürosu açılıyor," *Cumhuriyet*, April 9, 1935, 4; "Türk-Mısır dostluk cemiyeti," *Cumhuriyet*, January 28, 1935, 5; "Kahirede bir büro teşkil edildi," *Cumhuriyet*, May 19, 1935, 2.

41 "Iskenderiye vapur seferleri kalkıyor," *Cumhuriyet*, December 6, 1935, 1, 6.

42 "La navigation," *Bulletin Périodique de la Presse Turque*, No. 112 (December 1935–February 1936), 5–6.

43 "Mısır seferlerinin ihdası isteniyor," *Cumhuriyet*, December 18, 1935, 2; "Mısır seferlerinin kaldırılması," *Cumhuriyet*, December 21, 1935, 3; Yunus Nadi, "Denizyollarımızın İskenderiye seferleri Meselesi," *Cumhuriyet*, January 2, 1936, 1; "Mısır seferleri: Yeni gemi temin edilince tekrar başlıyacak," *Cumhuriyet*, January 3, 1936, 7; Abidin Daver, "İskenderiye Seferleri bir an Evvel başlamalıdır," *Cumhuriyet*, February 2, 1936, 1; "İskenderiye seferleri ne vakit başlıyacak," *Cumhuriyet*, February 5, 1936, 2; "Türkofis Mısır seferlerinin başlamasını istiyor," *Cumhuriyet*, May 20, 1936, 3; "İskenderiye seferleri başlamalıdır," *Cumhuriyet*, May 31, 1936, 7.

44 "İskenderiye seferleri ihya edilmelidir," *Cumhuriyet*, July 6, 1936, 7; "İskenderiye vapur seferleri," *Cumhuriyet*, September 12, 1936, 2; "Yeni vapurlar ve harici hatlar," *Cumhuriyet*, June 4, 1937, 2; "Turkey to Increase Merchant Fleet," *Financial Times*, April 23, 1938, 7.

45 "Rihlat al-Tulaba al-Misriyin ila' Uruba hadha al-'am," *al-Ahram*, July 9, 1936, 9.

46 BCA:30.10.0.0-200/367/10, July 29, 1936; "Le visite en Turquie des universitaires égyptiens," *Ankara*, July 23, 1936, 6; "Mısırlı Talebeler geldi," *Cumhuriyet*, July 17, 1936, 1, 7; "Kahire üniversitesi prefesör ve talebesinden mürekkep 100 kişilik bir gurup istanbulda," *Yeni Yol*, July 18, 1936, 1; "Mısırlı talebelerin ziyaretleri," *Cumhuriyet*, July 23, 1936, 2; "Tulaba al-Misriyun fi Turkiya," *al-Ahram*, July 25, 1936, 10; Majd al-Din Nasif, "al-Shabab al-Masri wa-Turkiya," *al-Ahram*, August 1, 1936, 1; "Şarkın Atası ve büyük inkılabları," *Cumhuriyet*, August 20, 1936, 2; "Atatürk Çanakkaleyi bir defa daha kurtardı," *Cumhuriyet*, July 20, 1936, 1; "Boğazların Askeri İşgali Dün Tamamlandı," *Cumhuriyet*, July 22, 1936, 1; "Mısırlı kardeşlerin ziyafetinde," *Cumhuriyet*, July 25, 1936, 2.

47 "Mısır Ordusu Müfettişi Aziz Paşanın beyanatı," *Cumhuriyet*, August 5, 1938, 1; "Egypte," *Bulletin Périodique de la presse Turque*, No. 125 (June–August 1938), 14.

48 BCA: 30.10.0.0-200/369/5, July 4, 1938; "Mısır Üniversitelileri şehrimizde," *Cumhuriyet*, July 6, 1938, 2; "al-Fariq al-Riyadi al-Masri fi Turkiya," *al-Ahram*, July 4, 1938, 8; "Vali, Mısırlı atletlere bir ziyafet Verdi," *Cumhuriyet*, July 6, 1938, 6; "Suriye matbuatının hedefi Arab alemini Türkiye aleyhine kışkırtmak istiyorlar," *Cumhuriyet*, June 17, 1938, 1.

49 Khanki Bey, *Turk wa-Ataturk*, 142–143.

50 Agatha Christie, *Murder on the Orient Express* (New York: Harper, 2011), 3–15.

51 "Le Simplon-Orient-Express," *Revue Générale des Chemins de fer*, Vol. 49, No. 5 (May 1930), 475–476; "Simplon-Orient Express to Run to Aleppo," *Times*, May 4, 1927, 11; "London to Mosul in a Week," *Times*, December 9, 1927, 13; "From Calais to Cairo," *Times*, February 7, 1928, 13; "Toros Ekspresi," *Cumhuriyet*, February 16, 1930, 3; Anastasiadou, *Constructing Iron Europe*, 159–162.

52 "Toros ekspresi," *Türk Sözü*, February 8, 1935, 1; "Les Voies ferréesde l'Asie Antérieure," *Revue Générale des Chemins de fer*, Vol. 56, No. 1 (July 1936), 65.

53 Türkofis Neşriyat ve Propaganda Servisi, *Turizm Raporu* (Ankara: 1935), 43; "Iraktan gezgin getirebilmek için ...," *Cumhuriyet*, May 11, 1935, 2; "Turizm böyle olur!," *Cumhuriyet*, July 1, 1935, 1; "Dün şehrimize gelen seyyahlar," *Cumhuriyet*, April 21, 1936, 2; Kandemir, "Turizm işleri üzerinde tetkikler: 2," *Cumhuriyet*, October 21, 1936, 2.

54 BCA: 30.10.0.0-200/369/3, June 24, 1938.

55 Baqir Amin al-Ward, *A'lam al-'Iraq al-Hadith* (Baghdad: Matba'at al-Ufsit al-Mina,' 1978), 1:283.

56 "Ma Shahadtuhu fi Turkiya: al-Hayat al-Diniya! (9)," *al-Istiqlal*, September 15, 1935, 1; "Ma Shahadtuhu fi Turkiya: al-Hayat al-Diniya! (10)," *al-Istiqlal*, September 17, 1935, 3; "Ma Shahadtuhu fi Turkiya: al-Hayat al-Diniya! (11)," *al-Istiqlal*, September 19, 1935, 3; "Ma Shahadtuhu fi Turkiya: al-Hala al-Siyasiya (13)," *al-Istiqlal*, September 22, 1935, 1.

57 "Ma Shahadtuhu fi Turkiya: al-Hala al-Siyasiya (14)," *al-Istiqlal*, September 23, 1935, 1; "Ma Shahadtuhu fi Turkiya: al-Hala al-Siyasiya (15)," *al-Istiqlal*, September 25, 1935, 1; "Ma Shahadtuhu fi Turkiya: al-Hala al-Siyasiya (16)," *al-Istiqlal*, September 29, 1935, 1; "Ma Shahadtuhu fi Turkiya: al-Shu'ur al-Qawmi (17)," *al-Istiqlal*, September 30, 1935, 1; "Ma Shahadtuhu fi Turkiya: al-Shu'ur al-Qawmi (19)," *al-Istiqlal*, October 2, 1935, 1; "Ma Shahadtuhu fi Turkiya: al-Mudafa'a (21)," *al-Istiqlal*, October 17, 1935, 1, 3.

58 Orit Bashkin, *The Other Iraq: Pluralism and Culture in Hashemite Iraq* (Stanford, CA: Stanford University Press, 2009), 52–69.

59 "Bahreyn Sultanı şehrimizde," *Cumhuriyet*, July 26, 1936, 2; "Suriye Başbakanı Parise Gitti," *Ulus Sesi*, November 30, 1937, 1; FO 371/21914/88, Loraine to Eden, December 30, 1937.

60 BCA: 30.10.0.0-258/740/6, June 4, 1931; "La politique asiatique de la Turquie," *Bulletin Périodique de la presse Turque*, No. 90 (December 1931), 14; "Irak Hariciye Nazırı," *Cumhuriyet*, September 4, 1936, 1.

61 FO 371/16889/7, Humphrys to Foreign Office, September 7, 1933; BCA: 30.10.0.0-200/368/5, October 22, 1937; "Irak Erkaıharbiye Reisi şehrimizde," *Cumhuriyet*, November 7, 1936, 1; "Tasrihat li-Taha al-Hashimi 'an al-Jaysh al-Turki," *al-Istiqlal*, November 11, 1936, 1; BCA: 30.10.0.0-259/745/10, November 23, 1936; 30.10.0.0-200/368/4, October 20, 1937.

62 M., "al-Islam wa-Kayfa Ya'rifuhu Katib Turki," *al-Risala*, January 10, 1938, 76; Gershoni and Jankowski, *Redefining the Egyptian Nation*, 63–64; Bashkin, *The Other Iraq*, 60.

63 Rainer Brünner, *Islamic Ecumenism in the 20th Century* (New York: Brill, 2004), 126.

64 'Abd al-Wahhab 'Azzam, "Bayna al-Qahira wa-Istanbul – 2," *al-Risala*, December 6, 1937, 1963–1964; 'Abd al-Wahhab 'Azzam, "Bayna al-Qahira wa-Istanbul – 3," *al-Risala*, December 6, 1937, 2062–2063; 'Abd al-Wahhab 'Azzam, "Bayna al-Qahira wa-Istanbul – 4," *al-Risala*, January 3, 1938, 14–16.

65 'Abd al-Wahhab 'Azzam, *Rihlat* (Cairo: Matba'at al-Risala, 1939), 272–298.

66 'Azzam, *Rihlat*, 253, 295.

67 For an interesting account on the operation of the Taurus Express after the British occupation of Syria and Iraq in 1941, see Richard Pearse, *Three Years in the Levant* (London: Macmillan, 1949), 101–114.

68 As, *Cumhuriyet Dönemi Ulaşım Politikaları*, 488, 508–509.

69 "Rabibat al-Ghazi fi Ziyarat al-Masajid al-Athariya," *al-Ahram*, October 17, 1933, 1; "Afet Hanım Mısırda," *Cumhuriyet*, October 22, 1933, 2.

70 Burhan Belge, "Mısırlı dostlarımız," *Ulus*, July 23, 1936, 2; Tekinalp, *Kemalizm*, 208–315.

Chapter 7 A Distant Neighbor

1 Hale, *Turkish Foreign Policy since 1774*, 53–54.

2 Ahmad, *Turkey: The Quest for Identity*, 90.

3 Oran, *Turkish Foreign Policy, 1919–2006*, 19.

4 Uzer, *Identity and Turkish Foreign Policy*, 89.

5 Bilgin, *Britain and Turkey*, 33–34.

6 Onur İşçi, "Russophobic Neutrality: Turkish Diplomacy, 1936–1945," unpublished PhD diss., Georgetown University, 2014, 97–100.

7 Y. Olmert, "Britain, Turkey and the Levant Question during the Second World War," *Middle Eastern Studies*, Vol. 23 (1987), 437–452; Nicholas Tamkin, *Britain, Turkey, and the Soviet Union, 1940–1945* (London: Palgrave, 2009), 54–55; Francis R. Nicosia, *Nazi Germany and the Arab World* (New York: Cambridge University Press, 2015), 197–198; Mogens Pelt, *Military Intervention and a Crisis of Democracy in Turkey* (London: I. B. Tauris, 2014), 37–39.

8 Erkin, *Dışişlerinde 34 Yıl*, 1:125.

9 Olmert, "Britain, Turkey and the Levant Question," 448–450.

10 Tevfik Rüştü Aras, *Görüşlerim* (Istanbul: Semih Lutfi Kitabevi, 1945), 21, 24, 31, 37, 131–132.

11 Hulusi Sidal, *Yakın Şarkta Ekonomik İşbirliği: Türkiye-Irak Gümrük Birliği ve Yakın Şark Federasyonu* (Istanbul, 1947).

12 Aptülahat Akşin, *Atatürk'ün Dış Politika İlkeleri ve Diplomasisi* (Ankara: Türk Tarik Kurumu, 1991), 210–214; Bilgin, *Britain and Turkey*, 75–137.

13 Darwaza, *Turkiya al-Haditha*, 7–8ff.

14 Basil Daqqaq, *Turkiya bayna Jabarayn* (Beirut: Dar al-Makshuf, 1947), 61–63, 81–86.

15 Amin Shakir et al., *Turkiya wa-al-Siyasa al-'Arabiya* (Cairo: Dar al-Ma'arif, 1954), 5–8.

16 Shakir, *Turkiya wa-al-Siyasa al-'Arabiya*, 32–33, 58, 71, 96–109, 122, 153–159.

17 Shakir Sabir, *Ta'rih al-Sadaqa bayna al-'Iraq wa-Turkiya* (Baghdad: Dar al-Ma'rifa, 1955), 1–16.

18 Sabir, *Ta'rih al-Sadaqa bayna al-'Iraq wa-Turkiya*, 17–19, 146–211.

19 Abd al-Majid al-Wandawi, *Al-Hilf al-Turki al-Bakistani wa-al-Mashari' al-Isti'mariya fi al-Sharq al-Awsat* (Baghdad: Matba'at al-Rabita, 1954), 11–13, 19–21, 32, 43–45.

20 For a detailed discussion of the politics of the Baghdad Pact, from Arab and Turkish perspectives, see Elie Podeh, *The Quest for Hegemony in the Arab World* (Leiden: Brill, 1995); Behçet Kemal Yeşilbursa, *The Baghdad Pact* (London: Frank Cass, 2005), 71–215.

21 Pelt, *Military Intervention*, 135–158.

22 "Faysel Hazretleri Şehri Dolaşıyor," *Son Posta*, July 11, 1931, 3.

23 Bashkin, *The Other Iraq*, 177–182.

24 "Ankara Şehir tiyatrosu Bağdada gidiyor," *Cumhuriyet*, March 24, 1938, 3; "al-Firqa al-Tamthiliya li-'Asimat Turkiya," *al-Istiqlal*, April 10, 1938, 3; BCA, 30.10.0.0-146/44/3, May 17, 1938.

25 Muhammad Jamil Bayhum, *al-ʿArab wa-al-Turk fi al-Siraʿ bayna al-Sharq wa-al-Gharb* (Cairo: al-Matbaʿa al-Wataniya, 1957), 223.

26 "Trabzon limanı ihale edildi," *Cumhuriyet*, October 17, 1945, 2; "Trabzon limanının inşası hazırlıkları," *Cumhuriyet*, January 23, 1946, 1; Yaşar Baytal, "Trabzon Limanı İnşası," *History Studies*, Vol. 5iii (June 2013), 28–31.

27 "Türk-İran yolları birbirine bağlanacak," *Milliyet*, October 15, 1956, 1; CENTO Public Relations Division, *The Story of the Central Treaty Organization* (Ankara, 1959), 24–30; "Amerika Muş-Tatvan Demiryolu inşaatına 6 milyon dolar veriyor," *Milliyet*, July 14, 1960, 1; "CENTO demiryolunun ilk kısmı bu hafta açılıyor," *Milliyet*, October 23, 1964, 7; Akçura, *Turizm Yıl Sıfır*, 115.

28 "Suez Spurs Talk of New Pipeline: Oil Concerns Again Consider Big Carrier to Bypass Some Mideast Countries through Pact Members," *New York Times*, August 10, 1956, 3; "Treaty Pledges Weighed for Proposed Pipeline to Bypass Suez Area," *Wall Street Journal*, March 22, 1957, 15; "Dulles Says US May Ask Treaty Protection for Mideast Oil Line," *Wall Street Journal*, March 27, 1957, 21; "Turkey, Iran Reach Accord on Pipeline," *Washington Post*, September 5, 1957, 5; "Pipeline Politics, a New Arab Game," *New York Times*, January 7, 1958, 68.

29 Suha Bolukbasi, "Turkey Copes with Revolutionary Iran," *Journal of South Asian and Middle Eastern Studies*, Vol. 13 (1989), 94–109.

30 "Syria under Pressure to Settle Oil Dispute," *London Times*, February 27, 1967, 5; "Turkey and Iran May Construct Pipeline to Avoid Arab Nations," *New York Times*, September 1, 1969, 26–27; "New Pipeline across Egypt Being Planned," *Washington Post*, June 15, 1971, 14; Alon Liel, *Turkey in the Middle East* (Boulder, CO: Lynne Rienner, 2001), 38–41.

31 Liel, *Turkey in the Middle East*, 155–176ff.

32 Zürcher, *Turkey*, 306–333.

33 Soner Cagaptay, *The Rise of Turkey: The Twenty-First Century's First Muslim Power* (Lincoln, NE: Potomac Books, 2014), 5–6, 17–18.

34 Mert Bilgin, "Energy Policy in Turkey: Security, Markets, Supplies and Pipelines," *Turkish Studies*, Vol. 12iii (2011), 399–417.

35 T. J. Howkins, "Changing Hegemonies and New External pressures: South East European Railway Networks in Transition," *Journal of Transport Geography*, Vol. 13 (2005), 187–197; Irene Anastasiadou and Aristotle Tympas, "Iron Silk Roads: Comparing Interwar and Post-war Transnational Asian Railway Projects," in Martin Schiefelbusch and Hans-Liudger Dienel, eds., *Linking Networks: The Formation of Common Standards and Visions for Infrastructure Development* (London: Routledge, 2014),169–185; "China, Turkey to Further Economy, to

Increase Investments," *DailySabah.com*, July 3, 2016 [retrieved: November 27, 2016]; Cagaptay, *The Rise of Turkey*, 24.

36 Aptülahat Akşin, *Türkiyenin 1945 den Sonraki Dış Gelişmeleri: Orta Doğu Meseleleri* (Istanbul: Kervan Matbaası, 1959), 125.

37 Khanki Bey, *Turk wa-Ataturk*, 34–35.

38 Patrick Seale, "The Rise and Rise of Turkey," *New York Times*, November 4, 2009, www.nytimes.com/2009/11/05/opinion/05iht-edseale.html; B. Senem Çevik, "Turkish Soap Opera Diplomacy," *Exchange: The Journal of Public Diplomacy*, Vol. 5i (2014), 78–103.

39 Annual exports to the Middle East in 2013 were $42 billion and in 2014 $41 billion. See the World Bank's "Product Exports by Turkey to Middle East & North Africa" for 2012–2015 in at http://wits.worldbank.org/CountryProfile/en/Country/TUR/Year/2015/TradeFlow/Export/Partner/MEA/Product/all-groups.

40 "High-Spending Arab Tourists Flock to Turkey," *Reuters*, July 6, 2011, www.reuters.com/article/uk-turkey-tourism-idUSLNE76505P2011 0706; "Steep Drop in Middle Eastern Tourists to Turkey," *Middle East Monitor*, January 4, 2017, www.middleeastmonitor.com/20170104-steep-drop-in-middle-eastern-tourists-to-turkey.

41 Oran, *Turkish Foreign Policy*, 19.

42 "Erdoğan: Lozan'ı Zafer diye yutturdular," *Yeni Şafak*, September 29, 2016, www.yenisafak.com/gundem/erdogan-lozani-zafer-diye-yutturdular-2538795; İbrahim Karagül, "Musul ve Halep'in kuzeyi Türkiye'ye devredilmeli ...," *Yeni Şafak*, October 24, 2016, www.yenisafak.com/yazarlar/ibrahimkaragul/musul-ve-halepin-kuzeyi-turkiyeye-devredilmeli-2033702; İbrahim Karagül, "Türkiye'yi durdurmak artık mümkün değildir," *Yeni Şafak*, December 2, 2016, www.yenisafak.com/yazarlar/ibrahimkaragul/turkiyeyi-durdurmak-artik-mumkun-degildir-2034557; Nick Danforth, "Turkey's New Maps Are Reclaiming the Ottoman Empire," *FP.com*, October 23, 2016, http://foreignpolicy.com/2016/10/23/turkeys-religious-nationalists-want-ottoman-borders-iraq-erdogan/.

43 Akşin, *Atatürk'ün Dış Politika İlkeleri*, 207–209.

44 Krüger, *Kemalist Turkey and the Middle East*, 168, 175.

45 Linke, "Turkey," 344–345.

46 Tripp, *A History of Iraq*, 86; "Death of a Dictator," *Times*, August 13, 1937, 13; M. Kalman, *Belge ve tanıklarıyla Dersim Direnişleri* (Istanbul: Nujen Yayıncılık, 1995), 237–239.

47 Henri J. Barkey and Ömer Taşpınar, "Republic of Turkey," in Mark Gasiorowski, ed., *The Government and Politics of the Middle East and North Africa*, 8th ed. (Boulder, CO: Westview Press, 2017), 222, 225.

Bibliography

Archives

Başbakanlık Cumhuriyet Arşivi [BCA], Ankara
Ben-Gurion Archives Online [BGAO], Sede Boqer (http://in.bgu.ac.il/en/
    bgarchives/Pages/archives.aspx)
Central Zionist Archives [CZA], Jerusalem
The National Archives [TNA], Kew, London
National Archives and Records Administration [NARA], College Park,
    Maryland, USA

Periodicals

al-Ahram (Cairo)
al-Istiqlal (Baghdad)
al-Jami'a al-'Arabiya (Jerusalem)
al-Jami'a al-Islamiya (Jaffa)
al-Kashkul (Cairo)
al-Ma'rid (Beirut)
al-Muqtataf (Cairo)
al-Musawwar (Cairo)
al-Risala (Cairo)
Ankara (Ankara)
Bayandırlık İşleri Dergisi (Ankara)
Bulletin Périodique de la presse Turque (Paris)
Cumhuriyet (Istanbul)
Davar (Tel Aviv)
Filastin (Jaffa)
Financial Times (London)
Hakimiyet-i Milliye (Ankara)
Journal of the Royal Central Asian Society (London)
L'Égyptienne (Cairo)
L'Humanité (Paris)
Le Petit Journal (Paris)
Life (New York, NY)

New York Times (New York, NY)
Palestine Post (Jerusalem)
Radikal (Ankara)
Ruz al-Yusuf (Cairo)
Son Posta (Istanbul)
The Times (London)
Time (New York)
Türk Sözü (Adana)
Türkiye Turing ve Ottomobil Klöbü Belleteni (Istanbul)
Ulus (Ankara)
Ulus Sesi (Mardin)
Urfada Milli Gazete (Urfa)
Varlık (Erzurum)
Wall Street Journal (New York, NY)
Washington Post (Washington, DC)
Yedi Gün (Istanbul)
Yeni Mersin (Mersin)
Yeni Yol (Trabzon)

Published Articles, Books, and Pamphlets

Abrahamian, Ervand. *A History of Modern Iran*. Cambridge: Cambridge University Press, 2008.

Ahmad, Feroz. "The Historical Background of Turkey's Foreign policy," in Lenore G. Martin and Dimitris Keridis, eds., *The Future of Turkish Foreign Policy*. Cambridge, MA: MIT Press, 2004. 9–33.

Turkey: The Quest for Identity. Oxford: Oneworld, 2003.

Akçura, Gökhan. *Turizm Yıl Sıfır*. Istanbul: Om Yayınevi, 2002.

Akşin, Aptülahat. *Atatürk'ün Dış Politika İlkeleri ve Diplomasisi*. Ankara: Türk Tarik Kurumu, 1991.

Türkiyenin 1945 den Sonraki Dış Gelişmeleri: Orta Doğu Meseleleri. Istanbul: Kervan Matbaası, 1959.

Alakom, Rohat. *Hoybun Örgütü ve Ağrı Ayaklanması*. Istanbul: Avesta Yayınları, 1998.

al-Bayyumi, Zakariya Sulayman. *Mawqif Misr min al-Mutaghayyirat fi Turkiya bayna al-Harbayn al-'Alimiyatayn*. Cairo: Dar al-Kitab al-Jami'i, 1989.

al-Difa' 'an al-Iskandaruna, Lajnat. *Al-Iskandaruna 'Arabiya Raghm Kul Quwwa*. Damascus: Matba'at Ibn-Zabdun, [1937].

al-Jamali, Muhammad Fadil. *Al-Tarbiya wa-al-Ta'lim fi Turkiya al-Haditha*. Baghdad: Matba'at al-Hukuma, 1938.

Allawi, Ali A. *Faisal I of Iraq*. New Haven, CT: Yale University Press, 2014.

al-Qabtan, Husayn Ramzi. *Mustafa Kamal wa-al-Harb al-Turkiya al-Yunaniya al-Akhira, aw Kayfa Jara' al-Hujum al-'Am.* Baghdad: Matba'at al-Furat, 1934.

Altuğ, Seda. "Secterianism in the Syrian Jazira: Community, Land and Violence in the Memories of World War I and the French Mandate (1915–1939)." Unpublished PhD diss., University of Utrecht, 2011.

al-Wandawi, Abd al-Majid. *Al-Hilf al-Turki al-Bakistani wa-al-Mashari' al-Isti'mariya fi al-Sharq al-Awsat.* Baghdad: Matba'at al-Rabita, 1954.

al-Wataniya al-Kurdiya, Jam'iyat Khoybun. *Al-Kurd Iza' al-'Afw al-'Am al-Turki* (1933).

Ambrosius, Gerold, and William H. Hubbard. *A Social and Economic History of Twentieth-Century Europe.* Cambridge, MA: Harvard University Press, 1989.

Amin, Camron Michael. "Globalizing Iranian Feminism, 1910–1950," *Journal of Middle East Women's Studies,* Vol. 4i (2008), 6–30.

Anastasiadou, Irene. *Constructing Iron Europe.* Amsterdam: University of Amsterdam Press, 2011.

Aras, Bülent. "Turkey's Rise in the Greater Middle East: Peace-Building in the Periphery," *Journal of Balkan and Near Eastern Studies,* Vol. 11i (2009), 29–41.

Aras, Bülent, and Aylin Görener. "National Role Conceptions and Foreign Policy Orientation: The Ideational Bases of the Justice and Development Party's Foreign Policy Activism in the Middle East," *Journal of Balkan and Near Eastern Studies,* Vol. 12, No. 1 (2010), 73–92.

Aras, Tevfik Rüştü. *Görüşlerim.* Istanbul: Semih Lutfi Kitabevi, 1945.

Atabaki, Touraj. *Azerbaijan: Ethnicity and the Struggle for Power in Iran.* New York: I. B. Tauris, 2000.

"Going East: The Ottomans' Secret Service Activities in Iran," in Touraj Atabaki, ed., *Iran and the First World War.* New York: I. B. Tauris, 2006. 29–42.

Atatürk'ün Söylev ve Demeçleri. 4 vols. Ankara: Türk Tarih Kurumu Basımevi, 1961.

[Atay], Falih Rıfkı. *Zeytindağı.* Ankara: Hakimiyeti Milliye Matbaası, 1932.

Ateş, Sabri. *Ottoman-Iranian Borderlands: Making a Boundary, 1843–1914.* New York: Cambridge University Press, 2013.

'Azmi, Mahmud. *Khabaya Siyasiya.* Cairo: Jaridat al-Masri, 1939.

'Azzam, 'Abd al-Wahhab. *Rihlat.* Cairo: Matba'at al-Risala, 1939.

Badran, Margot. *Feminists, Islam, and Nation.* Princeton, NJ: Princeton University Press, 1995.

Bainville, Jacques. *Les Dictateurs.* Paris: Les Éditions Denoël et Steele, 1935.

Baron, Beth. *Egypt as a Woman.* Berkeley: University of California Press, 2005.

Başgil, Ali Fuad. "La Constitution et le Régime politique," in *La Vie Juridique des Peuples: Turquie*. Paris: Librairie Delagrave, 1939. 9–38.

Bashkin, Orit. *The Other Iraq: Pluralism and Culture in Hashemite Iraq*. Stanford, CA: Stanford University Press, 2009.

Bayhum, Muhammad Jamil. *Al-'Arab wa-al-Turk fi al-Sira' bayna al-Sharq wa-al-Gharb*. Cairo: al-Matba'a al-Wataniya, 1957.

[Bayur], Yusuf Hikmet. *Yeni Türkiye Devletinin Harici Siyaseti*. Istanbul: Akşam Matbaası, [1934].

Bedr Kan, Sureya. *The Case of Kurdistan against Turkey*. Stockholm: Sara, 1995.

Ben-Gurion, David. *Zikhronot min Ha-'Izavon*. 6 vols. Tel Aviv: 'Am 'Oved, 1987.

Bharier, Julian. "A Note on the Population of Iran, 1900–1966," *Population Studies*, Vol. 22 ii (1968), 273–279.

Bilgin, Mustafa. *Britain and Turkey in the Middle East*. New York: Tauris Academic Studies, 2007.

Block, Alan A. "European Drug Traffic and Traffickers between the Wars," *Journal of Social History*, Vol. 23ii (1989), 315–337.

Bozdoğan, Sibel. *Modernism and Nation Building: Turkish Architectural Culture in the Early Republic*. Seattle: University of Washington Press, 2001.

Brünner, Rainer. *Islamic Ecumenism in the 20th Century*. New York: Brill, 2004.

Cagaptay, Soner. *Islam, Secularism and Nationalism in Modern Turkey: Who Is a Turk?* New York: Routledge, 2006.

The Rise of Turkey: The Twenty-First Century's First Muslim Power. Lincoln, NE: Potomac Books, 2014.

Cemil Paşa, Ekrem. *Muhtasar Hayatım*. Ankara: Beybun Yayınları, 1992.

CENTO Public Relations Division. *The Story of the Central Treaty Organization*. Ankara, 1959.

Conker, Orhan. *Les Chemins de Fer en Turquie et la Politique Ferroviaire Turque*. Paris: Librairie du Recueil Sirey, 1935.

Çetiner, Yusuf Turan. *Turkey and the West: From Neutrality to Commitment*. Lanham, MD: University Press of America, 2014.

Çetinsaya, Gökhan. "Atatürk Dönemi Türkiye-İran İlişkileri, 1926–1938," *Avrasya Dosyası*, Vol. 5iii (1999), 148–175.

Christie, Agatha. *Murder on the Orient Express*. New York: Harper, 2011.

Çiçek, M. Talha. "Erken Cumhuriyet Dönemi Ders Kitapları Çerçevesinde Türk Ulus Kimliği İnşası ve 'Arap İhaneti,'" *Divan*, Vol. 17, No. 32 (2012), 179–187.

Çin, Barış. *Türkiye-İran Siyasi İlişkileri (1923–1938)*. Istanbul: IQ Kültür Sanat Yayıncılık, 2007.

Çoşar, Nevin, and Sevtap Demirci. "The Mosul Question and the Turkish Republic: Before and after the Frontier Treaty of 1926," *The Turkish Yearbook of International Relations*, Vol. 35 (2004), 43–59.

Danielson, Virginia. *The Voice of Egypt*. Chicago: University of Chicago Press, 1997.

Daqqaq, Basil. *Turkiya bayna Jabarayn*. Beirut: Dar al-Makshuf, 1947.

Darwaza, Muhammad 'Izzat. *Turkiya al-Haditha*. Beirut: Matba'at al-Kashaf, 1946.

Daud, Sabiha al-Shaykh. *Awwal al-Tariq*. Baghdad, 1958.

Demir, Yaşar. *Fransa'nın Yakındoğu Politikaları: Suriye ve Hatay*. Istanbul: Mostar, 2013.

Department of Overseas Trade. *Economic Conditions in Turkey*. London: His Majesty's Stationery Office, 1930, 1932, 1934, 1937, 1939.

Deringil, Selim. *Turkish Foreign Policy during the Second World War*. New York: Cambridge University Press, 1989.

Dost-Niyego, Pınar. *Le Bon Dictateur: L'image de Mustafa Kemal Atatürk en France (1919–1938)*. Istanbul: Libra Yayınevi, 2014.

Erkin, Feridun Cemal. *Dışişlerinde 34 Yıl: Anılar – Yorumlar*. 2 vols. Ankara: Türk Tarih Kurumu, 1980.

Esendal, Memduh Şevket. *Tahran Anıları ve Düşsel Yazılar*. Ankara: Bilgi Yayınevi, 1999.

Fleischmann, Ellen. *The Nation and Its "New" Women*. Berkeley: University of California Press, 2003.

Fleury, Antoine. *La penetration allemande au Moyen Orient, 1919–1939*. Leiden: A. W. Sijthoff, 1977.

Ford, Guy Stanton. *Dictatorship in the Modern World*. Minneapolis: University of Minnesota Press, 1935.

Fromkin, David. *A Peace to End All Peace*. New York: Holt, 1989.

Gerede, Hüsrev. *Siyasi Hatıralarım I: Iran*. Istanbul: Vakit, 1952.

Gershoni, Israel, and James Jankowski. *Confronting Fascism in Egypt*. Stanford, CA: Stanford University Press, 2010.

Egypt, Islam, and the Arabs. New York: Oxford University Press, 1986.

Redefining the Egyptian Nation, 1930–1945. New York: Cambridge University Press, 1995.

Gingeras, Ryan. *Heroin, Organized Crime, and the Making of Modern Turkey*. New York: Oxford University Press, 2014.

Göçek, Fatma Müge. *The Transformation of Turkey*. London: I. B. Tauris, 2011.

Goldschmidt, Arthur. *Biographical Dictionary of Modern Egypt*. Boulder, CO: Lynne Reiner, 2000.

Gürol, Pelin. "Building for Women's Education during the Early Republican Period in Turkey: İsmet Paşa Girls' Institute in Ankara in the 1930s," unpublished MA thesis, Middle East Technical University, 2003.

Gürsoy, Özgür Burçak. "Losing Wealth or Restricting the Poison? Changing Opium Policies in Early Republican Turkey, 1923–1945," *Historia Agraria*, Vol. 61 (2013), 115–143.

Hale, William. *Turkish Foreign Policy since 1774*. 3rd ed. New York: Routledge, 2013.

Hanioğlu, M. Şükrü. *Atatürk: An Intellectual Biography*. Princeton, NJ: Princeton University Press, 2011.

Hershlag, Z. Y. *Introduction to the Modern Economic History of the Middle East*. Leiden: Brill, 1964.

Hourani, Albert. *Arabic Thought in the Liberal Age, 1798–1939*. New York: Cambridge University Press, 1983.

Ihrig, Stephan. *Atatürk in the Nazi Imagination*. Cambridge, MA: Harvard University Press, 2014.

Ireland, Philip Willard. "Berlin to Baghdad Up-to-date," *Foreign Affairs*, Vol. 19iii (1941), 665–670.

İşçi, Onur. "Russophobic Neutrality: Turkish Diplomacy, 1936–1945," unpublished PhD diss., Georgetown University, 2014.

Jacob, Wilson Chacko. *Working Out Egypt: Effendi Masculinity and Subject Formation in Colonial in Colonial Modernity, 1870–1940*. Durham, NC: Duke University Press, 2011.

Jahid, Burhan. *Al-Ghazi Mustafa Kamal wa-fursanihi al-Arba'a 1918*. Trans. Ra'fat al-Dajani. Jafa: Matba'at al-Kamal, 1935.

Jankowski, James. "Egyptian Regional Policy in the Wake of the Anglo-Egyptian Treaty of 1936: Arab Alliance or Islamic Caliphate?," in Michael J. Cohen and Martin Kolinsky, eds., *Britain and the Middle East in the 1930s*. New York: St. Martin's Press, 1992. 81–97.

Jongerden, Joost. *The Settlement Issue in Turkey and the Kurds*. Leiden: Brill, 2007.

Kalman, M. *Belge ve tanıklarıyla Dersim Direnişleri*. Istanbul: Nujen Yayıncılık, 1995.

Karaosmanoğlu, Ali. "The Evolution of the National Security Culture and the Military in Turkey," *Journal of International Affairs*, Vol. 54, No. 1 (2000), 199–216.

Kassir, Samir. *Beirut*. Berkeley: University of California Press, 2010.

Kezer, Zeynep. *Building Modern Turkey*. Pittsburgh, PA: University of Pittsburgh Press, 2015.

Khanki Bey, Aziz. *Turk wa-Ataturk*. Cairo: al-Matba'a al-Misriya, [1938].

Khatab, Sayed. *Understanding Islamic Fundamentalism*. Cairo: American University in Cairo Press, 2011.

Khatib-Shahidi, Rashid. *German Foreign Policy toward Iran before World War II*. New York: I. B. Tauris, 2012.

Khoury, Philip S. *Syria and the French Mandate*. Princeton, NJ: Princeton University Press, 1987.

Kop, Kadri Kemal. *Atatürk Diyarbakır'da*. Istanbul: Cumhuriyet Matbaası, 1938.

Kral, August Ritter, von. *Kamal Atatürk's land*. Vienna: Wilhelm Braumüller, 1938.

Krüger, Karl. *Kemalist Turkey and the Middle East*. London: Allen & Unwin, 1932.

Landau, Jacob. *Pan-Turkism: From Irredentism to Cooperation*. 2nd ed. Bloomington: Indiana University Press, 1995.

Lanfranchi, Sania Sharawi. *Casting Off the Veil*. London: I. B. Tauris, 2012.

League of Nations. *Question of the Frontier between Turkey and Iraq*. Geneva, 1924.

Statistical Year-book of the League of Nations, 1933–34. Geneva, 1934.

Lewis, Geoffrey. "An Ottoman Officer in Palestine, 1914–1918," in David Kushner, ed., *Palestine in the Late Ottoman Period*. Jerusalem: Yad Izhak Ben-Zvi Press, 1986. 402–415.

Libal, Kathryn. "Staging Turkish Women's Emancipation: Istanbul, 1935," *Journal of Middle East Women's Studies*, Vol. 4 (2008), 31–52.

Liel, Alon. *Turkey in the Middle East*. Boulder, CO: Lynne Rienner, 2001.

Linke, Lilo. "Turkey," in *Hitler's Route to Bagdad*. London: George Allen & Unwin, 1939.

Litvinoff, Barnet, ed. *The Letters and Papers of Chaim Weizmann*. 2 vols. New Brunswick, NJ: Transction, 1984.

Lukitz, Liora. *Iraq: The Search for National Identity*. London: Frank Cass, 1995.

Lust-Okar, Ellen Marie. "Failure of Collaboration: Armenian Refugees in Syria," *Middle Eastern Studies*, Vol. 32i (1996), 53–68.

Mafinezam, Alidad, and Aria Mehrabi. *Iran and Its Place among Nations*. Westport, CT: Praeger, 2008.

Marashi, Afshin. "Performing the Nation: The Shah's Official State Visit to Kemalist Turkey, June to July 1934," in Stephanie Cronin, ed., *The Making of Modern Iran*. New York: Routledge, 2003. 99–119.

Martin, Lenore G. "Turkey's Middle East Foreign Policy," in Lenore G. Martin and Dimitris Keridis, eds., *The Future of Turkish Foreign Policy*. Cambridge, MA: MIT Press, 2004. 157–189.

Mazower, Mark. *Dark Continent: Europe's Twentieth Century*. New York: Vintage, 2000.

McDowall, David. *A Modern History of the Kurds*. 3rd ed. New York: I. B. Tauris, 2005.

Menashri, David. *Education and the Making of Modern Iran*. Ithaca, NY: Cornell University Press, 1992.

Mikusch, Dagobert, von. *Mustafa Kamal: Al-Mathal al-A'la.'* Beirut: Matba'at al-Wafa,' 1933.

Millman, Brock. *The Ill-Made Alliance: Anglo-Turkish Relations 1939–1940.* Montreal: McGill-Queen's University Press, 1998.

Ministry of the Interior. *Press Department of Public Instruction in the Republic of Turkey.* Ankara, 1936.

Mochaver-ol-Memalek [Ali-Qoli Khan Ansari]. *Claims of Persia before the Conference of the Preliminaries of Peace at Paris.* Paris: Georges Cadet, 1919.

Mojtahed-Zadeh, Pirouz. *Boundary Politics and International Boundaries of Iran.* Boca Raton, FL: Universal, 2006.

Naqash, Shafiq, and 'Ali Khalifa. *Al-Haraka al-Kashfiyya fi al-Aqtar al-'Arabiyya.* Beirut: Mataba'at al-Kashaf, 1936.

Nelson, Cynthia. *Doria Shafik, Egyptian Feminist: A Woman Apart.* Gainesville: University of Florida Press, 1996.

Nicosia, Francis R. *Nazi Germany and the Arab World.* New York: Cambridge University Press, 2015.

O'Connell, John Morgan. *Alaturka: Style in Turkish Music (1923–1938).* Burlington, VT: Ashgate, 2013.

Olmert, Y. "Britain, Turkey and the Levant Question during the Second World War," *Middle Eastern Studies,* Vol. 23 (1987), 437–452.

Oran, Baskın, ed. *Turkish Foreign Policy, 1919–2006.* Salt Lake City: University of Utah Press, 2010.

Owen, Roger, and Şevket Pamuk. *A History of Middle East Economies in the Twentieth Century.* Cambridge, MA: Harvard University Press, 1999.

Özkan, Fulya. "The Role of the Trabzon-Erzurum-Bayezid Road in Regional Politics and Ottoman Diplomacy, 1850s–1910s," in Yaşar Cora et al., eds., *The Ottoman East in the Nineteenth Century.* New York: I. B. Tauris, 2016. 19–41.

Özkırımlı, Atilla. *Çağdaş Türk Edebiyatı,* ed. Turhan Baraz. Eskişehir: Anadolu Üniversitesi, 1993.

Pearse, Richard. *Three Years in the Levant.* London: Macmillan, 1949.

Pelt, Mogens. *Military Intervention and a Crisis of Democracy in Turkey.* London: I. B. Tauris, 2014.

Podeh, Elie. *The Quest for Hegemony in the Arab World.* Leiden: Brill, 1995.

Porath, Yehoshua. *In Search of Arab Unity, 1930–1945.* London: Frank Cass, 1986.

Press Department of the Ministry of Interior. *The Development of National Banking in Turkey.* Ankara, 1938.

Reynolds, Michael. *Shattering Empires: The Clash and Collapse of the Ottoman and Russian Empires 1908–1918.* New York: Cambridge University Press, 2011.

Ronart, Stephan. *Turkey To-day.* London: Robert Hale, 1938.

Rooke, Tetz. "Tracing the Boundaries: From Colonial Dream to National Propaganda," in Inga Brandell, ed., *State Frontiers: Borders and Boundaries in the Middle East*. London: I. B. Tauris, 2006. 123–139.

Sabir, Shakir. *Ta'rih al-Sadaqa bayna al-'Iraq wa-Turkiya*. Baghdad: Dar al-Ma'rifa, 1955.

Salami, Gholamreza, and Afsaneh Najmabadi. *Nahzat-e Nisvan-e Sharq*. Tehran: Shirazeh, 2005.

Sannu, Sa'id. *Turkiya al-Kamaliyah*. Beirut: Maktab al-Ashah wa-al-Nashr, 1938.

Sasson, Joseph. *Economic Policy in Iraq, 1932–1950*. New York: Frank Cass, 1987.

Sayari, Sabri. "Turkish Foreign Policy in the Post–Cold War Era: The Challenges of Multi-Regionalism," *Journal of International Affairs*, Vol. 54, No. 1 (2000), 169–184.

Sayegh, Salma. *Suwar wa-Dhikrayat*. Beirut: Dar al-Hadara, 1964.

Sayyid-Marsot, Afaf Lutfi. *Egypt's Liberal Experiment, 1922–1936*. Berkeley: University of California Press, 1977.

Schahgaldian, Nikola B. "The Political Integration of an Immigrant Community into a Composite Society," unpublished PhD diss., Columbia University, 1979.

Shaffer, Brenda. *Borders and Brethren: Iran and the Challenge of Azerbaijani Identity*. Cambridge, MA: MIT Press, 2002.

Shakir, Amin. *Turkiya wa-al-Siyasa al-'Arabiya*. Cairo: Dar al-Ma'arif, 1954.

Sha'rawi, Huda. *Dawr al-Mar'a fi Harakat al-Tatawwur al-'Alami*. Cairo, 1929.

　　Mudhakirat Huda Sha'rawi: Ra'idat al-Mar'a al-'Arabiya al-Haditha. Cairo: Dar al-Hilal, 1981.

Sharett, Moshe. *Yoman Medini*. 5 vols. Tel Aviv: Am Oved, 1971.

Shechter, Relli. *Smoking, Culture and Economy in the Middle East*. London: I. B. Tauris, 2006.

Sherrill, Charles H. *A Year's Embassy to Mustafa Kemal*. New York: Charles Scribner's Sons, 1934.

Shields, Sarah D. *Fezzes in the River*. New York: Oxford University Press, 2011.

Shimali, Fu'ad. *Turkiya al-Haditha*. Beirut: Dar al-Maktaba al-Ahliya, 1939.

Shissler, Ada Holland. "Beauty Is Nothing to Be Ashamed Of: Beauty Contests as Tools of Women's Liberation in Early Republican Turkey," *Comparative Studies of South Asia, Africa and the Middle East*, Vol. 24 iv (2004), 107–122.

Sidal, Hulusi. *Ykın Şarkta Ekonomik İşbirliğiş Türkiye-Irak Gümrük Birliği ve Yakın Şark Federasyonu*. Istanbul, 1947.

Silverfarb, Daniel. *Britain's Informal Empire in the Middle East.* New York: Oxford University Press, 1986.

Simon, Reeva Spector. *Iraq between the Two World Wars: The Militarist Origins of Tyranny.* Updated ed. New York: Columbia University Press, 2004.

Şimşir, Bilal N. *Atatürk ve Yabancı Devlet Başkanları.* 4 vols. Ankara: Türk Tarih Kurumu Basımevi, 2001.

Doğunun Kahramanı Atatürk. Ankara: Bilgi Yayınevi, 1999.

Sluglett, Peter. *Britain in Iraq: Contriving King and Country, 1914–1932.* New York: Columbia University Press, 2007.

Soysal, İsmail. "1937 Saadabad Pact," *Studies on Turkish-Arab Relations,* Vol. 3 (1988), 131–151.

Spearman, Diana. *Modern Dictatorship.* New York: Columbia University Press, 1939.

Strohmeier, Martin. *Crucial Images in the Presentation of Kurdish National Identity.* Leiden: Brill, 2003.

Tamkin, Nicholas. *Britain, Turkey, and the Soviet Union, 1940–1945.* London: Palgrave, 2009.

Tanpınar, Ahmet Hamdi. *Beş Şehir.* Ankara: Ülkü, 1946.

Tawfiq, Muhammad Muhammad. *Kamal Ataturk.* Cairo: Dar al-Hilal, 1936.

Tekinalp. *Le Kemalisme.* Paris: Alcan, 1937.

Kemalizm. Istanbul: Toplumsal Dönüşüm, 1998.

Ter Minassian, Taline. *Colporteurs du Komintern: l'Union soviétique et les minorités au Moyen-Orient.* Paris: Presses de Sciences Po, 1997.

Thabit, Munira. *Thawra fi . . . al-Burj al-'Aji.* Cairo: Dar al-Ma'arif lil-Tiba'a wa-al-Nashr, 1946.

Thomas, Martin. *Empires of Intelligence.* Berkeley: University of California Press, 2008.

Thompson, Elizabeth. *Colonial Citizens.* New York: Columbia University Press, 2000.

Thornburg, Max Weston, et al. *Turkey: An Economic Appraisal.* New York: Twentieth Century Fund, 1949.

Tongas, Gérard. *La Turquie: Centre de Gravité des Balkans et du Proche-Orient.* Paris: Librarie Orientaliste Paul Geuthner, 1939.

Tör, Vedat Nedim. *Yıllar Böyle Geçti.* Istanbul: Milliyet Yayınları, 1976.

Trabzon Ticaret ve Sanayı Odası. *Cumhuriyet'in 10 Yılında İktisat Meydanında Trabzon.* Trabzon: Şark Matbaası, 1933.

Tripp, Charles. *A History of Iraq.* 3rd ed. New York: Cambridge University Press, 2007.

Turkiya fi 1938. Istanbul: al-Jumhuriya, 1938.

Usta, Veysel. *Atatürk ve Trabzon.* Trabzon: Serander, 2011.

Uzer, Umut. *Identity and Turkish Foreign Policy*. New York: I. B. Tauris, 2011.

Watenpaugh, Keith David. *Being Modern in the Middle East*. Princeton, NJ: Princeton University Press, 2006.

Watt, D. Cameron. "The Saadabad Pact of 8 July 1937," in Uriel Dann, ed., *The Great Powers in the Middle East, 1919–1939*. New York: Holmes & Meier, 1988. 333–352.

Weber, Charlotte. "Between Nationalism and Feminism: The Eastern Women's Congresses of 1930 and 1932," *Journal of Middle East Women's Studies*, Vol. 4 (2008), 83–106.

———. "Unveiling Scheherazade: Feminist Orientalism in the International Alliance of Women, 1911–1950," *Feminist Studies*, Vol. 27 (2001), 125–157.

Webster, Donald Everett. *The Turkey of Atatürk*. Philadelphia: American Academy of Political and Social Sciences, 1939.

Werner, Christoph. "Drama and Operetta at the Red Lion and Sun: Theatre in Tabriz 1927–1941," in Bianca Devos and Christoph Werner, eds., *Culture and Cultural Politics under Reza Shah*. London: Routledge, 2013. 201–232.

White, Benjamin Thomas. *The Emergence of Minorities in the Middle East: The Politics of Community in French Mandate Syria*. Edinburgh: Edinburgh University Press, 2011.

Wien, Peter. *Iraqi Arab Nationalism: Authoritarian, Totalitarian, and Profascist Inclinations, 1923–1941*. London: Routledge, 2006.

Wilson, M. Brett. *Translating the Qur'an in an Age of Nationalism*. New York: Oxford University Press, 2014.

Wilson, Mary C. *King Abdullah, Britain and the Making of Jordan*. New York: Cambridge University Press, 1987.

Yavuz, Selim, ed. *Taşnak-Hoybun*. Istanbul: İleri Yayıncılık, 2005.

Yazıcı, Nevin. *Petrol Çerçevesinde Musul Sorunu (1926–1955)*. Istanbul: Ötüken, 2010.

Yeşilbursa, Behçet Kemal. *The Baghdad Pact*. London: Frank Cass, 2005.

Zu'aytir, Akram. *Min Mudhakkirat Akram Zu'aytir*. Vol. 1. Beirut: Al-Mu'assasa al-'Arabiya lil-Dirasat wa-al-Nashr, 1994.

Zürcher, Erik J. *Turkey: A Modern History*. New York: I. B. Tauris, 2004.

Index

A'zami, Ali al-, 208–210
Abalıoğlu, Yunus Nadi, 22, 195, 201
Abaza, Fikri, 153, 172, 186–187
Abbas Hilmi (ex-Khedive of Egypt),
    78–82
Abd al-Ilah (Regent of Iraq), 211
Abdallah (Emir of Transjordan / King
    of Jordan), 62, 77–79, 82, 90–91,
    95–96, 106, 168, 222
  visit to Turkey, 1937, 91–94
Abu al-Fath, Mahmud, 181–183
Adana, 43, 123, 157, 206, 213
Ahmed Barzani, 32–33
al-Ahram (newspaper), 68, 140, 144,
    150, 158, 168, 173–174, 177, 182,
    183, 188, 189, 203
Akşin, Aptülahat, 236, 238
Albania, Italian invasion of, 56, 100,
    105
Aleppo, 2, 10–11, 42–43, 46, 50,
    56–57, 59, 62, 76, 80, 105, 137,
    181, 204–206, 211–212, 218
Alexandretta, District of, 4, 5, 11, 13,
    42–46, 53–57, 76, 80, 89–94,
    97–100, 106, 117, 127, 128, 174,
    177, 215–216, 222, 224, 225–226,
    231, 232, 235
Amman, 77, 79, 91, 94, 96
Ankara Municipal Theater (Ankara
    Şehir Tiyatrosu), 229
Anschluss, 56, 57
Antalya, 12, 65
Arab Revolt (1916–1918), 1, 6, 20, 43,
    62, 74, 95, 203
Arab Revolt in Palestine, 1, 224
Aras, Tevfik Rüştü, 25, 40, 64, 72, 87,
    99, 115, 141, 169, 182, 184, 203,
    221
Arfa, Hasan, 39
Armenia, 8–10, 36

Armenian Genocide, 11, 48
Armenian Nationalism, 11, 13, 26–27,
    32, 46, 48–51, 60, 175
Armenian Revolutionary Federation
    (Dashnaktsutyun), 50–51
Armenians in Syria, 28, 42, 48–50,
    57–58, 75, 81
Armistice of Mudros, 8, 10, 12
Arslan, Adil, 94
Arslan, Shakib, 169
Assad, Bashar al-, 234
Assyrians (Nestorians), 13, 26–28, 48,
    65, 134
  in Iraq, 12–13, 28–34
  in Syria, 48, 49, 58, 75, 81
Atatürk, Mustafa Kemal
  image in the Middle East, 166–178
Atay, Falih Rıfkı, 21
Athens, 198
Azzam, Abd al-Wahhab, 168–169,
    211–213

Baghdad Pact, 222, 225, 226, 228, 230
Baghdad Railway, 11, 42, 110–111,
    123, 126–129, 137, 206
Bahrain, 210
Balkan Pact, 87, 89, 218
Başgil, Ali Fuad, 167
Basra, 124
Bayar, Celal, 107, 130, 134, 196, 222
Bayhum, Muhammad Jamil, 229
Bayur, Yusuf Hikmet, 142
Beirut, 1–2, 52, 54, 62, 79, 117, 206,
    210
Belge, Burhan Asaf, 20
Ben-Gurion, David, 229
Bitlis, 131
Bursa, 22, 180, 183, 189, 191, 200,
    203, 213
Buseiri, Abdul Salam al-, 141

Central Treaty Organization
  (CENTO), 228, 230
Çetinkaya, Ali, 118, 121, 128, 130
Christie, Agatha, 205
Churchill, Winston, 218
Circassians, 51–52, 57, 153
Cizre, 11, 42, 129, 131, 135
Cold War, 4–5, 216, 221–224,
  228–232
Constanţa, 122, 202
Cumhuriyet (newspaper), 22, 75, 128,
  135, 143, 158, 184, 195, 196, 197,
  200, 201, 207
Czechoslovakian Crisis, 56, 105

Dajani, Ra'fat al-, 175
Daqqaq, Basil, 224
Darwaza, 'Izzat, 224
Davaz, Suad, 3
Dersim Rebellion, 35, 53, 130,
  239

Eastern Women's Conferences,
  156–157
Ece, Keriman Halis (Miss Universe
  1932), 143–155, 186
Edhem the Circassian (Çerkes Edhem),
  51–52
Egyptian Feminist Union, 147–152,
  158, 161
Elazığ, 133, 135
Erdoğan, Recep Tayyip, 5, 21, 233–240
Erkin, Feridun Cemal, 1, 52, 220
Erzurum, 111, 114, 123
Ethiopia, Italian invasion of, 87, 88, 96

Faisal (King of Iraq), 34, 62, 73–75,
  227
  ambitions in Syria, 76–82, 90
  visit to Turkey, 1931, 75–76, 85, 87
Faisal bin 'Abd al-'Aziz Al Saud, 162
Farouk (King of Egypt), 97, 98–101,
  202
Fromkin, David, 3
Fuad (King of Egypt), 62, 68–71, 73,
  78, 80, 97

Gaziantep, 43
Greece, 8, 23, 87, 165, 186, 195, 196,
  200

Gülen, Fethullah, 234
Gulf of Iskenderun. See Alexandretta,
  District of

Haffar, Lutfi al-, 59
Haifa, 94, 108, 117, 125, 126, 129,
  206, 210, 231
Hakimiyet-i Milliye (Newspaper). See
  Ulus (newspaper)
Hakkari, 12, 13, 28, 29, 30, 31, 33, 34
Hamad bin 'Isa Al Khalifa (Ruler of
  Bahrain), 210
Hamada, Nur, 156
Hamza, Abd al-Malik, 67
Hashimi, Taha al-, 175, 211
Hashimi, Yasin al-, 211
Hatay. See Alexandretta, District of
Haydar, Rustam, 229
Hitler, Adolf, 85, 166, 170–171, 173,
  177, 218

İnan, Afet, 214
India, 108, 117, 121, 127, 131, 133,
  205, 235
İnönü, İsmet, 79, 93, 95–96, 105, 118,
  119, 128, 133, 134, 140, 162, 173,
  174, 177, 182, 184, 196, 221, 233
International Woman Suffrage Alliance
  (IWSA), 155, 158–161
Iskenderun. See Alexandretta, District
  of
Ismet Pasha Girls' Institute (İsmet Paşa
  Kız Enstitüsü), 162–165, 192
Istanbul-Alexandria Steamship Line,
  194–198, 200–202
al-Istiqlal (newspaper), 57, 88, 157,
  170, 208
Izmir, 22, 158, 180, 181, 183, 184,
  192, 193, 194, 198, 200, 226
  International Fair, 22, 207

Jamali, Muhammad Fadil al-, 176
al-Jami'a al-Islamiya (newspaper), 172,
  175
Jazira Region (Syria), 48, 57–59
Jeddah, 62
Jerusalem, 1, 59, 62, 91, 93, 94, 180
Justice and Development Party (Adalet
  ve Kalkınma Partisi), 233, 234,
  235, 236, 237, 238

Keriman Halis. *See* Ece, Keriman Halis (Miss Universe 1932)
Khanki, Aziz, 168, 173–174, 204
Khoybun (Xoybun), 49–51
Kirkuk, 125, 126, 205, 231, 232
Konya, 205, 206, 213
Kral, August Ritter von, 2
Kurdistan Workers' Party (Partiya Karkerên Kurdistanê), 233, 237
Kurtalan, 130, 134, 135, 136
Kuwait, 141, 231

Lake Van, 133
Lampson, Miles, 72
League of Nations, 8, 12, 28, 29, 31, 43, 48, 55, 58, 73, 82, 87, 88, 97, 99, 169

MacMichael, Harold, 95
Mahir, Ali, 104
Mahmud, Muhammad, 99, 102
Maraghi, Mustafa al-, 98
Mardin, 43, 129
Masiha, Kamil, 171
Menderes, Adnan, 222
Mersin, 181
Middle East Military Balance in the Interwar Period, 15–16
Mikusch, Dagobert von, 171
Mohammad Reza Pahlavi, 100
Molotov-Ribbentrop Pact, 104, 136, 217
Montreux Convention, 55, 88, 97, 105, 202
Mosul
  oil, 126–128
  territorial dispute, 10–13, 28–30, 35, 60, 74, 81–82, 238
  transportation, 42, 58, 115, 124–130, 205–206
Mount Ararat, Border Dispute and Rebellions, 35–41, 51, 114
Muhadenet (newspaper), 140, 145, 147, 186, 188, 196, 198
Muhammad, Ahmad al-Sawi, 150, 189–192
al-Muqtataf (newspaper), 170, 188, 190
Murder on the Orient Express (novel), 205

Muş, 133
Mussolini, Benito, 17, 85, 97, 170, 171, 173, 177
Mustafa Sabri Efendi, 173

Nabarawi, Saiza, 147, 160, 162
Nahhas, Mustafa al-, 71, 98, 99, 202
Najjar, Abd al-Wahhab al-, 198
Nasser, Gamal Abdel, 225, 228, 232
National Bloc (Syria), 53, 59, 92–94
National Pact (Misak-ı Milli), 10–12, 23, 25, 28–29, 58, 216, 238
NATO (North Atlantic Treaty Organization), 221, 225, 228

Ocalan, Abdullah, 233
Öngören, İbrahim Talî, 72
Opium, 108–110
Orient Express, 181, 205, 214

Pakistan, 222, 227, 228
Palestine, 1, 16, 21, 43, 47, 52, 54, 59, 91, 93, 117, 119, 125, 129, 199, 216, 222
  Arab Nationalists, 1, 2, 88, 158, 174–175, 224
  Zionists, 8, 21, 59, 158, 162, 210
Piraeus, 181, 194, 198, 200
Port Said, 210

Qatar, 235, 237

Remzi, Hüseyin, 140, 145, 147, 188
Republican People's Party (Cumhuriyet Halk Partisi), 19, 22, 192
Reza Shah Pahlavi, 15, 36, 37, 116, 170, 230
  visit to Turkey, 1934, 83–86, 115, 117
al-Risala (newspaper), 157, 170, 177, 212, 213
Romania, 87, 105, 122, 196, 217
Roosevelt, Franklin Delano, 171

Sabir, Shakir, 226
Said, Nuri al-, 56, 75, 76, 80, 210, 226
Şanlıurfa, 43, 157
Sannu, Sa'id, 163–165, 177
Saracoğlu, Şükrü, 229
Sarruf, Fuad, 162, 190

Saudi Arabia, 16, 88, 162, 222, 237
Sayf al-Din, Prince Ahmad, 71–73
Sayigh, Salma, 162
Sayyah, Fatimah, 165
Sèvres Syndrome, 26, 237
Sha'rawi, Huda, 150, 152, 156–164,
 167–169, 174, 191
Shafik, Doria, 150
Shahbandar, Abd al-Rahman, 59
Shakir, Amin, 225
Sherrill, Charles, 171
Shimali, Fuad, 172
Siirt, 133, 134
Simko. Ismail, 37–38
Suez Crisis, 228
Suffragist conference in Istanbul, 1935,
 157–161
Sulayman, Hikmat, 211
Sykes-Picot Agreement, 8, 11, 28

Tabriz-Trabzon Road, 112–122, 230
Tanpınar, Ahmet Hamdi, 114
Tatvan, 133, 135
Taurus Express, 181, 204–214, 230
Tawfiq, Muhammad Muhammad,
 172
Tekinalp, Munis (Moiz Kohen), 142,
 165, 168
Thabit, Munira, 165
Touring and Automobile Club of
 Turkey (Türkiye Turing ve
 Otomobil Kurumu), 180, 200, 203
Treaty of Ankara, 11
Treaty of Lausanne, 7, 12, 16, 25, 26,
 27, 28, 36, 42, 48, 55, 70, 180,
 226, 238
Treaty of Saadabad, 3, 16, 35, 89, 99,
 101, 106, 120, 129, 218, 222
Treaty of Sèvres, 8–11, 13, 26–28
Tripoli, 126, 129, 181, 206, 231
Turkey-Afghanistan relations, 3, 16,
 83, 120, 142
 Non-Aggression Pact, 86–90
Turkey-Britain relations, 17–18,
 90–96, 101–106, 217–221
Turkey-Egypt relations, 16–17, 69–70,
 80, 96–104, 232–240
 after end of Cold War, 232–240
 Cold War years, 221–224, 225–226,
 228–230, 232

Egyptian visitors to Turkey, 181–193,
 198–201, 202–205, 211–213
Fez Incident, 66–69
military ties, 101–104
Prince Ahmad Sayf al-Din Affair,
 71–73
trade and transportation, 18–19,
 107–110, 194–198, 200–202
Turkey-France relations, 17–18, 53–54,
 55–60, 90–96, 105–106, 217–221
Turkey-Germany relations, 17–18,
 217–221
Turkey-Iran relations, 16–17, 82–86,
 232–240
 after end of Cold War, 232–240
 border, 7, 35–41
 Cold War years, 221–224, 230–232
 Non-Aggression Pact, 3, 86–90
 trade and transportation, 18–19,
 109–110, 112–122, 128–135,
 136–138, 231–232
Turkey-Iraq relations, 16–17, 73–82,
 232–240
 after end of Cold War, 232–233,
 240
 border, 12–13, 28–35
 Cold War years, 221–224, 226–232
 Iraqi visitors to Turkey, 176,
 205–214
 Non-Aggression Pact, 3, 86–90
 trade and transportation, 18–19,
 123–135, 137–138, 213–214,
 230–232
Turkey-Italy relations, 12, 17, 96–97
Turkey-Soviet Union relations, 10, 17,
 104–105, 217–221, 228
Turkey-Syria relations, 16–17, 73–82,
 90–96, 232–240
 after end of Cold War, 232–233,
 240
 border, 11–12, 41–47, 53–54, 55–60,
 218–220
 Cold War Years, 221–224, 228–230,
 232
 trade and transportation, 18–19, 137
Türkofis, 108, 201

Ulus (newspaper), 21, 166, 201
Umar, Ahmed, 1
Urfa. *See* Şanlıurfa

Van, 131, 133

Wafd (political party), 68, 71, 97, 202
Wandawi, Abd al-Majid al-, 227

Yalova, 22, 180, 185, 186, 189, 200, 203

Young Men's Muslim Association (Jam'iyyat al-Shuban al-Muslimin), 198
Yugoslavia, 87, 109

Zawahiri, Ayman al-, 168
Zu'aytir, Akram, 174
Zürcher, Erik, 5